Krzysztof Fleszar

Network-Design Problems in Graphs and on the Plane

Krzysztof Fleszar

Network-Design Problems in Graphs and on the Plane

Würzburg
University Press

Dissertation, Julius-Maximilians-Universität Würzburg
Fakultät für Mathematik und Informatik, 2016
Gutachter: Dr. habil. Joachim Spoerhase, Prof. Dr. Alexander Wolff, Dr. habil. Jarosław Byrka

Impressum

Julius-Maximilians-Universität Würzburg
Würzburg University Press
Universitätsbibliothek Würzburg
Am Hubland
D-97074 Würzburg
www.wup.uni-wuerzburg.de

© 2018 Würzburg University Press
Print on Demand

Coverdesign: Jule Petzold
Coveridee: Krzysztof Fleszar

ISBN 978-3-95826-076-4 (print)
ISBN 978-3-95826-077-1 (online)
URN urn:nbn:de:bvb:20-opus-154904

Acknowledgments

I am very grateful to Joachim Spoerhase who led me into the intriguing field of approximation algorithms. It is a pleasure to work with him in this exciting area. I profited a lot from his expertise and his supervision.

I would also like to thank Alexander (Sascha) Wolff for offering me place in his group. He has always been very encouraging and helpful. His many good and practical advices as well as the extremely friendly atmosphere at the chair were very supporting when writing this thesis.

I thank my colleagues and my present and former collaborators Antonios Antoniadis, Sergey Bereg, Benedikt Budig, Jarosław Byrka, Steven Chaplick, Timothy M. Chan, Aparna Das, Thomas van Dijk, William S. Evans, Martin Fink, Christian Glaßer, Jan-Henrik Haunert, Ruben Hoeksma, Sigrid Keller, Philipp Kindermann, Stephen Kobourov, Fabian Lipp, Andre Löffler, Matthias Mnich, Dongliang Peng, Sergey Pupyrev, Alexander Ravsky, Christian Reitwießner, Bartek Rybicki, Noushin Saeedi, Kevin Schewior, Nadine Schwartges, Chansu Shin, José Soto, Sankar Veeramoni, Oleg Verbitsky and Maximilian Witek.

I further thank Jarosław Byrka, Kurt Mehlhorn, Chansu Shin and José Soto for my scientific stays in their groups, which gave me a lot of important experiences and opened new perspectives.

Finally, my thanks go to my family and my friends on whom I could always rely, especially to my wonderful wife for helping me polishing this book.

Krzysztof Fleszar

Preface

Networks such as road networks, public transport networks, supply networks, social networks, or computer networks play an ubiquitous role in our everyday life. Therefore, *designing* a network so that it meets the requirements for a specific range of use is a crucial task. The increasing size of networks call for automation of the design task by means of efficient *algorithms*.

In the research communities of *algorithms theory* and *discrete optimization*, a network is usually modeled in a graph-theoretic way by means of nodes that are connected via edges (links). A *network design* problem is concerned with finding a substructure in a given graph that meets certain mathematically defined requirements (such as connectivity) and that optimizes a certain objective function (such as cost).

In this thesis, Krzysztof Fleszar investigates several fundamental optimization problems in network design or closely related subjects (such as facility location). He makes progress or sheds new light on some of the central algorithmic questions related to these problems that have puzzled researchers in the algorithms and theory communities in the last years. Exemplarily, let me refer to the new results on the approximability of the capacitated k-median problem and the edge-disjoint paths problem that he developed in joint work with his coauthors. Additionally, Krzysztof Fleszar studies several new, interesting problems that arise in *geometric* network design or *graph drawing* where nodes are points on the plane and where edges are represented by line segments, polygonal chains, or more generally by Jordan curves.

It was a pleasure for me to supervise Krzysztof Fleszar's doctoral studies and to work together with him on some of the questions investigated in this thesis. I am convinced that some of the results or new problems proposed in this thesis will (and in parts they already have) inspire future researches and lead to new insights in the field of network design or more generally of discrete algorithms.

Joachim Spoerhase
Chair I – Algorithms, Complexity, and Knowledge-Based Systems
Institute of Computer Science
University of Würzburg
Germany

Contents

1. Introduction

Given a number of points in the plane, connect them using minimum ink. Though the task is simple to describe and easy to understand, it turns out to be very time consuming in the presence of many points. If one thinks about the problem for a while, one will come to the conclusion that any minimum drawing consists only of straight line segments between the given points and some newly added points. One will even observe that such a drawing has a simple and beautiful structure. However, the number of candidate drawings having this structure is so high that it takes impracticably long to go through all of them and pick a minimum one. As a matter of fact, one would settle the most prominent and important open problem in computer science, on whether P = NP, if one could describe a procedure to find such a minimum drawing in reasonable time. In other words, the task of finding such a minimum drawing is an NP-hard problem. Also better known as EUCLIDEAN STEINER TREE, it is a classic example of a geometric network design problem, carrying all the essence of this class of problems: luring with its simple and natural formulation and offering relentless resistance when directly approached. These problems emerge in many areas ranging from the construction of telecommunication and transportation networks to the design of circuit layouts of computer chips.

In general, network design problems are not constrained to points lying in the plane, but consist of abstract nodes with a predefined relationship among them. For instance, consider social networks where the nodes are persons and two nodes form an *edge* if they are friends. Or consider a model of a computer network where clients and routers are represented by nodes, and two nodes have an edge if there is a direct connection between them. Here, two nodes are said to be *connected* if there is a path in the graph connecting them. An often stated task in this context is: *Given a graph where some nodes are marked, select a minimum subset of the edges that connects all marked nodes.* This problem, a special variant of STEINER TREE IN GRAPHS, does not only resemble EUCLIDEAN STEINER TREE but is equivalent to it in terms of hardness.

Since most network design problems appearing in the real world are NP-hard, there is little hope to obtain an algorithm that is exact and efficient at the same time. Therefore, theoreticians usually embark on one of the following three approaches to tackle them.

(i) To consider special constrained variants that allow efficient exact algorithms. For instance, we could consider the special case of EUCLIDEAN STEINER TREE where we only allow to draw straight line segments between the input points. This variant, known as EUCLIDEAN MINIMUM SPANNING TREE, is solvable in $\Theta(n \log n)$ time where n is the number of input points [Kru56][1].

(ii) To consider efficient algorithms that approximate an optimum solution. Such approximation algorithms look for a "good" solution whose cost is guaranteed to lie

---

[1] Compute a so-called Delaunay triangulation and run Kruskal's [Kru56] algorithm on the obtained planar graph by using the Euclidean distance for edge weights.

within a factor of the optimum objective. For example, there is the following trivial α-approximation algorithm for EUCLIDEAN STEINER TREE that computes, for any instance, a solution that uses at most α times more ink than an optimum solution. The algorithm simply computes an Euclidean minimum spanning tree (MST) which is always a feasible solution to EUCLIDEAN STEINER TREE. Since the ratio between an MST and a minimum Euclidean Steiner tree is bounded from above by 1.21 [CG85], we have $\alpha = 1.21$. We call the factor α the *approximation ratio* of the algorithm. EUCLIDEAN STEINER TREE even admits a $(1 + \varepsilon)$-approximation algorithm for any positive constant ε [Aro98].

(iii) To consider exact algorithms with exponential run time thereby either keeping the exponent in the run time as low as possible or expressing the run time in dependence of the "complexity" of the input. We call the latter algorithms *fixed-parameter tractable* (FPT) if their run time is polynomial for constant parameters. For instance, STEINER TREE IN GRAPHS admits an FPT algorithm running in time $2^k \cdot n^{\mathcal{O}(1)}$ where k is the number of marked nodes and n the number of all nodes [CFK+15].

In this book, we will consider problems related to network design that belong to one of the following categories.

Spanning Trees. All three problems mentioned above, EUCLIDEAN STEINER TREE, STEINER TREE IN GRAPHS, and EUCLIDEAN MINIMUM SPANNING TREE, belong to this category. Given points in a metric space or nodes in a weighted graph, connect them while optimizing some objective function. The goal is not always to minimize the total length. For instance, when designing a computer network, one might be interested in keeping the maximum latency as low as possible while respecting the budget. Translated as a graph problem, one would like to obtain a spanning subgraph where the maximum distance between any two nodes is minimized while the weight of the subgraph is below some threshold. Many variants of spanning tree problems occur in practical settings. For instance, the rectilinear version of EUCLIDEAN STEINER TREE is important for VLSI circuits. In this book, we will consider a generalization of EUCLIDEAN STEINER TREE.

Flow problems. Here, we are given a graph where some nodes are called sources and sinks. Our goal is to send some flow from the sources to the sinks, where a flow is a set of weighted paths that connect sources to sinks. Each edge has an orientation and a fixed capacity that bounds from above the total amount of flow using this edge. In the MINIMUM EDGE-COST FLOW problem, we are given only one source and sink, but we have to pay an individual fee for each edge used by any flow path. Our goal is to send a flow of minimum cost such that the flow value is above some threshold. The NP-hard problem becomes efficiently solvable if the capacities have value 1. However, the problem gets NP-hard again if we only allow flow paths of unit weight between prescribed pairs of sources and sinks; even when all edges have cost 0. In that case, the hardness lies in deciding whether a certain number of disjoint paths between some given pairs of points exists. In this book, we will examine the optimization versions of such problems in more detail.

Facility Location Problems.   Problems of this group consist in general of two tasks. First, one has to open facilities on a subset of given locations. Secondly, one has to assign clients to open facilities. Facility location problems have a strong motivation in many real world applications and therefore attract considerable attention. Think for instance of opening a fixed number of fire departments on strategic locations such that the maximum distance a fire truck has to travel is minimized. For most facility location problems, the task of assigning the clients to facilities is easy to accomplish once the open facilities are given. The hardness lies in the right choice of where to open facilities. For problems of this group, various optimization criteria have been considered. The most prominent of these problem is the classic FACILITY LOCATION problem. Here, the objective is to minimize the sum of two cost functions that depend on the outcome of both tasks: the total cost of opening facilities and the total connection cost of the clients to the facilities they are assigned to. Hence, the first cost urges us to open as few facilities as possible, whereas the second cost pushes us in the contrary direction. Another interesting variant is k-MEDIAN. Here, only the connection cost of the clients to the facilities has to be minimized. The facilities are open for free, however we are only allowed to open a given number of them. In this book, we will study a variant where each facility has a capacity, that is, an upper bound on the number of clients it can serve.

Graph Drawing.   In many applications, from linguistics over cartography to bioinformatics, information is represented by means of relationships in graphs and networks. To make such data amenable to humans, graphs must be visualized such that the desired information can be extracted easily. Think of octilinear plans for metro and bus systems, of diagrams modeling object relationships in software engineering, or of sociograms visualizing social networks. Mostly, the graphs are drawn in the Euclidean plane by representing the edges by curves and the nodes by some geometric objects. Depending on the application, different optimization criteria are applied, but most of them attach importance to the aspect of comprehension: Minimizing the number of crossings to reduce the "visual clutter", maximizing the symmetry to make the graph easier to grasp, or limiting the number of bends on any edge so that the eyes can follow them smoothly. In this book, we consider a simple network, a cycle with edge constraints, that we want to draw as compact as possible; an algorithmically challenging task as we will see.

There are more problem categories related to network design for example, the category of *routing problems* that contains the prominent TRAVELING SALESMAN problem.

1.1   Outline of the Book

In this book, we study five problems from different areas of network design that will permit us to take a wide look on the broad field of network design problems. We can roughly classify our problems into two categories, problems on graphs and problems in the plane. On one hand, we will consider well-studied problems for which we obtain new results, on the other hand, we pose new natural questions that turn out to be difficult and intriguing. In addition, special variants of the five problems will be considered.

In most cases, we will develop approximation algorithms and, for some problems, we will simultaneously optimize two criteria. We will also obtain an FPT algorithm and we will exactly solve some special cases of our problems in polynomial time. The techniques applied will demonstrate various ways to round linear program (LP) relaxations. They will also involve dynamic programming in the context of exact, FPT and approximation algorithms. For some problems, we will also discuss their hardness and inapproximability.

The two categories of our problems are reflected in the structure of this book. In the first part, we consider two classic problems defined on graphs. In the second part, we examine new or recently-defined problems in the plane. Some essential notation will be explained in Chapter 2. At the end, in Chapter 7, we give a short summary of the obtained results and pose open questions.

1.1.1   Problems in Graphs

In Part I of the book, we consider network design problems related to graphs. We will make use of flow formulations and graph contraction. Our main technical tool will be based on rounding LP relaxations.

Disjoint Connecting Paths.   In Chapter 3, we examine two classical NP-hard flow problems, MAXIMUM EDGE DISJOINT PATHS (MAXEDP) and MAXIMUM NODE DISJOINT PATHS (MAXNDP). In both, we are given a graph of n nodes and a pairing of the nodes into k terminal pairs. For as many pairs as possible, we want to find paths connecting them such that each path connects only one pair and all paths are pairwise disjoint. Thereby, the definition of disjointness is the only difference in the formulation of the two problems. In MAXEDP, the selected paths are not allowed to go through a same edge, but they may share same nodes, in MAXNDP, the latter is not allowed.

Although being classic problems, their approximability is not well understood and there is a big gap between the best known approximation ratio and the best known lower bound. However, if one simplifies the instance and consider graphs that are trees (which are graphs that do not contain any paths that form cycles), then the problems become efficiently solvable.

We tackle the two problems by considering a parameter that measures how "far" the input graph is from being a tree. For this, we use the *feedback vertex set number*, which is the minimum number of nodes that one needs to remove from a graph until it becomes a tree. Our focus on the feedback vertex set number allows us to develop new algorithms with guaranteed bounds related to this parameter. As a consequence, we strengthen best known fundamental results for MAXEDP. In particular, we obtain two approximation algorithms where one of them is a bi-criteria algorithm allowing a bounded violation on the disjointness. Our main technical tools comprise a rounding procedure for multi-commodity flow LP solutions and the application of edge contractions to redundant edges. For MAXNDP, we show that, under reasonable complexity-theoretic assumptions, there is no FPT algorithm parametrized by the feedback vertex set number. However, we succeed in developing an FPT algorithm by combining the feedback vertex set number and the number of terminal pairs into one parameter.

The chapter is based on joint work with Matthias Mnich and Joachim Spoerhase [FMS18].

Capacitated Facility Location.   In Chapter 4, we consider capacitated k-FACILITY LOCA-
TION, which is a generalization of the two problems FACILITY LOCATION and k-MEDIAN that
we have briefly mentioned before. We are given a set of facility locations and a set of clients.
Both lie in a single metric space. We are also given an upper bound k on the number of
facilities that we are allowed to open. Furthermore, each facility location has an individual
opening cost and an individual capacity, where the capacity is an upper bound on the number
of clients that the facility can serve. A feasible solution opens at most k facilities and assigns
each client to a facility such that all capacities are respected. The goal is to find a feasible
solution of minimum cost where the cost is the sum of the total opening cost and the total
connection cost.

FACILITY LOCATION as well as k-MEDIAN are well-understood problems, however, the
capacitated variant of k-MEDIAN has been resistant to many algorithmic approaches and for a
long time little progress has been made. The only successful approach has been to round linear
program relaxations. However, using the known linear program relaxations, one is forced
to relax some constraints in order to obtain a bounded approximation ratio. The main two
approaches are to open a few facilities more than allowed, or to slightly violate the capacities.
In this book, we choose the latter approach and allow to open at most k facilities. Even more,
we consider the hard-capacitated variant where at most one facility can be build on a location.
Note that this constraint makes the problem even more general, as the input can specify
multiple distinct locations having the same distance values in the metric.

We present the first constant-factor algorithms for hard-capacitated k-MEDIAN and hard-
capacitated k-FACILITY LOCATION where only capacities are violated. For the former problem,
we consider arbitrary capacities and manage to bound the capacity violation by a factor of 3.
For the latter problem, we consider uniform capacities but allow arbitrary opening. We obtain
a bound of 2 on the capacity violation, which is the best-possible value when using the natural
LP relaxation.

Both algorithms begin with the same step of computing a solution to an LP relaxation.
They use the solution to select a subset of the clients as a backbone of a larger network defined
over the facilities and the clients. These networks eventually allow the algorithms to distribute
all clients among all facilities such that the capacity violation and the total cost is low.

This chapter is based on joint work with Jarosław Byrka, Bartosz Rybicki and Joachim
Spoerhase [BFRS15].

1.1.2   Problems on the Plane

In Part II of the book, we consider network design problems related to the Euclidean plane. Besides the usage of LP formulations, we will see various dynamic programs that take advantage
of the underlying geometry.

Stabbing Rectangles with Line Segments.   In Chapter 5, we initiate the study of a natural
geometric optimization problem that we call STABBING. We are given pairs of vertical line
segments in the plane and we want to connect each pair via a horizontal line segment. The
goal is to minimize the total length of all horizontal line segments. In contrast to MAXNDP
and MAXEDP, we do not require disjointness of the connectors, which would make the
problem trivial, but we allow horizontal line segments to connect multiple pairs. As we will

see in Chapter 5, the problem can be motivated by a resource allocation problem. It also has applications in batch processing [FJQS08] and geometric network design [DFK+18]. In some sense, STABBING can be seen as a geometric flow problem where the flow paths correspond to horizontal line segments. To the best of our knowledge, this natural problem has not been considered in its generality in setting of line segments so far.

In this book, we will focus on an equivalent definition of STABBING: We are given axis aligned rectangles in the plane and we want to *stab* all rectangles by horizontal line segments of total minimum length. A rectangle is stabbed by a horizontal line segment if the line segment connects the vertical edges of the rectangle. We show that the problem is NP-hard, and even APX-hard if the input prescribes a candidate set for the horizontal line segments. We discuss various techniques and approaches that on first glance seem to fail. But then we observe some structural properties of a special variant of the problem that immediately imply, by some known results, a constant-factor approximation algorithm. By showing that STABBING can be decomposed to this special variant, we obtain a constant-factor approximation algorithm also for the general case.

This chapter is based on joint work with Timothy Chan, Thomas C. van Dijk, Joachim Spoerhase and Alexander Wolff [CvDF+18].

Colored Steiner Problem.   In EUCLIDEAN STEINER TREE, the task is to connect all points in the plane with a tree of minimum total length. In Chapter 6, we define the following natural generalization, which, in some sense, is also a geometric version of MAXNDP/MAXEDP. Given a set of k-colored points in the plane, find k trees such that each tree connects all points of one color class, no two trees cross, and the total edge length of the trees is minimized. Note that this problem, which we call k-COLORED NON-CROSSING EUCLIDEAN STEINER FOREST, is equivalent to EUCLIDEAN STEINER TREE if $k = 1$.

We obtain the following results. For $k = 2$, we present a polynomial-time approximation scheme (PTAS), meaning that, for any fixed positive ε, there is an $(1 + \varepsilon)$-approximation algorithm. We achieve our algorithm by substantially modifying Arora's PTAS for EUCLIDEAN STEINER TREE [Aro98] that is based on dynamic programming. Building upon this result, we obtain an approximation algorithm with the slightly worse ratio $(5/3 + \varepsilon)$ for $k = 3$. For general k, we develop two approximation algorithms that make use of the geometry in different ways.

This chapter is based on joint work with Sergey Bereg, Philipp Kindermann, Sergey Pupyrev, Joachim Spoerhase and Alexander Wolff [BFK+15].

Drawing Rectilinear Polygons for Given Angle Sequences.   Eventually, in Chapter 7, we examine an interesting and natural problem that has been formulated only recently: MINIMUM RECTILINEAR POLYGON FOR GIVEN ANGLE SEQUENCE. Here, we are given a *simple rectilinear* polygon where the edges connecting adjacent points are axis parallel and non-crossing. The task is to find a *better* drawing of the polygon such that some natural criterion is minimized. The only freedom that we have is to vary the edge lengths between the points under the restriction that all points lie on the integer grid. The angles between consecutive edges may not change and no crossings are allowed. Therefore, we can interpret the problem also as follows: Given a sequence of left and right turns, draw a rectilinear polygon on the integer grid minimizing the respective objective.

In this book, we will consider the following three objectives that are related to compactness: Minimizing the perimeter, the area, and the area of the bounding box of the polygon. First, we show that all three problems are NP-hard. Then we focus on the special cases of x-monotone and xy-monotone rectilinear polygons. By using their geometric structure, we obtain efficient algorithms based on dynamic programming.

This chapter is based on joint work with William S. Evans, Philipp Kindermann, Noushin Saeedi, Chan-Su Shin and Alexander Wolff [EFK$^+$16].

2 Preliminaries

Before we begin our study on network design problems, we briefly recall some general notions that will be used within this book. The goal of this section is not to give a complete overview on the basics in computer science and graph theory but rather to fix some terminology that sometimes is defined in different ways or not commonly known.

For more details on the topics covered in this book, we refer to the following textbooks. *Introduction to Algorithms* by Cormen et al. [CLRS09] gives an introduction to basics in computer science and algorithms. For a deeper understanding of approximation algorithms and the application of linear programming in this field, we refer the reader to *Approximation Algorithms* by Vazirani [Vaz10] and to *The Design of Approximation Algorithms* by Williamson and Shmoys [WS11]. *Parameterized Complexity Theory* by Flum and Grohe [FG06] as well as the recently published textbook *Parameterized Algorithms* by Cygan et al. [CFK+15] introduce to the relatively young field of fixed-parameter algorithms. Fundamentals on computational complexity can be found in *Computational Complexity* by Papadimitriou [Pap94] and *Computational Complexity: A Modern Approach* by Arora and Barak [AB09]. More details on graph theory and graph drawing can be found in *Introduction to Graph Theory* by Trudeau [Tru93] and in the *Handbook of Graph Drawing and Visualization* edited by Tamassia [Tam16], respectively.

2.1 Mathematical Notation

Numbers and Vectors. We use $\mathbb{Z}$, $\mathbb{Q}$ and $\mathbb{R}$ to denote sets of integer, rational and real numbers, respectively. The superscript ≥ 0 restricts the sets to non-negative numbers; we define $\mathbb{N} = \mathbb{Z}^{\geq 0}$. If not stated differently, all numerical values throughout this book belong to $\mathbb{Q}$. For $x \in \mathbb{R}$, we define $\lfloor x \rfloor = \max\{z \in \mathbb{Z} \mid z \leq x\}$ and $\lceil x \rceil = \min\{z \in \mathbb{Z} \mid z \geq x\}$.

Vectors will be denoted by bold variables and their components will be written, using the same variable, in italic. For example, $\mathbf{x}$ is a vector and x_1 is its first component.

Chernoff bound. We will apply the following multiplicative forms of the *Chernoff bound*. Let X be the sum of some random variables taking values in $\{0,1\}$ and let $\mu = \mathbb{E}[X]$. The Chernoff bound states that

$$\mathbb{P}[X \geq (1+\delta)\mu] < \left(\frac{e^{\delta}}{(1+\delta)^{1+\delta}}\right)^{\mu} \tag{2.1}$$

holds for any positive $\delta \in \mathbb{R}$, and

$$\mathbb{P}[X \leq (1-\delta)\mu] \leq e^{-\frac{\mu\delta^2}{2}} \tag{2.2}$$

holds for $0 < \delta < 1$.

Big-O Notation and Functions.   Throughout the book, we will interpret the standard *asymptotic notations* $\mathcal{O}$, o, Ω, ω, and Θ, as sets of functions.

Definition 2.1. For functions $f, g \colon \mathbb{Q}^{\geq 0} \to \mathbb{R}^{\geq 0}$,

    (i) $f \in \mathcal{O}(g)$ if and only if there is a constant c with $f(n) \leq c\,g(n)$ for every n with $n \geq c$,

    (ii) $f \in \Omega(g)$ if and only if $g \in \mathcal{O}(f)$,

    (iii) $f \in \Theta(g)$ if and only if $f \in \mathcal{O}(g)$ and $f \in \Omega(g)$,

    (iv) $f \in o(g)$ if and only if $f \in \mathcal{O}(g)$ and $f \notin \Omega(g)$, and

    (v) $f \in \omega(g)$ if and only if $g \in o(f)$.

Following Knuth [Knu76], we use arithmetic operations appropriately in the context of asymptotic notations. Functions in such expressions will be interpreted as singleton sets and the arithmetic operations as elementwise operations on the sets. For instance,

$$\log n \cdot \mathcal{O}(n^2) + \sqrt{n} + 2^{\mathcal{O}(1/n)}$$

is the function set

$$\{\log n \cdot f(n) + \sqrt{n} + 2^{g(n)} \mid f \in \mathcal{O}(n^2), g \in \mathcal{O}(1/n)\}\,.$$

Furthermore, we redefine the equality symbol, $=$, as a one-way relation when used for expressions in the context of asymptotic notations: Given two such expressions E and F satisfying $E \subseteq F$, we say E *is* F and write $E = F$. For instance, $n^2 = \mathcal{O}(n^3)$. Note that this relation is transitive but not symmetric.

We use the following abbreviations. We let polylog denote the set of all polylogarithmic functions, that is,

$$\text{polylog} \;=\; \{p \circ \log \mid p \text{ is a polynomial}\}\,,$$

and, for any function $f \colon \mathbb{Q}^{\geq 0} \to \mathbb{R}^{\geq 0}$, we let $\tilde{\mathcal{O}}(f)$ denote the set $\text{polylog} \cdot \mathcal{O}(f)$.

2.2   Complexity

We fix our algorithmic computation model and recall some basics in complexity theory.

2.2.1   Algorithmic Model and Run Time

For our algorithms, we will use the algorithmic model of the random access machine (RAM) operating on registers attaining rational values and allowing only elementary arithmetic operations. The input and output consists of a sequence of rational numbers, each number occupying some well-defined register.

We define the *size* of a rational number r as the length of its encoding as a bit string and we let $|r|_s$ denote it. More specifically, we set $|r|_s = 1 + \lceil \log(|p|+1) \rceil + \lceil \log q \rceil$ where $r = p/q$ for two integers p, q with greatest common divisor 1 and $q \geq 1$. Analogously, we define the *size* of the input as the *total size* of all the numbers it contains, that is, as the sum of their sizes. Each single operation performed by the RAM consists of a number of steps which depends on the operation and the sizes of the numbers involved. In the *unit-cost* RAM, each operation consists of one step, whereas, in the *logarithmic-cost* RAM, the number of steps of an operation is defined as the total size of the numbers involved.

In this book, we consider only algorithms that terminate. We define *run time* as follows. The run time of an algorithm is a function that, given an integer $n \in \mathbb{Z}^{\geq 0}$, outputs the smallest upper bound on the total number of steps after which the algorithm terminates on every input of size n. In an analogous way, we define the *space consumption* (for short, *space*) of an algorithm as a function that upper bounds the total size of all numbers stored in the registers at any step over all inputs of the same size. We call a run time function f *constant*, *linear*, *polynomial* or *exponential* if $f \in O(g)$ where g is a constant or a linear, polynomial or exponential function, respectively. Further, we call an algorithm *efficient* if its run time is polynomial. In our discussions, we will be more interested in the asymptotic behavior of the run-time and the space consumption than their precise formulations. Therefore, we will mainly use asymptotic notations.

Recall that a unit-cost RAM runs each operation in one step, independently of the sizes of the numbers involved. Thus, it is more convenient to analyze the run time on this model than on models taking the number sizes into account. However, the run time analyzed on a unit-cost RAM may be asymptotically smaller than on a more *realistic* computational model like the logarithmic-cost RAM. For example, the algorithm repeating n times the operation $a = a \cdot a$ has run time $\Omega(2^n)$ on a logarithmic-cost RAM but needs only $O(n)$ time on a unit-cost RAM. Therefore, it is preferred to provide run time bounds based on the logarithmic-cost RAM. In the algorithms we consider, the sizes of all number are always bounded from above by a polynomial in the input size. Thus, up to logarithmic factors, both RAM models yield asymptotically equivalent run times for these algorithms. On account of this, we will analyze our algorithms implicitly assuming the unit-cost RAM model.

2.2.2 Problem Types, Complexity Classes, and Approximation

In this book, we will develop algorithms or discuss the hardness of finding algorithms for *optimization*, *decision* and *fixed-parameter tractable problems*. Among other properties, a problem always defines a countable set of *instances* and a *task*. An instance π is encoded as a sequence over a finite alphabet. Its *size* $|\pi|_s$ is the length of the sequence.

For example, an instance of EUCLIDEAN STEINER TREE is a description of a finite point set lying in the plane. The description could be a sequence of x and y-coordinates of the points in binary encoding. Throughout the book, we will not discuss the details of encoding an instance but rather see an instance as a sequence of rational number or other objects.

An algorithm *for* a problem is an algorithm that solves the task for every instance of the problem. For a run time function f, we say that a problem is *solvable in time* $O(f)$ if there is an algorithm for the problem with run time $O(f)$.

Optimization Problems. An optimization problems is either a minimization or maximization problem. Besides a set of instances, an optimization problem also defines, for each instance, a set of *feasible solutions*. It also defines an *objective function* that maps each solution to a rational number, called the *objective value*. An *optimum solution* is defined as a feasible solution with the *optimum* objective value. For minimization problems, the objective value is optimum if there is no other feasible solution with smaller objective value. Similarly, for maximization problems, the objective value is optimum if there is no feasible solution with larger objective value.

The algorithmic task for an optimization problem is to find an optimum solution to a given instance. For example, EUCLIDEAN STEINER TREE asks for a drawing of minimum total length. Note that any drawing connecting the input points is a feasible solution for this problem.

Decision Problems.   For problems in this group, the set of instances is partitioned into yes-instances and no-instances. The algorithmic task is to decide whether a given instance is a yes-instance. Hence, there is only one solution to each instance and it consists of the right answer.

Every optimization problem can be transformed into a decision problem in a straight-way manner. For example, consider a minimization problem with a set Π of instances. For the corresponding decision problem, we define $\{(\pi, k) \mid \pi \in \Pi, k \in \mathbb{Q}\}$ as the set Π' of instances. To this end, we call an instance $(\pi, k) \in \Pi'$ a yes-instance if the optimum objective value for π is bounded from above by k. For example, in the decision version of EUCLIDEAN STEINER TREE, an instance describes a finite number of points in the plane and specifies a value k. The task is to decide whether there exists a drawing of length at most k connecting all points.

Fixed-Parameter Tractable Problems.   A *parametrized* problem is a decision problem where each instance contains a *parameter*, which is a numerical value. A *fixed-parameter tractable* problem is solvable in time $f(k) \cdot n^{\mathcal{O}(1)}$ where f is any computable function and k is the parameter of the instance. We call an algorithm solving a fixed-parametrized problem in this time bound a *fixed-parameter (FPT) algorithm*.

For example, we can define the parametrized version of STEINER TREE IN GRAPHS by defining the parameter as the number k of terminals (marked nodes). As we have seen in the introduction, the problem is solvable in $2^k \cdot n^{\mathcal{O}(1)}$ time [CFK+15], hence, it is fixed-parameter tractable.

Complexity Classes.   A *complexity class* is a class of decisions problems that can be solved using the same *resource*, for example, run time or space. Of central importance for this book are the run-time complexity classes P and NP. The class P consists of all decision problems that are solvable in polynomial time. On the other hand, the class NP consists of all decision problems for which each yes-instance has an efficiently checkable 'proof' that it is a yes-instance. More formally, let A be a decision problem and let Π_A denote its instance set. It holds that A is in NP if and only if there exist a polynomial p and a decision problem $B \in P$ such that its instance set Π_B is a subset of

$$\{(\pi, k) \mid \pi \in \Pi_A, k \in \mathbb{Z}, |k|_s \leq p(|\pi|_s)\}$$

and, for every $\pi \in \Pi_A$, there is a k ('a proof for π') such that $(\pi, k) \in \Pi_B$.

Clearly, P is a subset of NP. The famous question of whether P = NP is one of the most important open problems in computer science. Since most theoreticians believe that the two classes are different [Gas12], many results are based on the assumption that P is a proper subset of NP. Also the results in this book will mainly build upon this conjecture.

Approximation Algorithms. For most of the optimization problems considered in the next chapters, efficient algorithms are believed to be unlikely as their existence would imply P = NP. Therefore, we will consider efficient algorithms that do not look for optimum solutions, though they may find them, but algorithms that compute any feasible solution whose objective value is *close* to the optimum one.

We call such an algorithm an *approximation* algorithm *for* the respective problem and we define the closeness by means of an *approximation ratio* which is a function mapping the input instances to the reals. In most cases of this book, an approximation ratio will be a constant or a function of the input size and some parameters. Let A be a minimization problem and let α be an approximation ratio defined on the instances of A. An approximation algorithm for A has approximation ratio α, if, for any instance π of the problem, the inequality

$$\alpha(\pi) \geq \frac{\text{ALG}}{\text{OPT}}$$

holds where ALG is the objective value of the solution to π produced by the algorithm and OPT is the optimum objective value for π. If A is a maximization problem, we define the approximation ratio analogously with the inequality

$$\alpha(\pi) \geq \frac{\text{OPT}}{\text{ALG}} \, .$$

We call the solution computed by an α-approximation algorithm an *approximation* as well as an α-approximation. An algorithm with approximation ratio α is also called an α-approximation algorithm.

A *polynomial-time approximation scheme (PTAS)* for an optimization problem A is an efficient algorithm that, given an instance of A and a positive constant ε, returns a $(1 + \varepsilon)$-approximation for A.

Randomized Algorithms. Some of our approximation algorithms will be also *randomized*. A randomized algorithm has access to an *oracle*, that uniformly at random returns 0 or 1 in constant time. The algorithm can use these values to make choices independent of the input. The performance of such algorithms, for example its running time or approximation ratio, is then expressed by a random variable. When analyzing such algorithms, we will determine the expected values of such variables or provide bounds for the variables that hold with constant probability.

2.2.3 Reducibility and Hardness

A *reduction* transforms an instance π of one problem A into an instance π' of another problem B in such a way that a solution to π' can be used to obtain a solution to π. The intuition behind a reduction is to show that B is at least as "hard" as A. If there is a reduction from A

to B, we also say that A *can be reduced to* B. Depending on the types of problems, we define a reduction as follows.

(1) Let A and B be two decision problems. A reduction from A to B is an efficient algorithm that, given an instance π of A, computes an instance π' of B such that π is a yes-instance of A if and only if π' is a yes-instance of B.

(2) Let A and B be two parametrized problems. A reduction from A to B is an algorithm that, given an instance π of A with parameter k, computes an instance π' of B with parameter k' such that

    (i) π is a yes-instance of A if and only if π' is a yes-instance of B,

    (ii) $k' \leq g(k)$ for some computable function g, and

    (iii) the run time is $f(k) \cdot n^{\mathcal{O}(1)}$ for some computable function f.

Such a reduction is called an *FPT-reduction*.

(3) Let A and B be two optimization problems. A reduction from A to B consists of two positive constants α and β and two efficiently computable functions f and g such that:

    (i) If π is an instance of A, then $f(\pi)$ is an instance of B,

    (ii) if s is a solution to $f(\pi)$, then $g(s)$ is a solution to π,

    (iii) for the optimum objective values $\mathrm{OPT}_A(\pi)$ and $\mathrm{OPT}_B(f(\pi))$ of the instances π and $f(\pi)$, respectively, we have

$$\mathrm{OPT}_B(f(\pi)) \leq \alpha \cdot \mathrm{OPT}_A(\pi),$$

    and

    (iv) for the objective values $\mathrm{cost}(s)$ of s and $\mathrm{cost}(g(s))$ of $g(s)$ we have

$$|\mathrm{cost}(g(s)) - \mathrm{OPT}_A(\pi)| \leq \beta \cdot |\mathrm{cost}(s) - \mathrm{OPT}_B(f(\pi))|.$$

Such a reduction is called an *L-reduction (linear reduction)* [PY91]. A nice property is that it implies a PTAS for problem A if there is a PTAS for problem B.

We call a problem *hard* for some complexity class $\mathcal{A}$ if it is at least as "hard" as every problem belonging to $\mathcal{A}$. If there is a complexity class $\mathcal{B}$ that is a proper subset of $\mathcal{A}$, then a problem that is $\mathcal{A}$-hard does not belong to $\mathcal{B}$. For example, if $\mathrm{P} \subsetneq \mathrm{NP}$ is true, then efficient algorithms for NP-hard problems do not exist. Below, we define the hardness of several interesting complexity classes in more detail.

NP-Hardness. A decision problem A is called NP-hard if every problem of NP can be reduced to it. If A even belongs to NP, then it is called NP-complete. In order to show that a problem is NP-hard, it suffices to reduce an NP-hard problem to it.

We call an NP-hard problem *strongly* NP-*hard* if either all instances are given in unary notation or as sequences of numbers whose *values* are bounded from above by a polynomial of the length of the sequence. An NP-complete problem is *strongly* NP-*complete* if it is strongly NP-hard.

An optimization problem is called NP-*hard* if one can reduce an NP-hard (decision) problem to it. To show NP-hardness of an optimization problem, it suffices to show NP-hardness of its natural decision version.

FPT and W[1]-hardness. The complexity class FPT consists of all problems that are fixed-parameter tractable. It equals the first class W[0] of the W-hierarchy, a collection of complexity classes W[0] ⊆ W[1] ⊆ ... It is unknown whether W[0] = W[1] (for more details, see the literature [FG06, CFK+15]). Similar to NP-hardness and NP-completeness, we can define W[1]-hardness and W[1]-completeness by means of FPT-reductions. Analogously, we can show W[1]-hardness by an FPT-reduction from a W[1]-hard problem. If we show that a problem is W[1]-hard, then we can conclude that it is intractable in its parameter assuming FPT ⊊ W[1].

APX-hardness. The complexity class APX contains all optimization problems that admit a constant-factor approximation algorithm. Similar to NP-hardness, we can define APX-hardness by means of a so called *PTAS reduction* [Cre97]. The existence of such a reduction follows from the existence of an L-reduction. Unless P = NP, there are problems that cannot be approximated below a constant implying that an APX-hard problem does not admit a PTAS.

In this book, we will briefly mention several other complexity classes. For their definition, we refer to the aforementioned textbooks [Pap94, AB09].

2.3 Graphs

We use standard graph terminology. A *graph* G consists of a set $V(G)$ of *vertices* and a set $E(G)$ of *edges*, and it is called *non-empty* if it contains at least one vertex. We interchangeably refer to the vertices also as *nodes*. In some contexts, we will call some nodes *terminals* in order to distinguish them from the remaining ones. Every edge e consists of two nodes, called *endpoints of e*, that either form a set or a tuple: If the graph is *undirected*, then

$$E(G) \subseteq \{\{u, v\} \subseteq V(G) \mid u \neq v\} .$$

If the graph is *directed*, then

$$E(G) \subseteq \{(u, v) \in V(G) \times V(G) \mid u \neq v\} .$$

To simplify the notation, we refer to an edge $\{u, v\}$ of an undirected graph also by (u, v) and (v, u). If we don't specify that a graph is *directed*, then it is *undirected*.

An edge is *incident* to its endpoints, and a node is *incident* to every edge of which it is an endpoint. The endpoints of an edge are called *adjacent*. Similarly, two edges are called adjacent if they share an endpoint. Otherwise, they are called *disjoint* or *independent*. We say that an edge is *between* its endpoints.

A graph *with multiple edges* contains two nodes with more than one edge between them. In such graphs the edge set is a multiset. We will also consider graphs where we relax the definition of the edges a little and allow edges consisting of only one endpoint. We will call such an edge a *loop*. A graph is *simple* if it neither has multiple edges nor loops. If not specified differently, we always assume graphs to be simple.

A *complete* graph contains every possible edge.

Degrees and Directed Edges.   The *degree* $\deg(v)$ of a node v is the number of edges incident to v. Let G be a directed graph and (u, v) an edge in $E(G)$. We say that (u, v) *goes from u to v* and we say that (u, v) *is directed from u to v*. We call (u, v) an *outgoing edge of u* and an *incoming edge of v*. The *indegree* of a node is the number of its incoming edges, and the *outdegree* of a node is the number of its outgoing edges.

Subgraphs, Contractions, and Minors.   Let G be a graph. A *subgraph H of G* is a graph with $V(H) \subseteq V(G)$ and $E(H) \subseteq E(G)$. We call H an *induced* subgraph of G if H contains exactly those edges of G that have both endpoints in $V(H)$. Note that for a given subset of the nodes, there is only one induced subgraph. Let $V' \subseteq V(G)$. We denote by $G - V'$ the induced subgraph of G with the node set $V(G) \setminus V'$.

Informally, a *contraction* of an edge merges its two endpoints to a new vertex while deleting the edge between them. Formally, a contraction of an edge e with endpoints u and v of a graph G is an operation that creates a new graph H with a new vertex $w \notin V(G)$ and new edges that are incident to w. For $y \in \{u, v\}$ and for each edge $(x, y) \in E(G) \setminus \{e\}$, the operation creates a new edge (x, w) for $E(H)$. Similarly, for $y \in \{u, v\}$ and for each edge $(y, x) \in E(G) \setminus \{e\}$, the edge (w, x) is created for $E(H)$. Thereby, multiple edges might be created if u and v are adjacent to a common node making $E(H)$ a multiset. The remaining edges of $E(H)$ are all those edges in $E(G)$ that were not incident to u or v.

A *minor* of a graph G is a graph H that is obtained by successively contracting edges from a subgraph of G and deleting any occurring loops. A class $\mathcal{G}$ of graphs is *minor-closed* if, for any graph in $\mathcal{G}$, all its minors belong to $\mathcal{G}$. Notable, the Robertson–Seymour theorem [RS04] states that for every minor-closed class of graphs there exists a finite set of *forbidden minors* such that a graph belongs to the class if and only if it does not have any of the forbidden minors. For example, the class of *planar* graphs, which are graphs that admit crossing-free drawings, is fully described by just two forbidden minors: the complete graph with five nodes (K_5) and the complete bipartite graph with six nodes ($K_{3,3}$).

Paths and Cycles.   A *walk* is a sequence $(v_1, \ldots, v_k)$ of k nodes, $k \geq 1$, where any two consecutive nodes are adjacent. We say that an edge (u, w) is *contained* in a walk if we have $(u, w) = (v_i, v_{i+1})$ for some i with $1 \leq i \leq k - 1$. In directed graphs, a walk is *directed*, if (v_i, v_{i+1}) is an edge for every i with $1 \leq i \leq k - 1$.

A *cycle* is a walk of at least three nodes where the first node and the last node are the same, and a cycle is *simple* if all other nodes appear at most once. A *path* is a walk where each node appears at most once. (Note that some authors refer to paths by 'simple paths' and to walks simply by 'paths'.) We call the first node and the last node of a path π *endpoints* of π. Two paths are *edge disjoint* if they share no common edge. Similarly, two paths are *node disjoint* if they share no common node.

The *length of a walk* is one less than the length of its node sequence. Thus, for paths and cycles, thire length is the number of edges they contains.

Connectivity and Connected Components. If u is the first node and v the last node of a path π, then we say they are *connected by* π. If π is directed, then we also say that u is *connected to v by* π. We say that two nodes are *connected* in a (directed) graph if the graph contains a (directed) path connecting both nodes. We call a graph *connected* if all nodes are pairwise connected in it.

A *connected component* of a graph G is a connected non-empty subgraph H of G such that there is no edge in $E(G)$ connecting a node in $V(H)$ and with a node in $V(G) \setminus V(H)$. For short, we will often call connected components simply components.

Forests, Trees, and Acyclic Graphs. A *forest* is a graph without cycles and a *tree* is a connected forest. For directed graphs, we call forests also *acyclic graphs*. A *rooted* tree is a tree with a designated node called the *root of T*. In a tree, all nodes of degree 1 are called *leaves* and all other nodes are called *inner nodes*. In any tree, the number of inner nodes is one less than the number of leaves. An *in-tree* is a directed rooted tree where every node is connected to the root.

For a rooted tree T and a node $v \in V(T)$, we let $T[v]$ denote *the subtree of T rooted at v* which is the induced subgraph of T containing all nodes that are connected to the root of T with a path that contains v. Note that $T[v]$ is also a tree, and if T is an in-tree, then $T[v]$ is an in-tree with the root v.

Weights and Coloring. In some contexts, a graph also defines numerical values for each edge or node. Typical such values are *weights* for edges. We call a graph with edge weights a *weighted graph*. Also other objects can be associated with such values. For instance, in the context of flows, we will assign *weights* to paths.

A *node coloring* of a graph *G with c colors* is a function that assigns to each node in $V(G)$ a *color*, where a color is a number in $\{1, \ldots, c\}$. A node coloring is called *proper* if any two adjacent nodes have different colors. Similarly, an *edge coloring* of a graph *G with c colors*, for short, a *c-edge-coloring*, is a function that assigns to each edge in $E(G)$ a *color*, where again a color is a number in $\{1, \ldots, c\}$. An edge coloring is called *proper* if any two adjacent nodes have different colors.

We call a graph *c-colorable* if there exists a proper node coloring with c colors for it, and we call a graph *c-edge-colorable* if there exists a proper edge coloring with c colors for it.

Bipartite Graphs and Matchings. A graph G is *bipartite* if $V(G)$ can be partitioned into two sets such that no two nodes of the same set are adjacent. We refer to the two sets of the partition by *partite sets*. It holds that a graph is bipartite if and only if it is 2-colorable. We define *matching* in the context of sets. Let S be a set whose elements are two-element sets or tupels. A matching of S is a subset of S where all elements are pairwise disjoint. Thus, a matching of the edge set of a graph is a subset where all edges are pairwise disjoint.

Vertex Cover and Feedback Vertex Set.   We say that an edge e is *covered* by a subset V' of the nodes if V' contains an endpoint of e. A *vertex cover* of a graph is a subset of the nodes that covers all edges. A *feedback vertex set* of a graph G is a subset V' of the nodes such that $G - V'$ is a forest.

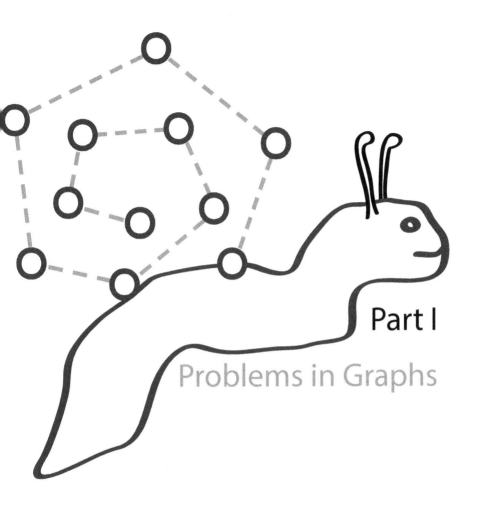

Part I

Problems in Graphs

3 New Algorithms for Maximum Disjoint Paths Based on Tree-Likeness

We study the classical NP-hard problems of finding maximum-size subsets from given sets of k terminal pairs that can be routed via edge-disjoint paths (MAXEDP) or node-disjoint paths (MAXNDP) in a given graph. The approximability of MAXEDP/MAXNDP is currently not well understood. There is a significant gap between the best known lower and upper bound, and closing this gap is currently one of the big open problems in approximation algorithms.

In this chapter, we strengthen fundamental results for these problems. We provide new bounds formulated in terms of the *feedback vertex set number* r of a graph, which measures its vertex deletion distance to a forest. In particular, we obtain the following results:

- For MAXEDP, we give an $\mathcal{O}(\sqrt{r}\log kr)$-approximation algorithm. Up to a logarithmic factor, our result strengthens the best known ratio $\mathcal{O}(\sqrt{n})$ by Cherkuri et al. [CKS06], as $r \leq n$.

- Further, we show how to route $\Omega(\text{OPT}^*)$ pairs with congestion $\mathcal{O}(\log kr/\log\log kr)$, strengthening the bound obtained by the classic approach of Raghavan and Thompson.

- For MAXNDP, we give an algorithm that gives the optimal answer in $(k + r)^{\mathcal{O}(r)} \cdot n$ time. This result is a substantial improvement on the run time of $2^k r^{\mathcal{O}(r)} \cdot n$, which can be obtained via an algorithm by Scheffler [Sch94].

We complement these positive results by various hardness bounds.

3.1 Introduction

In this chapter, we study disjoint paths routing problems. In this setting, we are given an undirected graph G and a collection $\mathcal{M} = \{(s_1, t_1), \cdots, (s_k, t_k)\}$ of vertex pairs, called *terminal pairs*, that can be thought of being source-destination pairs. The goal is to select a maximum-sized subset $\mathcal{M}' \subseteq \mathcal{M}$ of the pairs that can be *feasibly routed*, where a routing of $\mathcal{M}'$ is a collection $\mathcal{P}$ of paths such that, for each pair $(s_i, t_i) \in \mathcal{M}'$, there is a path in $\mathcal{P}$ connecting s_i to t_i. In the MAXIMUM EDGE DISJOINT PATHS (MAXEDP) problem, a routing $\mathcal{P}$ is feasible if its paths are pairwise edge-disjoint, and in the MAXIMUM NODE DISJOINT PATHS (MAXNDP) problem, a routing $\mathcal{P}$ is feasible if its paths are pairwise node-disjoint. Throughout this chapter, a *solution* to MAXEDP or MAXNDP is a feasible routing $\mathcal{P}$ of a subset $\mathcal{M}' \subseteq \mathcal{M}$.

Disjoint paths problems are fundamental problems with a long history and significant connections to optimization and structural graph theory. The decision versions EDP of MAXEDP and NDP of MAXNDP ask whether all of the pairs can be routed. When the number of pairs is part of the input, EDP and NDP are NP-complete [Kar75, EIS75]. In undirected graphs, MAXEDP and MAXNDP are solvable in polynomial time when the number of pairs is a fixed constant; this fact is a very deep result of Robertson and Seymour [RS95] that builds on several fundamental results in structural graph theory from their graph minors project.

In this chapter, we consider the optimization problems MaxEDP and MaxNDP when the number of pairs is part of the input. In this setting, the best approximation ratio for MaxEDP is achieved by an $\mathcal{O}(\sqrt{n})$-approximation algorithm [CKS06, KS04], that is, by an algorithm that routes $\Omega(\text{OPT}/\sqrt{n})$ pairs, where OPT is the number of pairs in an optimum routing and n is the number of nodes. However, the best known lower bound for undirected graphs is only $2^{\Omega(\log^{1-\varepsilon} n)}$ for any positive constant ε unless $\text{NP} \subseteq \text{RTIME}(n^{\text{polylog } n})$ [CKN18]. Bridging this gap is a fundamental open problem that seems quite challenging.

Most of the results for routing on disjoint paths use a natural multi-commodity flow relaxation as a starting point. A well-known integrality gap instance due to Garg et al. [GVY97] shows that this relaxation has an integrality gap of $\Omega(\sqrt{n})$, and this fact is the main obstacle for improving the $\mathcal{O}(\sqrt{n})$-approximation ratio in general graphs. This led Chekuri et al. [CNS13a] to study the approximability of MaxEDP with respect to the *treewidth* of the underlying graph. In particular, they pose the following conjecture:

Conjecture 1 ([CKS09]). *The integrality gap of the standard multi-commodity flow relaxation for MaxEDP is $\Theta(w)$, where w is the treewidth of the graph.*

Recently, Ene et al. [EMPR16] showed that MaxEDP admits an $\mathcal{O}(w^3)$-approximation algorithm on graphs of treewidth at most w. Theirs is the best known approximation ratio in terms of w, improving on an earlier $\mathcal{O}(w \cdot 3^w)$-approximation algorithm due to Chekuri et al. [CNS13a]. These results show that the problem seems more amenable on "tree-like" graphs.

However, for $w = \omega(n^{1/6})$, the bound is weaker than the bound of $\mathcal{O}(\sqrt{n})$. In fact, EDP remains NP-hard even for graphs of *constant* treewidth, namely treewidth $w = 2$ [NVZ01]. This further rules out the existence of a fixed-parameter algorithm for MaxEDP parameterized by treewidth, assuming $P \neq NP$. Therefore, to obtain fixed-parameter tractability results as well as better approximation guarantees, one needs to resort to parameters stronger than treewidth.

Another route to bridge the large gap between approximation lower and upper bounds for MaxEDP is to allow the paths to have *congestion c*: that is, instead of requiring the routed paths to be pairwise disjoint, at most c paths can use an edge. We can also think of this problem that each edge has a *capacity c*; thus, on unit-capacity graphs we ask for solutions without congestion. In their groundbreaking work, Raghavan and Thompson [RT87] introduced the technique of randomized rounding of LPs to obtain polynomial-time approximation algorithms for combinatorial problems. Their approach allows to route $\Omega(\text{OPT}^*)$ pairs of paths with congestion $\mathcal{O}(\log n/\log\log n)$, where OPT^* denotes the value of an optimum solution to the multi-commodity flow relaxation. This extensive line of research [And10, Chu16, KK10] has culminated in a $\log^{\mathcal{O}(1)} k$-approximation algorithm with congestion 2 for MaxEDP [CL16]. A slightly weaker result also holds for MaxNDP [CE13].

3.1.1   Motivation and Contribution

The goal of this work is to study disjoint paths problems under another natural measure for how "far" a graph is from being a tree. In particular, we propose to examine MaxEDP and MaxNDP under the *feedback vertex set number*. It denotes the smallest size r of a *feedback vertex set* of a graph G, which is a subset R of nodes for which $G - R$ is a forest. Note that the treewidth of G is at most $r + 1$. Therefore, given the NP-hardness of EDP for treewidth $w = 2$ and the current gap between the best known upper bound $\mathcal{O}(w^3)$ and the linear upper bound suggested by Conjecture 1, it is interesting to study the stronger restriction of bounding the feedback vertex set number r of the input graph. Our approach is further motivated by the fact that MAXEDP is efficiently solvable on trees by means of the algorithm of Garg, Vazirani and Yannakakis [GVY97]. Similarly, MAXNDP is easy on trees (see Theorem 3.3). Throughout this work, the parameter r will denote the feedback vertex set number of a graph.

Our main insight is that one can in fact obtain bounds in terms of r that either strengthen the best known bounds or are almost tight (see Table 3.1). It therefore seems that the parameter r correlates quite well with the "difficulty" of disjoint paths problems.

Our first result allows the paths to have small congestion: in this setting, we strengthen the result, obtained by the classic randomized LP-rounding approach of Raghavan and Thompson [RT87], that with constant probability one can always route $\Omega(\text{OPT}^*)$ pairs with congestion $\mathcal{O}(\log n / \log \log n)$.

Theorem 3.1. *There is a polynomial-time algorithm for MAXEDP that produces—with constant probability—a routing of $\Omega(\text{OPT}^*)$ paths with congestion $\mathcal{O}(\log kr / \log \log kr)$ where OPT^* is the value of an optimum solution to the multi-commodity flow relaxation, k is the number of terminal pairs and r is the feedback vertex set number.*

In other words, we show that there is an $\mathcal{O}(1)$-approximation algorithm for MAXEDP with congestion $\mathcal{O}(\log kr / \log \log kr)$.

Our second main result builds upon Theorem 3.1 and uses it as a subroutine. We show how to use a routing for MAXEDP with low congestion to obtain a polynomial-time approximation algorithm for MAXEDP *without congestion* that performs well in terms of r.

Theorem 3.2. *There is a polynomial-time algorithm for MAXEDP that produces—with constant probability—a routing of $\text{OPT}^* / \mathcal{O}(\sqrt{r} \log kr)$ paths with no congestion where OPT^* is the value of an optimum solution to the multi-commodity flow relaxation, k is the number of terminal pairs and r is the feedback vertex set number.*

In particular, our algorithm strengthens the best known approximation algorithm for MAXEDP on general graphs [CKS06] as always $r \leq n$, and indeed it matches that algorithm's performance up to a logarithmic factor. Substantially improving upon our bounds would also improve the current state of the art of MAXEDP. Conversely, the result implies that it suffices to study graphs with close to linear feedback vertex set number in order to improve the currently best upper bound of $\mathcal{O}(\sqrt{n})$ on the approximation ratio [CKS06].

Our algorithmic approaches harness the forest structure of $G - R$ for any feedback vertex set R. However, the technical challenge comes from the fact that the edge set running between $G - R$ and R is unrestricted. Therefore, the "interaction" between R and $G - R$ is non-trivial, and flow paths may run between the two parts in an arbitrary manner and multiple times. In fact, we show that MAXEDP is already NP-hard if R consists of a *single node* (Theorem 3.5); this result contrasts the efficient solvability on forests [GVY97].

In order to overcome the technical hurdles, we propose several new concepts, which we believe could be of interest in future studies of disjoint paths or routing problems.

In the randomized rounding approach of Raghavan and Thompson [RT87], it is shown that the probability that the congestion on any fixed edge is larger than $c \log n / \log \log n$ for some constant c is at most $1/n^{\mathcal{O}(1)}$. Combining this with the fact that there are at most n^2 edges, yields that every edge has bounded congestion with high probability. The number of edges in the graph may, however, be unbounded in terms of r and k. Hence, in order to prove Theorem 3.1, we propose a non-trivial *preprocessing step* of the optimum LP solution that is applied prior to the randomized rounding. In this step, we aggregate the flow paths by a careful rerouting so that the flow "concentrates" in $\mathcal{O}(kr^2)$ nodes (so-called *hot spots*) in the sense that if all edges incident on hot spots have low congestion, then so have all edges in the graph. Unfortunately, for any such hot spot the number of incident edges carrying flow may still be unbounded in terms of k and r. We are, however, able to give a refined probabilistic analysis that suitably relates the probability of exceeding the congestion bound to the amount of flow on the respective edge. Since the total amount of flow traversing any given hot spot is at most k, the probability that there is an edge incident on this hot spot that violates the congestion bound is inverse polynomial in r and k.

The known $\mathcal{O}(\sqrt{n})$-approximation algorithm for MaxEDP by Chekuri et al. [CKS06] employs a clever LP-rounding approach. If there are many long flow paths in the LP solution, then there must be a single node carrying a significant fraction of the total flow and a good fraction of this flow can be realized by integral paths by solving a single-source flow problem. If the LP solution contains many short flow paths, then greedily routing these short paths yields the bound. Essentially, this fact follows from the observation that routing a short path blocks only a small amount of flow. In order to prove Theorem 3.2, we also distinguish two cases. We are interested, however, in the number of nodes in R that a flow path is visiting rather than in its length. In the first case, there are many paths, each of which is visiting a large number of nodes in R. Here, we reduce to a single-source flow problem in a similar way to the approach of Chekuri et al. The second case where a majority of the flow paths visit only a few nodes in R turns out to be more challenging, since any such path may still visit an unbounded number of edges in terms of k and r. We use two main ingredients to overcome these difficulties. First, we apply our Theorem 3.1 as a building block to obtain a solution with logarithmic congestion while losing only a constant factor in the approximation ratio. Secondly, we introduce the concept of *irreducible routings with low congestion* which allows us to exploit the structural properties of the graph and the congestion property to identify a sufficiently large number of flow paths blocking only a small amount of flow.

Note that the natural greedy approach of always routing the shortest conflict-free path gives only an approximation ratio of $\mathcal{O}(\sqrt{m})$ for MaxEDP, where m is the number of edges. We believe that it is non-trivial to obtain our bounds via a more direct or purely combinatorial approach.

Our third result is a fixed-parameter algorithm for MaxNDP in $k + r$.

Theorem 3.3. *MaxNDP can be solved in time $(k + r)^{\mathcal{O}(r)} \cdot n$ on graphs with k terminal pairs, feedback vertex set number r, and n vertices. When a minimum feedback vertex set is given, it can be even solved in time $(8k + 8r)^{2r+3} \cdot \mathcal{O}(n)$.*

This run time is polynomial for constant r. We also note that, for small r, our algorithm is asymptotically significantly faster than the fastest known algorithm for NDP, by Kawarabayashi and Wollan [KW10], which requires time at least *quadruple-exponential* in k [AKK$^+$11]. Namely, if r is asymptotically less than triple-exponential in k, our algorithm is asymptotically faster than theirs. We achieve this result by the idea of so-called *essential pairs* and *realizations*, which characterizes the "interaction" between the feedback vertex set R and the paths in an optimum solution. Note that in our algorithm of Theorem 3.3 the parameter k does not appear in the exponent of the run time at all. Hence, whenever $r = o(k/\log k)$, our algorithm is asymptotically faster than reducing MAXNDP to NDP by guessing the subset of pairs to be routed (at an expense of 2^k in the run time) and using Scheffler's [Sch94] algorithm for NDP with run time $2^{\mathcal{O}(r \log r)} \cdot n$; for $r = \Omega(k/\log k)$, our algorithm is asymptotically not slower.

Once a fixed-parameter algorithm for a problem has been obtained, the existence of a polynomial-size kernel comes up. Here we note that MAXNDP does not admit a polynomial kernel for the combined parameter $k + r$, unless NP $\subseteq$ coNP/poly [BTY11].

Another natural question is whether the run time $f(k, r) \cdot n$ in Theorem 3.3 can be improved to $f(r) \cdot n^{\mathcal{O}(1)}$. We answer this question in the negative, ruling out the existence of a fixed-parameter algorithm for MAXNDP parameterized by r (assuming FPT $\neq$ W[1]):

Theorem 3.4. *MAXNDP in unit-capacity graphs is* W[1]*-hard parameterized by feedback vertex set number.*

This theorem contrasts the known result that NDP is fixed-parameter tractable in feedback vertex set number [Sch94]—which further stresses the relevance of understanding this parameter.

For MAXEDP, we prove that the situation is, in a sense, even worse:

Theorem 3.5. *MAXEDP is* NP*-hard for unit-capacity graphs with feedback vertex set number* $r = 1$ *and EDP is* NP*-hard for unit-capacity graphs with feedback vertex set number* $r = 2$.

This theorem also shows that our algorithms are relevant for small values of r, and that they nicely complement the NP-hardness for MAXEDP in capacitated trees [GVY97].

Our results are summarized in Table 3.1.

Table 3.1: Summary of results obtained in this chapter.

	EDP	MAXEDP	NDP	MAXNDP
const.				
$r = 0$	poly [GVY97]	poly [GVY97]	poly [Sch94]	poly (Thm. 3.3)
$r = 1$	poly [GOS17]	NP-hard (Thm. 3.5)	poly [Sch94]	poly (Thm. 3.3)
$r \geq 2$	NP-hard (Thm. 3.5)	NP-hard (Thm. 3.5)	poly [Sch94]	poly (Thm. 3.3)
param.	para-NP-hard (Thm. 3.5)		FPT [Sch94]	W[1]-hard (Thm. 3.4)
in r	$\mathcal{O}(\sqrt{r} \log kr)$-approx (Thm. 3.2)		exact $(k + r)^{\mathcal{O}(r)} n$ (Thm. 3.3)	
	$\mathcal{O}(1)$-approx. w. cg. $\mathcal{O}\left(\frac{\log kr}{\log \log kr}\right)$ (Thm. 3.1)			

Related Work. Our study of the parameter feedback vertex set number is in line with the general attempt to obtain bounds for MaxEDP (or related problems) that are independent of the input size. Besides the above-mentioned works that provide bounds in terms of the

(a) A terminal s. Assume that it appears in three terminal pairs $(s, t_1), (s, t_2), (s, t_3)$.

(b) Three copies s_1, s_2, and s_3 of the terminal s attached as leaves to it. We replace the terminal pairs of s by (s_1, t_1), (s_2, t_2), and (s_3, t_3) and define s as a normal vertex.

Figure 3.1: We can assume that M forms a matching and all terminals are leaves.

treewidth of the input graph, Günlük [Gün07] and Chekuri et al. [CSW13] give bounds on the *flow-cut gap* for the closely related integer multi-commodity flow problem; their bounds are logarithmic with respect to the *vertex cover number* of a graph. This improved upon earlier bounds of $\mathcal{O}(\log n)$ [LR99] and $\mathcal{O}(\log k)$ [AR98, LLR95]. As every vertex cover is in particular a feedback vertex set of a graph, our results for disjoint path problems address a generalization of graphs with bounded vertex cover number. Bodlaender et al. [BTY11] showed that NDP does not admit a polynomial kernel parameterized by vertex cover number *and* the number k of terminal pairs, unless NP $\subseteq$ coNP/poly; therefore, NDP is unlikely to admit a polynomial kernel in $k + r$ either. Ene et al. [EMPR16] showed that MaxNDP is W[1]-hard parameterized by tree-depth, which is another restriction of treewidth that is incomparable to feedback vertex set number.

The basic gap in understanding the approximability of MaxEDP has led to several improved results for special graph classes, and also our results can be seen in this light. For example, polylogarithmic approximation algorithms are known for graphs whose global minimum cut value is $\Omega(\log^5 n)$ [RZ10], for bounded-degree expanders [BFSU99, BFU94, Fri01, KR96, LR99], and for Eulerian planar or 4-connected planar graphs [KK10]. Constant factor approximation algorithms are known for capacitated trees [CMS07, GVY97], grids and grid-like graphs [AR95, AGLR94, KT95, KT98]. For planar graphs, there is a constant-factor approximation algorithm with congestion 2 [SCS11]. Recently, Chuzhoy et al. [CKL16] gave a $\tilde{\mathcal{O}}(n^{9/19})$-approximation algorithm for MaxNDP on *planar* graphs. However, improving the $\mathcal{O}(\sqrt{n})$-approximation algorithm for MaxEDP remains elusive even for planar graphs.

Very recently, Ganian et al. [GOS17] positively confirmed a conjecture posed in our extended abstract [FMS18]. They showed that EDP can be solved in polynomial time if $r = 1$.

3.2   Preliminaries

For an instance $(G, \mathcal{M})$ of MaxEDP/MaxNDP, we refer to the vertices participating in the pairs $\mathcal{M}$ as *terminals*. It is convenient to assume that $\mathcal{M}$ forms a matching on the terminals; this can be ensured by making several copies of the terminals and attaching them as leaves as depicted in Fig. 3.1. Hence, we can also assume that all terminals are leaves.

Multi-commodity flow relaxation.   We use the following standard multi-commodity flow relaxation for MaxEDP that we will call MaxEDP LP (there is an analogous relaxation for MaxNDP). We use $\mathcal{P}(u, v)$ to denote the set of all paths in G from u to v, for each pair (u, v) of nodes. Since the pairs in $\mathcal{M}$ form a matching, the sets in $\{\mathcal{P}(s_i, t_i) \mid (s_i, t_i) \in \mathcal{M}\}$ are

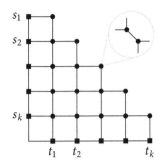

Figure 3.2: An instance with an integrality gap of $\Omega(\sqrt{n})$ for MaxEDP [GVY97]: Any integral routing routes at most one pair, whereas a fractional multi-commodity flow can send $1/2$ unit of flow for each pair (s_i, t_i) along the canonical path from s_i to t_i in the grid.

pairwise disjoint. Let $\mathcal{P} = \bigcup_{i=1}^{k} \mathcal{P}(s_i, t_i)$. The LP has a variable $f(P)$ for each path $P \in \mathcal{P}$ representing the amount of flow on P. For each pair $(s_i, t_i) \in \mathcal{M}$, the LP has a variable x_i denoting the total amount of flow routed for the pair (in the corresponding integer program, x_i denotes whether the pair is routed or not). The LP imposes the constraint that there is a flow from s_i to t_i of value x_i. Additionally, the LP has constraints that ensure that the total amount of flow on paths using a given edge (respectively node for MaxNDP) is at most 1.

$$
\begin{aligned}
\text{maximize} \quad & \sum_{i=1}^{k} x_i \\
\text{subject to} \quad & \sum_{P \in \mathcal{P}(s_i, t_i)} f(P) = x_i \le 1 \quad \text{for each } i = 1, \cdots, k; \\
& \sum_{P \in \mathcal{P}: \, e \in P} f(P) \le 1 \qquad \text{for each } e \in E(G); \\
& f(P) \ge 0 \qquad \text{for each } P \in \mathcal{P}.
\end{aligned}
$$

It is well-known that the relaxation MaxEDP LP can be solved in polynomial time, since there is an efficient separation oracle for the dual LP (alternatively, one can write a compact relaxation). We use $(f, \mathbf{x})$ to denote a feasible solution to MaxEDP LP for an instance $(G, \mathcal{M})$ of MaxEDP.

As noted in the introduction, MaxEDP LP has an integrality gap of $\Omega(\sqrt{n})$ as shown by Garg et al. [GVY97]. The integrality instance on an $n \times n$ grid (of treewidth $\Theta(\sqrt{n})$) exploits a topological obstruction in the plane that prevents a large integral routing; see Fig. 3.2.

We will use the following result by Chekuri et al. [CKS06, Sect. 3.1]; see also Proposition 3.3 of Chekuri et al. [CNS13b].

Proposition 3.1 (Chekuri et al. [CKS06]). *Let $(f, \mathbf{x})$ be a fractional solution to the LP relaxation of a MaxEDP instance $(G, \mathcal{M})$. If some node v is contained in all flow paths of f, then we can find an integral routing of size at least $\sum_i x_i/12$ in polynomial time.*

As a corollary of Theorem 3.2, we immediately obtain the following proposition about the integrality gap of MaxEDP LP.

Corollary 3.1. *The integrality gap of the multi-commodity flow relaxation for MaxEDP with k terminal pairs is $\mathcal{O}(\sqrt{r}\log kr)$ for graphs with feedback vertex set number r.*

Let f be a multi-commodity flow assigning to each path $P \in \mathcal{P}$ a non-negative flow value $f(P)$. The flow f is said to have *congestion c* if it satisfies a modification of MaxEDP LP where we replace, for each edge $e \in E(G)$, the constraint $\sum_{P \in \mathcal{P}:\, e \in P} f(P) \le 1$ by the constraint $\sum_{P \in \mathcal{P}:\, e \in P} f(P) \le c$. In the particular case where f is integral we also speak of a *routing f with congestion c*.

3.3   Bi-Criteria Approximation for MaxEDP with Low Congestion

We present a randomized rounding algorithm that will lead to the proof of Theorem 3.1. First we will modify a fractional solution to the multi-commodity flow relaxation and then run a randomized rounding procedure.

3.3.1   Algorithm

Consider an instance $(G, \mathcal{M})$ of MaxEDP. Let k denote the number of terminal pairs in $\mathcal{M}$, and let R be a feedback vertex set of G that we construct by taking the union of the terminals in $\mathcal{M}$ and any 2-approximate minimum feedback vertex set; note that such an approximation can be obtained in polynomial time [BBF99]. Thus, $|R| \le 2r + 2k$.

First, solve the corresponding MaxEDP LP. We obtain an optimal extreme point solution $(f, \mathbf{x})$. For each $(s_i, t_i) \in \mathcal{M}$, this gives us a set $\mathcal{P}'(s_i, t_i)$ of positive weighted paths that satisfy the LP constraints. Formally,

$$\mathcal{P}'(s_i, t_i) = \{P \in \mathcal{P}(s_i, t_i) \mid f(P) > 0\}\,.$$

Since we have an extreme point solution, the number of tight constraints is not smaller than the number of variables. Hence, given the numbers of constraints and variables, the number of constraints that are not tight is polynomially bounded in the input size. Consequently, the same bound holds for the cardinality of the set $\mathcal{P}' = \bigcup_{i=1}^{k} \mathcal{P}'(s_i, t_i)$. In what follows, we will modify $\mathcal{P}'$ and then select an (unweighted) subset $\mathcal{P}'_{\text{Sol}}$ of $\mathcal{P}'$ that will form our integral solution.

Each $P \in \mathcal{P}'$ has the form $(r_1, \ldots, r_2, \ldots, r_\ell)$ where $r_1, \ldots, r_\ell$ are the nodes in R that are traversed by P in this order. For every j with $1 \le j \le \ell - 1$, we call the path $(r_j, \ldots, r_{j+1})$ a *subpath of P*. For every subpath P' of P, we set $f(P') = f(P)$. Let $\mathcal{S}$ be the multi-set of all subpaths of all paths in $\mathcal{P}'$. Let $F = G - R$ be the forest obtained by removing R.

We now modify some paths in $\mathcal{P}'$, one by one, and at the same time, we incrementally construct a subset $H_{\text{Alg}} \subseteq V(F)$ in several steps. We will refer to the nodes in H_{Alg} as *hot spots*. When the construction of H_{Alg} is complete, every subpath in $\mathcal{S}$ will contain at least one hot spot, that is, a node in H_{Alg}.

Initially, let $H_{\text{Alg}} = \varnothing$. Consider any tree T in F and fix any of its nodes as a root. Then let $\mathcal{S}_T$ be the multi-set of all subpaths in $\mathcal{S}$ that, excluding the endpoints, are contained in T. For each subpath $P \in \mathcal{S}_T$, define its *highest node $h(P)$* as the node on P closest to the root.

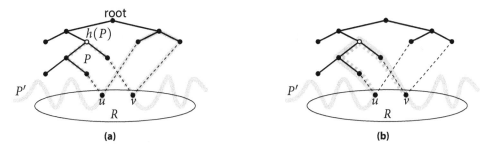

Figure 3.3: Example of the flow aggregation step: (a) A subpath P (highlighted in dashed gray) enters a tree (solid black edges) where $h(P)$ (white node) is its closest node to the root. A path P' (highlighted in solid gray) contains a different subpath with the same endpoints $u, v \in R$ as P. (b) We reroute P' by replacing its subpath between u and v with a copy of P.

Note that $P \cap T$ equals $P \cap F$ and that $P \cap T$ is a path. Now, pick a subpath $P \in \mathcal{S}_T$ that does not contain any node in H_{Alg} and whose highest node $h(P)$ is *farthest away* from the root. Consider the multi-set $\mathcal{S}[P]$ of all subpaths in $\mathcal{S}_T$ that are identical to P (but may be subpaths of different flow paths in $\mathcal{P}'$). Note that the weight $f(\mathcal{S}[P])$ of $\mathcal{S}[P]$ defined as $\sum_{P \in \mathcal{S}[P]} f(P)$ is at most 1 by the constraints of the LP. Let $u, v \in R$ be the endpoints of P. We define $\mathcal{S}_{uv}$ as the set of all subpaths in $\mathcal{S} \setminus \mathcal{S}[P]$ that have u and v as their endpoints and that do not contain any node in H_{Alg}.

Intuitively speaking, we now aggregate flow on P by rerouting as much flow as possible from $\mathcal{S}_{uv}$ to P. To this end, we repeatedly perform the following operation as long as $f(\mathcal{S}[P]) < 1$ and $\mathcal{S}_{uv} \neq \emptyset$. We pick a path P' in $\mathcal{S}$ that contains a subpath in $\mathcal{S}_{uv}$; see Fig. 3.3. We reroute flow from P' by creating a new path P'' that arises from P' by replacing its subpath between u and v with a new path identical to P, and assign it the weight

$$f(P'') = \min\{f(P'), 1 - f(\mathcal{S}[P])\}.$$

Then we set the weight of (the original path) P' to $\max\{0, f(P') + f(\mathcal{S}[P]) - 1\}$. We update the sets $\mathcal{P}', \mathcal{P}'(s_i, t_i), \mathcal{S}, \mathcal{S}_T, \mathcal{S}[P]$ and $\mathcal{S}_{uv}$ accordingly.

As soon as $f(\mathcal{S}[P]) = 1$ or $\mathcal{S}_{uv} = \emptyset$, we mark $h(P)$ as a hot spot and add it to H_{Alg}. Then, we proceed with the next $P \in \mathcal{S}_T$ that does not contain a hot spot and whose highest node $h(P)$ is farthest away from the root. If no such P is left, we consider the next tree T in F.

At the end, we create our solution $\mathcal{P}'_{\text{Sol}}$ by randomized rounding: We route every terminal pair (s_i, t_i) with probability x_i. In case (s_i, t_i) is routed, we randomly select a path from $\mathcal{P}'(s_i, t_i)$ and add it to $\mathcal{P}'_{\text{Sol}}$ where the probability that the path P is taken is $f(P)/x_i$.

3.3.2   Analysis

First, observe that **x** did not change during our modifications of the paths, as the total flow between any terminal pair did not change. Thus, the expected number of pairs routed in our solution $\mathcal{P}'_{\text{Sol}}$ is $\sum_{i=1}^{k} x_i \geq \text{OPT}^*$. Using the Chernoff bound, the probability that we route less than $\text{OPT}^*/2$ pairs is at most $e^{-1/8\,\text{OPT}^*} < 1/2$, assuming $\text{OPT}^* > 8$.

In the above algorithm, we guarantee that when we aggregate flow on a path P, then the total amount of all flow paths containing P as a subpath has increased to at most 1. Nevertheless, the flow f may have congestion greater than 1 after this modification. This is because P may intersect flow paths that contain only a proper subset of the edges of P. For instance, consider the situation where we increase $f(\mathcal{S}[P'])$ for a subpath P' that initially contained a tight edge e (that is, an edge e with $\sum_{P\in\mathcal{P}:\, e\in P} f(P) = 1$). After increasing $f(\mathcal{S}[P'])$, the total amount of flow paths going through e is greater than 1. However, the congestion of the modified flow f is always at most 2 as shown by the following lemma.

Lemma 3.1. *The congestion of the flow f is at most 2.*

Proof. In our algorithm, we increase the flow only along flow subpaths that are pairwise edge-disjoint. To see this, consider two distinct flow subpaths P and P' on which we increase the flow. If there were an edge e lying on P and P', then both subpaths traverse the same tree in the forest F. Assume, without loss of generality, that P was considered before P' by the algorithm. Then the path from e to the root would first visit $h(P)$ and then $h(P')$. Hence, $h(P)$ would be an internal node of P'. This membership yields a contradiction, as $h(P)$ was already marked as a hot spot when P' was considered. This argument shows that we increased the flow along any edge by at most one unit. Hence, f has congestion at most 2. $\square$

We now bound the congestion of the integral solution obtained by randomized rounding. In the algorithm, we constructed a set H_{Alg} of hot spots. As a part of the analysis, we will now extend this set to a set H as follows. Initially, $H = H_{\mathrm{Alg}}$. We build a sub-forest F' of F consisting of all edges of F that lie on a path connecting two hot spots. Then we add to H all nodes that have degree at least 3 in F'. Since the number of nodes of degree 3 in any forest is at most its number of leaves and since every leaf of F' is a hot spot, it follows that this can at most double the size of H to $2|H_{\mathrm{Alg}}|$. Finally, we add all nodes of the feedback vertex set R to H and mark all nodes in H as hot spots.

Lemma 3.2. *The number $|H|$ of hot spots is at most $2k|R|^2 + |R|$.*

Proof. To this end, fix two nodes $u, v \in R$ and consider the set of flow subpaths with endpoints u and v for which we added their hot spots to H_{Alg}. Due to the aggregation of flows in our algorithm, all except possibly one of the subpaths are saturated, that is, they carry precisely one unit of flow. Since no two of these subpaths are contained in a same flow path of f and since the flow value of f is bounded from above by k, we added at most k hot spots for the pair u, v. Since there are at most $|R|^2$ pairs in R, the claim follows. $\square$

Definition 3.1. A hot spot $u \in H$ is *good* if the congestion on any edge incident on u is bounded by $12 \log k|R|/ \log\log k|R|$; otherwise, u is *bad*.

Lemma 3.3. *Let $u \in H$ be a hot spot. The probability that u is bad is bounded from above by $1/(k^2|R|^3)$.*

Proof. Let $e_1 = uv_1, \ldots, e_\ell = uv_\ell$ be the edges incident on u and, for each i with $1 \le i \le \ell$, let f_i be the total flow on the edge uv_i. Since any flow path visits at most two of the edges incident on u, the total flow $\sum_{i=1}^{\ell} f_i$ on the edges incident on u is at most $2k$.

For any i with $1 \le i \le \ell$, we have $f_i = \sum_{P:P \ni e_i} f(P)$, where P runs over the set of all paths connecting some terminal pair and containing e_i. For $1 \le j \le k$, we define

$$f_{ij} = \sum_{P \in \mathcal{P}(s_j, t_j):P \ni e_i} f(P)$$

as the total amount of flow sent across e_i by the terminal pair (s_j, t_j). Recall that x_j is the total flow sent for tdp/main-edp.the terminal pair (s_j, t_j). The probability that the randomized rounding procedure picks a certain path $P \in \mathcal{P}(s_j, t_j)$ is precisely $x_j \cdot (f(P)/x_j) = f(P)$. Given the disjointness of the respective events, the probability that the pair (s_j, t_j) routes a path across e_i is precisely f_{ij}. Let X_{ij} be the binary random variable indicating whether the pair (s_j, t_j) routes a path across e_i. Then $\mathbb{P}\left[X_{ij} = 1\right] = f_{ij}$. Let $X_i = \sum_{j=1}^{k} X_{ij}$ be the number of paths routed across e_i by the algorithm. By linearity of expectation,

$$\mathbb{E}\left[X_i\right] = \sum_{j=1}^{k} \mathbb{E}\left[X_{ij}\right] = \sum_{j=1}^{k} f_{ij} = f_i \,.$$

In the following, we assume that k is sufficiently big ($k \ge e^{e^e}$). Note that this assumption is feasible as MaxEDP can be efficiently solved when k is constant [RS95]. Fix any edge e_i. Set

$$\delta = 6 \cdot \frac{\log k|R|}{\log \log k|R|}$$

and $\delta' = 2\delta/f_i - 1$. Note that, for fixed i, the variables in $\{X_{ij} \mid 1 \le j \le k\}$ are independent. Hence, by the Chernoff bound (see Equation 2.1 in Chapter 2.1) , we have

$$\mathbb{P}\left[X_i \ge 2\delta\right] \le \mathbb{P}\left[X_i \ge (1 + \delta')f_i\right]$$

$$< \left(\frac{e^{\delta'}}{(1 + \delta')^{1+\delta'}}\right)^{f_i}$$

$$\le \left(\frac{f_i}{2}\right)^{2\delta} \cdot \left(\frac{e}{\delta}\right)^{2\delta}$$

$$\le \frac{f_i}{2} \cdot \left(\frac{f_i}{2}\right)^{2\delta - 1} \cdot \delta^{-\delta}$$

$$\le \frac{f_i}{2} \cdot e^{-\delta \log \delta}$$

$$\le \frac{f_i}{2} \cdot e^{-6 \cdot \frac{\log k|R|}{\log \log k|R|} \log\left(6 \cdot \frac{\log k|R|}{\log \log k|R|}\right)}$$

$$\le \frac{f_i}{2} \cdot e^{-6 \cdot \frac{\log k|R|}{\log \log k|R|} \log\left(\frac{\log k|R|}{\log \log k|R|}\right)} \tag{3.1}$$

$$\le \frac{f_i}{2k^3|R|^3} \,. \tag{3.2}$$

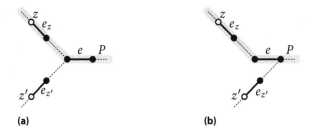

Figure 3.4: Two examples of an edge e with two hot spots z and z' (white nodes) being direct to e. Note that there is no hot spot in between z and z'. Any path routed by our algorithm that visits e must visit e_z or $e_{z'}$. Such a path P is highlighted in gray.

For Equation 3.1, we use $f_i \leq 2$ (see Lemma 3.1) and $e/\delta \leq \delta^{-1/2}$. For Equation 3.2, we use

$$\frac{\log\log\log k|R|}{\log\log k|R|} \leq \frac{1}{e} < \frac{1}{2}.$$

Now, applying the union bound, we can infer that the probability that any of the edges incident on u carries more than 2δ paths, that is, more than $12\log k|R|/\log\log k|R|$ paths, is at most

$$\sum_i \frac{f_i}{2k^3|R|^3} \leq \frac{2k}{2k^3|R|^3} = \frac{1}{k^2|R|^3}. \qquad \square$$

Lemma 3.4. *If every hot spot is good, then the congestion on every edge is bounded from above by* $24\log k|R|/\log\log k|R|$.

Proof. Consider an arbitrary edge $e = uv$ that is not incident on any hot spot. In particular, this means that e lies in the forest $F = G - R$. A hot spot z in F is called *direct* to e if the path in F from z to e excluding e does not contain any hot spot other than z.

We claim that there can be at most two distinct hot spots z, z' direct to e. If there were a third hot spot z'' direct to e, then consider the unique node $z_0 \in V(F)$ such that no two of the hot spots z, z', z'' are connected in $F - z_0$. Such a node z_0 exists, since z, z', z'' cannot lie on a common path in F as they are all direct to e. The node z_0, however, would be added as a hot spot at the latest when H was built. Now this is a contradiction, because then one of the paths connecting z, z' or z'' to e would contain z_0 and thus one of these hot spots would not be direct to e.

Now we show the lemma assuming that there are two distinct hot spots z, z' direct to e. If there were only one or no hot spot direct to e, then we can apply a similar argument as the following one.

Now, let P be an arbitrary path that is routed by our algorithm and that traverses e, and let $P' \in S$ be the subpath of P visiting e; see Fig. 3.4. Consider the two paths in F connecting z to e and z' to e. Let e_z and $e_{z'}$ be the edges on these paths incident on z and z', respectively. By our construction, P' must visit a hot spot in F. If P' visited neither z nor z', then P' would contain a hot spot direct to u or to v that is distinct from z and z'—a contradiction. Hence P' and thus also P visit e_z or $e_{z'}$. The claim now follows from the facts that, first, this holds for any path traversing e, and that, secondly, z and z' are good, and that, thirdly, therefore altogether at most $2 \cdot (12 \log k|R| / \log \log k|R|)$ paths visit e_z or e'_z. □

Now we are ready to prove Theorem 3.1.

Proof of Theorem 3.1. We show that the algorithm presented in Sect. 3.3.1 produces—with constant probability—a routing with $\Omega(\mathrm{OPT}^*)$ paths with congestion $\mathcal{O}(\log kr / \log \log kr)$. As argued above, the probability that we route less than $\mathrm{OPT}^*/2$ paths is at most $1/2$. By Lemma 3.2, the number of hot spots is at most $2k|R|^2 + |R| \leq 3k|R|^2$. Thus, Lemma 3.3 implies an upper bound of $3k|R|^2/(k^2|R|^3) = 3/(k|R|)$ on the probability that at least one of these hot spots is bad. Hence, by Lemma 3.4, we route with probability

$$1 - 1/2 - 3/(k|R|)$$

at least $\mathrm{OPT}^*/2$ pairs with congestion at most $24 \log k|R| / \log \log k|R|$. Since the probability is bounded from below by a positive constant for sufficiently big k, the statement of the theorem follows by using $|R| \leq 2r + 2k$ and $|R| \geq r$. □

3.4   Refined Approximation Bound for MaxEDP

In this section, we provide an improved approximation guarantee for MaxEDP *without* congestion, thereby proving Theorem 3.2.

3.4.1   Irreducible Routings with Low Congestion

We first develop the concept of *irreducible routings with low congestion*, which is (besides Theorem 3.1) a key ingredient of our strengthened bound on the approximability of MaxEDP based on feedback vertex set number.

Consider any multigraph G and any set $\mathcal{P}$ of (not necessarily simple) paths in G with congestion c. We say that an edge e is *redundant in* $\mathcal{P}$ if there is an edge $e' \neq e$ such that the set of paths in $\mathcal{P}$ covering (containing) e is a subset of the set of paths in $\mathcal{P}$ covering e'. For instance, if G contains at least two edges, then any edge that is not covered by any path in $\mathcal{P}$ is redundant in $\mathcal{P}$.

Definition 3.2. The set $\mathcal{P}$ is called an *irreducible routing with congestion c* if each edge belongs to at most c paths of $\mathcal{P}$ and there is no edge redundant in $\mathcal{P}$.

In contrast to a feasible routing of a MaxEDP instance, we do not require an irreducible routing to connect a set of terminal pairs. If there is an edge e redundant in $\mathcal{P}$, we can apply the following *reduction rule*: We contract e in G and we contract e in every path of $\mathcal{P}$ that covers e. By this, we obtain a minor G' of G and a set $\mathcal{P}'$ of paths that consists of all the contracted paths and of all paths in $\mathcal{P}$ that were not contracted. Thus, there is a one-to-one correspondence between the paths in $\mathcal{P}$ and $\mathcal{P}'$.

We make the following observation about $\mathcal{P}$ and $\mathcal{P}'$.

Observation 3.1. *A subset of paths in $\mathcal{P}'$ is edge-disjoint in G' if and only if the corresponding subset of paths in $\mathcal{P}$ is edge-disjoint in G.*

As applying the reduction rule strictly decreases the number of redundant edges, an iterative application of this rule yields an irreducible routing on a minor of the original graph.

Theorem 3.6. *Let $\mathcal{G}$ be a minor-closed class of multigraphs and let $p_{\mathcal{G}}$ be a positive integer. If for each graph $G \in \mathcal{G}$ and every non-empty irreducible routing $\mathcal{P}$ on G with congestion c there exists a path in $\mathcal{P}$ of length at most $p_{\mathcal{G}}$, then the average length of the paths in $\mathcal{P}$ is at most $c \cdot p_{\mathcal{G}}$.*

Proof. Take a path P_0 of length at most $p_{\mathcal{G}}$. Contract all edges of P_0 in G and obtain a minor $G' \in \mathcal{G}$ of G. For each path in $\mathcal{P}$ contract all edges shared with P_0 to obtain a set $\mathcal{P}'$ of paths. Remove P_0 along with all degenerated paths from $\mathcal{P}'$, thus $|\mathcal{P}'| < |\mathcal{P}|$. Note that $\mathcal{P}'$ is an irreducible routing on G' with congestion c. We repeat this reduction procedure recursively on G' and $\mathcal{P}'$ until $\mathcal{P}'$ is empty; this happens after at most $|\mathcal{P}|$ steps. At each step, we decrease the total path length by at most $c \cdot p_{\mathcal{G}}$. Hence, the total length of paths in $\mathcal{P}$ is at most $|\mathcal{P}| \cdot c \cdot p_{\mathcal{G}}$. □

As a consequence of Theorem 3.6, we get the following result for forests.

Lemma 3.5. *Let F be a forest and let $\mathcal{P}$ be a non-empty irreducible routing on F with congestion c. The average path length in $\mathcal{P}$ is at most $2c$.*

Proof. We show that $\mathcal{P}$ contains a path of length at most 2. Then the lemma follows immediately by applying Theorem 3.6 and using the fact that (simple) forests are minor-closed.

Take any tree in F, root it with any node and consider a leaf v of maximum depth. If v is adjacent to the root, then the tree is a star and every path in the tree has length at most 2. Otherwise, let e_1 and e_2 be the first two edges on the path from v to the root. By the definition of irreducible routing, the set of all paths covering e_1 is not a subset of the paths covering e_2; hence, e_1 is covered by a path which does not cover e_2. Since all other edges incident to e_1 end in a leaf, this path has length at most 2. □

Note that the bound provided in Lemma 3.5 is actually tight up to a constant. Let c be an arbitrary integer greater than one. Consider a graph that is a path of length $c - 1$ with a star of $c - 1$ leaves attached to one of its endpoints. The $c - 1$ paths of length c together with the $2c - 2$ paths of length 1 form an irreducible routing with congestion c. The average path length is

$$\frac{(c-1)c + (2c-2)}{3c-3} = \frac{c+2}{3}.$$

3.4.2 Approximation Algorithm

Consider an instance $(G, \mathcal{M})$ of MaxEDP with k terminal pairs. Let R be a 2-approximate minimum feedback vertex set in G; recall that we can obtain R in polynomial time [BBF99]. Furthermore, let $c = \mathcal{O}(\log kr / \log \log kr)$ be the bound on the congestion of our algorithm in Theorem 3.1.

We solve the corresponding MaxEDP LP and obtain an optimal extreme point solution $(f, \mathbf{x})$ of total flow $|f| = \mathrm{OPT}^*$. By the same argument as in Sect. 3.3, the number of all paths with a positive flow value is polynomially bounded in the input size. Let $\rho = \sqrt{|R|}/c$ and let $\mathcal{P}$ be the set of all paths with a positive flow value that visit at most ρ nodes of R.

Below we argue how to use R, $\mathcal{P}$ and f to obtain a feasible routing of $\Omega\left(|f|/(c\sqrt{|R|})\right)$ paths, which yields an overall approximation ratio of $\mathcal{O}(\sqrt{r}\log kr)$; that will prove Theorem 3.2.

We distinguish the following two cases.

Case 1:   The total flow of $\mathcal{P}$ is at least $|f|/2$. We compute a new flow (f', x'), where we set $f'(P) = f(P)$ for every path P in $\mathcal{P}$, and $f'(P) = 0$ for any other path P. Thus, we have $|f'| \geq |f|/2$. By applying our algorithm of Sect. 3.3 on (f', x'), we efficiently compute with constant probability a routing $\overline{\mathcal{P}}$ with congestion c containing $\Omega(|f'|) = \Omega(|f|)$ paths. Note that all paths in $\overline{\mathcal{P}}$ visit at most ρ nodes of R. Initialize $\mathcal{P}'$ with $\overline{\mathcal{P}}$. As long as there is an edge e not adjacent to R that is redundant in $\mathcal{P}'$, we iteratively apply the reduction rule (see Sect. 3.4.1) on e by contracting e in the graph as well as in every path that covers it. Let G' be the obtained minor of G with forest $F' = G' - R$. Note that F' is simple (in contrast to G' that might contain multiple edges) as we contracted edges only in the (simple) forest $G - R$. The obtained set $\mathcal{P}'$ is a set of (not necessarily simple) paths in G' corresponding to $\overline{\mathcal{P}}$. In order to obtain a feasible routing for $(G, \mathcal{M})$ of size Ω $(|f|/(c\rho))$, it suffices by iterated application of Observation 3.1 to $\overline{\mathcal{P}}$ and $\mathcal{P}'$ that we efficiently find a subset $\mathcal{P}'_{\text{Sol}} \subseteq \mathcal{P}'$ of pairwise edge-disjoint paths of size $|\mathcal{P}'_{\text{Sol}}| = \Omega\left(|\overline{\mathcal{P}}|/(c\rho)\right)$.

To obtain $\mathcal{P}'_{\text{Sol}}$, we first bound the total path length in $\mathcal{P}'$. Removing R from G' "decomposes" the set $\mathcal{P}'$ into a set $\mathcal{S}$ of subpaths lying in F', that is,

$$\mathcal{S} = \{S \text{ is a connected component of } P \cap F' \mid P \in \mathcal{P}'\} \, .$$

Observe that $\mathcal{S}$ is an irreducible set of F' with congestion c, as the reduction rule is not applicable anymore. (Note that a single path in $\mathcal{P}'$ may lead to many paths in the cover $\mathcal{S}$ which are considered distinct.) Thus, by Lemma 3.5, the average path length in $\mathcal{S}$ is at most $2c$.

Let P be an arbitrary path in $\mathcal{P}'$. Each edge on P that is *not* in a subpath in $\mathcal{S}$ is incident on a node in R, and each node in R is incident on at most two edges in P. Together with the fact that P visits less than ρ nodes in R, there are less than 2ρ edges of P outside $\mathcal{S}$. By the same fact, P contributes at most ρ subpaths to $\mathcal{S}$. Given that the average length of the subpaths in $\mathcal{S}$ is at most $2c$, we can upper bound the total path length $\sum_{P \in \mathcal{P}'} |P|$ by $|\mathcal{P}'|\rho(2c + 2)$. Let $\mathcal{P}''$ be the set of the $|\mathcal{P}'|/2$ shortest paths in $\mathcal{P}'$. Hence, each path in $\mathcal{P}''$ has length at most $4\rho(c + 1)$.

We greedily construct a feasible solution $\mathcal{P}'_{\text{Sol}}$ by iteratively picking an arbitrary path P from $\mathcal{P}''$, adding it to $\mathcal{P}'_{\text{Sol}}$ and removing all paths from $\mathcal{P}''$ that share some edge with P (including P itself). We stop when $\mathcal{P}''$ is empty. As $\mathcal{P}''$ has congestion c, we remove at most $4\rho c(c + 1)$ paths from $\mathcal{P}''$ per iteration. Thus,

$$|\mathcal{P}'_{\text{Sol}}| \geq |\mathcal{P}''|/(4\rho c(c + 1)) = \Omega\left(|\overline{\mathcal{P}}|/(c\sqrt{|R|})\right) \, .$$

Case 2:   The flow of $\mathcal{P}$ is less than $|f|/2$. Then, the flow of all paths visiting at least ρ nodes of R is at least $|f|/2$. Let $\mathcal{P}'$ be the subset of these paths and let f' be the sum of all these flows. Note that f' provides a feasible solution to relaxation MaxEDP LP for (G, M) of value at least $|f|/2$. Since every flow path in f' has length at least ρ, the total inflow of the nodes in R is at least $|f'|\rho$. By averaging, there must be a node $v \in R$ of inflow at least $\rho|f'|/|R| = |f'|/(c\sqrt{|R|})$. Let f'' be the subflow of f' consisting of all flow paths visiting v. This subflow corresponds to a feasible solution $(f'', \mathbf{x}'')$ of the LP relaxation of value at least $|f'|/(c\sqrt{|R|}) \geq |f|/(2c\sqrt{|R|})$. Using Proposition 3.1, we can recover an integral feasible routing of size at least

$$\sum_i x_i''/12 \geq |f|/(24c\sqrt{|R|}) = \Omega\left(|f|/(c\sqrt{|R|})\right).$$

This case completes the proof of Theorem 3.2. □

3.5   Fixed-Parameter Algorithm for MaxNDP

In this section, we give a fixed-parameter algorithm for MAXNDP that solves any instance $(G, \mathcal{M})$ in time $(k + r)^{O(r)} \cdot n$, where r denotes the feedback vertex set number of G, $k = |\mathcal{M}|$ and $n = |V(G)|$. We note that a feedback vertex set R of size r can be computed in time $r^{O(r)} \cdot n$ [LRS18].

By the matching assumption (see Sect. 3.2), each terminal in $\mathcal{M}$ is a leaf. We can thus assume that none of the terminals is contained in R.

Consider an optimal routing $\mathcal{P}$ of the given MAXNDP instance and the set $\mathcal{M}_R \subseteq \mathcal{M}$ of terminal pairs that are connected via $\mathcal{P}$ by a path that visits at least one node in R. Let $P \in \mathcal{P}$ be a path connecting a terminal pair $(s_i, t_i) \in \mathcal{M}_R$. This path has the form

$$(s_i, \ldots, r_1, \ldots, r_2, \ldots, r_\ell, \ldots, t_i),$$

where $r_1, \ldots, r_\ell$ are the nodes in R that are traversed by P in this order. The pairs (s_i, r_1) and (r_ℓ, t_i) as well as (r_j, r_{j+1}) for $j = 1, \ldots, \ell - 1$ are called *essential* pairs *for* P. A node pair is called *essential* if it is essential for some path in $\mathcal{P}$. Let $\mathcal{M}_e$ be the set of essential pairs.

Let F be the forest that arises when deleting R from the input graph G. Let (u, v) be any pair of nodes in G. A path P in G with endpoints u and v is said to *realize* (u, v) if all internal nodes of P lie in F. A set $\mathcal{P}'$ of paths is said to *realize* a set of node pairs if every pair in this set is realized by some path in $\mathcal{P}'$ and if two paths in $\mathcal{P}'$ can only intersect at their endpoints. Note that the optimal routing $\mathcal{P}$ induces a realization of $\mathcal{M}_e$ in a natural way: The realization consists of all maximal subpaths of paths in $\mathcal{P}$ whose internal nodes all lie in F. Conversely, for any realization $\mathcal{P}'$ of $\mathcal{M}_e$, we can concatenate paths in $\mathcal{P}'$ to obtain a feasible routing that connects all terminal pairs in $\mathcal{M}_R$. Therefore, we consider $\mathcal{P}'$ (slightly abusing notation) also as a feasible routing for $\mathcal{M}_R$.

In our algorithm, we first guess the set $\mathcal{M}_e$ of essential pairs, which implies the set $\mathcal{M}_R$ as well as the set $\overline{\mathcal{M}}_R$ that we define as $\overline{\mathcal{M}}_R = \mathcal{M} \smallsetminus \mathcal{M}_R$. Then, by dynamic programming, we construct two sets of paths, $\mathcal{P}_e$ and $\mathcal{P}_F$, where $\mathcal{P}_e$ realizes $\mathcal{M}_e$ and $\mathcal{P}_F$ routes in F a subset of $\overline{\mathcal{M}}_R$. In our algorithm, the set $\mathcal{P}_e \cup \mathcal{P}_F$ forms a feasible routing that maximizes $|\mathcal{P}_F|$ and routes all pairs in $\mathcal{M}_R$. Recall that we consider the realization $\mathcal{P}_e$ of $\mathcal{M}_e$ as a feasible routing for $\mathcal{M}_R$.

Now assume that we correctly guessed $\mathcal{M}_e$. Below, we will describe an algorithm that uses a dynamic programming table to compute an optimum routing in $2^{O(r)}(k + r)^{O(1)} \cdot n$ time. For the sake of easier presentation, first we describe how to compute the cardinality of such a routing. Then we argue how to find such a routing without a significant increase in the run time.

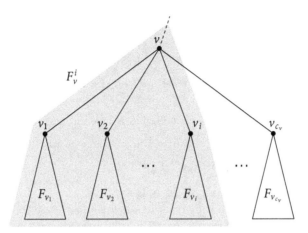

Figure 3.5: Subtree F_v^i consists of v and subtrees $F_{v_1}, \ldots, F_{v_i}$. Recall that only leaf nodes can be terminals or neighbors of R.

3.5.1   Dynamic Programming Table

Before we describe the dynamic programming table, we make several technical assumptions that help to simplify the presentation. First, we modify the input instance as follows. We subdivide every edge incident on a node in R by introducing a single new node on this edge. Note that this modification yields an instance equivalent to the input instance. As a result, every neighbor of a node in R that lies in F, that is, every node in $N_G(R)$, is a leaf in F. Moreover, the set R is an independent set in G. Also recall that we assumed that every terminal is a leaf and that therefore R does not contain any terminal. We also assume that the forest F is a rooted tree by introducing a dummy node (which plays the role of the root) and arbitrarily connecting this node to every connected component of F by an edge. In our dynamic programming table, we will take care that no path visits this root node. We also assume that F is an ordered tree by introducing an arbitrary order among the children of every node.

For any node v, let F_v be the subtree of F rooted at v. Let c_v be the number $\deg_F(v) - 1$ of children of v and let $v_1, \ldots v_{c_v}$ be the (ordered) children of v. Then, for $i = 1, \ldots, c_v$, let F_v^i denote the subtree of F_v induced by the union of v with the subtrees $F_{v_1}, \ldots, F_{v_i}$; see Fig. 3.5. If v is a leaf, we have $F_v = v$ and we define F_v^0 as F_v.

We introduce a dynamic programming table T. It contains an entry for every F_v^i and every subset $\mathcal{M}_e'$ of $\mathcal{M}_e$. Roughly speaking, the value of such an entry is the solution to the subproblem, where we restrict the forest to F_v^i, and the set of essential pairs to $\mathcal{M}_e'$. More precisely, table T contains five parameters: Parameters v and i describing F_v^i, a parameter $\mathcal{M}_e'$ describing the set of essential pairs, and two more parameters u and b. The parameter u is either a terminal or a node in R, and b is in one of the three states: *free, to-be-used,* or *blocked.* The value $T[v, i, \mathcal{M}_e', u, b]$ is the maximum cardinality of a set $\mathcal{P}_F$ of paths with the following properties:

1. The set $\mathcal{P}_F$ is a feasible routing of some subset of $\overline{\mathcal{M}_R}$.

2. The set $\mathcal{P}_F$ is completely contained in F_v^i.

3. There is an additional set $\mathcal{P}_e$ of paths with the following properties:

    (a) The set $\mathcal{P}_e$ is a realization of $\mathcal{M}'_e \cup \{(u,v)\}$ if $b = to\text{-}be\text{-}used$. Else, it is a realization of $\mathcal{M}'_e$.

    (b) The set $\mathcal{P}_e$ is completely contained in $F_v^i \cup R$ and node-disjoint from the paths in $\mathcal{P}_F$.

4. If $b = free$, there is no path in $\mathcal{P}_e \cup \mathcal{P}_F$ visiting v.

If no such set $\mathcal{P}_F$ exists, then $T[v, i, \mathcal{M}'_e, u, b]$ is $-\infty$.

Note that the parameter u is only relevant when $b = to\text{-}be\text{-}used$ (otherwise, it can just be ignored). One can think of the three states of b as follows: If $b = free$, then there is no path in $\mathcal{P}_e \cup \mathcal{P}_F$ visiting v, hence, in the future we might consider to add a path through v. If $b = to\text{-}be\text{-}used$, then v is visited by some path in $\mathcal{P}_e$ (connecting u to v) and we cannot add a new path through v. Eventually, if $b = blocked$, we may add a path to $\mathcal{P}_e \cup \mathcal{P}_F$ that goes through v. Hence, v is "blocked" for the future because of the possibility of having been already visited. Thus, we have

$$T[v, i, \mathcal{M}'_e, u, blocked] \geq T[v, i, \mathcal{M}'_e, u, free] \geq T[v, i, \mathcal{M}'_e, u, to\text{-}be\text{-}used] .$$

Below, we describe how to compute the entries of T in a bottom-up manner. Having computed T, we obtain the cardinality of the optimum routing $\mathcal{P}$ by $|\mathcal{M}_R| + T[v, c_v, \mathcal{M}_e, u, free]$, where v is the dummy root node and u is an arbitrary terminal.

Base case.   In the base case, the node v is a leaf and we have $\mathcal{P}_F = \emptyset$. Thus, every entry for v has value either 0 or $-\infty$, depending on whether $\mathcal{M}_e$ can be routed. When $b = free$, no path can visit v and, hence, also $\mathcal{P}_e = \emptyset$. Thus we set

$$T[v, 0, \emptyset, u, free] = 0 .$$

Then we set

$$T[v, 0, \mathcal{M}'_e, u, blocked] = 0$$

if $\mathcal{M}'_e$ is either empty, or consists of a single pair of nodes in $R \cap N_G(v)$, or consists of a single pair where one node is v and the other one is in $R \cap N_G(v)$. Finally, we set

$$T[v, 0, \emptyset, u, to\text{-}be\text{-}used] = 0$$

if $u = v$ or u is in $R \cap N_G(v)$. For all the other cases where v is a leaf, we set

$$T[v, i, \mathcal{M}'_e, u, b] = -\infty .$$

Induction step.   For the inductive step, we first consider $i = 1$. We have

$$T[v, 1, \mathcal{M}'_e, u, to\text{-}be\text{-}used] = T[v_1, c_v, \mathcal{M}'_e, u, to\text{-}be\text{-}used] ,$$

since the path in $\mathcal{P}_e$ realizing (u, v) has to start at a leaf node of F_{v_1}. For the other states of b, recall that every path in $\mathcal{P}_e \cup \mathcal{P}_F$ connects two leaves in F_v^1. Since v has degree 1 in F_v^1, there is no path in $\mathcal{P}_e \cup \mathcal{P}_F$ visiting v, and we have

$$T[v, 1, \mathcal{M}'_e, u, blocked] = T[v, 1, \mathcal{M}'_e, u, free] = T[v_1, c_v, \mathcal{M}'_e, u, blocked].$$

Now, let i be greater than 1. In a high level view, we guess which part of $\mathcal{M}'_e$ is realized in $F_v^{i-1} \cup R$ and which part is realized in $F_{v_i} \cup R$. For this, we consider every partition $\mathcal{M}'_{e1} \uplus \mathcal{M}'_{e2}$ of $\mathcal{M}'_e$. By our dynamic programming table, we find a partition that maximizes our objective. In the following, we assume that we guessed $\mathcal{M}'_{e1} \uplus \mathcal{M}'_{e2}$ correctly. Let us consider the different states of b in more detail.

1. When $b = free$, node v is not allowed to be visited by any path, especially by any path in $F_v^{i-1} \cup R$. Hence, $T[v, i, \mathcal{M}'_e, u, free]$ is equal to

$$T[v, i-1, \mathcal{M}'_{e1}, u, free] + T[v_i, c_{v_i}, \mathcal{M}'_{e2}, u, blocked].$$

2. When $b = to\text{-}be\text{-}used$, we have to realize (u, v) in $F_v^i \cup R$. For this, there are two possibilities: Either (u, v) is realized by a path in $F_v^{i-1} \cup R$, or there is a realizing path that first goes through $F_{v_i} \cup R$ and then reaches v via the edge (v_i, v). Hence, for the first possibility, we consider

$$T[v, i-1, \mathcal{M}'_{e1}, u, to\text{-}be\text{-}used] + T[v_i, c_{v_i}, \mathcal{M}'_{e2}, u, blocked],$$

for the second possibility, we consider

$$T[v, i-1, \mathcal{M}'_{e1}, u, free] + T[v_i, c_{v_i}, \mathcal{M}'_{e2}, u, to\text{-}be\text{-}used].$$

Maximizing over both, we obtain $T[v, i, \mathcal{M}'_e, u, to\text{-}be\text{-}used]$.

3. When $b = blocked$, we will also consider two cases. In the first one, there is no path in $\mathcal{P}_e \cup \mathcal{P}_F$ going through edge (v_i, v), hence, we get the term

$$T[v, i-1, \mathcal{M}'_{e1}, u, blocked] + T[v_i, c_{v_i}, \mathcal{M}'_{e2}, u, blocked].$$

In the second case, there is a path P in $\mathcal{P}_e \cup \mathcal{P}_F$ going through edge (v_i, v). Since P is connecting two leaves in F_v^i, a part of P is in $F_v^{i-1} \cup R$ and the other part is in $F_{v_i} \cup R$. If $P \in \mathcal{P}_e$, then it is realizing a pair of $\mathcal{M}'_e$. Hence, for every pair $(u_1, u_2) \in \mathcal{M}'_e$, we have to consider the term

$$T[v, i-1, \mathcal{M}'_{e1} - (u_1, u_2), u_1, to\text{-}be\text{-}used]$$
$$+ T[v_i, c_{v_i}, \mathcal{M}'_{e2} - (u_1, u_2), u_2, to\text{-}be\text{-}used]$$

and the symmetric term where we swap u_1 and u_2. If $P \in \mathcal{P}_F$, then it is realizing a terminal pair of $\overline{\mathcal{M}_R}$. Hence, for every pair $(u_1, u_2) \in \overline{\mathcal{M}_R}$ we get the term

$$1 + T[v, i-1, \mathcal{M}'_{e1}, u_1, to\text{-}be\text{-}used] + T[v_i, c_{v_i}, \mathcal{M}'_{e2}, u_2, to\text{-}be\text{-}used]$$

and the symmetric term where we swap u_1 and u_2. Note that we count the path realizing (u_1, u_2) in our objective. Maximizing over all the terms of the two cases, we obtain $T[v, i, \mathcal{M}'_e, u, \text{to-be-used}]$.

3.5.2   Analysis

Let us analyze the run time of the algorithm described above. Given R, the forest F can be computed in time $\mathcal{O}(r \cdot n)$. In order to guess $\mathcal{M}_e$, we enumerate all potential sets of essential pairs. To bound the number of potential sets of essential pairs, first recall that each pair contains at least one node in R. On the other hand, each node in R appears in at most two pairs and, consequently, $|\mathcal{M}_e| \leq 2r$. Thus, an upper bound on the number of potential sets for $\mathcal{M}_e$ is the number of ways to choose up to two pairs for each node in R. As each node in R is paired with a terminal node or another node in R, there are at most $(2k + r - 1)$ candidate pairs for it. Hence, there are at most $(2k + r)^{2r}$ candidate sets to consider. For each particular guess for $\mathcal{M}_e$, we run the dynamic program above. The number of entries in T—as specified by the five parameters v, i, $\mathcal{M}'_e$, u and b—for each fixed guess for $\mathcal{M}_e$ is at most

$$\left(\sum_{v \in V(F)} \deg_F(v) \right) \cdot 2^{2r} \cdot (2k + r) \cdot 3 = 2^{2r} \cdot (2k + r) \cdot \mathcal{O}(n) .$$

Among the different entries, those with $b = \textit{blocked}$ and $i > 1$ have the highest run time in the worst case. There, we do not only consider all partitions of $\mathcal{M}'_e$, but for every partition we also consider every possible node pair that is either an essential pair in $\mathcal{M}'_e$ or a terminal pair in $\overline{\mathcal{M}_R}$. As there are at most 2^{2r} partitions of $\mathcal{M}'_e$, at most $2r$ essential pairs in $\mathcal{M}'_e$ and at most k terminal pairs in $\overline{\mathcal{M}_R}$, we consider at most

$$2^{2r} + 2 \cdot 2^{2r} \cdot (k + 2r) \leq 2^{2r+1} \cdot (2k + 2r)$$

different terms, including the symmetric terms, for computing an entry. For each term, we need constant time for look-up. Hence, altogether, this gives a run time of

$$r \cdot (2k + r)^{2r} \cdot 2^{2r} \cdot (2k + r) \cdot 2^{2r+1} \cdot (2k + 2r) \cdot \mathcal{O}(n) = (8k + 8r)^{2r+3} \cdot \mathcal{O}(n)$$

assuming that R is given. By computing R in time $r^{\mathcal{O}(r)} \cdot n$, we can bound the total run time by $(k + r)^{\mathcal{O}(r)} \cdot n$.

3.5.3   Reconstruction of an Optimal Routing

Above, we computed only the cardinality of the routing $\mathcal{P}$. Now we discuss how to compute an optimal routing of size $|\mathcal{P}|$ without asymptotically increasing the total run time. For every non-leaf entry of T, we take a term that maximized its value and define the (at most two) entries appearing in the term as its children. We can do this while computing T without increasing the asymptotic run time. By considering all the children that (recursively) contributed to the entry with the optimum value of the root node, we obtain a *computation tree*. Going over the computation tree from bottom to top, we compute for each entry of the tree its set of paths $\mathcal{P}_e \cup \mathcal{P}_F$. We store the set as a linked list with pointers to the paths which themselves are stored as linked lists of their nodes. Whenever we concatenate two lists, we will not create a new copy but reuse one of them. This will give us constant time for concatenation. Note that for almost all entries we obtain $\mathcal{P}_e \cup \mathcal{P}_F$ by just taking the union of the paths of its children. Hence, we just concatenate the lists of its children (at most two) in constant time. The only exception are entries where $b = blocked$ and a path P is going through the node given by the first parameter v of the entry. Here, we obtain P by concatenating two paths, where each one belongs to a different child of the entry. Then we add the concatenated path to the union of the remaining paths of the children. The operation to find the two paths that we want to concatenate takes $\mathcal{O}(|\mathcal{P}_e \cup \mathcal{P}_F|) = \mathcal{O}(k + r)$ time. The remaining steps to compute $\mathcal{P}_e \cup \mathcal{P}_F$ also take constant time. Thus, for each entry of the tree, we can bound the run time by $\mathcal{O}(k + r)$. Note that in the computation tree there is exactly one entry for each subtree F_v^i, hence, in total there are $\mathcal{O}(n)$ entries. Thus, our approach takes additional time of $(k + r) \cdot \mathcal{O}(n)$ to compute the paths $\mathcal{P}_e \cup \mathcal{P}_F$. Finally, the time needed to accordingly concatenate the paths in $\mathcal{P}_e$ to get a routing for $\mathcal{M}_R$ takes at most $\mathcal{O}(|\mathcal{P}_e|^2) = \mathcal{O}(r^2)$ time. Hence, in time $(8k + 8r)^{2r+3} \cdot \mathcal{O}(n)$, we can compute an optimal routing, asymptotically matching the time needed to compute its cardinality .

This discussion finishes the proof of Theorem 3.3. $\hfill\square$

3.6 Parameterized Intractability of MaxNDP for the Parameter r

In this section, we prove Theorem 3.4, that is, we show that MAXNDP is $W[1]$-hard parameterized by feedback vertex set number. This reduction was originally devised for the parameter tree-depth by Ene et al. [EMPR16]; we notice that the same reduction also works for the parameter r. (Both tree-depth and feedback vertex set number are restrictions of treewidth, but they are incomparable to each other.)

For sake of completeness, we include the reduction here, and argue about the feedback vertex set number of the reduced graph. The reduction is from the $W[1]$-hard MULTICOLORED CLIQUE problem [FHRV09], where given a graph G and a partition of $V(G)$ into q independent sets $V^1, \cdots, V^q$, we are to check if there exists a q-clique in G with exactly one vertex in every set V^i. By adding dummy vertices, we can assume $q \geq 2$ and $|V^i| = n$ for some n with $n \geq 2$ and every i with $1 \leq i \leq q$.

Construction.   Given an instance $(G, (V^i)_{i=1}^q)$ of MULTICOLORED CLIQUE, we aim at constructing an equivalent instance $(H, \mathcal{M}, \ell)$ of MAXNDP consisting of a graph H with feedback vertex set number bounded by a function of q, a set M of terminal pairs, and an integer ℓ. The graph H will contain ℓ node-disjoint paths, each one routing a distinct terminal pair in M, if and only if $(G, (V^i)_{i=1}^q)$ is a "yes"-instance.

We start by constructing for every set V^i a gadget W^i as follows. First, for every $v \in V^i$, we construct a path X_v^i of length $q - 2$ on the vertex set

$$\{x_{v,j}^i \mid j \in \{1, \cdots, q\} \setminus \{i\}\} ,$$

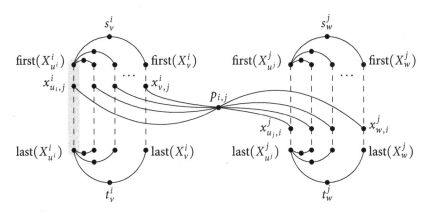

Figure 3.6: Part of the construction of the graph H: The gadgets W^i and W^j connected via $p_{i,j}$. On the left side, the path $X^i_{u^i}$ is highlighted.

where the vertices are connected in any order. Let $\text{first}(X^i_v)$ denote any one of the two endpoints of X^i_v, and let $\text{last}(X^i_v)$ denote the other endpoint of X^i_v. Secondly, we select an arbitrary vertex $u^i \in V^i$. Thirdly, for every $v \in V^i \setminus \{u^i\}$, we add a vertex s^i_v and a vertex t^i_v. We make s^i_v adjacent to $\text{first}(X^i_v)$ and to $\text{first}(X^i_{u^i})$. Similarly, we make t^i_v adjacent to $\text{last}(X^i_v)$ and to $\text{last}(X^i_{u^i})$; see Fig. 3.6. We set (s^i_v, t^i_v) as a terminal pair. This concludes the description of the gadget W^i. Let $\mathcal{M}_{st}$ denote the set of terminal pairs constructed in this step.

To encode adjacencies in G, we proceed as follows. For every i and j with $1 \le i < j \le q$, we add a vertex $p_{i,j}$ adjacent to all vertices in $\{x^i_{v,j} \mid v \in V^i\}$ and in $\{x^j_{w,i} \mid w \in V^j\}$; see Fig. 3.6. For every edge $vw \in E(G)$ with $v \in V^i$ and $w \in V^j$, we add a terminal pair $(x^i_{v,j}, x^j_{w,i})$. Let $\mathcal{M}_x$ be the set of terminal pairs constructed in this step; we have $\mathcal{M} = \mathcal{M}_{st} \cup \mathcal{M}_x$.

Finally, we set the required number ℓ of paths to $q(n-1) + \binom{q}{2}$. This concludes the description of the instance $(H, \mathcal{M}, \ell)$.

From a clique to disjoint paths. Assume that the given instance of Multicolored Clique is a "yes"-instance, and let $\{v^i \mid i \in \{1, \cdots, q\}\}$ be a clique in G such that v^i belongs to V^i for each $i \in \{1, \cdots, q\}$. We construct a family of ℓ node-disjoint paths as follows. First, for every $i \in \{1, \cdots, q\}$ and every $v \in V^i \setminus \{u^i\}$, we route a path from s^i_v to t^i_v through the path X^i_v if $v \ne v^i$, and through the path $X^i_{u^i}$ if $v = v^i$. Note that in this step we have created $q(n-1)$ node-disjoint paths connecting terminal pairs, and in every gadget W^i the only unused vertices are vertices on the path $X^i_{v^i}$. To construct the remaining $\binom{q}{2}$ paths, for every i and j with $1 \le i < j \le q$, we take the 3-vertex path from $x^i_{v^i,j}$ to $x^j_{v^j,i}$ through $p_{i,j}$; note that the assumption $v^i v^j \in E(G)$ ensures that $(x^i_{v^i,j}, x^j_{v^j,i})$ is indeed a terminal pair in $\mathcal{M}$.

From disjoint paths to a clique. In the other direction, let $\mathcal{P}$ be a family of ℓ node-disjoint paths connecting terminal pairs in H. Let $\mathcal{P}_{st} \subseteq \mathcal{P}$ be the set of paths connecting terminal pairs from $\mathcal{M}_{st}$, and, in an analogous way, let $\mathcal{P}_x \subseteq \mathcal{P}$ be the set of paths connecting terminal pairs from $\mathcal{M}_x$. Eventually, let $P = \{p_{i,j} \mid 1 \le i < j \le q\}$. First, observe that P separates every terminal pair from $\mathcal{M}_x$. Hence, every path from $\mathcal{P}_x$ contains at least one vertex from P. Since $|P| = \binom{q}{2}$, we have $|\mathcal{P}_x| \leq \binom{q}{2}$, and, consequently,

$$|\mathcal{P}_{st}| \geq \ell - \binom{q}{2} = q(n-1) = |\mathcal{M}_{st}|.$$

Thus, $\mathcal{P}_{st}$ routes all terminal pairs in $\mathcal{M}_{st}$ and $\mathcal{P}_x$ routes $\binom{q}{2}$ pairs from $\mathcal{M}_x$. Since $|\mathcal{P}_x| = |P|$, every vertex in P is contained in a path from $\mathcal{P}_x$. Consequently, the paths in $\mathcal{P}_{st}$ cannot use any vertex in P. Therefore, every path in $\mathcal{P}_{st}$ lies inside one gadget W^i.

Observe that a shortest path between terminals s_v^i and t_v^i inside W^i is either $X_{u^i}^i$ or X_v^i prolonged with the terminals at endpoints, and thus contains $q+1$ vertices. Furthermore, a shortest path between two terminals in $\mathcal{M}_x$ contains three vertices. We infer that the total number of vertices on paths in $\mathcal{P}$ is at least

$$|\mathcal{P}_{st}| \cdot (q+1) + |\mathcal{P}_x| \cdot 3 = q(n-1)(q+1) + 3\binom{q}{2}$$

$$= q((n-1)(q+1) + (q-1)) + \binom{q}{2} = |V(H)|.$$

We infer that every path in $\mathcal{P}_{st}$ consists of $q+1$ vertices, and every path in $\mathcal{P}_x$ consists of three vertices. In particular, for every $i \in \{1, \cdots, q\}$ and every $v \in V^i \smallsetminus \{u^i\}$, the path in $\mathcal{P}_{st}$ that connects s_v^i and t_v^i goes either through X_v^i or $X_{u^i}^i$. Consequently, for each $i \in \{1, \cdots, q\}$ there exists a vertex $v^i \in V^i$ such that the path $X_{v^i}^i$ is not contained in any path from $\mathcal{P}_{st}$. Even more, $X_{v^i}^i$ contains all the vertices of W^i that do not lie on any path from $\mathcal{P}_{st}$.

We claim that $\{v^i \mid i = 1, \cdots, q\}$ is a clique in G. To this end, consider any $p_{i,j} \in P$. Since we have $|\mathcal{P}_x| = |P|$, there exists a path in $\mathcal{P}_x$ that goes through $p_{i,j}$. Moreover, this path has exactly three vertices. Since the only neighbors of $p_{i,j}$ that are not used by paths from $\mathcal{P}_{st}$ are $x_{v^i,j}^i$ and $x_{v^j,i}^j$, we infer that $(x_{v^i,j}^i, x_{v^j,i}^j)$ is a terminal pair in $\mathcal{M}$ and, consequently, $v^i v^j \in E(G)$. This fact concludes the proof of the correctness of the construction.

Bounding the feedback vertex set number. We are left with a proof that H has bounded feedback vertex set number in q.

First, observe that $H - P$ consists of q components, where each component is a gadget W^i, for some $i \in \{1, \cdots, q\}$. Secondly, consider the endpoints of the path $X_{u^i}^i$ from the gadget W^i. Observe that the deletion of both vertices breaks W^i into n components where each component is a path. Consequently, H has the feedback vertex set

$$P \cup \{\text{first}(X_{u^i}^i), \text{last}(X_{u^i}^i) \mid i = 1, \cdots, q\}$$

of size $\mathcal{O}(q^2)$.

This observation finishes the proof of Theorem 3.4. □

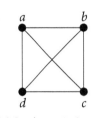
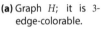

(a) Graph H; it is 3-edge-colorable.

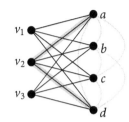

(b) Graph G obtained from H with $r = 2$.

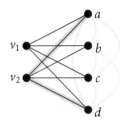

(c) Graph G obtained from H with $r = 1$.

Figure 3.7: The reduction from an Edge 3-Coloring-instance H to an EDP/MaxEDP-instance $(G, \mathcal{M})$. Dotted curves depict which terminals form a pair in $\mathcal{M}$. The path highlighted in gray connects the terminal pair $\{a, d\}$.

3.7 Hardness of Edge-Disjoint Paths in Almost-Forests

In this section, we show that EDP is NP-hard already in graphs that become forests after deleting two nodes. Though this immediately implies NP-hardness for MaxEDP in such graphs, we show that MaxEDP is NP-hard even in graphs that become forests after deleting just one node. Thus, we prove Theorem 3.5.

Proof of Theorem 3.5. We first show NP-hardness of EDP for $r = 2$. We reduce from the problem EDGE 3-COLORING in cubic graphs, which is NP-hard [Hol81]. Given a cubic graph H, we construct a complete bipartite graph G, where one of the two partite sets of $V(G)$ consists of three nodes $\{v_1, v_2, v_3\}$, and the other partite set consists of $V(H)$; see Figs. 3.7a and 3.7b. As for the set $\mathcal{M}$ of terminal pairs, let $\mathcal{M} = \{(s, t) \mid \{s, t\} \in E(H)\}$; in words, we want to connect a pair of nodes by a path in G if and only if they are connected by an edge in H. This completes the construction of the instance $(G, \mathcal{M})$ of MaxEDP. Note that G has feedback vertex set number $r = 2$; removing from G any two vertices of $\{v_1, v_2, v_3\}$ yields a forest.

Regarding correctness of the reduction, we show that H is 3-edge-colorable if and only if *all* pairs in $\mathcal{M}$ can be routed in G.

In the forward direction, suppose that there is a proper 3-edge-coloring $\varphi \colon E(H) \to \{1, 2, 3\}$. For every $c \in \{1, 2, 3\}$, let $E_c \subseteq E(H)$ be the set of edges that receive color c under φ. There is a routing in G that, for every $c \in \{1, 2, 3\}$, routes all terminal pairs $\{(s, t) \in \mathcal{M} \mid \{s, t\} \in E_c\}$ exclusively via the node v_c (and thus via paths of length 2). Note that this routing indeed yields edge-disjoint paths. Otherwise there were an edge $\{s, v_c\}$ in $E(H)$ contained in at least two paths that route two terminal pairs $\{s, t_1\}$ and $\{s, t_2\}$. Hence, the two edges in $E(H)$ corresponding to $\{s, t_1\}$ and $\{s, t_2\}$ would receive the same color c in φ; a contradiction to the proper edge-coloring φ as both edges are incident on s.

In the backward direction, suppose that all terminal pairs in $\mathcal{M}$ can be routed in G. Since H is cubic, any node $s \in V(H)$ is contained in three terminal pairs. Therefore, no path of the routing can have a node in $V(H)$ as an internal node and thus all paths in the routing have length 2. Then this routing naturally corresponds to a proper 3-edge-coloring φ of H, where any terminal pair $\{s, t\}$ routed via $v_c \in \{v_1, v_2, v_3\}$ means that we color the edge $\{s, t\} \in E(H)$ with color c under φ.

In order to show NP-hardness of MAXEDP for $r = 1$, we also reduce from EDGE 3-COLORING in cubic graphs and perform a similar construction as described above: This time, we construct a bipartite graph G with one subset of the partition being $\{v_1, v_2\}$, the other being $V(H)$, and the set $\mathcal{M}$ of terminal pairs being again specified by the edges of H; see Figs. 3.7a and 3.7c. This completes the reduction. The resulting graph G has feedback vertex set number $r = 1$.

We claim that H is 3-colorable if and only if we can route $n = |V(H)|$ pairs in G.

In the forward direction, suppose that there is a proper 3-edge-coloring $\varphi: E(H) \to \{1, 2, 3\}$. For $c \in \{1, 2, 3\}$, let $E_c \subseteq E(H)$ be the set of edges that receive color c under φ. There is a routing in G that, for every $c \in \{1, 2\}$, routes all terminal pairs $\{(s, t) \in \mathcal{M} \mid \{s, t\} \in E_c\}$ exclusively via the node v_c (and thus via paths of length 2). Note that the terminals corresponding to edges receiving color 3 remain unrouted. The reasoning that the resulting routing is feasible is analogous to the case of $r = 2$. To see that precisely n terminal pairs are routed overall, observe that, for each of the n terminals, exactly two of the three terminal pairs are routed.

In the backward direction, suppose that n terminal pairs in $\mathcal{M}$ can be routed in G. Since every terminal v in G has degree two, at most two paths can be routed for v. As n terminal pairs are realized, this also means that *exactly* two paths are routed for each terminal. Hence, none of the paths in the routing has length more than two. Otherwise, it would contain an internal node in $V(H)$, which then could not be part of two other paths in the routing. Then this routing naturally corresponds to a partial edge-coloring of H, where any terminal pair $\{s, t\}$ routed via $v_c \in \{v_1, v_2\}$ implies that we color the edge $\{s, t\} \in E(H)$ with color c. Since each terminal v in $V(H)$ is involved in exactly two paths in the routing, exactly one terminal pair for v remains unrouted. Hence, exactly one edge incident on v in H remains uncolored in the partial coloring. We color all uncolored edges in H by color 3 to obtain a proper 3-edge-coloring. $\qquad\square$

Thus, we almost close the complexity gap for EDP with respect to the size of a minimum feedback vertex set, only leaving the complexity of the case $r = 1$ open.

3.8 Concluding Remarks

In this chapter, we examined the problems of routing terminal pairs by edge- and node-disjoint paths in graphs of bounded feedback vertex set number r. We observed that our obtained approximability bounds, expressed in terms of r, either strengthen best known bounds or they are almost tight. This fact leads us to the conclusion that the parameter r in fact captures the "difficulty" of disjoint paths problems.

In particular, for MAXEDP, we obtained a constant-factor approximation algorithm with congestion logarithmic in $k + r$, where k is the number of terminal pairs. This result strengthens the bound obtained by directly applying the randomized rounding technique for LPs introduced by Raghavan and Thompson [RT87]. Though also we applied this technique, beforehand we appropriately modified the fractional LP solution by making use of the forest that one obtains when removing the feedback vertex set from the graph. For our next result, we used the solution above to extract $\text{OPT}^* / \mathcal{O}(\sqrt{r} \log kr)$ edge-disjoint paths out of it, where OPT^* denotes the value of an optimum fractional solution. This approach strengthens, up to a logarithmic factor, the best known bound of $\text{OPT}^* / \mathcal{O}(\sqrt{n})$ [CKS06]. We achieved our result by contracting "redundant" edges in the input graph and in the routing which lead to an "irreducible" routing from which we could greedily pick up our solution. The result shows that in order to improve the best known bound it suffices to focus only on graphs with feedback vertex set number close to n.

We also complemented the upper bounds with hardness results. We observed that the complexities of both problems, routing node-disjoint paths and edge-disjoint-paths, differ when r is constant. Whereas NDP [Sch94] and MaxNDP are efficiently solvable for any constant r, EDP and MaxEDP are NP-hard even for $r = 2$ and $r = 1$, respectively. When considering r as part of the input, we can separate NDP and MaxNDP (if FPT $\neq$ W[1]). We showed W[1]-hardness of MaxNDP when parameterized by r, whereas NDP is fixed-parameterized tractable in r [Sch94]. However, we were able to provide a fixed-parameter algorithm for the combined parameter $k + r$.

4

Approximating Hard-Capacitated k-Facility Location Problems

The k-FACILITY LOCATION problem is a generalization of the classical problems k-MEDIAN and FACILITY LOCATION. The goal is to select a subset of at most k facilities that minimizes the total cost of opened facilities and established connections between clients and opened facilities. In this chapter, we present the first constant-factor approximation algorithms for the hard-capacitated variants of the problem. In this setting, a single facility may only serve a limited number of clients and creating multiple copies of a facility is not allowed.

For uniform capacities, we obtain a $(2 + \varepsilon)$-capacity violating algorithm with approximation ratio $\mathcal{O}(1/\varepsilon^2)$; our result has not yet been improved. Then, for non-uniform capacities, we consider the case of k-MEDIAN, which is equivalent to k-FACILITY LOCATION with uniform opening cost of the facilities. Here, we obtain a $(3 + \varepsilon)$-capacity violating algorithm with approximation ratio $\mathcal{O}(1/\varepsilon)$.

Our algorithms are based on rounding a fractional solution to the standard LP. We first use the clustering of Charikar et al. [CGTS99] to partition the facilities into sets where the total fractional opening in each set is at least $1 - 1/\ell$ for some fixed ℓ. Then we exploit the technique of Levi, Shmoys, and Swamy [LSS12] developed for the capacitated FACILITY LOCATION problem, which is to locally group the demand from clients to obtain a system of single-demand-node instances. Next, depending on the setting, we either use a dedicated routing tree on the demand nodes (for non-uniform opening cost), or we work with stars of facilities (for non-uniform capacities), to redistribute the demand that cannot be satisfied locally within the clusters.

4.1 Introduction

In metric location problems, the input consists of a set $\mathcal{C}$ of clients, a set $\mathcal{F}$ of facilities and a metric distance function d on $\mathcal{C} \cup \mathcal{F}$. The goal is to select a subset $\mathcal{F}' \subseteq \mathcal{F}$ of facilities, and an assignment of clients to the selected facilities, that together minimize a certain problem-specific cost function. One can think of $\mathcal{F}$ being a set of potential facility locations, whereas $\mathcal{F}'$ contains locations where we decided to open (build) facilities.

In the k-MEDIAN setting, we search for a subset $\mathcal{F}' \subseteq \mathcal{F}$ of cardinality at most k and want to minimize the total cost of assigning clients in $\mathcal{C}$ to facilities in $\mathcal{F}'$, where the cost of assigning a client $s \in \mathcal{C}$ to a facility $i \in \mathcal{F}'$ equals their metric distance $d(s, i)$. The k-MEDIAN problem is a classical NP-hard problem appearing in a number of realistic optimization scenarios. Consider, for example, the location of actual facilities such as voting points during elections, or power plants in an electrical grid. It also appears in the context of clustering data, where one wishes to partition objects into a fixed number of groups containing similar items.

Similar to k-MEDIAN is the k-CENTER problem, where a subset of k facilities is selected but the objective is to minimize the maximum distance between a client and its assigned facility. Another related setting is the FACILITY LOCATION problem, where instead of the strict constraint of opening at most k facilities, we pay a certain cost f_i for opening a facility in location $i \in \mathcal{F}$. A common generalization of k-MEDIAN and FACILITY LOCATION is k-FACILITY LOCATION, where there are both, the location specific facility opening cost and the upper bound of k on the number of open facilities. Note that k-MEDIAN is equivalent to k-FACILITY LOCATION with uniform opening costs[1].

In this chapter, we consider the capacitated versions of k-MEDIAN and k-FACILITY LOCATION. In this generalization, each facility $i \in \mathcal{F}$ has a capacity u_i that constrains us to assign at most u_i clients to i. If all capacities are the same, we call such a location problem *uniform*, and, if there are no restrictions on the capacities, we call such problems *general* or *non-uniform*. We focus on the versions with *hard capacities*, where each facility may be opened at most once, and with *splittable demand*, where a single client may be served from more than one facility. In the simple case of unit demand clients and integral capacity of facilities, the splittability of demands is not important as we discuss in Section 4.2. The case of unit demand clients carries the essence of capacitated location problems with splittable demand, and, hence, for the simplicity of the argument, we will only consider unit demands. The case of hard capacities is a generalization of the case of *soft capacities*, where one may open multiple copies of the same facility. We will call such location problems *hard-capacitated* and *soft-capacitated*, respectively. In the setting of uniform capacities, the soft- and hard-capacitated versions of k-MEDIAN are equivalent up to a constant factor in the approximation ratio [Li17].

All these mathematical formulations of location problems, although modeling essentially the same clustering task, behave very differently in the context of approximation.

Best understood is the k-CENTER problem, for which Hochbaum and Shmoys [HS85] gave a simple and best possible 2-approximation algorithm. In recent past, Cygan et al. [CHK12] gave a constant-factor approximation algorithm for the capacitated version of the k-CENTER problem. The approximation ratio was subsequently improved to 9 by an algorithm of An et al. [ABC+15] that is based on a natural LP relaxation of capacitated k-CENTER. This result narrows down the integrality gap of the natural LP relaxation to either one of the three integers[2] 7, 8, or 9. The best-known lower bound on the approximation factor is 3 [CHK12].

After a long line of research, the approximability of the uncapacitated FACILITY LOCATION problem has been nearly resolved. The 1.488-approximation algorithm of Li [Li13] almost closed the gap with the approximability lower bound of 1.463 by Guha and Khuller [GK99]. The approximability of the capacitated variant is much less clear. We know that the soft-capacitated problem admits a 2-approximation by Jain et al. [JMM+03], which matches the integrality gap of the standard LP. However, the integrality gap of the standard LP for hard-capacitated FACILITY LOCATION is unbounded and, for a while, the only successful approach has been local search, which yields a 3-approximation for uniform capacities [ALB+13] and a 5-approximation for general capacities [BGG12]. Recently, An, Singh and Svensson [ASS17] were successful in obtaining an LP relaxation that yielded a constant-factor approximation algorithm. By this, they answered one of the ten open questions posed in a textbook of Wiliamson and Shmoys [WS11]. Of interest for our results is an LP-based 5-approximation algorithm for the case with uniform opening costs that was given by Levi et al. [LSS12]. We

---

[1] To reduce k-FACILITY LOCATION to k-MEDIAN, guess the number of opened facilities in the optimal solution and use this number as k. In the other direction, set all opening costs to 0.

[2] Cygan et al. [CHK12] give a simple argument that it suffices to consider tree-metrics on unweighted graphs where the optimum solution has length 1. Then any solution has an integral value.

will partly build on their techniques in the construction of our algorithm for capacitated k-MEDIAN.

Despite the simple formulation, k-MEDIAN appears to be the most difficult to handle of the problems above. The first constant-factor approximation algorithm for the uncapacitated k-MEDIAN was achieved by Charikar et al. [CGTS99] and had an approximation ratio of $6\frac{2}{3}$. For a long time, the best approximation ratio was $3 + \varepsilon$ for any positive ε, which was obtained by a local-search method [AGK+01]. Then, not long ago, Charikar and Li [CL12] gave a 3.25-approximation algorithm by directly rounding the fractional solution to the standard LP. Next, Li and Svensson gave an LP-based algorithm [LS16] with approximation ratio $(1 + \sqrt{3} + \varepsilon) \approx 2.73 + \varepsilon$, in which they turn a pseudo-approximation algorithm opening a few too many facilities into an algorithm opening at most k facilities. Eventually, two ingredients of this algorithm were optimized by Byrka et al. [BPR+17] to obtain a 2.675-approximation algorithm for k-MEDIAN.

Until recently, all constant-factor approximation algorithms for capacitated k-MEDIAN were based on the standard LP. Since the standard LP has an unbounded integrality gap, it forces to relax some of the constraints. A natural relaxation is to either allow a violation of the capacities by a small factor (we call the factor *capacity violation*), or to allow opening slightly more than k facilities. Note that in the well-known integrality gap example [DL16], an integral solution must either violate the capacities by at least a factor of $2 - \varepsilon$ or open at least $(2 - \varepsilon)k$ facilities in order to have the connection cost within a constant of the optimal solution cost to the standard LP, even for uniform soft capacities.

The relaxation led to constant-factor approximation algorithms where the factor violating the relaxed constraint is bounded by a constant. Charikar et al. [CGTS99] obtained such a bi-factor approximation algorithm for the setting of uniform soft capacities. They presented a 16-approximation algorithm by violating the capacities by a factor of 3. Later, Chuzhoy and Rabani [CR05] gave the first constant-factor approximation algorithm for the non-uniform soft-capacitated case, bounding the capacity violation and the approximation ratio by two-digit constants. Only recently further progress was made. Aardal et al. [AvdBGL15] designed a $(7 + \varepsilon)$-approximation algorithm for the case of general hard capacities using at most $2k + 1$ facilities and respecting all capacity constraints.

Our results. We present two algorithms for hard-capacitated k-FACILITY LOCATION that are based on the standard LP, one with general opening costs, and one with general capacities. Our aim is to *not* violate the number of open facilities and, simultaneously, to keep the capacity violation as low as possible.

First, in Section 4.3, we present an algorithm for uniform k-FACILITY LOCATION that is still the best known one in its setting. Its capacity violation of at most $2 + \varepsilon$, for any positive ε, meets the lower bound enforced by the integrality gap example. We note that the presentation in our extended abstract [BFRS15] had some inaccuracies, as pointed out by Grover et al. [GGP17b, GGP17a]. In parallel to our preparation of this chapter, Grover et al. were able to achieve a slightly higher violation factor of 3 avoiding the issues in our extended abstract [BFRS15]. Independently of them, we fixed the issue by making a distinction between *strict* and *relaxed* solutions of stars instances in Section 4.2. We could also improve the approximation factor by a constant in comparison to the extended abstract. In particular, we obtain the following result:

Theorem 4.1. *For any ℓ with $\ell \geq 2$, there is an approximation algorithm for uniform hard-capacitated k-Facility Location that computes a solution of cost $8(\ell + 1)^2 \cdot \text{OPT}^*$ which violates the capacities by a factor at most $2 + 3/(\ell - 1)$, where OPT^* is the cost of an optimum solution to the standard LP relaxation.*

Next, we examine the non-uniform k-Facility Location problem with uniform opening costs. Recall that this problem is equivalent to non-uniform k-Median. In Section 4.4, we describe the first constant-factor approximation algorithm for the hard-capacitated variant of this problem, and achieve a capacity violation at most $3 + \varepsilon$ for any sufficiently small positive ε. More specifically, we prove the following.

Theorem 4.2. *For any ε with $0 < \varepsilon \leq 1$, there is an approximation algorithm for non-uniform hard-capacitated k-Median that computes a solution of cost $540/\varepsilon \, \text{OPT}^* + 144\, \text{OPT}^*$ which violates the capacities by a factor at most $3 + \varepsilon$, where OPT^* is the cost of an optimum solution to the standard LP relaxation.*

Both our results for k-Facility Location are built on the idea of Levi et al. [LSS12] to decompose the instance into single-demand-node instances. We exploit this in Section 4.2 where we present the tools used by our algorithms.

Subsequent Work.   Since the publication of our extended abstract [BFRS15], new results were announced. Li [Li17] introduces a novel LP relaxation for uniform hard-capacitated k-Median. This allows him to open only $k(1 + \varepsilon)$ facilities while respecting all capacity constraints. He further develops the LP relaxation and generalizes the result to the case of non-uniform soft capacities [Li16]. Byrka et al. [BRU16] use the LP relaxation for uniform hard capacities to open at most k facilities and to violate the capacities only by $1 + \varepsilon$. The same outcome is achieved by Demirci and Li [DL16] for the non-uniform hard-capacitated case. We believe that our results are still of interest as they are based on the substantially simpler standard LP relaxation. Besides that analyzing this relaxation is an interesting question in its own right, the resulting algorithms might also be advantageous in practical applications. Also our approximation ratio has a better asymptotic dependence on $1/\varepsilon$, which may lead to better solutions for medium violation factors.

4.2   Star Clusters and Star Instances

Given a capacitated k-Facility Location instance $(\mathcal{C}, \mathcal{F}, k, d, u)$, we will partition the facilities of $\mathcal{F}$ into *star clusters* (similar to Charikar and Li [CL12]). For this, we first solve the following natural LP relaxation denoted by Ck-FL LP, where the variable y_i encodes the opening value (opening) of the facility i, and the variable x_{it} encodes the assignment of the client t to the facility i. The variable x_{it} can also be viewed as the *LP demand* of the client t that is send to the facility i. Recall that we consider unit demands, that is, the total LP demand of the client t is $\sum_{i \in \mathcal{F}} x_{it} = 1$. Throughout this chapter, we fix an integral parameter $\ell \geq 2$ and an optimal fractional solution $(\mathbf{x}^*, \mathbf{y}^*)$ to Ck-FL LP and denote its objective value by OPT^*.

$$\text{minimize} \sum_{i \in \mathcal{F}, t \in \mathcal{C}} d(i,t)x_{it} + \sum_{i \in \mathcal{F}} y_i f_i$$

$$\text{subject to} \sum_{i \in \mathcal{F}} y_i \leq k; \tag{LP-1}$$

$$\sum_{i \in \mathcal{F}} x_{it} = 1 \qquad \text{for each } t \in \mathcal{C}; \tag{LP-2}$$

$$x_{it} \leq y_i \qquad \text{for each } i \in \mathcal{F}, t \in \mathcal{C}; \tag{LP-3}$$

$$\sum_{t \in \mathcal{C}} x_{it} \leq u_i y_i \qquad \text{for each } i \in \mathcal{F}; \tag{LP-4}$$

$$x_{it}, y_i \geq 0 \qquad \text{for each } i \in \mathcal{F}, t \in \mathcal{C}.$$

A *solution with capacity violations* to Ck-FL LP is a solution that satisfies the weaker version of Ck-FL LP where we drop Constraint (LP-4). In such a solution, the *capacity violation of a facility* $i \in \mathcal{F}$ is

$$\frac{\sum_{t \in \mathcal{C}} x_{it}}{u_i y_i}.$$

We call such a solution also a *solution with capacity violation* γ if $\gamma \geq \max_{i \in \mathcal{F}} \gamma_i$.

As noted in Section 4.1, in order to find a solution, it suffices to compute a feasible integral opening vector for the facilities and a possibly fractional assignment of the clients to the open facilities.

Lemma 4.1. *Given a subset $\mathcal{F}' \subseteq \mathcal{F}$ of open facilities for which an assignment of the clients exists, we can efficiently compute such an assignment with minimum cost and splittable demands. Moreover, if the capacities are integral, we can obtain a minimum-cost assignment where no demand is split.*

Proof. Given $\mathcal{F}'$, we fix the corresponding facility openings in Ck-FL LP and solve the LP to obtain a minimum-cost assignment that possibly is fractional. If the capacities are integral and we wish to obtain an integral assignment, we model our problem as a minimum-cost flow problem. For this, we take the complete bi-partite graph with the partite sets $\mathcal{C}$ and $\mathcal{F}'$, orient all edges from $\mathcal{C}$ to $\mathcal{F}'$ and set their capacities to 1 (or any larger integer value) and their costs corresponding to their length in the metric d. Then we introduce a source node that we connect to every client in $\mathcal{C}$ via an edge of cost 0 and capacity 1, and, similarly, we introduce a sink node to which we connect every facility $i \in \mathcal{F}'$ via an edge of cost 0 and capacity u_i. We set the required flow to the number of clients.

Since all capacities and the flow are integral, there is a minimum-cost flow that is integral and we find it efficiently [Tar85]. Hence, each client is "assigned" by the flow to exactly one facility. □

In order to upper bound the connection cost of assignments returned by Lemma 4.1, we will provide possibly suboptimal, fractional assignments of the clients to the open facilities. By upper bounding these, we obtain an upper bound for the assignment obtained by the lemma.

Preliminaries. Before obtaining an integral opening value for every facility, our algorithms will operate on smaller subsets of facilities with possibly fractional openings. To ease the description of these procedures, we introduce some helpful notation.

Definition 4.1. An *opening vector* $\mathbf{z}$ for a subset $\mathcal{F}' \subseteq \mathcal{F}$ of facilities contains an opening value $z_i \in [0,1]$ for each facility $i \in \mathcal{F}'$ and it contains not other values. We say, a facility $i \in \mathcal{F}'$ is

- *closed in* $\mathbf{z}$ if $z_i = 0$,

- *supporting in* $\mathbf{z}$ if $z_i \in (0,1]$,

- *fractional in* $\mathbf{z}$ if $z_i \in (0,1)$,

- and *open in* $\mathbf{z}$ if $z_i = 1$.

We define the *volume* $\mathrm{vol}(\mathbf{z})$ of $\mathbf{z}$ as $\sum_{i \in \mathcal{F}'} z_i$, and, for any $\mathcal{F}'' \subseteq \mathcal{F}'$, we use $\mathrm{vol}_{\mathbf{z}}(\mathcal{F}'')$ to denote $\sum_{i \in \mathcal{F}''} z_i$. We call $\mathbf{z}$ *almost integral* if at most one $i \in \mathcal{F}'$ is fractional in $\mathbf{z}$.

Let $\mathcal{F}', \mathcal{F}'' \subseteq \mathcal{F}$ be two disjoint sets and $\mathbf{z}'$ an opening vector for $\mathcal{F}'$ and $\mathbf{z}''$ an opening vector for $\mathcal{F}''$. The *union* of $\mathbf{z}'$ and $\mathbf{z}''$ is an opening vector $\mathbf{z}$ for $\mathcal{F}' \cup \mathcal{F}''$ with $z_i = z_i'$ for each $i \in \mathcal{F}'$, and $z_i = z_i''$ for each $i \in \mathcal{F}''$.

Definition 4.2. For any set $\mathcal{F}' \subseteq \mathcal{F}$ of facilities, we define its *volume* as $\mathrm{vol}_{\mathbf{y}^*}(\mathcal{F}')$.

In the metric d, a node can have the same distance to multiple nodes. To avoid ambiguity, we could arbitrarily define one of the multiple nodes to be its *closest* node. However, our algorithms will need a stronger property: We will have to avoid cycles of length more than two where, for each node of the cycle, its closest node is its neighbor in a fixed orientation. We can achieve this by assigning to every edge $\{s, t\} \subseteq \mathcal{C} \cup \mathcal{F}$ a distinct priority $p_d(\{s, t\})$. Now, informally speaking, the closest node t to a node s is the node with the smallest distance to s and, among all the nodes with the smallest distance to s, it is the node whose edge connecting to s has the smallest value in p_d. Suppose there is a cycle as described above, then all its edges have the same distance and exactly one of the edges has the smallest priority value. Both its endpoints are thus closest to each other, implying that the cycle is of length 2; a contradiction. We define the notion of *closeness* more precisely.

Definition 4.3. Let $A \subseteq \mathcal{C} \cup \mathcal{F}$ be a non-empty set and let $s \in \mathcal{C} \cup \mathcal{F}$. If $s \in A$, then the *closest* node *in A to s* is s. Otherwise, let

$$A_s^{\min} = \{t \in A \mid \nexists t' \in A : d(s, t') < d(s, t)\}.$$

The *closest* node *in A to s* is $\arg\min_{t \in A_s^{\min}} p_d(\{s, t\})$. If t is the closest node in A to s, we also say: $t \in A$ *is closest to s*.

Graphs on Clients and Facilities. To simplify the description of our algorithms, we will build directed acyclic graphs based on either the clients or the facilities. First, we fix some notations and then present a procedure that we will use to construct forests of rooted in-trees.

Definition 4.4. Let (s, t) be an edge of a directed acyclic graph G. We call s a *son* of t, and t a *father* of s. Sons of the same father are called *brothers*. Any node in G with outdegree 0 is called a *root*.

Below, we present a procedure that, given two disjoint subsets $A, B \subseteq \mathcal{F} \cup \mathcal{C}$, constructs a directed forest, where each node in A has either a directed edge to its closest distinct node in $A \cup B$, or is a root (recall Definition 4.3). We will show that its components are in-trees. The procedure assumes that A is not empty and $A \cup B$ contains at least two elements.

Procedure Short-Trees(A, B)

Create G with initially $V(G) = A$ and $E(G) = \varnothing$
foreach $s \in A$ **do**
    select $s' \in A \cup B \setminus \{s\}$ closest to s
    add s' to $V(G)$ if not already contained
    add the directed edge (s, s') to $E(G)$
foreach $(s, s'), (s', s) \in E(G)$ **do**
    remove the edge (s, s') from G
return G

Let G be the output of Procedure Short-Trees(A, B) on any disjoint subsets $A, B \subseteq \mathcal{F} \cup \mathcal{C}$. We establish the following properties of G.

Lemma 4.2. *Let* $s, s', s'' \in V(G)$. *If* $(s, s'), (s', s'') \in E(G)$, *then* $d(s, s') \geq d(s', s'')$.

Proof. We have $s \neq s''$ because the algorithm removes one edge from each cycle of length 2. By the construction of the edge set, s'' is the closest node in $V(G)$ to s'. Therefore, we have $d(s', s'') \leq d(s, s')$. □

Lemma 4.3. *The graph G is a forest of in-trees and $A \subseteq V(G)$.*

Proof. By construction, $A \subseteq V(G)$. Furthermore, every node in the graph has outdegree at most 1. Suppose there is a cycle. Then, by Lemma 4.2, all edges have the same length. Recall Definition 4.3 and consider the edge (s, s') on the cycle that yields the smallest priority value $p_d(\{s, s'\})$. By the definition of closeness, both endpoints s and s' are the closest nodes to each other. By the construction of the edge set, the cycle must contain (s, s') and (s', s); a contradiction as cycles of length 2 have been removed by the procedure. □

Lemma 4.4. *Every root in G has at least one son, and one of its sons is the closest node in $A \cup B$ to the root. Furthermore, all nodes in $B \cap V(G)$ are roots.*

Proof. During the construction of G, every node receives an outgoing edge to its closest node. Since the root of an in-tree does not contain any outgoing edge in the returned graph, its outgoing edge is removed at the end of the construction. Given the condition on which an edge is deleted, the node closest to the root is one of its sons.

The second claim follows from the fact that A and B are disjoint and that we therefore never add an outgoing edge to a node in B. □

Star Clusters.   Central for our algorithms is the following quantity. For every client $t \in C$, we define $d_{av}(t) = \sum_{i \in F} x_{it}^* d(i, t)$ as *its connection cost in* $(\mathbf{x}^*, \mathbf{y}^*)$. In general, connection cost refers to the cost $w \cdot l$ of sending w units of demand along a distance l.

We select a subset $C_{sc} \subseteq C$ of clients that are *far away* from each other with respect to their connection cost. Beginning with $C_{sc} = \varnothing$ and $C' = C$, we select a client $s \in C'$ with minimum $d_{av}(s)$ (ties are broken arbitrarily) and remove it from C' along with every client t with $d(s, t) \le 2\ell d_{av}(t)$, and add s to C_{sc}. We repeat this procedure until C' is empty. We call the clients in C_{sc} *star centers*.

Lemma 4.5. *The following holds:*

1. *For any* $s, s' \in C_{sc}$, $s \ne s'$, *the inequality* $d(s, s') > 2\ell \max\{d_{av}(s), d_{av}(s')\}$ *holds.*

2. *For any* $t \in C \smallsetminus C_{sc}$, *there is a client* $s \in C_{sc}$ *with* $d(s, t) \le 2\ell d_{av}(t)$.

3. *For any* $s \in C_{sc}$ *and any* $t \in C$, *the inequality* $d_{av}(s) \le 2d_{av}(t)$ *holds if either* $|C_{sc}| = 1$ *or* $d(s, t) \le \min\{d(s, s') \mid s' \in C_{sc}, s' \ne s\}/2$.

Proof. Let $s, s' \in C_{sc}$. Without loss of generality, s was added before s' into C_{sc} and thus we have $d_{av}(s) \le d_{av}(s')$. Since s' was not removed from C' when s was added to C_{sc}, we also have $2\ell d_{av}(s') < d(s, s')$, and Claim 1 follows.

Next, let $t \in C \smallsetminus C_{sc}$. As $t \notin C_{sc}$, it was removed from C' when a client s was added to C_{sc}. Thus, we have $d(s, t) \le 2\ell d_{av}(t)$ and Claim 2 follows.

Now, let $s \in C_{sc}$ and $t \in C$. If $|C_{sc}| = 1$, then s is the only star center in C_{sc}. Then we know that t was removed from C' when s was added to C_{sc} (and possibly $s = t$). Hence, our greedy construction of C_{sc} implies $d_{av}(s) \le d_{av}(t)$, and the claim follows. Otherwise, $|C_{sc}| \ge 2$ and let $R = \min\{d(s, s') \mid s' \in C_{sc}, s' \ne s\}/2$. By assumption, $d(s, t) \le R$. As a consequence of Claim 1, $R > 0$. Thus, $d(s, t) < 2R$, and either $t = s$ or $t \in C \smallsetminus C_{sc}$. In the first case, the claim follows immediately. In the second case, Claim 2 gives us a client $s' \in C_{sc}$ with $d(s', t) \le 2\ell d_{av}(t)$. If $s = s'$ and s is the only such client for t, then t was removed from C' when s was added to C_{sc}. As discussed above, this event implies the claim. Otherwise, there is a star center $s' \in C_{sc}$ with $d(s', t) \le 2\ell d_{av}(t)$ and $s' \ne s$. By the minimality of R and the triangle inequality, we have

$$2R \le d(s', s) \le d(s', t) + d(t, s) \le 2\ell d_{av}(t) + R .$$

Consequently, $R \le 2\ell d_{av}(t)$. Claim 1 implies $\ell d_{av}(s) < R$. Thus, altogether, $\ell d_{av}(s) < 2\ell d_{av}(t)$ and Claim 3 follows. □

Definition 4.5. For each star center $s \in C_{sc}$, we define the star cluster $\mathcal{F}_s \subseteq \mathcal{F}$ as the set of all facilities that are closest to s, that is,

$$\mathcal{F}_s = \{i \in \mathcal{F} \mid s \text{ is the closest node in } C_{sc} \text{ to } i\} .$$

Recall that by our definition of closeness (Definition 4.3), each facility has a unique closest star center. Therefore, the star clusters partition all facilities in $\mathcal{F}$.

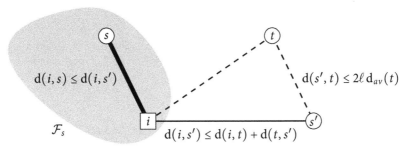

Figure 4.1: Let $s \in C_{sc}$, $t \in C$, $i \in \mathcal{F}_s$, and $s' \in C_{sc}$ be the closest star center to i. The distance $d(i, s)$ (bold edge) is bounded by the distance $d(i, s')$ (solid edge), which in turn is bounded by the detour over t (dashed path).

Lemma 4.6. *For any $s \in C_{sc}$, $t \in C$ and $i \in \mathcal{F}_s$, the following holds:*

1. $d(i, s) \leq d(i, t) + 2\ell d_{av}(t)$.

2. $d(s, t) \leq 2d(i, t) + 2\ell d_{av}(t)$.

Proof. Let $s' \in C_{sc}$ be the star center closest to t (possibly $s' \in \{s, t\}$). If $t \notin C_{sc}$, then, by Lemma 4.5.2, $d(s', t) \leq 2\ell d_{av}(t)$. Otherwise, $s' = t$, and the same inequality holds. Consider Fig. 4.1. Since i belongs to $\mathcal{F}_s$, we have

$$d(i, s) \leq d(i, s') \leq d(i, t) + d(t, s') \leq d(i, t) + 2\ell d_{av}(t)$$

and

$$d(s, t) \leq d(s, i) + d(i, t) \leq 2d(i, t) + 2\ell d_{av}(t) . \qquad \square$$

Next, we bound the volume of facilities that are close to their star centers.

Lemma 4.7. *For any positive R and any $s \in C_{sc}$, let $\mathcal{F}_s^R = \{i \in \mathcal{F}_s \mid d(i, s) \leq R\}$. The volume satisfies $\mathrm{vol}_{y^*}(\mathcal{F}_s^R) \geq 1 - d_{av}(s)/R$.*

Proof. Note that at most a portion $d_{av}(s)/R$ of the LP demand $\sum_{i \in \mathcal{F}} x_{is}^*$ of s can be served by the facilities in $\mathcal{F} \setminus \mathcal{F}_s^R$. Otherwise,

$$d_{av}(s) = \sum_{i \in \mathcal{F}} x_{is}^* d(i, s) \geq R \cdot \sum_{i \in \mathcal{F} \setminus \mathcal{F}_s^R} x_{is}^* > R \cdot d_{av}(s)/R = d_{av}(s) ;$$

a contradiction. Hence at least a portion $1 - d_{av}(s)/R$ of the LP demand of s is served by the facilities in $\mathcal{F}_s^R$. Hence, by Constraint (LP-3),

$$\mathrm{vol}_{y^*}(\mathcal{F}_s^R) = \sum_{i \in \mathcal{F}_s^R} y_i^* \geq \sum_{i \in \mathcal{F}_s^R} x_{is}^* \geq 1 - d_{av}(s)/R . \qquad \square$$

Our last result implies the following bound on the volume of star clusters, which has also been shown by Charikar et al. [CGTS99].

Corollary 4.1 ([CGTS99]). *The volume of every star cluster is at least $1 - 1/\ell$.*

Proof. By Lemma 1, any facility $i \in \mathcal{F}$ lying within the radius $\ell d_{av}(s)$ around a star center $s \in \mathcal{C}_{sc}$ belongs to $\mathcal{F}_s$. If $d_{av}(s) = 0$, then, by the definition of $d_{av}(s)$, all facilities serving s must have distance 0 to s. Thus, $\mathrm{vol}_{y^*}(\mathcal{F}_s^R) \geq 1$. If $d_{av}(s) > 0$, then we set $R = \ell d_{av}(s)$ and apply Lemma 4.7. $\square$

In our algorithms and in their analyses, we will charge portions of OPT^* to the star centers. These portions are described by the following quantities.

Definition 4.6. For every star center $s \in \mathcal{C}_{sc}$, we define the *budgets*

- $b_s^f = \sum_{i \in \mathcal{F}_s} y_i^* f_i$ as the *opening cost budget*,

- $b_s^d = \sum_{i \in \mathcal{F}_s} \sum_{t \in C} x_{it}^* d(i,t)$ as the *direct connection cost budget*, and

- $b_s^r = \sum_{i \in \mathcal{F}_s} \sum_{t \in C} x_{it}^* d_{av}(t)$ as the *relative connection cost budget*.

The idea for these quantities is to distribute the total opening and connection cost among the star centers. Then these cost portions can be used by each star center to upper bound some local solutions. Consequently, the total cost of all these solutions will be bounded from above by a function of OPT^*. For the first two budgets, we split the total cost evenly between the facilities. For a star center $s \in \mathcal{C}_{sc}$, the budget b_s^f is the total opening cost of the facilities in $\mathcal{F}_s$, and b_s^r is the total connection cost of transporting demand to facilities in $\mathcal{F}_s$. For the third budget, we split the total connection cost proportional to the amount of demand that is served by the facilities of the star clusters. To see this, consider the contribution of any client $t \in C$ to b_s^r. It is $d_{av}(t) \sum_{i \in \mathcal{F}_s} x_{it}^*$. This quantity corresponds to the connection cost $d_{av}(t)$ of t weighted by the LP demand that t sent to $\mathcal{F}_s$. Our observations about the quantities are confirmed by the following lemma.

Lemma 4.8. *The following holds:*

1. $\sum_{s \in \mathcal{C}_{sc}} b_s^f + b_s^d = \mathrm{OPT}^*$.

2. $\sum_{s \in \mathcal{C}_{sc}} b_s^r \leq \mathrm{OPT}^*$.

Proof. Both statements follow directly from the definitions of the budgets and the fact that the star clusters partition $\mathcal{F}$:

1.
$$\sum_{s \in \mathcal{C}_{sc}} b_s^f + b_s^d = \sum_{s \in \mathcal{C}_{sc}} \sum_{i \in \mathcal{F}_s} \left(y_i^* f_i + \sum_{t \in C} x_{it}^* d(i,t) \right)$$
$$= \sum_{i \in \mathcal{F}} y_i^* f_i + \sum_{t \in C} \sum_{i \in \mathcal{F}} x_{it}^* d(i,t)$$
$$= \mathrm{OPT}^* .$$

2.
$$\sum_{s\in C_{sc}} b_s^r = \sum_{s\in C_{sc}} \sum_{i\in F_s} \sum_{t\in C} x_{it}^* d_{av}(t)$$
$$= \sum_{t\in C} \sum_{i\in F} x_{it}^* d_{av}(t)$$
$$= \sum_{t\in C} d_{av}(t) \underbrace{\sum_{i\in F} x_{it}^*}_{=1}$$
$$= \sum_{t\in C} \sum_{i\in F} x_{it}^* d(i,t)$$
$$\leq \text{OPT}^* .$$

$\square$

Star instances. We will now introduce a notion that will help us to locally modify facility openings. Following the approach of Levi et al. [LSS12], we "move" the total demand served by facilities of a star cluster F_s to its center s. We call the so-obtained single-demand-node instances *star instances*. We will see that extreme point solutions to such star instances have a particular nice structure. This will enable us later to round these solutions to integral solutions with small constant capacity violation at the expense of only a constant factor in the connection and opening cost. On the other hand, we will show that we can decompose the original instance into a collection of star instances and that we pay only a constant factor in approximation when applying this reduction.

Definition 4.7. Every star center $s \in C_{sc}$ defines one star instance S_s. It consists of

- the set F_s that we obtained when computing the star centers,
- the *demand* $w_s = \sum_{i\in F_s} \sum_{t\in C} x_{it}^*$,
- the *strict budget* $b_s^I = b_s^f + b_s^d + 2\ell b_s^r$,
- and the *relaxed budget* $b_s^{II} = 2b_s^f + 2b_s^d + 2\ell b_s^r$.

A star instance asks for a *solution*, which is either a *strict solution* or a *relaxed solution*. A *strict solution* to the star instance S_s is an opening vector $\mathbf{z}$ for the facilities in F_s that satisfies the following constraints:

$$\sum_{i\in F_s} u_i z_i \geq w_s \tag{4.1}$$
$$\sum_{i\in F_s} (f_i + d(i,s)u_i)z_i \leq b_s^I . \tag{4.2}$$

A *relaxed solution* to the star instance S_s is an opening vector $\mathbf{z}$ for the facilities in F_s that contains exactly one supporting facility $\hat{i} \in F_s$ and satisfies Constraint (4.1) as well as the following constraint:

$$f_{\hat{i}} z_{\hat{i}} + d(\hat{i},s)w_s \leq b_s^{II} . \tag{4.3}$$

In a strict sense, the problem of finding a relaxed solution is not always a "relaxation" of finding a strict solution, in contrast to what the name might suggest. However, we will use relaxed solutions in the context of almost integral opening vectors of volume at most 1. In such cases, any restricted solution is also a relaxed solution.

We defined star instances only on star centers. Therefore, when referring to a star instance S_s, or to one of its quantities w_s, b_s^I, or b_s^{II}, we will implicitly assume that $s \in C_{sc}$. We will also call w_s the *demand* of the star center s, opposed to the LP demand of s that refers to the unit demand of s in the context of Ck-FL LP.

Throughout the chapter, Constraints (4.1)–(4.3) will refer to the constraints defined by a star instance, whereas Constraints (LP-1)–(LP-4) refer to the constraints defined by Ck-FL LP.

As a corollary of Lemma 4.8, we immediately get the following bounds on the total budgets of all star centers.

Corollary 4.2. *The following holds:*

1. $\sum_{s \in C_{sc}} b_s^I \leq (1 + 2\ell) \, \mathrm{OPT}^*$.

2. $\sum_{s \in C_{sc}} b_s^{II} \leq (2 + 2\ell) \, \mathrm{OPT}^*$.

In the following central lemma, we show how to compute a strict solution to a star instance of bounded volume.

Lemma 4.9. *For any star instance S_s, we can efficiently construct a strict solution $\mathbf{z}$ to S_s such that the volume satisfies $\mathrm{vol}(\mathbf{z}) \leq \mathrm{vol}_{y^*}(\mathcal{F}_s)$.*

Proof. The demand w_s is given by $w_s = \sum_{i \in \mathcal{F}_s} \sum_{t \in C} x_{it}^*$. For $i \in \mathcal{F}_s$, we charge $\sum_{t \in C} x_{it}^*$ units of w_s to the facility i by opening it by an amount of $z_i = (\sum_{t \in C} x_{it}^*)/u_i$. Then we have $z_i \leq y_i^*$ by Constraint (LP-4). Thus $\mathbf{z}$ is an opening vector satisfying Constraint (4.1) and the inequality $\mathrm{vol}(\mathbf{z}) \leq \mathrm{vol}_{y^*}(\mathcal{F}_s)$.

Now we prove that also Constraint (4.2) is satisfied. By Lemma 4.6.1, for every client $t \in C$ and every facility $i \in \mathcal{F}_s$, the inequality $d(i, s) \leq d(i, t) + 2\ell d_{av}(t)$ holds. So we have

$$\sum_{i \in \mathcal{F}_s} (f_i + d(i, s) u_i) z_i$$
$$= \sum_{i \in \mathcal{F}_s} z_i f_i + \sum_{i \in \mathcal{F}_s} \sum_{t \in C} d(i, s) x_{it}^*$$
$$\leq \sum_{i \in \mathcal{F}_s} y_i^* f_i + \sum_{i \in \mathcal{F}_s} \sum_{t \in C} (d(i, t) + 2\ell d_{av}(t)) x_{it}^*$$
$$= b_s^I .$$
$\square$

Note that the strict solution provided by Lemma 4.9 may have volume strictly smaller than that of the underlying star cluster and consequently also smaller than $1 - 1/\ell$ (see Corollary 4.1). However, in our algorithm for k-FACILITY LOCATION with uniform capacities, we will be interested in solutions of volume at least $1 - 1/\ell$. Therefore, we prove the following lemma.

Lemma 4.10. *For any a star instance S_s with uniform capacities that admits a strict solution $\mathbf{z}$ with $\mathrm{vol}(\mathbf{z}) \leq \min\{1, \mathrm{vol}_{y^*}(\mathcal{F}_s)\}$, we can efficiently construct a relaxed solution $\mathbf{z}'$ to S_s with $\mathrm{vol}(\mathbf{z}') = \min\{1, \mathrm{vol}_{y^*}(\mathcal{F}_s)\}$ where the only supporting facility $\hat{i} \in \mathcal{F}_s$ satisfies the distance bound $d(\hat{i}, s) \leq \ell d_{av}(s)$.*

Proof. We first construct an opening vector $\mathbf{z}'$ with the required volume and distance properties and then show that it is a relaxed solution to S_s.

Let $R = \ell d_{av}(s)$. Let $\mathcal{F}_s^R$ be the set $\{i \in \mathcal{F} \mid d(i, s) \leq R\}$ of facilities lying within the radius R around s. First, we show that $\mathcal{F}_s^R$ is not empty by observing $\text{vol}_{y^*}(\mathcal{F}_s^R) > 0$. If $d_{av}(s) = 0$,
then $\text{vol}_{y^*}(\mathcal{F}_s^R) \geq 1$ as discussed before. Otherwise, $R > 0$ and Lemma 4.7 assures

$$\text{vol}_{y^*}(\mathcal{F}_s^R) \geq 1 - d_{av}(s)/R = 1 - 1/\ell \geq 1/2 \, ;$$

the last inequality follows from $\ell \geq 2$. Consequently $\mathcal{F}_s^R$ is not empty.

Among the facilities in $\mathcal{F}_s^R$, pick a facility $\hat{i}$ that minimizes the opening cost $f_{\hat{i}}$. We define
the following opening vector $\mathbf{z}'$ for $\mathcal{F}_s$. We set $z_{\hat{i}}' = \min\{1, \text{vol}_{y^*}(\mathcal{F}_s)\}$ and, for every other
facility $i \in \mathcal{F}_s$, we set $z_i' = 0$. Thus, we have the two properties $\text{vol}(\mathbf{z}') = \min\{1, \text{vol}_{y^*}(\mathcal{F}_s)\}$
and $d(\hat{i}, s) \leq \ell d_{av}(s)$.

To this end, we show that $\mathbf{z}'$ is a relaxed solution. Since the solution $\mathbf{z}$ fulfills Constraint (4.1),
we have

$$u \, \text{vol}(\mathbf{z}) = \sum_{i \in \mathcal{F}_s} u z_i \geq w_s \, .$$

Thus, also $\mathbf{z}'$ fulfills Constraint (4.1), as

$$\text{vol}(\mathbf{z}') = \min\{1, \text{vol}_{y^*}(\mathcal{F}_s)\} \geq \text{vol}(\mathbf{z}) \, .$$

To show Constraint (4.3), we first show $z_{\hat{i}}' \cdot f_{\hat{i}} \leq b_s^f$ and then $d(\hat{i}, s) w_s \leq 2 b_s^d + 2\ell b_s^r$.
Recall that $b_s^f = \sum_{i \in \mathcal{F}} f_i y_i^*$. By using the minimality of $\hat{i}$, we infer

$$b_s^f \geq \sum_{i \in \mathcal{F}_s^R} f_i y_i^* \geq f_{\hat{i}} \sum_{i \in \mathcal{F}_s^R} y_i^* = f_{\hat{i}} \cdot \text{vol}_{y^*}(\mathcal{F}_s^R) \, .$$

Above we have shown $\text{vol}_{y^*}(\mathcal{F}_s^R) \geq 1/2$. Thus, $b_s^f \geq f_{\hat{i}}/2$ and our bound on $z_{\hat{i}}' \cdot f_{\hat{i}}$ holds
as $f_{\hat{i}} \geq z_{\hat{i}}' \cdot f_{\hat{i}}$.

Next, we show $d(\hat{i}, s) w_s \leq 2 b_s^d + 2\ell b_s^r$. In fact, we will prove the stronger inequality

$$R w_s \leq 2 b_s^d + 2\ell b_s^r \, ,$$

which implies the first one as $d(\hat{i}, s) \leq R$. Let P denote the set $\mathcal{F}_s \times C$ of pairs. By our definitions,

$$R w_s = \sum_{(i,t) \in P} x_{it}^* R$$

and

$$2 b_s^d + 2\ell b_s^r = \sum_{(i,t) \in P} x_{it}^* (2d(i, t) + 2\ell d_{av}(t)) \, .$$

Observe that each pair $(i, t) \in P$ contributes an amount $x_{it}^* R$ to the left side of the inequality
and an amount $x_{it}^*(2d(i, t) + 2\ell d_{av}(t))$ to the right side of the inequality. Therefore, to show
the inequality, it suffices to show

$$R \leq 2d(i, t) + 2\ell d_{av}(t)$$

for each $(i, t) \in P$. Consider any $(i, t) \in P$. We distinguish two cases.

In the first case, $d(s, t) < R$. If $|\mathcal{C}_{sc}| \geq 2$, then, by Lemma 4.5.1, we have $R \leq d(s', s)/2$ for any $s' \in \mathcal{C}_{sc}$ with $s' \neq s$. Hence,

$$d(s, t) < \frac{1}{2} \cdot \min\{d(s, s') \mid s' \in \mathcal{C}_{sc}, s' \neq s\}.$$

Thus, independently of the size of $|\mathcal{C}_{sc}|$, Lemma 4.5.3 implies $d_{av}(s) \leq 2d_{av}(t)$. Consequently,

$$R = \ell d_{av}(s) \leq 2\ell d_{av}(t).$$

In the second case, $R \leq d(s, t)$. By Lemma 4.6.2, $d(s, t) \leq 2d(i, t) + 2\ell d_{av}(t)$ and the claim follows. □

The next lemma shows that we can always assume that a strict solution to a star instance has at most two fractional facilities.

Lemma 4.11. *For any strict solution $\mathbf{z}$ to a star instance S_s, we can efficiently construct a strict solution $\mathbf{z}'$ to S_s which has at most two fractional facilities and satisfies $\mathrm{vol}(\mathbf{z}') \leq \mathrm{vol}(\mathbf{z})$.*

Proof. Let S_s be any star instance with a strict solution $\mathbf{z}$. Consider the LP for the star instance with Constraints (4.1), (4.2) and the *additional constraints*

$$0 \leq z_i \quad \text{and} \quad z_i \leq 1 \quad \text{for each } i \in \mathcal{F}_s$$

(which implicitly hold for opening vectors), and the objective

$$\text{minimize} \sum_{i \in \mathcal{F}_s} z_i.$$

Clearly $\mathbf{z}$ is a feasible solution to this LP with objective $\mathrm{vol}(\mathbf{z})$. Now consider an optimal extreme point solution $\mathbf{z}'$ to this LP. Of course, $\mathrm{vol}(\mathbf{z}') \leq \mathrm{vol}(\mathbf{z})$ is satisfied. The number of variables in the LP is $|\mathcal{F}_s|$. Since $\mathbf{z}'$ is an extreme point solution, at least $|\mathcal{F}_s|$ many of the LP constraints are tight. This means that at least $|\mathcal{F}_s| - 2$ of the additional constraints are tight. As for each $i \in \mathcal{F}_s$, at most one of its two additional constraints are tight ($z_i = 0$ and $z_i = 1$ are mutually exclusive events), there are at most two facilities in $\mathcal{F}_s$ whose both additional constraints are not tight. □

For the case of uniform capacities, we can even assume that a strict solution contains at most one fractional facility.

Lemma 4.12. *For any strict solution $\mathbf{z}$ to a star instance S_s with uniform capacities, we can efficiently construct an almost integral strict solution $\mathbf{z}'$ to S_s with $\mathrm{vol}(\mathbf{z}') = \mathrm{vol}(\mathbf{z})$.*

Proof. Let S_s be any star instance with a strict solution $\mathbf{z}$. The idea is to take the volume of $\mathbf{z}$ and transfer it greedily to the facility $i \in \mathcal{F}_s$ that minimizes $d(i, s)u + f_i$ among all facilities that are not yet open.

In more detail, we compute an opening vector $\mathbf{z}'$ for $\mathcal{F}_s$ of volume equal to $\mathrm{vol}(\mathbf{z})$ that minimizes $\sum_{i \in \mathcal{F}_s}(f_i + d(i, s)u_i)z_i'$. For this, we define for each facility $i \in \mathcal{F}_s$ its *weight* as $d(i, s)u + f_i$ and order the facilities non-decreasingly by their weights. Then we create an opening vector $\mathbf{z}'$ for $\mathcal{F}_s$, where we set the first $\lfloor \mathrm{vol}(\mathbf{z}) \rfloor$ facilities to 1, the $(\lfloor \mathrm{vol}(\mathbf{z}) \rfloor + 1)$-th facility (if it exists) to $\mathrm{vol}(\mathbf{z}) - \lfloor\mathrm{vol}(\mathbf{z})\rfloor$, and all remaining facilities to 0. Thus, we have an almost integral opening vector with $\mathrm{vol}(\mathbf{z}') = \mathrm{vol}(\mathbf{z})$ and

$$\sum_{i \in \mathcal{F}_s} (f_i + d(i,s)u_i)z_i' \leq \sum_{i \in \mathcal{F}_s} (f_i + d(i,s)u_i)z_i \leq b_s^{\mathrm{l}} .$$

Thus, Constraints (4.1) and (4.2) are fulfilled and $\mathbf{z}'$ is a strict solution to S_s. □

For technical reasons, we prove the following two lemmas which are crucial for our later analysis. The statement of the first lemma is a little surprising. For any star instance with a relaxed solution $\mathbf{z}$, we can take a fraction $1 - \mathrm{vol}(\mathbf{z})$ of its demand and send it to its closest star center. Independently of the distance, we can bound the connection cost with the budget of the star instance. We show this claim by observing that, in the Ck-FL LP solution, at least a fraction $1 - \mathrm{vol}(\mathbf{z})$ of the LP demand of the corresponding star center was sent to facilities that were very far away. The corresponding connection cost sufficiently sized the budget of the star instance. The proof follows the ideas of the proof of Lemma 4.10.

Lemma 4.13. *Assume $|\mathcal{C}_{sc}| \geq 2$. Consider any star instance S_s with uniform capacities and any relaxed solution $\mathbf{z}$ to S_s with $\mathrm{vol}(\mathbf{z}) = \mathrm{vol}_{y^*}(\mathcal{F}_s)$. Let $\hat{i}$ be the single supporting facility in $\mathbf{z}$ and let $s' \in \mathcal{C}_{sc} \setminus \{s\}$ be the distinct star center closest to s. We have*

$$(1 - z_{\hat{i}})w_s d(s,s') \leq 4(b_s^{\mathrm{d}} + \ell b_s^{\mathrm{r}}) .$$

Proof. Let $P = \mathcal{F}_s \times C$. Then

$$(1 - z_{\hat{i}})w_s d(s,s') = \sum_{(i,t)\in P} x_{it}^*(1 - z_{\hat{i}})d(s,s')$$

and

$$4(b_s^{\mathrm{d}} + \ell b_s^{\mathrm{r}}) = \sum_{(i,t)\in P} x_{it}^* 4(d(i,t) + \ell d_{\mathrm{av}}(t)) .$$

To show the inequality, it suffices to show $(1 - z_{\hat{i}})d(s,s') \leq 4(d(i,t) + \ell d_{\mathrm{av}}(t))$ for each pair $(i,t) \in P$. Consider any $(i,t) \in P$. Similarly, as in the proof of Lemma 4.10, we distinguish the two cases where $d(s,t)$ is smaller or larger than a value R, respectively. We set $R = d(s,s')/2$, thus $R > 0$.

First, assume $d(s,t) \leq R$. Then, by Lemma 4.5.3, $d_{\mathrm{av}}(s) \leq 2d_{\mathrm{av}}(t)$. Note that every facility within radius R around s belongs to $\mathcal{F}_s$. Applying Lemma 4.7, we obtain that the volume of $\mathcal{F}_s$ is at least $1 - d_{\mathrm{av}}(s)/R$. Given $z_{\hat{i}} = \mathrm{vol}(\mathbf{z})$ and our assumption $\mathrm{vol}(\mathbf{z}) = \mathrm{vol}_{y^*}(\mathcal{F}_s)$, we have $1 - z_{\hat{i}} \leq d_{\mathrm{av}}(s)/R$. Hence, $(1 - z_{\hat{i}})d(s,s')$ is bounded from above by

$$d_{\mathrm{av}}(s)/R \cdot 2R = 2d_{\mathrm{av}}(s) \leq 4d_{\mathrm{av}}(t) .$$

Secondly, suppose $R \leq d(s,t)$. By Lemma 4.6.2, $d(s,t) \leq 2d(\hat{i},t) + 2\ell d_{\mathrm{av}}(t)$. We therefore have

$$(1 - z_{\hat{i}})d(s,s') \leq 2R \leq 2d(s,t)$$
$$\leq 4(d(\hat{i},t) + \ell d_{\mathrm{av}}(t)) . □$$

The next lemma is essential to our decomposition of the problem to star instances. It will justify our assumption that all the demand of the clients is accumulated in the star centers.

Lemma 4.14. *We can distribute the LP demand of the clients among the star centers such that each star center s receives precisely w_s units of demand and such that the total connection cost is at most $(2\ell + 2)\,\mathrm{OPT}^*$.*

Proof. Let $t \in C$ be an arbitrary client and i be a facility lying in a star instance S_s for any $s \in C_{sc}$. We ship precisely x_{it}^* units of flow from t to s. By Lemma 4.6.2, we upper bound the distance $d(s, t)$ by $2d(i, t) + 2\ell d_{av}(t)$. Performing this operation for any client-facility pair $t \in C$, $i \in \mathcal{F}_s$, we ensure that the star center s collects $\sum_{t \in C} \sum_{i \in \mathcal{F}_s} x_{it}^*$ units of demand, which is precisely w_s.

The total cost of transporting w_s to the star center s is at most

$$\sum_{t \in C} \sum_{i \in \mathcal{F}_s} x_{it}^*(2d(i, t) + 2\ell d_{av}(t))$$
$$= 2b_s^d + 2\ell b_s^r \, .$$

Thus, the total cost of this flow over all star instances is bounded from above by

$$2 \sum_{s \in C_{sc}} b_s^d + 2\ell \sum_{s \in C_{sc}} b_s^r$$

which is upper bounded by $(2\ell + 2)\,\mathrm{OPT}^*$ according to Lemma 4.8. $\square$

4.2.1   The Dependent Rounding Approach

In our algorithm for hard-capacitated k-FACILITY LOCATION, we will apply the dependent rounding approach of Gandhi et al. [GKPS06] that is based on pipage rounding [AS04]. For the sake of completeness, we give now an overview of this approach and state some properties that we will use.

The dependent rounding procedure iteratively rounds a given vector $\mathbf{y} \in [0, 1]^N$, for any number N of components, until all components are in $\{0, 1\}$. It works as follows. Suppose the current version of the rounded vector is $\mathbf{v} \in [0, 1]^N$; initially, $\mathbf{v}$ is set to $\mathbf{y}$. When we describe the random choice made in a step below, this choice is made independently of all such choices made thus far. If every component of $\mathbf{v}$ lies in $\{0, 1\}$, we are done, so let us assume that there is at least one component $v_i \in (0, 1)$. The first (simple) case is that there is exactly one fractional component v_i; we round v_i in the natural way—to 1 with probability v_i, and to 0 with complementary probability $1 - v_i$; letting V_i denote the rounded version of v_i, we note that

$$\mathbb{E}[V_i] = v_i$$

holds. This simple step is called a *Type I iteration*, and it completes the rounding process. The remaining case is that of a *Type II iteration*: there are at least two components of $\mathbf{v}$ that lie in $(0, 1)$. In this case, we choose two such components, v_i and v_j, in an arbitrary manner. Let ε and δ be the positive constants such that: (a) $v_i + \varepsilon$ and $v_j - \varepsilon$ lie in $[0, 1]$, with at least one of these two quantities lying in $\{0, 1\}$, and (b) $v_i - \delta$ and $v_j + \delta$ lie in $[0, 1]$, with at least one of these two quantities lying in $\{0,1\}$. Such strictly-positive ε and δ exist and are trivial to compute. We then update (v_i, v_j) to a random pair (V_i, V_j) as follows:

- with probability $\delta/(\varepsilon + \delta)$, set $(V_i, V_j) = (v_i + \varepsilon, \ v_j - \varepsilon)$;

- with the complementary probability $\varepsilon/(\varepsilon + \delta)$, set $(V_i, V_j) = (v_i - \delta, \ v_j + \delta)$.

The main properties of *Type II iteration* that we need are:

(i) $\mathbb{P}\left[V_i + V_j = v_i + v_j\right] = 1$;

(ii) $\mathbb{E}\left[V_i\right] = v_i$ and $\mathbb{E}\left[V_j\right] = v_j$.

We iterate the iteration above until we obtain a rounded vector with at most one component in $(0,1)$. Since each iteration rounds at least one additional variable, we need at most N iterations.

Note that the description above does not specify the order in which the elements are rounded. Observe that we may use a predefined laminar family of subsets to guide the rounding procedure. That is, we may first apply Type II iterations to elements of the smallest subsets, then continue applying Type II iterations for smallest subsets among those still containing more than one fractional entry, and eventually round the at most one remaining fractional entry with a Type I iteration. The following lemma shows that by executing the dependent rounding procedure in this manner, we almost preserve the sum of entries within each of the subsets of our laminar family.

For any subset $L \subseteq \{1, \dots, N\}$ of component indices and any vector $\mathbf{v} \in [0,1]^N$, let $\mathrm{vol}_\mathbf{v}(L)$ denote the total volume $\sum_{j \in L} v_j$ of the components of $\mathbf{v}$ whose indices are in L.

Lemma 4.15. *Let* $\mathbf{y} \in [0,1]^N$, *and let* $L_1 \subset \cdots \subset L_l$ *be any laminar sequence of subsets of the component indices* $\{1, \dots, N\}$ *of* $\mathbf{y}$. *In the order* $i = 1, \dots, l$, *we repeatedly run the Type II iteration on the components of* $\mathbf{y}$ *that are given by* L_i *until at most one element of* L_i *points to a fractional component. Let* $\bar{\mathbf{y}} \in [0,1]^N$ *be the resulting rounded vector.*
The following holds: For each i with $1 \le i \le l$, there are at least $\lfloor \mathrm{vol}_\mathbf{y}(L_i) \rfloor$ elements of L_i that have value 1 in $\bar{\mathbf{y}}$.

Proof. Consider any $i \in \{1, \dots, l\}$ and the moment when the Type II iteration has just finished rounding elements in L_i. Let $\mathbf{v} \in [0,1]^N$ be the current version of the rounded vector. Until this moment, only elements of L_i had been considered, given the laminar property $L_j \subseteq L_i$ for every j and i with $1 \le j \le i$. Thus, by the main properties of Type II iteration, the volume of L_i preserved completely and we have $\mathrm{vol}_\mathbf{v}(L_i) = \mathrm{vol}_\mathbf{y}(L_i)$. Recall that at most one element j in L_i has value $v_j \in (0,1)$. Thus there are exactly $\lfloor \mathrm{vol}_\mathbf{y}(L_i) \rfloor$ elements of L_i that have value 1 in $\mathbf{v}$. Since the dependent rounding procedure never changes integral values, at least a portion $\lfloor \mathrm{vol}_\mathbf{y}(L_i) \rfloor$ of the volume of L_j remains until the end. □

4.3   Algorithm for Uniform Hard-Capacitated k-Facility Location

In this section, we prove Theorem 4.1. For any positive ε, we show that we can efficiently compute a solution to the hard-capacitated k-FACILITY LOCATION problem with capacity violation $2 + \varepsilon$ and cost bounded by a factor $\mathcal{O}(1/\varepsilon^2)$ of the cost of an optimum LP solution.

In what follows, we fix the parameter ℓ to any value at least 2 (see Section 4.2) and let u denote the uniform capacity of the facilities. Given ℓ and the optimum solution $(\mathbf{x}^*, \mathbf{y}^*)$ to Ck-FL LP, we obtain the set $\mathcal{C}_{sc}$ of star centers and, for each star center $s \in \mathcal{C}_{sc}$, its corresponding star instance S_s, as described in Section 4.2. By the following lemma, we will assume that there are at least two star centers.

Lemma 4.16. *If $\mathcal{C}_{sc}$ contains only one star center s, we can efficiently compute an approximation with capacity violation 2 and connection cost $(4\ell + 6)\,\mathrm{OPT}^*$ to the underlying k-FACILITY LOCATION instance.*

Proof. By Lemmas 4.9 and 4.12, we compute an almost integral strict solution $\mathbf{z}$ to S_s. If its volume is at least 1, we round any fractional facility down and take the rounded vector as our solution. Otherwise, by Lemma 4.10, we compute a relaxed solution $\mathbf{z}'$ and claim that the single supporting facility is open. We take it as our solution. Lemma 4.1 gives us an assignment of the clients to the open facilities.

We show that our solution is feasible and satisfies the bound on the connection cost. First, we assume $\mathrm{vol}(\mathbf{z}) \geq 1$. Then our solution contains $\lfloor \mathrm{vol}(\mathbf{z}) \rfloor$ open facilities and $\lfloor \mathrm{vol}(\mathbf{z}) \rfloor \geq 1$ holds. If we scale the capacities up by 2, the total capacity of our solution will be $2u \cdot \lfloor \mathbf{z} \rfloor$. This is enough to serve the total demand, which is at most $u\,\mathrm{vol}(\mathbf{z})$; see Constraint (4.1). Next, we assume $\mathrm{vol}(\mathbf{z}) < 1$. By Lemma 4.10, the volume of our relaxed solution $\mathbf{z}'$ satisfies $\mathrm{vol}(\mathbf{z}') = \min\{1, \mathrm{vol}_{\mathbf{y}^*}(\mathcal{F}_s)\}$. Since s is the only star center, we have $\mathcal{F}_s = \mathcal{F}$. By Constraints (LP-2) and (LP-3), $\mathrm{vol}_{\mathbf{y}^*}(\mathcal{F}_s) \geq 1$. Thus, we obtain

$$\mathrm{vol}(\mathbf{z}') \;=\; \min\{1, \mathrm{vol}_{\mathbf{y}^*}(\mathcal{F}_s)\} \;=\; 1\,.$$

Hence, there is a single open facility and it can serve the total demand without capacity violation. In the latter case, the cost of distributing w_s and opening the facilities is at most b_s^{II} by Constraint (4.3). In the former case, it is at most $2b_s^{\mathrm{I}}$ given the capacity blow-up of 2 and Constraint (4.2). Hence, observing $b_s^{\mathrm{II}} \leq 2b_s^{\mathrm{I}}$ and using Corollary (4.2), the distribution and opening cost is bounded by $(2\ell + 4)\,\mathrm{OPT}^*$. The cost to move all the demand of the clients to s is at most $(2\ell + 2)\,\mathrm{OPT}^*$ by Lemma 4.14. The claim follows. □

4.3.1   Constructing a Star Forest

In the first step of our algorithm for the uniform capacitated k-FACILITY LOCATION problem, we decomposed the instance into a set of star instances. Subsequently, we introduce the concept of a *star tree* which imposes a suitable structure on the star instances and facilitates our description of the algorithm as the demand will be routed only along edges of the star tree. We show that in order to obtain a bi-factor approximation algorithm for capacitated k-FACILITY LOCATION it suffices to appropriately "round" a star tree.

A star tree is build up of so called *stars*, which are star instances with solutions. We will distinguish between stars whose solutions have small or big volume and consider only those that have a lower bound on their volume.

Definition 4.8. A star (S_s, z) consists of a star instance S_s and an almost integral solution z to S_s. The *demand of a star* (S_s, z) is the demand w_s of S_s, and the *volume of a star* (S_s, z) is the volume of z. A star is *small* if it has volume at most 1 and at least $1 - 1/\ell$, and z is a relaxed solution. A star is *big* if it is has volume greater than 1 and z is a strict solution.

Note that any small star has exactly one supporting facility. Also note that each star contains at most one fractional facility.

Definition 4.9. A star tree is any rooted in-tree T whose node set C_T is a subset of C_{sc} and that is associated with following components satisfying the following properties. The components are the set $\mathcal{F}_T$ defined as $\bigcup_{s \in C_T} \mathcal{F}_s$, and a metric d_T on $C_T \cup \mathcal{F}_T$ where $s \in C_T$ and $i \in \mathcal{F}_s$ imply $d_T(i, s) = d(i, s)$. The properties are:

(i) Each $s \in C_T$ is associated with a small or a big star (S_s, z).

(ii) Each $s \in C_T$ has indegree at least 2 and the root r has indegree exactly 1.

(iii) For any consecutive edges $(s, s'), (s', s'')$, we have $d_T(s, s') \geq d_T(s', s'')$.

(iv) Consider any $s, s' \in C_T$, $s \neq s'$, where s is associated with a small star. Let $\hat{i}$ be the single supporting facility of s. We have $d_T(\hat{i}, s) \leq d_T(s, s')/2$.

(v) Consider any $s \in C_T$ associated with a small star (S_s, z). Let $\hat{i}$ be the single supporting facility of s. If s is the root of T, let s' be the single son of s, otherwise, let s' be the father of s. We have

$$(1 - z_i)w_s d_T(s, s') \leq 8(b_s^d + \ell b_s^r).$$

The *budget* $b(T)$ of the star tree T is $\sum_{s \in C_T} b_s^{II}$. The *volume* $\mathrm{vol}(T)$ of the star tree is given by the sum of the volumes of its stars.

A *solution to T with capacity violation y* is a set $\mathcal{F}' \subseteq \mathcal{F}_T$ and an assignment $(a_{is})_{i \in \mathcal{F}', s \in C_T}$ satisfying the following constraints:

$$\sum_{i \in \mathcal{F}'} a_{is} \geq w_s \quad \text{for each } s \in C_T$$

$$\sum_{s \in C_T} a_{is} \leq yu \quad \text{for each } i \in \mathcal{F}'$$

$$a_{is} \geq 0 \quad \text{for each } i \in \mathcal{F}', s \in C_T.$$

The *cost* of the solution is

$$\sum_{i \in \mathcal{F}'} f_i + \sum_{i \in \mathcal{F}'} \sum_{s \in C_T} a_{is} d_T(i, s).$$

Summarized, a star tree is a binary tree whose nodes are associated with small or big stars. The edge lengths are non-increasing towards the root which has degree 1. Furthermore, every small star $(S_s, \mathbf{z})$ has its single supporting facility $\hat{i}$ relatively close to its center. Moreover, we can afford sending a fraction $1 - z_{\hat{i}}$ of the demand of s to its closest neighbor. We can interpret the last property also as follows: If the probability is $1 - z_{\hat{i}}$ that s sends all its demand to its closest neighbor, and otherwise it does not send any demand, then we can bound the expected connection cost by a constant multiple of its budget. A star tree also defines a set of facilities which is the set of all facilities of its stars. By the construction of the star clusters, each facility of a star tree appears in exactly one of stars of the tree.

Definition 4.10. A *star forest* H is a collection of disjoint star trees. The *budget* $b(H)$ and the *volume* $\mathrm{vol}(H)$ of a star forest H are given by the sum of budgets and the sum volumes of its star trees, respectively. A *solution* to a star forest provides a solution to each of its star trees and additionally satisfies the constraint that the total number of open facilities is no more than $\lceil \mathrm{vol}(H) \rceil$. The *cost* of a solution to a star forest H is the total cost of the solutions that it provides to each star tree of H.

Creating Star Trees.   The motivation for considering star trees is given by the following theorem. It states that in order to get a constant-factor approximation algorithm for uniform capacitated k-FACILITY LOCATION, it is sufficient to appropriately "round" a star forest.

Theorem 4.3. *If there is an efficient algorithm that computes for a given star forest H a solution of cost at most $c \cdot b(H)$ for some constant $c > 0$ with capacity violation γ, then there is a $(2\ell + 2)(c + 1)$-approximation algorithm for capacitated k-FACILITY LOCATION with capacity violation γ.*

Before we prove the theorem, we first describe how to build a star forest H from a solution to Ck-FL LP where the total volume $\mathrm{vol}(H)$ is bounded from above by k. We begin by defining the node set and proving Property (i).

As the node set of the forest, we take the set $\mathcal{C}_{sc}$ of all star centers. Since the star clusters defined by the star centers partition the set $\mathcal{F}$ of all facilities, our forest will contain all facilities of $\mathcal{F}$. Recall that each $s \in \mathcal{C}_{sc}$ defines the star instance S_s. By Lemma 4.9, we compute a strict solution $\mathbf{z}$ to S_s with $\mathrm{vol}(\mathbf{z}) \le \mathrm{vol}_{y^*}(\mathcal{F}_s)$. If $\mathrm{vol}(\mathbf{z}) > 1$, we apply Lemma 4.12 to obtain an almost integral strict solution $\mathbf{z}'$ with $\mathrm{vol}(\mathbf{z}') = \mathrm{vol}(\mathbf{z})$. Thus, $(S_s, \mathbf{z}')$ is a big star and we associate it with s. Otherwise, if $\mathrm{vol}(\mathbf{z}) \le 1$, then we have $\mathrm{vol}(\mathbf{z}) \le \min\{1, \mathrm{vol}_{y^*}(\mathcal{F}_s)\}$. We apply Lemma 4.10 to obtain a relaxed solution $\mathbf{z}'$ with $\mathrm{vol}(\mathbf{z}') = \min\{1, \mathrm{vol}_{y^*}(\mathcal{F}_s)\}$ where the only supporting facility $\hat{i} \in \mathcal{F}_s$ satisfies $d(\hat{i}, s) \le \ell d_{\mathrm{av}}(s)$. By Corollary 4.1, $\mathrm{vol}_{y^*}(\mathcal{F}_s) \ge 1 - 1/\ell$ and so $\mathrm{vol}(\mathbf{z}') \ge 1 - 1/\ell$. Consequently $(S_s, \mathbf{z}')$ is a small star. We associate it with s and conclude that Property (i) holds.

Note that every star $(S_s, \mathbf{z})$ constructed above has a volume at most $\mathrm{vol}_{y^*}(\mathcal{F}_s)$. Thus, the total volume in the star forest that we are constructing is at most k, in particular, $\lceil \mathrm{vol}(H) \rceil \le k$. In the following, we describe how to connect the nodes together and how to compute a metric in each obtained star tree so that the remaining properties are satisfied.

As a first step, we build a directed forest G on the node set $\mathcal{C}_{sc}$ by running Procedure Short-Trees$(\mathcal{C}_{sc}, \varnothing)$ (see Section 4.2). By Lemma 4.3, its components are all in-trees, which we will call *short center trees*. We cannot take the short center trees as our star trees, as the indegrees of their nodes may be unbounded. Therefore, we change the structure of each short center tree to obtain a *binary center tree*, in which the indegree of each node is at most 2. Figure 4.2 depicts

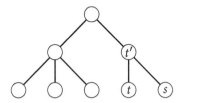 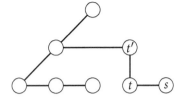

Figure 4.2: Making a tree binary: The left side shows one of the trees returned by Procedure Short-Trees($\mathcal{C}_{sc}$, ∅); the right side shows the corresponding tree after modification by Procedure Binary-Trees(G). Observe that the father t' of s has been replaced by the left brother t of s.

this process that we describe below. By showing that all remaining properties of Definition 4.9 are fulfilled, we will prove that the constructed binary center tree is a star tree.

Consider the Procedure Binary-Trees(G) that takes as input the forest G of short center trees returned by Short-Trees($\mathcal{C}_{sc}$, ∅). Each short center tree T in G is separately modified as follows. For each node $t \in V(T)$, we sort all incoming edges of t from left to right by non-decreasing length. In the case that t is the root of T, the leftmost edge is set to be the incoming edge from its closest son. (Note that there might exist multiple incoming edges with the same smallest length, therefore, we use the uniqueness of closeness; see Definition 4.3.) Having defined the order, we remove all incoming edges of t except the leftmost one. In the next step, the procedure adds for each son s of t an edge from s to its left brother (if there exists one). Note that no edge is added to the leftmost son of t. The resulting forest of binary center trees is denoted by H.

Procedure Binary-Trees(G)

$H = $ ∅
foreach short tree T in G **do**
    foreach node $t \in V(T)$ **do**
        sort all sons of t from left to right by non-decreasing distance to t
        if t is the root of T **then**
            place the son of t closest to t on the leftmost position in the ordering
        remove all incoming edges of t from T except the leftmost one
        add a directed edge from each son of t to its left brother (if there exists one)
    add T to H
return H

Every binary center tree satisfies the following useful property.

Lemma 4.17. *The root of a binary center tree has exactly one son and its son is its closest star center.*

Proof. By Lemma 4.4, the node closest to the root is one of its sons in the short center tree. During the construction of the binary center tree, this node becomes the only son of the root. □

Consider any binary center tree T'. Let $\mathcal{C}_{T'}$ be its node set and let $\mathcal{F}_{T'}$ be the set $\bigcup_{s \in \mathcal{C}_{T'}} \mathcal{F}_s$ of all facilities in T'. Let T be the short center tree from which T' was derived. We show that T' is a star tree. For technical reasons, we first define a new metric $d_{T'}$ on $\mathcal{F}_{T'} \cup \mathcal{C}_{T'}$ for T', before we consider the remaining properties.

The metric $d_{T'}$ will be a tree metric where the underlying tree is the binary center tree T' (for this purpose considered undirected) with an additional edge for each facility that connects it to its star center. Recall that, in a tree metric, the distance between any two nodes is the weight of the path connecting the two nodes. For each additional edge between a facility i and its star center s, we set its weight to $d(i, s)$; hence $d_{T'}(i, s) = d(i, s)$ and we fulfill the requirement imposed by Definition 4.9 on $d_{T'}$. For each edge (s, t) of the binary center tree T', we set its weight to $2d(s, t')$, where t' is the closest node in $\mathcal{C}_{sc} \setminus \{s\}$ to s, or stated equivalently, where t' is the father of s in the short center T; see Fig. 4.2. Hence, $d_{T'}(s, t) = 2d(s, t')$. The new metric $d_{T'}$ is never smaller than the underlying metric d, as the next lemma shows.

Lemma 4.18. *The metric $d_{T'}$ satisfies $d_{T'}(s, t) \geq d(s, t)$ for every $s, t \in \mathcal{C}_{T'} \cup \mathcal{F}_{T'}$.*

Proof. It suffices to show the claim for each edge of the tree that underlies the metric. For each edge between a facility and its star center, the claim directly holds by definition. Thus, consider any edge $(s, t) \in E(T')$. By definition of $d_{T'}$, we have $d_{T'}(s, t) = 2d(s, t')$, where t' is the father of s in the short center tree T. To prove the claim, we show $d(s, t) \leq 2d(s, t')$. There are two cases: Either t is the father of s in T, or it is the left brother of s in T. The first case is trivial as $d(s, t) \leq 2 \cdot d(s, t)$. In the second case, the node t' is the common father of s and t in T; see Fig. 4.2. Since t is the left brother of s in T, we have $d(t, t') \leq d(s, t')$. Hence $d(s, t) \leq d(s, t') + d(t', t) \leq 2 \cdot d(s, t')$. $\qquad\square$

Now that the metric $d_{T'}$ is defined, we prove that T' satisfies all properties of a star tree.

Lemma 4.19. *The binary center tree T' with the metric $d_{T'}$ is a star tree.*

Proof. Recall that our construction of the node set and their associated stars already implies Property (i) for T'.

The next two properties are related to the tree structure of a binary center tree. We provide bounds on the degree of the nodes and show that edge lengths towards the root are non-increasing.

We show Property (ii). Any node s in T' has at most two incoming edges: One from its closest son in T and one from its right brother in T. By Lemma 4.17, the root has exactly one son in T'.

Next, we show Property (iii). Let (s, s') and (s', s'') be any consecutive edges in T'. We have to prove $d_{T'}(s, s') \geq d_{T'}(s', s'')$. In the tree T, let t be the father of s, and let t' be the father of s'. Recall that, by the definition of $d_{T'}$, the equations $d_{T'}(s, s') = 2d(s, t)$ and $d_{T'}(s', s'') = 2d(s', t')$ hold. Therefore, it suffices to show $d(s, t) \geq d(s', t')$. If s' is the father of s in T, then $s' = t$ and the claim holds by Lemma 4.2. If s' is the left brother of s in T, then $t' = t$ and the claim holds by the construction of binary center trees.

The remaining two properties are related to small stars. We show how to bound the distance of a node to its only supporting facility and how to bound the cost of transporting its demand to the next node.

Consider any small star $(S_s, \mathbf{z})$ with $s \in C_{T'}$. Let $\hat{i}$ be the only supporting facility in $(S_s, \mathbf{z})$. We show Property (iv). Let $s' \in C_{T'} \setminus \{s\}$ be any node distinct to s. By the definition of $d_{T'}$, we have $d_{T'}(\hat{i}, s) = d(\hat{i}, s)$. Recall that our construction of small stars guarantees that $\hat{i}$ satisfies $d(\hat{i}, s) \leq \ell d_{\text{av}}(s)$. By Lemmas 4.5.1 and 4.18, we obtain

$$\ell d_{\text{av}}(s) < d(s', s)/2 \leq d_{T'}(s', s)/2.$$

Next, we show Property (v). If $\text{vol}(\mathbf{z}) = 1$, we are done. Therefore, we assume $\text{vol}(\mathbf{z}) < 1$ which implies $\text{vol}(\mathbf{z}) = \text{vol}_{\mathbf{y}^*}(\mathcal{F}_s)$ by our construction of small stars. Let $s' \in C_{\text{sc}} \setminus \{s\}$ be the star center distinct from s that is closest to s. If s is the root of T', then, by Lemma 4.17, s' is the son of s. Thus, by the definition of $d_{T'}$, $d_{T'}(s', s) = 2d(s', s)$ and Lemma 4.13 implies the claim. If s is not the root, let t be the father of s. Then, by the definition of $d_{T'}$, we have $d_{T'}(s, t) = 2d(s, s')$. Therefore, it suffices to show the inequality

$$(1 - z_{\hat{i}})w_s d(s, s') \leq 4(b_s^{\text{d}} + \ell b_s^{\text{r}})$$

to prove the claim. The inequality holds by Lemma 4.13.   □

We have now shown that all properties of star trees as required in Definition 4.9 are actually satisfied by the binary center tree T'. This fact implies that all our binary center trees are star trees, and, hence, that our constructed forest H is in fact a star forest. Thus, we are ready to prove Theorem 4.3.

Proof of Theorem 4.3. Given a capacitated *k*-FACILITY LOCATION instance, we compute the corresponding star forest H and use the black box algorithm to obtain a solution to H of cost $c \cdot b(H)$ and capacity violation γ. Note that the solution opened at most $\lceil \text{vol}(H) \rceil \leq k$ facilities. Then, by solving a minimum-cost flow problem (see Lemma 4.1), we efficiently compute an optimal assignment of the clients to facilities opened by the solution.

To bound the cost of the solution, we give a suboptimal fractional flow of demand that uses the edges in the star forest and that satisfies the claimed cost bound. The flow is constructed in two steps. First the demand of the clients is transported to the star centers so that each node $s \in C_{\text{sc}}$ collects precisely w_s units of demand. By Lemma 4.14, this can be accomplished at cost at most $(2 + 2\ell) \cdot \text{OPT}^*$. To transport the demand collected at the star centers to the actual facilities, we use the assignment provided by the solution to the star forest. By definition, this assignment transports for each $s \in C_{\text{sc}}$ precisely w_s units of demand to the facilities opened by the solution. The cost of this assignment, together with the costs for opening the facilities, is

$$c \cdot b(H) = c \cdot \sum_{s \in C_{\text{sc}}} b_s^{\text{II}} \leq c \cdot (2\ell + 2)\,\text{OPT}^*$$

by Corollary 4.2. Altogether, we obtain $(c + 1) \cdot (2\ell + 2)\,\text{OPT}^*$ as an upper bound of the solution cost.   □

4.3.2   Solving a Star Forest

We now show how to solve any given star forest H. We describe a deterministic rounding procedure which is tuned to minimize the capacity violation while allowing a large connection and opening cost that is still bounded by a constant multiple of the budget $b(H)$. Together with Theorem 4.3, this will imply, for any positive ε, an $\mathcal{O}(1/\varepsilon^2)$-approximation algorithm for the uniform hard-capacitated k-Facility Location problem with capacity violation $2 + \varepsilon$.

In the first step, the algorithm forms groups of $\ell \geq 2$ nodes in each star tree. In the next step, at the cost of loosing some accuracy with distances, we simplify the graph structure within each of the groups. Eventually, we use a dependent rounding routine to decide the actual openings of facilities, and argue that there is sufficient capacity open up every tree to serve all demand coming from below, and, hence, on every star tree there exists a feasible routing of its total demand.

To the end of this section, let $\mathbf{z}$ denote the union of the solutions of all stars in the star forest. For the sake of easier presentation, we will refer to each star $(S_s, \mathbf{z}')$ just by its instance S_s and use $\mathbf{z}$ when referring to the opening values of its facilities. Also to the end of this section, we fix any star tree T of our forest with a root r. Let $\mathcal{C}_T$ be the set of its nodes, $\mathcal{F}_T$ the set of its facilities, and d_T its metric on $\mathcal{C}_T \cup \mathcal{F}_T$.

Building groups.   The nodes of the star tree T will be grouped by a top-down greedy procedure starting from the root r; see Fig. 4.3a. When forming a new group, a single node s (having all its descendants yet not grouped) will be selected as a root of the new group. Then new nodes will be added to the group in a greedy fashion until either the group has reached the size of ℓ nodes, or all descendants of s are already included. The greedy choice of the next node to include will be to take one which is connected to the already included nodes by a cheapest tree edge. When a group is complete, we exclude the selected nodes from participating in the later formed groups. As long as not all nodes of the tree are grouped, we select a top-most one s and build a group G_s rooted at s.

Definition 4.11.   A group G_s is a *child* of a group G_t and G_t is a *parent* of G_s if there is a directed edge in T from s to a node in G_t. The group G_r is the *root group* and every other group is a *non-root group*.

Observation 4.1.   *If G_t has at least one child, then it contains exactly ℓ nodes, otherwise (if it has no children) G_t may have less nodes. Moreover, each group has at most $\ell + 1$ children.*

The next lemma is implied by Property (iii) and the way in which the algorithm selects nodes to a group.

Lemma 4.20.   *Consider any group G_t that has a child group G_s. Let $e_s \in E(T)$ be the edge from s (the root of G_s) to its father in G_t. For any edge e in G_t and any edge e' in G_s, we have $d_T(e) \leq d_T(e_s) \leq d_T(e')$.*

Group modification.   To facilitate rounding of facility openings within groups, we will modify the tree structure within groups to obtain a new in-tree T' from the initial star tree T. The partition of nodes into groups will stay unchanged and the parent-child relation between groups will also be preserved. The modification within a single group is as follows.

Consider a group of nodes G_s and the order in which the nodes were added to the group by the greedy procedure. In the modified tree T', the group G_s will form a chain graph directed

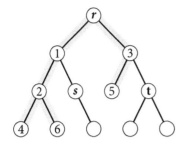

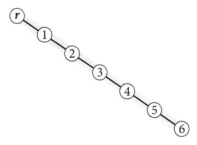

(a) Building groups: Edges highlighted in gray form a new group G_r with the root node r; nodes s and t are roots of groups G_s and G_t, respectively. G_r is parent group of G_s and G_t. The numbers indicate a possible order in which the nodes have been added to G_r.

(b) The group G_r after the modification step: The group is now a chain and nodes are ordered from top to bottom in the order they were added to the group, that is, with non-decreasing distances to their fathers in the star tree.

Figure 4.3: Building groups and the modification step.

towards its root s, with the nodes closer to s being those selected earlier by the group forming algorithm; see Fig. 4.3b. Finally, for any group G_s which is a child of a group G_t, let the edge outgoing from s point to the lowest vertex in G_t in T'.

Clearly, such modification of the tree structure may interfere with routing demand along edges of the used tree. Nevertheless, we will argue that we may bound this influence to only a constant multiplicative growth in the routing distance.

Recall that the lengths of edges of T were monotone non-increasing on any directed path towards the root node r. We will no longer have this property in T', but we will now exploit the monotonicity of d_T on edges of directed paths in T to bound distances on T'.

Lemma 4.21. *Let s and t be any nodes of the same group such that t lies above s in T'. Let t' be the father of s in T. It holds $d_T(s, t) \le (\ell - 1) \cdot d_T(s, t')$.*

Proof. Since t lies above s in the same group as s in T', we have that s was added later to this group than t. Hence every edge on the path (ignoring edge directions) from s to t in T has length at most $d_T(s, t')$; see Fig. 4.3 and consider $s = 5$, $t = 2$ and $t' = 3$. Since no more than $\ell - 1$ edges lie on this path and since d_T is a metric, the claim follows. □

Lemma 4.22. *Let s be the root of any non-root group, let t' be its father in T, and let t be any node in the parent group of s. It holds $d_T(s, t) \le \ell \cdot d_T(s, t')$.*

Proof. By triangle inequality,

$$d_T(s, t) \le d_T(s, t') + d_T(t', t) .$$

If $t' = t$, we are done. Otherwise, there is an edge (t', s') in T. By Lemma 4.21,

$$d_T(t', t) \le (\ell - 1) \cdot d_T(t', s')$$

and, by Lemma 4.20, $d_T(t', s') \le d_T(s, t')$. □

Lemma 4.23. *Let (s, s') and (t, t') be any two edges in T. If t lies above s in T', then we have $d_T(s, s') \geq d_T(t, t')$.*

Proof. If s and t do not belong to the same group in T, then the claim follows by Lemma 4.20. Otherwise, our greedy choice in the construction of the group implies the claim.   □

Rounding the facility openings.   In the previous step of our algorithm, we have computed, for T as well as every other star tree of our star forest H, a new in-tree with modified groups. Now, to decide the eventual openings of facilities, we use the dependent rounding procedure described in Section 4.2.1 that we apply on all facilities of the star forest together. We will refer to the randomized rounding algorithm by *rounding procedure*. Later, we show how to derandomize it.

The rounding procedure starts with the opening vector $\mathbf{z}$. In each step, it computes a new opening vector that is used as the input for the next step. In the first iterative phase (Type II iteration), the procedure considers, step by step, pairs of still fractional facilities. In such a pair of facilities, the procedure pumps one of the openings up and the other one down randomly choosing the one to increase. As a result of this step, at least one of the two facilities becomes either closed or open. The Type II iteration phase ends when at most one fractional facility is left in H. Based on its current opening value, we randomly decide whether to close or to open it (Type I iteration).

In the first phase, the procedure preserves the sum of facility openings (hence, their volume). Therefore, we will open either $\lfloor \text{vol}(H) \rfloor$ or $\lceil \text{vol}(H) \rceil$ facilities at the end. Moreover, the probability of eventually opening the facility i equals the opening value that it had at the beginning of the random procedure, that is, it equals z_i.

On top of these standard properties, we will also exploit that we may guarantee to almost preserve the volume in a number of chosen subsets of facilities, provided that the subsets form a laminar family (see Lemma 4.15). Here, rather than explicitly defining the family of subsets, we will directly say in which order the pairs of fractional facilities should be chosen.

The rounding will proceed first within the groups until at most one fractional facility is left in each of the groups. Within each group, the rounding procedure will always select the top-most pair of currently fractional facilities. Please note that modifying the shape of the tree inside the groups into chain graphs we have made the choice of the top-most pair unambiguous. When there is at most one fractional facility left in each group, the rounding may be continued in an arbitrary order. At the end, there is at most one fractional facility left in the whole star forest. We open it with probability equal to its current opening.

In more detail, consider any group G_s. In each step, we select among all the facilities of G_s the two top-most fractional ones. Here, we say a facility lies above another one, if the node it belongs to lies above the node of the other facility in the chain graph of G_s. Then we round this pair as described in the Type II iteration (see Section 4.2.1). As a result, one of both facilities gets either open or closed and their total volume remains the same. Eventually, we are left with at most one fractional facility in G_s.

During the next discussions, the (unchanged) opening vector on which the rounding procedure started is still denoted by $\mathbf{z}$. Also the volume of a star remains defined by $\mathbf{z}$. However, when referring to the opening value of a facility without specifying the opening vector, we will refer to its opening in the opening vector returned by the rounding procedure.

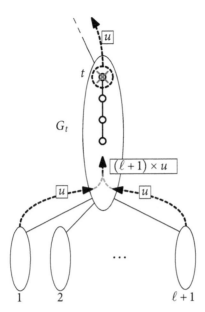

Figure 4.4: A parent group G_t with $\ell + 1$ children groups. The groups are depicted as ovals with edges connecting them. Each child group sends at most u units of demand to its parent group (dashed arrows). Thus, G_t receives at most $(\ell + 1)u$ units of demand from its children. Inside G_t, the root t is a small star whose supporting facility has been closed. The demand of t, which is at most u, gets routed to the parent of G_t (assuming that it exists). Any other demand of G_t and all demand coming from its children is served within G_t.

The following lemma shows that, independently of the outcome of the rounding procedure, the distribution of the volume has a nice property: For any node, the total volume of the stars above the node is almost entirely preserved. Later, this will ensure that enough facilities are open above every node without open facilities to serve its demand.

Lemma 4.24. *Consider any group and let l be the number of it nodes. For $1 \leq m \leq l$, let $\mathcal{F}_m$ denote the set of all facilities of the first m nodes from the top, and let v_m denote the volume of $\mathcal{F}_m$ in $\mathbf{z}$.*
The following is true: For each m with $1 \leq m \leq l$, the rounding procedure opens at least $\lfloor v_m \rfloor$ facilities in $\mathcal{F}_m$.

Proof. By our greedy choice of always selecting the top-most pair of fractional facilities, we exhaustively applied Type II iteration on each set $\mathcal{F}_m \in \mathcal{F}_1, \ldots, \mathcal{F}_l$ in this order until at most one fractional facility remained in $\mathcal{F}_m$. Note that $\mathcal{F}_1 \subset \cdots \subset \mathcal{F}_l$ forms a laminar sequence. Thus, the claim follows directly by the sum preservation shown in Lemma 4.15 and the fact that once opened facilities will not be closed at any step later by the rounding procedure. □

Routing and analysis.   Once the facilities are opened, a minimum-cost assignment of clients to facilities can be found, for example, by a minimum-cost flow computation in the original graph. Nevertheless, for the purpose of the analysis, we will consider a suboptimal assignment where the demand is routed along the edges of the in-tree T'.

We will make sure that the demand of any node $s \in C_T$ will be satisfied not farther than at the root of the group of the parent of s, which is not too far by Lemmas 4.20 and 4.21. We will show that after scaling up the capacity of each facility by a factor of $2 + 3/(\ell - 1)$, each non-root group will send up at most u units of demand to its parent group; see Fig. 4.4. Then we will argue that the excess capacity of at least $(\ell + 1)u$ in a group is sufficient to serve the demand sent up from its child groups. The tricky part is to control the demand transportation within groups. Note that once we let a unit of demand travel along an edge of T', then, by paying only ℓ times more, we may let it travel further as long as it stays within the same group. Therefore, it is essential to make sure that inside each group sufficient capacity is provided by the open facilities above a node to collect its demand.

Lemma 4.25. *For any group G_s, we can assign its total demand such that each open facility receives at most $2u$ units of demand, the demand of each big star gets completely assigned to its own open facilities and the following holds for every small star $S_{s'}$:*

(i) *If $S_{s'}$ has an open facility, its demand gets completely assigned to its open facility.*

(ii) *Otherwise, if s' is the root of T', its demand gets completely assigned to open facilities that belong to its son. (Note that the son exists.)*

(iii) *Otherwise, if s' is the root of G_s, its demand remains completely unassigned.*

(iv) *Otherwise, the demand of $S_{s'}$ gets completely assigned to open facilities that belong to nodes lying above s' in G_s.*

Proof. In the following, we call a small star *closed* if it contains no open facility in the opening vector returned by the rounding procedure.

We set the capacity of each open facility to $2u$, hence, each open facility can serve a demand up to $2u$. Consider any big star. By definition, it has some volume v larger than 1 and an almost integral solution. Thus, it contains $\lfloor v \rfloor$ open facilities in $\mathbf{z}$ and at least the same number in the output of the rounding procedure. By Constraint (4.1), its demand is at most vu. Using the fact $2u \cdot \lfloor v \rfloor \geq uv$, we assign the demand of every big star to its own open facilities such that each facility receives at most $2u$ units of demand. Next, consider any small star. It has some volume v and a demand of size at most $uv \leq u$. Hence, if a small star is not closed, then we assign its demand to its own open facility.

We now show how we assign the demand of closed small stars. Let $s_1, \ldots, s_l$ be the nodes as they are ordered in the group G_s from top to bottom. First assume that at least one of the two statements is true: (a) S_{s_1} is not a small star, or (b) s_1 is not the root of T'. We prove the claim of the lemma by induction for every subgroup $s_1, \ldots, s_m$ where $m = 1, \ldots, l$.

Consider first the base case $m = 1$. If S_{s_1} is a closed small star, then, by assumption, S_{s_1} is not the root of T'. We don't route its demand and the claim holds. Otherwise the star serves its own demand as shown above and the claim also holds.

Next, consider the inductive step with $m \geq 2$. By induction hypothesis, we compute an assignment σ that satisfies the claim for the subgroup $s_1, \ldots, s_{m-1}$. We will extend this assignment to S_{s_m}. Let v be the total volume of the stars $S_{s_1}, \ldots, S_{s_m}$. By Lemma 4.24, the number of open facilities in the stars $S_{s_1}, \ldots, S_{s_m}$ is at least $\lfloor v \rfloor$, and, hence, their total capacity is at least $2u \cdot \lfloor v \rfloor$. By Constraint (4.1), the total demand located at these stars is at most uv. Since $m \geq 2$ and since each star has volume at least $1 - 1/\ell \geq 1/2$ (Definition 4.8), we have $v \geq 1$. Consequently, $2u \cdot \lfloor v \rfloor \geq uv$. Let v' be the volume in the stars $S_{s_1}, \ldots, S_{s_{m-1}}$. Since the assignment σ distributes at most uv' units of demand, the leftover capacity in the stars $S_{s_1}, \ldots, S_{s_m}$ is at least $2u \cdot \lfloor v \rfloor - uv'$. This amount is larger than the demand of S_{s_m}, which is at most $u(v - v') = uv - uv'$. Therefore, if S_{s_m} is a small star whose fractional facility has been closed, we assign the demand of S_{s_m} in an arbitrary manner to the leftover capacity. In all other cases, the star serves its demand itself as argued above. Thus, we get a new assignment for the subgroup $s_1, \ldots, s_m$ satisfying the claim.

Now, consider the case that S_{s_1} is a small star and s_1 is the root of T'. By Property (ii), the root of T' has a son and thus $l \geq 2$. Again, we prove the claim of the lemma by induction for every subgroup $s_1, \ldots, s_m$ where $m = 2, \ldots, l$.

For the base case $m = 2$, the claim immediately holds if neither S_{s_1} nor S_{s_2} is a closed small star as then the stars serve their demands by themselves. Otherwise, at least one of the stars is a closed small star. Let v be the total volume of S_{s_1} and S_{s_2} in $\mathbf{z}$. Recall, by Lemma 4.24, that there are at least $\lfloor v \rfloor$ open facilities in the two stars. Thus, the open facilities in the stars provide a capacity of at least $2u \cdot \lfloor v \rfloor$. As every star has volume at least $1 - 1/\ell \geq 1/2$, we have $\lfloor v \rfloor \geq 1$. This fact implies two observations. First, at least one facility is open. Hence, exactly one of the two stars is a closed small star. Secondly, the capacity provided by the open facilities is enough to serve their total demand, which is at most vu. Thus, we obtain a feasible assignment by assigning the demand of the closed small star in an arbitrary manner to the leftover capacity of the other star.

For the inductive step with $m \geq 3$, we apply the same arguments as in the inductive step described above. Hence, we obtain an assignment for the whole group G_s that satisfies the claim. $\qquad\square$

The lemma above shows that, within each group, we can satisfy the demand of all its nodes, except perhaps the root node of the group. If the demand of the root of a group G_s is not satisfied, then, by Lemma 4.25, the root s is associated with a small star and s is not the root of T'. Consequently, the unsatisfied demand is at most u and there exists a parent group for G_s. To satisfy the demand of s, we will forward it to the parent group. Thus, we have to show that the parent group G_t has enough capacity left to serve the demand sent from G_s and from every other of its children. As G_t is a non-leaf group, it contains ℓ stars. Since each star has volume at least $1 - 1/\ell$ (see Definition 4.8), the volume v of G_t is at least $\ell - 1$. By Lemma 4.24, there are $\lfloor v \rfloor$ open facilities in G_t. After scaling the capacities with $(2 + 3/(\ell - 1))$ and using $\lfloor v \rfloor \geq \ell - 1$, we can lower bound the total capacity in G_t by

$$\begin{aligned}
&(2 + 3/(\ell-1)) \lfloor v \rfloor u \\
&= \lfloor v \rfloor u + (1 + 3/(\ell-1)) \lfloor v \rfloor u \\
&\geq (v - 1)u + (1 + 3/(\ell-1))(\ell-1)u \\
&\geq vu + (\ell+1)u \ .
\end{aligned}$$

From this capacity, at most vu is used for the demand from G_s. Consequently, at least $(\ell + 1)u$ capacity remains to be potentially used by demand forwarded from the child groups. Since there are at most $\ell + 1$ child groups and each of them forwards at most u units of demand, the remaining capacity is sufficient. Thus, we assign the demand coming from the children arbitrarily on the facilities in G_t that still have some capacity left; see Fig. 4.4.

We summarize the properties of our assignment as follows.

Lemma 4.26. *We can assign the total demand in T' such that each open facility receives at most $2 + 3/(\ell - 1)u$ units of demand, the demand of each big star gets completely assigned to its own open facilities and the following holds for every small star S_s:*

(i) *If S_s has an open facility, its demand gets completely assigned to its open facility.*

(ii) *Otherwise, if s is the root of T', its demand gets completely assigned to open facilities that belong to its son.*

(iii) *Otherwise, if s is the root of a group, its demand gets completely assigned to open facilities that belong to nodes lying in the parent group of s.*

(iv) *Otherwise, the demand of S_s gets completely assigned to open facilities that belong to nodes lying above s in the same group as s.*

Expected Cost.   Now, we examine the expected cost of the assignment above, that is, the cost of placing facilities in T' and routing demand within T'.

Consider any outcome of the rounding procedure together with our assignment given by Lemma 4.26. We will split the cost over all facilities such that each facility is charged with some cost portion: Every facility pays its own opening cost as well as the connection cost of the demand that it receives directly from its star center. If the single facility i of a small star is closed, it pays the connection cost of distributing the demand of its star S_s on other star centers. If a receiving star center t belongs to a small star S_t, then i even pays for forwarding the demand to the single open facility in S_t. If S_t is big, then each facility i' receiving a demand portion from s pays for the last stretch of moving the demand from t to i'. Note that by this charging schema, we have completely split the cost over all facilities.

In what follows, we upper bound the cost contribution of each facility i depending on whether i is open or closed in the outcome of the rounding procedure. For the case that i is open, we use c_i^1 to denote its upper bound, otherwise, we use c_i^0. Thus, for any opening vector $\bar{z}$ returned by the rounding procedure, the total cost of the solution to T will be bounded from above by *the gross cost of T* that we define as follows.

Definition 4.12. The gross cost of T is $\sum_{i \in \mathcal{F}_T} \bar{z}_i\, c_i^1 + (1 - \bar{z}_i)\, c_i^0$.

Consider any facility i and assume that it belongs to a big star S_s. For the case that i is closed, i is not charged and we set $c_i^0 = 0$. For the case that i is open, it has to pay for its opening cost f_i as well as for moving from its star center all the demand that it receives. By Lemma 4.26, i receives at most $(2 + 3/(\ell - 1))u$ units of demand. Thus, we set $c_i^1 = f_i + (2 + 3/(\ell - 1))u\, d_T(i, s)$.

Now, assume that i belongs to a small star S_s. If i is not the single supporting facility $\hat{i}$ of S_s in z, it will remain closed and therefore not charged. We set $c_i^1 = c_i^0 = 0$. Otherwise, consider $i = \hat{i}$. For the case that $\hat{i}$ is open, it has to pay for its opening cost as well as for moving the demand that it receives directly from its star center. Since a small star has at most one open facility, $\hat{i}$ has to pay for the full demand w_s of s. Recall that it is not charged for receiving demand originating from other stars. Thus, we set $c_i^1 = f_i + w_s d_T(\hat{i}, s)$.

For the case that $\hat{i}$ is closed, it has to pay for distributing the demand w_s on other stars. We distinguish two cases.

First, assume that s is the root of T and let s' be its single son in T (see Property (ii)), which is the same in T'. By Lemma 4.26, all the demand of S_s gets assigned to facilities in $S_{s'}$. Thus, we move the demand to s' over the distance $d_T(s, s')$. If $S_{s'}$ is a small star, we further route the demand to the single open facility in $S_{s'}$. By Property (iv), we traversed in total a distance at most $(1 + 1/2)d_T(s, s')$. Generously, we set $c_i^0 = w_s(\ell + 1/2)d_T(s, s')$.

Next, assume that s is not the root of T. Let s' be the father of s in T. Fix a portion $\hat{w}_s$ of the demand that is routed to some star S_t. By Lemma 4.26, t has to lie above s in T'. If s is the root of its group, then t belongs to the parent group of G_s. Otherwise, if s is not the root of its group, then t belongs to the same group as s. By Lemmas 4.21 and 4.22, we know that the distance between s and t is at most $\ell d_T(s, s')$. If S_t is a big star, we just route $\hat{w}_s$ to t. If S_t is a small star, we further route $\hat{w}_s$ to its single open facility $\hat{i}'$.

Assume that t is not the root of T. Let t' be the father of t in T. Since t lies above s in T', we have $d_T(t, t') \leq d_T(s, s')$ by Lemma 4.23. Thus, by Property (iv), the distance from t to $\hat{i}'$ is at most

$$d_T(t, t')/2 \leq d_T(s, s')/2.$$

Now, if t is the root of T, then let t' be the single son of t in T and T'. If t' lies above s in T', then Lemma 4.23 implies $d_T(t, t') \leq d_T(s, s')$. Otherwise, $t' = s$, and thus $(t', t) = (s, s')$. Again, by Property (iv), we have

$$d_T(\hat{i}, t) \leq d_T(t, t')/2 \leq d_T(s, s')/2.$$

Hence, the total distance for $\hat{w}_s$ is at most $(\ell + 1/2)d_T(s, s')$. Since this bound holds for any portion of the demand w_s, we set $c_i^0 = w_s(\ell + 1/2)d_T(s, s')$.

We summarize our bounds:

Definition 4.13. Let C_T^b denote the set of all star centers of big stars in C_T, and let C_T^s denote the set of all star centers of small stars in C_T.

- For every $s \in C_T^b$ and $i \in F_s$, we set

$$c_i^1 = f_i + (2 + 3/(\ell - 1))u d_T(i, s) \quad \text{and} \quad c_i^0 = 0.$$

- For every $s \in C_T^s$ and the only supporting facility $\hat{i}$ of S_s in $\mathbf{z}$, we set

$$c_i^1 = f_i + w_s d_T(\hat{i}, s) \quad \text{and} \quad c_i^0 = w_s(\ell + 1/2)d_T(s, s'),$$

where s' is the son of s if s is the root, and the father of s in T' otherwise.

- For every other facility $i \in F_T$, we set

$$c_i^1 = 0 \quad \text{and} \quad c_i^0 = 0.$$

Now we are ready to bound the expected gross cost.

Lemma 4.27. *The expected gross cost of our solution to T is at most $(4\ell + 3)b(T)$.*

Proof. For every $s \in C_T^s$, we define $\hat{\imath}(s)$ as the single supporting facility of S_s in **z**. Recall that every facility $i \in \mathcal{F}_T$ is opened with probability equal to z_i by the rounding procedure. Using our definitions, the expected gross cost is

$$\sum_{i \in \mathcal{F}_T} z_i\, c_i^1 + (1 - z_i)\, c_i^0$$

$$= \sum_{s \in C_T^b} \sum_{i \in \mathcal{F}_s} z_i\, c_i^1 + \sum_{s \in C_T^s} z_{\hat{\imath}(s)}\, c_{\hat{\imath}(s)}^1 + (1 - z_{\hat{\imath}(s)})\, c_{\hat{\imath}(s)}^0 \ .$$

Next, we separately bound the cost contribution of facilities belonging to big and small stars. Thereby, we will use $d(i, s) = d_T(i, s)$ for every $s \in C_T$ and $i \in \mathcal{F}_s$, which holds by the definition of d_T.

For each $s \in C_T^b$, we have

$$\sum_{i \in \mathcal{F}_s} z_i\, c_i^1$$

$$= \sum_{i \in \mathcal{F}_s} z_i f_i + (2 + 3/(\ell - 1))u \sum_{i \in \mathcal{F}_s} z_i d_T(i, s)$$

$$\leq (2 + 3/(\ell - 1))b_s^I$$

$$\leq 5b_s^I \ ,$$

where the first inequality follows from Constraint (4.2) for solutions to star instances, and the second one follows from $\ell \geq 2$.

For each $s \in C_T^s$ with the single supporting facility $\hat{\imath}$ in **z**, we have

$$z_{\hat{\imath}}\, c_{\hat{\imath}}^1$$

$$= z_{\hat{\imath}} f_{\hat{\imath}} + z_{\hat{\imath}} w_s d_T(\hat{\imath}, s)$$

$$\leq z_{\hat{\imath}} f_{\hat{\imath}} + w_s d_T(\hat{\imath}, s)$$

$$\leq b_s^{II} \ ,$$

where the last inequality follows from Constraint (4.3). If s is the root of T', then let s' be the son of s, otherwise, let s' be the father of s. We have

$$(1 - z_{\hat{\imath}})\, c_{\hat{\imath}}^0$$

$$= (1 - z_{\hat{\imath}})w_s(\ell + 1/2)d_T(s, s')$$

$$\leq 8(\ell + \frac{1}{2})(b_s^d + \ell b_s^r)$$

$$\leq (4\ell + 2)(2b_s^d + 2\ell b_s^r)$$

$$\leq (4\ell + 2)b_s^{II} \ ,$$

where the first inequality follows from Property (v). Thus,

$$z_i\, c_i^1 + (1 - z_i)\, c_i^0 \;\leq\; (4\ell + 3) b_s^{\mathrm{II}}\,.$$

Given $(4\ell + 3) b_s^{\mathrm{II}} \geq 5 b_s^{\mathrm{I}}$ for each $s \in C_T$, we infer the following upper bound on the expected cost:

$$\sum_{i \in \mathcal{F}_T} z_i\, c_i^1 + (1 - z_i)\, c_i^0$$
$$\leq \sum_{i \in \mathcal{F}_T} (4\ell + 3) b_s^{\mathrm{II}}$$
$$= (4\ell + 3) b(T)\,. \qquad\square$$

The result on the trees directly extends to the forest H, as no demand is routed between any two star trees. Here, we define the *gross cost of H* as the sum of the gross costs of its star trees.

Corollary 4.3. *The expected gross cost of our solution to the star forest H is bounded from above by $(4\ell + 3) b(H)$.*

Note that the same upper bound also applies on the expected cost of our solution since the gross cost is always an upper bound on the actual cost.

Derandomization. Let $\mathcal{F}_H$ denote the set of all facilities in H. Consider any step of the rounding procedure and let $\tilde{z}$ be the current opening vector at the beginning of the step. From this step on, the rounding procedure guarantees that each facility $i \in \mathcal{F}_H$ will be opened with probability $\tilde{z}_i$. Hence, from this step on, the expected value of the gross cost is exactly $\sum_{i \in \mathcal{F}_H} \tilde{z}_i\, c_i^1 + (1 - \tilde{z}_i)\, c_i^0$. This value is an upper bound for the expected gross cost of at least one of the choices in the current step. This fact leads us directly to the following derandomization algorithm: At each step of the rounding procedure, compute the expected value of the gross cost for each of the two choices of rounding. Greedily make the choice with the smaller expected value, or make an arbitrary choice if both values are equal. At the end, we deterministically obtain a solution to H whose gross cost is at most the expected gross cost of our rounding procedure.

Using Corollary 4.3, we summarize our discussion in the following theorem.

Theorem 4.4. *For any value at least 2 for the parameter ℓ, there is an efficient algorithm that computes for a given star forest H a solution with capacity violation at most $2 + 3/(1 - \ell)$ and cost at most $(4\ell + 3) \cdot b(H)$.*

Combining this result with Theorem 4.3, we obtain Theorem 4.1.

4.4 Algorithm for Non-uniform Hard-Capacitated k-Median

In this section, we describe a bi-factor approximation algorithm for the k-MEDIAN problem with non-uniform hard capacities that will prove Theorem 4.2. Note that this problem is equivalent to k-Facility Location with uniform opening costs. Moreover, its standard LP relaxation, denoted by Ck-MED LP, is a special case of Ck-FL LP where all opening costs $(f_i)_{i \in \mathcal{F}}$ are set to 0.

During our algorithm, we will obtain, step by step, a series of solutions where the initially fractional openings are more and more restricted until we finally arrive at an integral solution to Ck-MED LP with bounded capacity violation. We will consider the following two types of solutions.

Definition 4.14. A solution $(\widetilde{\mathbf{x}}, \widetilde{\mathbf{y}})$ to Ck-MED LP is called a $[1/2, 1]$-*solution* if, for every $i \in \mathcal{F}$, we have $\widetilde{y}_i \in \{0\} \cup [1/2, 1]$. Similarly, a solution $(\widetilde{\mathbf{x}}, \widetilde{\mathbf{y}})$ to Ck-MED LP is called a $\{1/2, 1\}$-*solution* if, for every $i \in \mathcal{F}$, we have $\widetilde{y}_i \in \{0, 1/2, 1\}$.

Recall that a solution with capacity violations has to satisfy all constraints of Ck-MED LP with the exception of Constraint (LP-4). In this section, we will consider an even weaker type of solutions.

Definition 4.15. A solution $(\widetilde{\mathbf{x}}, \widetilde{\mathbf{y}})$ to the weaker version of Ck-MED LP where we drop Constraints (LP-3) and (LP-4) is called a *weak solution* to Ck-MED LP.

Let $(\mathbf{x}^*, \mathbf{y}^*)$ be the optimum solution to Ck-MED LP that we fixed in Section 4.2. Similarly to the algorithm of the previous section, we partition all facilities into star clusters and, for each corresponding star instance, we compute a strict solution of volume bounded by a function of ℓ. In doing so, we set the parameter $\ell = 2$. Note that we do not consider relaxed solutions. We then proceed as follows.

In Section 4.4.1, we modify the solution to each star instance by moving openings between facilities such that all supporting facilities are open or all but one of the facilities are closed. The union of these solutions will help us to obtain a $[1/2, 1]$-solution $(\mathbf{x}', \mathbf{y}')$ where fractional facilities have capacity violation at most $1 + \varepsilon$ and open facilities have capacity violation at most $2 + \varepsilon$, for any sufficiently small constant ε.

Then, in Section 4.4.2, we construct a weak $\{1/2, 1\}$-solution $(\hat{\mathbf{x}}, \hat{\mathbf{y}})$: By some greedy rule, we either round each opening in $\mathbf{y}'$ down to $1/2$ or up to 1. Thereby, we might violate Constraint (LP-3) and therefore obtain only a weak solution. Also the capacity violation might increase slightly, but not more than up to $2 + 2\varepsilon$. The connection cost of $(\hat{\mathbf{x}}, \hat{\mathbf{y}})$ remains the same as in $(\mathbf{x}', \mathbf{y}')$.

Eventually, in Section 4.4.3, we round $(\hat{\mathbf{x}}, \hat{\mathbf{y}})$ into an integral solution. We do this by building so called *facility trees* and cutting them to smaller instances which are easier to round. By this procedure, we obtain an integral solution $(\bar{\mathbf{x}}, \bar{\mathbf{y}})$ to Ck-MED LP with capacity violation $3 + 3\varepsilon$.

4.4.1   Obtaining a $[1/2, 1]$-Solution with Capacity Violations

In this section, we describe how to obtain a solution $(\mathbf{x}', \mathbf{y}')$ with capacity violations such that the opening of every supporting facility is in $[1/2, 1]$. Let ε be an arbitrary constant with $0 < \varepsilon \leq 1$.

In the following, we consider a star instance S_s. By Lemmas 4.9 and 4.11, we compute a strict solution $\mathbf{z}$ to S_s with at most two fractional facilities and the bound $\mathrm{vol}(\mathbf{z}) \leq \mathrm{vol}_{\mathbf{y}^*}(\mathcal{F}_s)$. Since $\mathbf{z}$ satisfies Constraint (4.1), we can completely distribute the demand w_s on the facilities in $\mathcal{F}_s$ such that each facility i serves a demand d_i of size at most $z_i u_i$. We fix such a distribution of w_s and define d_i as the demand that the facility i has to serve; thus $\sum_{i \in \mathcal{F}_s} d_i = w_s$. Note that there is no capacity violation in our distribution and that the cost of moving d_i to the facility i is at most $d(i, s)d_i \leq d(i, s)z_i u_i$. Hence, by Constraint (4.2), the connection cost of our distribution, that is, the cost of sending w_s from the star center s to the facilities, is upper bounded by the strict budget $b_s^!$.

Next, we compute a new opening vector $\mathbf{z}'$ for the facilities in $\mathcal{F}_s$ where either all supporting facilities are open, or there is one fractional facility and all other facilities are closed. In parallel, we assign each facility a demand d_i' such that the new distribution of w_s has cost $\mathcal{O}(b_s^!)$ and capacity violation $\mathcal{O}(1 + \varepsilon)$. Depending on the size of $\text{vol}(\mathbf{z})$, we compute $\mathbf{z}'$ in one of two different ways.

Small Volume. First, we consider the case when $\text{vol}(\mathbf{z}) \leq 1$, which is always true for star instances whose star clusters have volume at most 1, and might sometimes also hold star instances with star clusters of volume greater than 1. If there is only one fractional facility $\hat{i}$, we just set $z_i' = \min\{1, \text{vol}_{y^*}(\mathcal{F}_s)\}$ and $d_i' = d_i$. Then $z_i' \geq \text{vol}(\mathbf{z}) = z_{\hat{i}}$ and we have no capacity violation. If there are exactly two fractional facilities $\hat{i}_1$ and $\hat{i}_2$, then we close one of them and move its demand and opening to the other one. In fact, we can do so without any increase of capacity violation as the next lemma shows.

Lemma 4.28. *Let $i, i' \in \mathcal{F}_s$ satisfy $z_i + z_{i'} \leq 1$. For at least one $i'' \in \{i, i'\}$, there is no capacity violation if we set the opening of i'' to $z_i + z_{i'}$ and its demand to $d_i + d_{i'}$.*

Proof. Take $i'' \in \{i, i'\}$ with $u_{i''} = \max\{u_i, u_{i'}\}$ and observe $(z_i + z_{i'})u_{i''} \geq d_i + d_{i'}$.   □

Unfortunately, the connection cost might be unbounded in the lemma above. However, if we allow a slight capacity violation, we can control the cost.

Lemma 4.29. *Let ε' satisfy $0 < \varepsilon' \leq 1$ and let $i, i' \in \mathcal{F}_s$ satisfy $z_i + z_{i'} \leq 1$. The following is true for at least one $i'' \in \{i, i'\}$: If we set the opening of i'' to $z_i + z_{i'}$ and its demand to $d_i + d_{i'}$, then its capacity violation is at most $1 + \varepsilon'$ and we get $d_i + d_{i'} \leq (1 + \varepsilon')/\varepsilon' \cdot d_{i''}$.*

Proof. If for both choices of i'' the resulting capacity violation is at most $1 + \varepsilon'$, we choose a facility $i'' \in \{i, i'\}$ with maximum $d_{i''}$. Then $(d_i + d_{i'})/d_{i''} \leq 2 \leq (1 + \varepsilon')/\varepsilon'$ and the claim holds.

Now, assume that for one of the choices, say i', we have capacity violation γ greater than $1 + \varepsilon'$. Then, by Lemma 4.28, the other choice for i'' has no capacity violation at all. Thus, we choose $i'' = i$. Note that γ satisfies $\gamma u_{i'}(z_i + z_{i'}) = (d_i + d_{i'})$. Given $u_{i'}z_{i'} \geq d_{i'}$, we obtain

$$\frac{z_{i'}}{z_i + z_{i'}} \cdot \frac{d_i + d_{i'}}{d_{i'}} \geq \gamma > 1 + \varepsilon'.$$

The inequality leads to $(d_i + d_{i'})/d_{i'} > 1 + \varepsilon'$. Together with $1 - d_{i'}/(d_i + d_{i'}) = d_i/(d_i + d_{i'})$, we obtain $(d_i + d_{i'})/d_i < (1 + \varepsilon')/\varepsilon'$ for the demand increase of i.   □

By Lemma 4.29 and choosing $\varepsilon' = \varepsilon$, we select an appropriate facility $\hat{i} \in \{\hat{i}_1, \hat{i}_2\}$, set its opening $z'_i = \min\{1, \mathrm{vol}_{y^*}(\mathcal{F}_s)\}$, its demand $d'_i = w_s$ and close the other facility. Thus, we have $z'_i \geq \mathrm{vol}(\mathbf{z})$ and the capacity bound still holds. Given $d'_i \leq (1 + \varepsilon)/\varepsilon \cdot d_i$ and given

$$d_i d(\hat{i}, s) \leq z_i u_i d(\hat{i}, s) \leq b^{\mathrm{I}}_s$$

by Constraint (4.2), the connection cost is at most $(1 + \varepsilon)/\varepsilon \cdot b^{\mathrm{I}}_s$.

Big Volume.   Next, we consider the case when $\mathrm{vol}(\mathbf{z}) > 1$, which is only true for star instances whose star clusters have volume greater than 1. If there are no fractional facilities, then we just set $\mathbf{z}' = \mathbf{z}$ and $d'_i = d_i$ for each $i \in \mathcal{F}_s$.

Otherwise, consider two supporting facilities $\hat{i}_1$ and $\hat{i}_2$ with smallest openings. Since we have at most two fractional facilities, the remaining supporting ones are open.

Lemma 4.30. *Let $i, i' \in \mathcal{F}_s$ satisfy $z_i + z_{i'} \geq 1$. For at least one of the two facilities the following is true: If we open the facility and set its demand to $d_i + d_{i'}$, then its capacity violation and demand increase by a factor at most 2.*

Proof. Choose a facility i'' in $\{i, i'\}$ with the demand $\max\{d_i, d_{i'}\}$ and observe that the capacity violation is at most $z_{i''}/(z_i + z_{i'}) \cdot (d_i + d_{i'})/d_{i''} \leq (d_i + d_{i'})/d_{i''} \leq 2$ and the connection cost is $(d_i + d_{i'})d(i'', s) \leq 2 d_{i''} d(i'', s)$. □

If $z_{\hat{i}_1} + z_{\hat{i}_2} \geq 1$, we choose one of them by Lemma 4.30 to be open in $\mathbf{z}'$ and close the other one. Otherwise, if $z_{\hat{i}_1} + z_{\hat{i}_2} < 1$, then there is an open facility $\hat{i}$ in the star instance.

Lemma 4.31. *Let $i, i', i'' \in \mathcal{F}_s$ satisfy $z_i = 1$ and $z_{i'} + z_{i''} < 1$. For at least one of the three facilities the following is true: If we open the facility and set its demand to $d_i + d_{i'} + d_{i''}$, then its capacity violation increases by a factor at most $2 + \varepsilon$ and its demand increases by a factor of a most $2 + 4/\varepsilon$.*

Proof. By Lemma 4.29 and choosing $\varepsilon' = \varepsilon/2$, we select one of $\{i', i''\}$, say i', such that its capacity violation is at most $1 + \varepsilon'$ and its demand is at most $(1 + \varepsilon')/\varepsilon' \cdot d_{i'}$

Then we apply Lemma 4.30 on i and i' using as the opening and demand of i' the quantities $z_{i'} + z_{i''}$ and $d_{i'} + d_{i''}$, respectively. In the worst case, we choose to open i' and get capacity violation at most $2(1 + \varepsilon') = 2 + \varepsilon$ and a total increase of demand by a factor at most $2(1 + \varepsilon')/\varepsilon' = 2 + 4/\varepsilon$. □

By Lemma 4.31, we choose one of the three facilities in $\{\hat{i}, \hat{i}_1, \hat{i}_2\}$ to be open in $\mathbf{z}'$ and close the other two. In both cases, we route the demand of the closed facilities to the chosen one. The resulting capacity violation is at most $2 + \varepsilon$. Since we do not change the openings and demands of any other facilities of the star instance, and only increase the demand of one facility by a factor at most $2 + 4/\varepsilon$, the total connection cost is at most $\sum_{i \in \mathcal{F}_s} d(i, s)(2 + 4/\varepsilon)d_i$. By Constraint (4.2), this cost is at most $(2 + 4/\varepsilon)b^{\mathrm{I}}_s$. Note that $\mathrm{vol}(\mathbf{z}') \leq \mathrm{vol}(\mathbf{z}) \leq \mathrm{vol}_{y^*}(\mathcal{F}_s)$ is satisfied.

The discussion of the two cases of $\mathrm{vol}(\mathbf{z})$ can be summarized as follows.

Lemma 4.32. *We can compute an opening vector $\mathbf{z}'$ for $\mathcal{F}_s$ with $\mathrm{vol}(\mathbf{z}') \leq \mathrm{vol}_{\mathbf{y}^*}(\mathcal{F}_s)$ where*

- *there is only one supporting facility $i \in \mathcal{F}_s$ and $z'_i = \mathrm{vol}_{\mathbf{y}^*}(\mathcal{F}_s)$, or*
- *all supporting facilities are open.*

Furthermore, we can distribute the demand w_s on the facilities supporting in $\mathbf{z}'$ such that

- *each fractional facility $i \in \mathcal{F}_s$ has capacity violation at most $1 + \varepsilon$, and*
- *each open facility $i \in \mathcal{F}_s$ has capacity violation at most $2 + \varepsilon$.*

The connection cost of the distribution is at most $(2 + 4/\varepsilon)b_s^l$.

Corollary 4.4. *For any ε with $0 < \varepsilon \leq 1$, we can efficiently compute a $[1/2, 1]$-solution $(\mathbf{x}', \mathbf{y}')$ with capacity violations such that $\mathrm{vol}(\mathbf{y}') \leq k$ holds, fractional facilities have capacity violation at most $1 + \varepsilon$, open facilities have capacity violation at most $2 + \varepsilon$, and the total connection cost is at most $20/\varepsilon \, \mathrm{OPT}^* + 16 \, \mathrm{OPT}^*$.*

Proof. To construct a feasible solution $(\mathbf{x}', \mathbf{y}')$ to Ck-MED LP with the claimed capacity violation bounds, we first apply the procedure of Lemma 4.32 to compute an opening vector for each star instance. Let $\mathbf{y}'$ be the union of all these opening vectors. We have the inequality

$$\mathrm{vol}(\mathbf{y}') \leq \sum_{s \in \mathcal{C}_{sc}} \mathrm{vol}_{\mathbf{y}^*}(\mathcal{F}_s) \leq \sum_{i \in \mathcal{F}} y_i^* \leq k,$$

where the second last inequality follows from the fact that each facility belongs to exactly one star instance. Thus, Constraint (LP-1) is fulfilled.

Next, we construct a feasible assignment $\mathbf{x}'$ suitable for $\mathbf{y}'$. For every facility $i \in \mathcal{F}$, let d'_i be its demand given by Lemma 4.32. For every star instance S_s and every client $t \in \mathcal{C}$, we define x_t^s as the total LP demand $\sum_{i' \in \mathcal{F}_s} x_{i't}^*$ of t that is served by the facilities of S_s in $\mathbf{x}^*$. Then we send the fraction d'_i/w_s of x_t^s to every facility $i \in \mathcal{F}_s$, that is, we set $x'_{it} = d'_i/w_s \cdot x_t^s$.

Hence, Constraint (LP-2) holds, as each client $t \in \mathcal{C}$ is fully served:

$$\sum_{i \in \mathcal{F}} x'_{it} = \sum_{s \in \mathcal{C}_{sc}} x_t^s \sum_{i \in \mathcal{F}_s} d_i/w_s = \sum_{s \in \mathcal{C}_{sc}} x_t^s = 1.$$

The assignment also implies the satisfaction of Constraint (LP-3). To see this, consider any client $t \in \mathcal{C}$, star instance $s \in \mathcal{C}_{sc}$ and facility $i \in \mathcal{F}_s$. If $y'_i = 1$, then the constraint immediately holds. Otherwise, by Lemma 4.32, we have

$$y'_i = \mathrm{vol}_{\mathbf{y}^*}(\mathcal{F}_s) = \sum_{i' \in \mathcal{F}_s} y_{i'}^* \geq \sum_{i' \in \mathcal{F}_s} x_{i't}^* = x_t^s \geq x'_{it}.$$

Observe that the facility i serves a total amount of

$$\sum_{t \in \mathcal{C}} x'_{it} = d'_i/w_s \sum_{t \in \mathcal{C}} x_t^s = d'_i.$$

Hence, the bounds on capacity violation of Lemma 4.32 still hold.

Consequently, $(\mathbf{x}', \mathbf{y}')$ is a feasible solution with capacity violations. Let us recall that Lemma 4.32 restricts the openings of the facilities. For each facility $i \in \mathcal{F}$, we have either $y_i' \in \{0,1\}$ or $y_i' = \mathrm{vol}_{\mathbf{y}^*}(\mathcal{F}_s)$, where $\mathcal{F}_s$ is the star cluster containing i. Furthermore, by Corollary 4.1 and $\ell = 2$, we know that every star cluster $\mathcal{F}_s$ has volume $\mathrm{vol}_{\mathbf{y}^*}(\mathcal{F}_s)$ at least $1 - 1/\ell = 1/2$. Thus, $(\mathbf{x}', \mathbf{y}')$ is even a $[1/2, 1]$-solution.

Regarding the connection cost of $\mathbf{x}'$, we can assume that we first move the demands of the clients to the star centers and then move them from there to the supporting facilities. The cost of the first step is at most $(2 + 2\ell)\,\mathrm{OPT}^*$ as Lemma 4.14 implies. The cost of the second step, for each star center s, is at most $(2 + 4/\varepsilon)b_s^{\mathrm{I}}$ by Lemma 4.32. Since we know that the total strict budget over all star instances is upper bounded by $\sum_{s \in \mathcal{C}_{sc}} b_s^{\mathrm{I}} \leq (1 + 2\ell)\,\mathrm{OPT}^*$ (Corollary 4.2), the total cost is at most

$$(2 + 4/\varepsilon)(1 + 2\ell)\,\mathrm{OPT}^* + (2 + 2\ell)\,\mathrm{OPT}^*$$
$$= 20/\varepsilon\,\mathrm{OPT}^* + 16\,\mathrm{OPT}^* \,. \qquad \square$$

4.4.2   Computing a Weak $\{1/2, 1\}$-Solution

Let $(\mathbf{x}', \mathbf{y}')$ be a $[1/2, 1]$-solution with capacity violations obtained by Corollary 4.4. We will now transform it into a weak $\{1/2, 1\}$-solution $(\hat{\mathbf{x}}, \hat{\mathbf{y}})$.

Definition 4.16. We define

- $N_1 = \{i \in \mathcal{F} \mid y_i' = 1\}$, and

- $N_2 = \{i \in \mathcal{F} \mid 1/2 \leq y_i' < 1\}$.

For each facility $i \in N_2$, let $d_i' = \sum_{t \in C} x_{it}'$ be the demand served by i and let $s(i)$ be its closest facility in $N_1 \cup N_2 \setminus \{i\}$ (recall Definition 4.3).

Lemma 4.33. *We can efficiently compute a weak $\{1/2, 1\}$-solution $(\hat{\mathbf{x}}, \hat{\mathbf{y}})$ of volume $\mathrm{vol}(\hat{\mathbf{y}}) \leq k$ and connection cost of at most $20/\varepsilon\,\mathrm{OPT}^* + 16\,\mathrm{OPT}^*$ where the capacity violation of every facility is at most $2 + 2\varepsilon$. Moreover, the following inequality holds:*

$$\sum_{i \in N_2} d_i'(1 - \hat{y}_i)d(s(i), i) \leq \sum_{i \in N_2} d_i'(1 - y_i')d(s(i), i) \,.$$

Proof. For each facility $i \in N_1$, set $\hat{y}_i = 1$. If $k \geq |N_1| + |N_2|$, then also set $\hat{y}_i = 1$ for each facility $i \in N_2$. Thus, the volume $\mathrm{vol}(\hat{\mathbf{y}})$ is bounded from above by k, and the claimed inequality holds, as the left side adds up to 0.

If $k < |N_1| + |N_2|$, then $|N_2| > 2k - 2|N_1| - |N_2|$. For each facility $i \in N_2$, we define the *weight of the facility* i as $d_i' d(s(i), i)$. Sort all facilities in N_2 non-increasingly by their weights. Then set the openings of the first $2k - 2|N_1| - |N_2|$ facilities of N_2 to 1, and the openings of the remaining facilities to $1/2$. By this assignment of openings, the volume of $\hat{\mathbf{y}}$ is exactly

$$\mathrm{vol}(\hat{\mathbf{y}}) = |N_1| + (2k - 2|N_1| - |N_2|) + \frac{1}{2}(|N_2| - (2k - 2|N_1| - |N_2|)) = k \,.$$

Observe that among all opening vectors $\mathbf{v}$ for $\mathcal{F}$ satisfying the two conditions,

(i) $\text{vol}_\mathbf{v}(N_2) \le k - |N_1|$, and

(ii) $v_i \ge 1/2$

for every $i \in N_2$, vector $\hat{\mathbf{y}}$ attains the maximum value for the objective $\sum_{i \in N_2} d'_i \hat{y}_i d(s(i), i)$. Also observe that $\mathbf{y}'$ fulfills the two conditions (i) and (ii). Thus, we have

$$\sum_{i \in N_2} d'_i y'_i d(s(i), i) \le \sum_{i \in N_2} d'_i \hat{y}_i d(s(i), i),$$

which is equivalent to the inequality claimed in the lemma statement.

Next, we set $\hat{\mathbf{x}} = \mathbf{x}'$ and thus have the same cost as $\mathbf{x}'$. Consider the facility openings that decreased. Since these openings changed by a factor not smaller than $1/2$, we can bound the capacity violation of their facilities by $2(1 + \varepsilon)$. The capacity violation of other facilities did not increase. Now, open facilities have in worst case capacity violation

$$\max\{1 + \varepsilon, 2 + \varepsilon\} \le 2 + 2\varepsilon. \qquad \square$$

Definition 4.17. We define

- $\hat{N}_1 = \{i \in \mathcal{F} \mid \hat{y}_i = 1\}$, and
- $\hat{N}_2 = \{i \in \mathcal{F} \mid \hat{y}_i = 1/2\}$.

We have $\hat{N}_1 \cup \hat{N}_2 = N_1 \cup N_2$, and in particular $\hat{N}_2 \subseteq N_2$. Thus, $s(i)$ is well defined for every $i \in \hat{N}_2$ and we have $s(i) \in \hat{N}_1 \cup \hat{N}_2$.

4.4.3   Rounding a Weak $\{1/2, 1\}$-Solution $\hat{y}$ to an Integral Solution $\bar{y}$

In the last section, we obtained a weak $\{1/2, 1\}$-solution $(\hat{\mathbf{x}}, \hat{\mathbf{y}})$ by Lemma 4.33. In this section, we describe how to round this solution to an integral solution $(\bar{\mathbf{x}}, \bar{\mathbf{y}})$. For the sake of easier presentation, we assume that the demands of the clients have been moved to the facilities via the solution $(\hat{\mathbf{x}}, \hat{\mathbf{y}})$ so that every facility $i \in \hat{N}_1 \cup \hat{N}_2$ carries the demand d'_i. We will describe how to obtain an integral opening vector $\bar{\mathbf{y}}$ and how to further reroute the demand to facilities that are open in $\bar{\mathbf{y}}$. We will give an upper bound of $3 + 3\varepsilon$ on the capacity violation and analyze the cost of the rerouting.

Combining the rerouting with the assignment $\hat{\mathbf{x}}$, we obtain $\bar{\mathbf{x}}$. Altogether, this leads to the solution $(\bar{\mathbf{x}}, \bar{\mathbf{y}})$ to the original instance (where the demand resides in the clients) with capacity violation $3 + 3\varepsilon$. The cost of this solution is the total cost of $(\hat{\mathbf{x}}, \hat{\mathbf{y}})$ and the rerouting.

Building facility trees.   In a similar way as in related works [CGTS99, Li14], we construct a directed forest of in-trees spanning the facilities in $\hat{N}_2$. For this, we run Procedure Short-Trees$(\hat{N}_2, \hat{N}_1)$ as described in Section 4.2. By the construction, nodes in $\hat{N}_1$ may appear only as roots (Lemma 4.4), and each node $i \in \hat{N}_2$ has either a directed edge to its closest node $s(i)$ in $\hat{N}_1 \cup \hat{N}_2 \setminus \{i\}$, or is a root of an in-tree. In the following, we will call the in-trees facility trees.

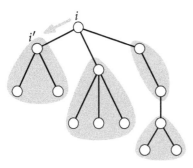
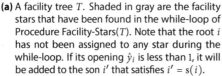
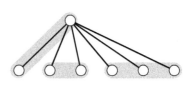

(a) A facility tree T. Shaded in gray are the facility stars that have been found in the while-loop of Procedure Facility-Stars(T). Note that the root i has not been assigned to any star during the while-loop. If its opening $\hat{y}_i$ is less than 1, it will be added to the son i' that satisfies $i' = s(i)$.

(b) A facility star. Shaded in gray is a partition of the fractional facilities into pairs and triples. Here, also the root is a fractional facility. In each tuple, only one facility with the highest demand will be opened. It serves the demand of its closed partners.

Figure 4.5: A facility star decomposed into facility stars, and a facility star partitioned into tuples.

Decomposing facility trees to rooted facility stars. We cut each facility tree T into *facility stars* consisting of a root and a group of leaves. To this end, we greedily choose the leaf node i that has the largest number of edges on the path to the root of its tree. Then we remove the subtree rooted at $s(i)$. We call the removed subtree a facility star and use $Q_{s(i)}$ to denote it. See Procedure Facility-Stars(T) and Fig. 4.5a.

Procedure Facility-Stars(T)

> **while** there are at least two nodes in T **do**
> > choose a leaf node i with the largest number of edges on the path from i to the root
> > consider the subtree rooted at $s(i)$ as a rooted facility star $Q_{s(i)}$, and remove this subtree
>
> **if** only one node i is left and $\hat{y}_i < 1$ **then**
> > add i to the star rooted at $s(i)$ as a child of $s(i)$

There is a special case, when only one facility i is left in T. If $\hat{y}_i = 1$, we just ignore this node, otherwise $\hat{y}_i < 1$ and we have $i \in \hat{N}_2$. Note that i can only be the root of T. Then, by Lemma 4.4, $s(i)$ was a son of i. Since $s(i)$ was removed from T but its father i was not, $s(i)$ must be the root of a facility star. Hence, we just add i to $Q_{s(i)}$.

Rounding facility stars. Using the facility stars, we will round $\hat{y}$ and reroute the demand to obtain our integral solution $(\bar{x}, \bar{y})$. First, we open all facilities in $\hat{N}_1$ that do not belong to any facility star. Each of them is serving its own demand. Then we apply the following procedure on each facility star Q_r to open at most $\left\lfloor \sum_{i \in Q_r} \hat{y}_i \right\rfloor$ facilities in each of them:

If Q_r contains at least two fractional facilities, we partition all fractional facilities into pairs and triples; see Fig.. 4.5b. In each pair and triple, we open a facility i that has the biggest demand d'_i, close all other facilities in its tuple and route the demand of the closed facilities to i. If Q_r also contains a facility i in $\hat{N}_1$, we open it and let it serve its own demand.

If Q_r contains exactly one fractional facility i, then Q_r contains also an open facility i' of $\hat{N}_1$. If $d'_{i'} < 2d'_i$, we open the facility i, close i' and move the demand of i' to i. Otherwise, if $d'_{i'}/2 \geq d'_i$, we open the facility i', close i and move the demand of i to i'.

Next, we show that our solution $(\bar{x}, \bar{y})$ has at most k open facilities and small capacity violation.

Lemma 4.34. *In the integral solution $\bar{y}$, at most k facilities are open and every facility has capacity violation at most $3 + 3\varepsilon$.*

Proof. Observe that every facility star Q_r contains at most $\lfloor \sum_{i \in Q_r} \hat{y}_i \rfloor$ open facilities in $\bar{y}$. Among the facilities that do not belong to any facility star, we open only those that already had opening 1 in $\hat{y}$. So we have $\sum_{i \in F} \bar{y}_i \leq \sum_{i \in F} \hat{y}_i \leq k$ which implies the first claim.

In the solution $(\hat{x}, \hat{y})$, the capacity violation of each facility $i \in \hat{N}_1 \cup \hat{N}_2$ is at most $2 + 2\varepsilon$. To bound the capacity violation in $(\bar{x}, \bar{y})$ by $3 + 3\varepsilon$, it suffices to bound the increase of capacity violation by the factor $3/2$.

Consider any facility $i \in \hat{N}_2$ that we opened in $\bar{y}$. By our choice to open it, we sent at most $2d'_i$ units of demand to it, either from closed facilities in its tuple, or from the root r of its facility star. Thus, the demand of i increased by a factor at most 3. Given that we simultaneously increased its opening by the sfactor 2, the capacity violation of i increased by a factor at most $3/2$.

Next, consider any facility in $i \in \hat{N}_1$ that we opened. If i serves only its own demand, its capacity violation did not increase. Otherwise, i is also serving the demand of some facility $i' \in \hat{N}_2$ and we have $d'_i/2 \geq d'_{i'}$. Thus, the demand of i increased by a factor at most $3/2$, and so its capacity violation. □

To this end, we bound the cost of our solution $(\bar{x}, \bar{y})$. For this, we need to bound the rerouting cost. We will do it in two steps. First we provide an upper bound that depends on the facility demands and the distances within facility stars. In the second step, we relate this upper bound to OPT*.

Lemma 4.35. *The cost of rerouting the demand from the facilities that are supporting in $\hat{y}$ to the facilities that are open in $\bar{y}$ is at most $2 \sum_{i \in \hat{N}_2} d'_i d(s(i), i)$.*

Proof. Consider any facility star Q_r. To bound the rerouting cost, we assume, by triangle inequality, that demand is rerouted only along the edges of Q_r. For each such edge (i, r), we have $r = s(i)$ and $i \in \hat{N}_2$. We don't have $i \in \hat{N}_1$ as nodes of $\hat{N}_1$ can appear only as a roots. Thus, it suffices to show that each edge (i, r) carries at most $2d'_i$ units of demand. Consider any such edge (i, r). If i is closed, it sends its demand d'_i along (i, r) to r (from where the demand might be further routed) and no other demand is routed along (i, r). If i is opened, it receives at most $2d'_i$ units of demand as discussed in the proof of Lemma 4.34, and no other demand is routed along (i, r). □

Before we further bound the term $\sum_{i \in \hat{N}_2} d'_i d(s(i), i)$, we first show the following helpful inequality.

Lemma 4.36. *For every $t \in C$, we have*

$$\sum_{i \in N_2} x'_{it}(1 - y'_i)d(s(i), i) \le 2 \sum_{i \in N_1 \cup N_2} x'_{it}d(i, t) .$$

Proof. Fix any $t \in C$. By Constraint (LP-3), we have

$$1 - y'_i \le 1 - x'_{it} = \sum_{i' \in N_1 \cup N_2 \setminus \{i\}} x'_{i't}$$

for every $i \in N_2$, and thus

$$\sum_{i \in N_2} x'_{it}(1 - y'_i)d(s(i), i)$$

$$\le \sum_{i \in N_2} x'_{it} \sum_{i' \in N_1 \cup N_2 \setminus \{i\}} x'_{i't}d(s(i), i) .$$

By the definition of $s(i)$, $d(s(i), i) \le d(i', i)$ for every $i' \in N_1 \cup N_2 \setminus \{i\}$. Using this, we can further upper bound the expression above by

$$\sum_{i \in N_2} x'_{it} \sum_{i' \in N_1 \cup N_2 \setminus \{i\}} x'_{i't}d(i', i)$$

$$\le \sum_{i \in N_2} x'_{it} \sum_{i' \in N_1 \cup N_2 \setminus \{i\}} x'_{i't}(d(i', t) + d(i, t)) \qquad \text{(Triangle inequality)}$$

$$= \sum_{i \in N_2} x'_{it} \sum_{i' \in N_1 \cup N_2 \setminus \{i\}} x'_{i't}d(i', t) + \sum_{i \in N_2} x'_{it} \sum_{i' \in N_1 \cup N_2 \setminus \{i\}} x'_{i't}d(i, t)$$

$$\le \sum_{i' \in N_1 \cup N_2} x'_{i't}d(i', t) \sum_{i \in N_2} x'_{it} + \sum_{i \in N_2} x'_{it}d(i, t) \sum_{i' \in N_1 \cup N_2 \setminus \{i\}} x'_{i't}$$

$$\le \sum_{i' \in N_1 \cup N_2} x'_{i't}d(i', t) + \sum_{i \in N_2} x'_{it}d(i, t)$$

$$\le 2 \sum_{i \in N_1 \cup N_2} x'_{it}d(i, t) ,$$

where the second last inequality follows from $\sum_{i \in N_1 \cup N_2} x'_{it} = 1$ for each $t \in C$, given by Constraint (LP-2). $\qquad\square$

We are ready to relate the rerouting cost to OPT*.

Lemma 4.37. *The sum $\sum_{i \in \hat{N}_2} d'_i d(s(i), i)$ is at most $80/\varepsilon \, \mathrm{OPT}^* + 64 \, \mathrm{OPT}^*$.*

Proof. For each $i \in \hat{N}_2$, we have $\hat{y}_i = 1/2$, so

$$d'_i d(s(i), i) = 2d'_i(1 - \hat{y}_i) \mathrm{vol}_{s(i)}(i) .$$

Thus,

$$\sum_{i\in\hat{N}_2} d'_i d(s(i), i)$$

$$= 2 \sum_{i\in\hat{N}_2} d'_i (1 - \hat{y}_i) d(s(i), i)$$

$$\leq 2 \sum_{i\in N_2} d'_i (1 - \hat{y}_i) d(s(i), i) \qquad\qquad (\hat{N}_2 \subseteq N_2)$$

$$\leq 2 \sum_{i\in N_2} d'_i (1 - y'_i) d(s(i), i) \qquad\qquad \text{(Lemma 4.33)}$$

$$= 2 \sum_{t\in C} \sum_{i\in N_2} x'_{it} (1 - y'_i) d(s(i), i) \qquad\qquad \text{(Definition of } (d'_i)_{i\in\mathcal{F}})$$

$$\leq 4 \sum_{t\in C} \sum_{i\in N_1 \cup N_2} x'_{it} d(i, t) \qquad\qquad \text{(Lemma 4.36)}$$

$$\leq 4 \left(20/\varepsilon \, \text{OPT}^* + 16 \, \text{OPT}^* \right) \qquad\qquad \text{(Corollary 4.4)}$$

$$= 80/\varepsilon \, \text{OPT}^* + 64 \, \text{OPT}^* \, . \qquad\qquad\qquad \square$$

Now we have all the ingredients to bound the cost of our solution and to prove Theorem 4.2.

Proof of Theorem 4.2. From Lemma 4.33, we know that the cost of solution $(\hat{\mathbf{x}}, \hat{\mathbf{y}})$ is bounded from above by $20/\varepsilon \, \text{OPT}^* + 16 \, \text{OPT}^*$. This corresponds also to the cost of sending the demand from the clients to the facilities supporting in $\hat{\mathbf{y}}$. Using Lemmas 4.35 and 4.37, we bound the cost of rerouting the demand to the facilities open in $\bar{\mathbf{y}}$ by

$$2(80/\varepsilon \, \text{OPT}^* + 64 \, \text{OPT}^*) \, .$$

Summing this up, we obtain
$$180/\varepsilon \, \text{OPT}^* + 144 \, \text{OPT}^*$$

as an upper bound for the cost of our solution $(\bar{\mathbf{x}}, \bar{\mathbf{y}})$ with capacity violation $3 + 3\varepsilon$. $\square$

4.5 Concluding Remarks and Open Questions

In this chapter, we gave the first approximation algorithms for hard-capacitated k-FACILITY LOCATION problems, where we considered either non-uniform capacities or non-uniform opening costs. Both algorithms are based on the standard LP relaxation, a reduction to single-demand-node instances, and a tree structure to guide the distribution of demand.

Our results imply two insights on the integrality gap of the standard LP: For uniform capacities, the 2 barrier on capacity violation is tight up to an arbitrarily small constant. For non-uniform capacities, the barrier is located between 2 and 3; it would be interesting to pinpoint it tighter.

It also remains open to construct an algorithm for the generalization of the two settings above, that is, for hard-capacitated k-FACILITY LOCATION where both, the capacities and openings, are non-uniform. For such an algorithm, it would be appealing to base it on a new LP relaxation like the one introduced by Li [Li16].

Finally, the big open question is whether capacitated k-MEDIAN admits a constant-factor approximation algorithm without any violations.

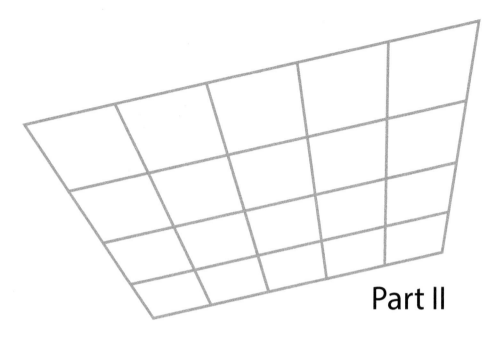

Part II

Problems on the Plane

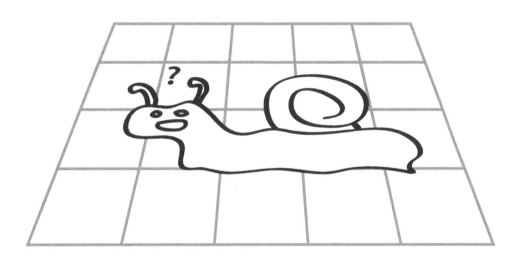

5 Stabbing Rectangles by Line Segments

Consider the following natural problem: *Given a set of axis-aligned rectangles in the plane, find a set of horizontal line segments of minimum total length so that every rectangle is stabbed by some line segment.* Here, a line segment stabs a rectangle if it intersects its left and its right edge. In this chapter, we initiate the study of this geometric optimization problem, which we call STABBING.

We interpret STABBING as a weighted geometric set cover problem and examine structural relations to existing geometric set cover problems. We show that our problem is strongly NP-hard. A constrained variant of STABBING turns out to be APX-hard. These negative results suggest investigating the approximability of STABBING, and in particular, its *shallow-cell* complexity. Chan et al. [SODA'12] showed that *weighted* geometric set cover instances of low shallow-cell complexity admit constant-factor approximation algorithms. However, as we observe, the shallow-cell complexity of STABBING instances can be high. We still achieve a constant-factor approximation by decomposing general instances into what we call *laminar* instances that have low enough complexity.

5.1 Introduction

In this chapter, we study the following geometric optimization problem, which we call STAB-BING. The input is a set R of n axis-aligned rectangles in the plane. The objective is to find a set S of horizontal line segments of minimum total length $\|S\|$, where $\|S\| = \sum_{s \in S} \|s\|$, such that each rectangle $r \in R$ is stabbed by some line segment $s \in S$. Here, we say that s stabs r if s intersects the left and the right edge of r (see Fig. 5.1). The length of a line segment s is denoted by $\|s\|$. Throughout this chapter, rectangles are assumed to be axis-aligned and segments are horizontal line segments (unless explicitly stated otherwise).

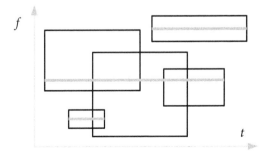

Figure 5.1: An instance of Stabbing (rectangles) with an optimal solution (gray line segments).

Our problem can be viewed as a resource allocation problem. Consider a server that receives a number of communication requests. Each request r is specified by a time window $[t_1, t_2]$ and a frequency band $[f_1, f_2]$. In order to satisfy the request r, the server has to open a communication channel that is available in the time interval $[t_1, t_2]$ and operates at a fixed frequency within the frequency band $[f_1, f_2]$. Therefore, the server has to open several channels over time so that each request can be fulfilled. Requests may share the same channel if their frequency bands and time windows overlap. Each open channel incurs a fixed cost per time unit and the goal is to minimize the total cost. Consider a t–f coordinate system. A request r can be identified with a rectangle $[t_1, t_2] \times [f_1, f_2]$. An open channel corresponds to horizontal line segments and the operation cost equals its length. Satisfying a request is equivalent to stabbing the corresponding rectangle.

To the best of our knowledge, general STABBING has not been studied, although it is a natural problem. Finke et al. [FJQS08] consider the special case of the problem where the left sides of all input rectangles lie on the y-axis. They derive the problem from a practical application in the area of batch processing and give a polynomial time algorithm that solves this special case of STABBING to optimality. Das et al. [DFK+18] describe an application of STABBING in geometric network design. They obtain a constant-factor approximation for a slight generalization of the special case of Finke et al. in which rectangles are only constrained to *intersect* the y-axis. This result constitutes the key step for an $\mathcal{O}(\log n)$-approximation algorithm to the GENERALIZED MINIMUM MANHATTAN NETWORK problem.

We also consider the following variant of our problem, which we call CONSTRAINED STABBING. Here, the input additionally consists of a set F of horizontal line segments of which any solution S must be a subset.

Related Work.   STABBING can be interpreted as a weighted geometric set cover problem where the rectangles play the role of the elements, the potential line segments correspond to the sets and a segment s "contains" a rectangle r if s stabs r. The weight of a segment s equals its length $\|s\|$. SET COVER is one of the classical NP-hard problems. The greedy algorithm yields a ln n-approximation (where n is the number of elements) and this is known to be the best possible approximation ratio for the problem unless P = NP [Fei98, DS14]. It is an important research direction of computational geometry to surpass the lower bound known for general SET COVER in geometric settings. In their seminal work, Brönniman and Goodrich [BG95] gave an $\mathcal{O}(\log \mathrm{OPT})$-approximation algorithm for *unweighted* SET COVER, where OPT is the size of an optimum solution, for the case when the underlying VC-dimension[1] is constant. This property holds in many geometric settings. Numerous subsequent works have improved upon this result in specific geometric settings. For example, Aronov et al. [AES10] obtained an $\mathcal{O}(\log \log \mathrm{OPT})$-approximation algorithm for the problem of piercing a set of axis-aligned rectangles with the minimum number of points (HITTING SET for axis-aligned rectangles) by means of so-called *ε-nets*. Mustafa and Ray [MR10] obtained a PTAS for the case of piercing pseudo-disks by points. A limitation of these algorithms is that they only apply to *unweighted* geometric SET COVER; hence, we cannot apply them directly to our problem. In a break-through, Varadarajan [Var10] developed a new technique, called

---

[1]   Informally, the VC-dimension of a set cover instance $(U, \mathcal{F})$ is the size of a largest subset $X \subseteq U$ such that X induces in $\mathcal{F}$ the set cover instance $(X, 2^X)$.

quasi-uniform sampling, that gives sub-logarithmic approximation algorithms for a number of *weighted* geometric set cover problems (such as covering points with weighted fat triangles or weighted disks). Subsequently, Chan et al. [CGKS12] generalized Varadarajan's idea. They showed that quasi-uniform sampling yields a sub-logarithmic performance if the underlying instances have low shallow-cell complexity. Bansal and Pruhs [BP14] presented an interesting application of Varadarajan's technique. They reduced a large class of scheduling problems to a particular geometric set cover problem for anchored rectangles and obtained a constant-factor approximation via quasi-uniform sampling. Recently, Chan and Grant [CG14] and Mustafa et al. [MRR15] settled the APX-hardness status of all natural weighted geometric SET COVER problems where the elements to be covered are points in the plane or space.

Gaur et al. [GIK02] considered the problem of stabbing a set of axis-aligned rectangles by a minimum number of axis-aligned *lines*. They obtain an elegant 2-approximation algorithm for this NP-hard problem by rounding the standard LP-relaxation. Kovaleva and Spieksma [KS06] considered a generalization of this problem involving weights and demands. They obtained a constant-factor approximation for the problem. Even et al. [ELR+08] considered a *capacitated* variant of the problem in arbitrary dimension. They obtained approximation ratios that depend linearly on the dimension and extended these results to approximate certain lot-sizing inventory problems. Giannopoulos et al. [GKRW13] investigated the fixed-parameter tractability of the problem where given translated copies of an object are to be stabbed by a minimum number of lines (which is also the parameter). Among others, they showed that the problem is W[1]-hard for unit-squares but becomes FPT if the squares are disjoint.

Our Contribution.   We are the first to investigate STABBING in this general form: horizontal line segments stabbing axis-aligned rectangles without further restrictions. We examine the complexity and the approximability of this problem.

We rule out the possibility of efficient exact algorithms by showing that STABBING is NP-hard; see Section 5.5. CONSTRAINED STABBING and CARDINALITY STABBING turn out to be even APX-hard; see Section 5.6. Another negative result is that STABBING instances can have high shallow-cell complexity so that a direct application of the quasi-uniform sampling method yields only the same logarithmic bound as for arbitrary set cover instances; see Section 5.3.2.

Our main result is a constant-factor approximation algorithm for STABBING; see Section 5.3. Our algorithm is based on the following three ideas. First, we show a simple decomposition lemma that implies a constant-factor approximation for (general) set cover instances whose set family can be decomposed into two disjoint sub-families each of which admits a constant-factor approximation. Second, we show that STABBING instances whose segments have a special *laminar* structure have low enough shallow-cell complexity so that they admit a constant-factor approximation by quasi-uniform sampling. Third, we show that an arbitrary instance can be transformed in such a way that it can be decomposed into two disjoint laminar families. Together with the decomposition lemma, this transformation establishes the constant-factor approximation.

Another (this time more obvious) application of the decomposition lemma gives also a constant-factor approximation for the variant of STABBING where we allow horizontal and vertical stabbing segments. Also in this case, a direct application of quasi-uniform sampling gives only a logarithmic bound as there are laminar families of horizontal *and* vertical segments that have high shallow-cell complexity. This and two further applications of the decomposition lemma are sketched in Section 5.4.

The above results provide two natural examples for the fact that the property of having low shallow-cell complexity is *not* closed under the union of the set families. In spite of this, constant-factor approximations are still possible. Our results also show that the representation as a union of low-complexity families may not be obvious at first glance. We therefore hope that our approach helps to extend the reach of quasi-uniform sampling beyond the concept of low shallow-cell complexity also in other settings. Our results for STABBING may also lead to new insights for other related geometric problems such as the GENERALIZED MINIMUM MANHATTAN NETWORK problem [DFK+18].

As a side remark, we explore the relationship of STABBING to well-studied geometric set cover (or equivalently hitting set) problems; see Section 5.2. We show that STABBING can be seen as (weighted) HITTING SET for axis-aligned boxes in three dimensions. This immediately implies an $\mathcal{O}(\log \log n)$-approximation algorithm for CARDINALITY STABBING, the unweighted variant. The embedding does not yield a sub-logarithmic performance for STABBING, however. A similar embedding is not possible in two dimensions: There are set cover instances that can be realized as instances of our problem but not as instances of HITTING SET for axis-aligned rectangles. We also show that natural greedy approaches for STABBING fail to beat the logarithmic bound.

5.2   Structural Properties and Applicability of Existing Techniques

Since our problem is—at least in its general form in the setting of line segments—new, we investigate the applicability of existing techniques for (geometric) SET COVER. We provide instances of STABBING where the greedy algorithm (and natural variants of it) have performance $\Omega(\log n)$; see Section 5.2.1. Then we explore the structural relation of STABBING to existing geometric set cover (or, equivalently, hitting set) problems; see Section 5.2.2.

5.2.1   Greedy Algorithm for Set Cover

The greedy algorithm has approximation ratio ln n for SET COVER on n elements. It is known that this result is the best possible unless P = NP [Fei98].

The greedy algorithm—translated to STABBING—works as follows. Start with an empty set S of segments. Pick a segment s that minimizes the cost efficiency $\|s\| / n_s$ where n_s is the number of rectangles that are stabbed by s. Add s to S and remove the rectangles that are stabbed by s from R. Repeat these steps until R becomes empty. Eventually, output the resulting set S. This algorithm certainly has approximation ratio $\mathcal{O}(\log n)$ for STABBING.

While the bound $\mathcal{O}(\log n)$ is tight for general SET COVER, this fact does not immediately imply tightness for STABBING as well. Unfortunately, there are instances of STABBING where the greedy algorithm (and natural variants of it) have ratio $\Omega(\log n)$.

Consider the instance shown in Fig. 5.2. We introduce two segments t and b of length 1. Then we construct a set B of nested rectangles that are all stabbed by b. The set B is subdivided into levels $0, 1, \ldots, \ell$ according to the nesting hierarchy (see the figure). At level i, there

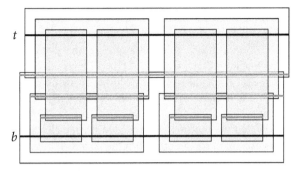

Figure 5.2: Instance where the greedy algorithm has performance $\Omega(\log n)$. The black segments belong to the optimum solution and the gray segments belong to the output of the greedy algorithm. To make the drawing easier to read, we moved the rectangles of T (those stabbed by t) slightly to the right and to the bottom. In our instance, the bottom edges of the rectangles in T coincide with the top edges of their counterparts in B (which are stabbed by b), and there are no two top edges with the same vertical projection.

are 2^i pairwise disjoint rectangles of width $(1 - i\varepsilon)/2^i$ for a sufficiently small positive ε. We slightly perturb the top edges of the rectangles in B so that the top edges of the rectangles in B have pairwise different y-coordinates. Next, we construct a set T of rectangles. For each rectangle $r \in B$ we create a corresponding rectangle r' in T of the same width such that the bottom edge of r' coincides with the top edge of r and r' is stabbed by t.

We now analyze how the greedy algorithm performs on this instance. First, we verify that the first segment s picked by the algorithm contains the top edge of some rectangle $r \in B$ and has endpoints that lie on the left and right edge of some rectangle $r' \in B$. If s were not containing the top edge of any rectangle in B, then we could vertically move it until it contains such a top edge and simultaneously stabs one rectangle more than before; a contradiction to the greedy choice. On the other hand, if the endpoints of s were not lying on a left and right edge of the same rectangle, then, by our construction, there would be a small positive interval on s which is not contained in the rectangles stabbed by s. We could cut the interval out of s and obtain one or two new line segments, where at least one of them has a better cost efficiency than s; a contradiction.

Now, consider a segment s that is lying on the top edge of some rectangle $r \in B$ and is containing the vertical boundaries of some rectangle $r' \in B$. Let $i \in \{0, \ldots, \ell\}$ be the level of r'. Observe that s has length $(1 - i\varepsilon)/2^i$ and stabs $\sum_{j=0}^{\ell-i} 2^j + 1 = 2^{\ell-i+1}$ many rectangles. (Note that s also stabs the rectangle corresponding to r in T.) Therefore, s has cost efficiency $(1 - i\varepsilon)/2^{\ell+1}$, which is minimized for the biggest-possible value of i. From this we can conclude that the algorithms picks s such that r' belongs to the highest level i, which implies that r' and r coincide. Thus, s is the top edge of some rectangle in B with the highest level i. In subsequent iterations, the algorithm continues selecting the top edge of a rectangle in B that has the highest level among the remaining rectangles. Overall the algorithm produces a solution that consists of all top edges of rectangles in B which has cost $\Omega(\log n)$ since the highest level ℓ is in $\Omega(\log n)$. The solution $\{t, b\}$, however, has only cost 2, which completes our claim.

The example above suggests the following natural variation of the greedy algorithm. In each step, pick the segment that minimizes the ratio of its length to the total *width* of the (previously unstabbed) rectangles it stabs. We can easily modify the instance so that also this algorithms performs bad. In the first step, we remove all rectangles of odd levels and do not change the level enumeration. Thus, all levels are now even. In the second step, we create copies of each rectangle so that a rectangle at level i has multiplicity $\lceil 2^i/(1-i\varepsilon) \rceil$. This multiplicity will ensure that the total weight of equivalent rectangles is roughly 1 and not smaller than 1. Note that the number of levels is still in $\Omega(\log n)$ although we increased the number n of rectangles.

To this end, we show that the modified greedy algorithm picks again all top edges of the rectangles in B, always greedily picking one from the currently highest level. Suppose this were not the case and consider the first segment s not picked in this manner. By the same discussion as in the unweighted case, the segment s lies on a top edge of a rectangle $r \in B$ and is touching the horizontal boundaries of a rectangle $r' \in B$. Let i be the level of r'. By our assumption, i is not the highest level, hence, the highest level is at least $i+2$ (as all levels are even). Thus, we can find a segment s' that lies on a top edge of some rectangle $r'' \in B$ and, at the same time, touches the horizontal boundaries of some rectangle of level $i+2$.

Let w be the total width of the rectangles stabbed by s' excluding the rectangles of T corresponding to r''. Note that the total width of those excluded rectangles is at least 1. Hence, the cost efficiency of s' is at most

$$\frac{1-(i+2)\varepsilon}{2^{i+2}(w+1)}.$$

Next, consider s. The total width of r' and its copies is at most

$$\left\lceil \frac{2^i}{1-i\varepsilon} \right\rceil \cdot \frac{1-i\varepsilon}{2^i} < 1 + \frac{1-i\varepsilon}{2^i}.$$

The same bound holds for the total width of the rectangles of T corresponding to r as the level of r is not smaller than i. Thus, the total width of the rectangles stabbed by s is at most

$$4w + 2\left(1 + \frac{1-i\varepsilon}{2^i}\right) < 4w + 4.$$

Hence, the cost efficiency of s' is greater than

$$\frac{1-i\varepsilon}{2^i(4w+4)} = \frac{1-i\varepsilon}{2^{i+2}(w+1)}$$

and thus bigger than the cost efficiency of s'; a contradiction to the greedy choice.

Note that none of the segments returned by the algorithm is redundant so that a post-processing that removes unnecessary segment parts does not help.

5.2.2 Relation to Piercing

In this section, we consider how our stabbing problems relate to the well-studied hitting set problem for axis-aligned rectangles (or boxes in higher dimensions), which we call PIERCING. In this problem, we are given a set R of axis-aligned rectangles (or boxes) and a set P of points. We want to hit all rectangles using a minimum number of points from P. We also consider the weighted version where each point has a positive weight and we want to minimize the total weight of the points selected. Similarly to STABBING, also this problem can be expressed naturally in terms of SET COVER: The rectangles are the elements to be covered, and the piercing points are the sets. This correspondence allows us to compare stabbing and piercing by asking whether a given set cover instance has a realization as either of them. We will show that every stabbing instance corresponds directly in this way to a piercing instance in dimension three. Just in dimension two, however, not every stabbing instance can be realized as a piercing instance. This shows that STABBING is structurally different from two-dimensional PIERCING.

Theorem 5.1. *Any set cover instance* $(U, \mathcal{F})$ *arising from* STABBING *can be realized as an instance of weighted* PIERCING *in dimension 3.*

Proof. Starting with a (2-dimensional) stabbing instance, we will translate it to a 3-dimensional piercing instance: Every rectangle becomes an axis-aligned box and every stabbing line segment becomes a piercing point. Note that a stabbing line segment is defined by an interval $[x_1, x_2]$ and a height y. We lift it to the 3-dimensional point (x_1, x_2, y) and assign it the weight $x_2 - x_1$. Consider a rectangle $[x_{\min}, x_{\max}] \times [y_{\min}, y_{\max}]$. The line segment stabs this rectangle if and only if

$$x_1 \leq x_{\min}, \quad x_{\max} \leq x_2, \quad \text{and} \quad y \in [y_{\min}, y_{\max}] . \tag{5.1}$$

These inequalities describe an axis-aligned box that is unbounded on one side of x_1 on the first coordinate axis and on one side of x_2 on the second coordinate axis. We can observe that an optimal solution does not need to use any line segments with endpoints to the left of all rectangles or to the right of all rectangles. This fact limits the relevant values of x_1 and x_2 and we can bound the box on all sides. □

Aronov et al. [AES10] describe an $\mathcal{O}(\log \log \mathrm{OPT})$-approximation algorithm for unweighted PIERCING in dimension 3, where OPT is the size of an optimum solution. This algorithm immediately gives us the same bound for CARDINALITY STABBING. Their result does not carry over to weighted PIERCING, so we cannot use it to solve STABBING.

Corollary 5.1. *There is an* $\mathcal{O}(\log \log \mathrm{OPT})$-*approximation algorithm for* CARDINALITY STABBING, *where OPT is the size of an optimum solution.*

Now, we show that such a correspondence does not exist in dimension 2: There exist stabbing instances that have no corresponding piercing instance. A set $S \in \mathcal{F}$ in a set cover instance $(U, \mathcal{F})$ is called *universal* if $S = U$. Note that the universal set (if there exists any) is not necessarily an optimum solution since we are dealing with weighted SET COVER.

Lemma 5.1. *Let* $(U, \mathcal{F})$ *be a* SET COVER *instance on n elements that arises from a* PIERCING *instance and contains the universal set. For any k,* $\mathcal{F}$ *contains* $\mathcal{O}(n)$ *distinct sets of cardinality k.*

Proof. Consider the faces of the arrangement on the plane induced by the set R of n rectangles of the PIERCING instance. Any points in the same face pierce exactly the same set of rectangles and are therefore the same set in terms of $\mathcal{F}$. Call the number of rectangles pierced by points in a face the *depth* of the face. Since it is given that C contains the universal set, there must be

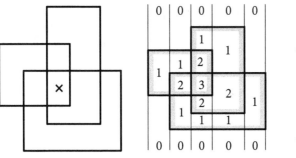 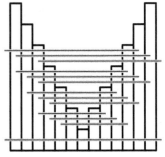

(a) A Piercing instance with a uni- **(b)** Slabs with depth values. **(c)** A Stabbing instance with many lines
versal point.   of equal cardinality.

Figure 5.3: Some structural properties of Piercing and Stabbing.

a face of depth n. This face contains a point $p_u \in P$ and this point pierces all rectangles. See Fig. 5.3a for an example, where × indicates p_u.

Now, we consider a vertical line at every left and right edge of a rectangle. These lines cut the plane into $\mathcal{O}(n)$ vertical slabs and within each slab, all faces are rectangles (see Fig. 5.3b). In each slab, the topmost face has depth zero. Traversing downward until the height of p_u, every next face *increases* the depth by at least one. Traversing further downward *decreases* the depth by at least one for each face. Hence, for any k, there are at most two faces with depth k in a slab. The number of faces of a certain depth bounds the number of distinct sets of that size, and the claimed bound follows. □

Lemma 5.2. *For every odd n, there exist SET COVER instances on n elements arising from STABBING instances that contain the universal set and $\Omega(n^2)$ distinct sets of equal cardinality.*

Proof. Let ℓ be arbitrarily large and even. For each $i \in \{-\ell, .., \ell\}$, we introduce a rectangle r_i. Thus, we have $n = 2\ell + 1$ rectangles, and we will place them in a double staircase as follows; see Fig. 5.3c. All rectangles have width 1 and touch the x-axis with their bottom edges. For each $i \in \{-\ell, .., \ell\}$, the left edge of rectangle r_i has x-coordinate i and height $|i| + 1$. Call the rectangles with negative index *left* and the ones with positive index *right*. A stabbing line is said to have *level i* if its y-coordinate is in $(i, i + 1)$. At level 0, we add a stabbing line that stabs every rectangle.

Let $k = \ell/2$. Now, we construct k stabbing lines on each of the levels 1 through $k + 1$, each stabbing $k + 1$ rectangles. Consider level i. For every j with $1 \le j \le k$, the stabbing line $s_{i,j}$ stabs j many left rectangles and $k + 1 - j$ many right rectangles. This construction is uniquely defined, enough rectangles exist on these levels, and all of these line segments stab distinct sets of $k + 1$ rectangles. Thus, the lemma holds: by construction, we have a universal set, and $k \cdot (k + 1) = \Omega(n^2)$. □

Theorem 5.2. *There exist SET COVER instances that are realizable as 2-dimensional STABBING but not as 2-dimensional PIERCING.*

Proof. Consider an arbitrarily large SET COVER instance on n elements from Lemma 5.2. It is realizable as a STABBING instance, has the universal set, and contains $\Omega(n^2)$ distinct sets of equal size. If it is large enough, then, by Lemma 5.1, it does not have a realization as PIERCING.   □

5.3   A Constant-Factor Approximation Algorithm for Stabbing

In this section, we present a constant-factor approximation algorithm for STABBING. First, we model STABBING as a set cover problem, and we revisit the standard linear programming relaxation for set cover and the concept of shallow-cell complexity; see Sections 5.3.1 and 5.3.2. Then, we observe that there are STABBING instances with high shallow-cell complexity. This limiting fact prevents us from obtaining any constant approximation factor if applying the generalization of Chan et al. [CGKS12] in a direct way; see Section 5.3.2. In order to bypass this limitation, we decompose any STABBING instance into two disjoint families of low shallow-cell complexity. Before describing the decomposition in Section 5.3.5, we show how to merge solutions to these two disjoint families in an approximation-factor preserving way; see Section 5.3.3. Then, in Section 5.3.4, we observe that these families have sufficiently small shallow-cell complexity to admit a constant-factor approximation.

5.3.1   Set Cover and Linear Programming

An instance $(U, \mathcal{F}, c)$ of weighted SET COVER is given by a finite universe U of n elements, a family $\mathcal{F}$ of subsets of U that covers U, and a cost function $c: \mathcal{F} \to \mathbb{Q}^+$. The objective is to find a sub-family $\mathcal{S}$ of $\mathcal{F}$ that also covers U and minimizes the total cost $c(\mathcal{S}) = \sum_{S \in \mathcal{S}} c(S)$.

An instance (R, F) of CONSTRAINED STABBING, given by a set R of rectangles and a set F of line segments, can be seen as a special case of weighted SET COVER where the rectangles in R are the universe U, the line segments in F form the sets in $\mathcal{F}$, and a line segment $s \in F$ "covers" a rectangle r if and only if s stabs r. Unconstrained STABBING can be modeled by SET COVER as follows. We can, without loss of generality, consider only feasible solutions where the end points of any line segment lie on the left or right boundaries of rectangles and where each line segment touches the top boundary of some rectangle. Thus, we can restrict ourselves to feasible solutions that are subsets of a set F of $\mathcal{O}(n^3)$ candidate line segments. This shows that STABBING is a special case of CONSTRAINED STABBING and, hence, of SET COVER.

The standard LP relaxation $\mathrm{LP}(U, \mathcal{F}, c)$ for a SET COVER instance $(U, \mathcal{F}, c)$ is as follows:

$$\text{Minimize} \quad \sum_{S \in \mathcal{F}} c(S) z_S$$

$$\text{subject to} \quad \sum_{S \in \mathcal{F}, S \ni e} z_S \geq 1 \quad \text{for all } e \in U,$$

$$z_S \geq 0 \quad \text{for all } S \in \mathcal{F}.$$

The optimum solution to this LP provides a lower bound on OPT. An algorithm is called *LP-relative α-approximation algorithm* for a class Π of set cover instances if it rounds any feasible solution $\mathbf{z} = (z_S)_{S \in \mathcal{F}}$ to the above standard LP relaxation for some instance $(U, \mathcal{S}, c)$ in this class to a feasible integral solution $\mathcal{S} \subseteq \mathcal{F}$ of cost $c(\mathcal{S}) \leq \alpha \sum_{S \in \mathcal{F}} c(S) z_s$.

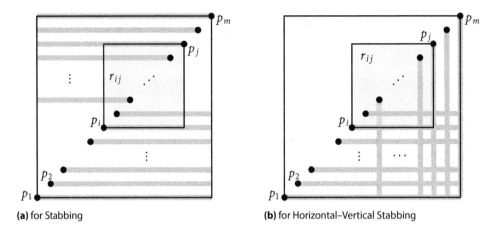

(a) for Stabbing   **(b)** for Horizontal–Vertical Stabbing

Figure 5.4: Instances with high shallow-cell complexity.

5.3.2   Shallow-Cell Complexity

We define the shallow-cell complexity for classes that consist of instances of weighted SET COVER. Informally, the shallow-cell complexity is a bound on the number of equivalent classes of elements that are contained in a small number of sets. Here is the formal definition.

Definition 5.1 (Chan et al. [CGKS12]). Let $f(m, k)$ be a function non-decreasing in m and k. An instance $(U, \mathcal{F}, c)$ of weighted SET COVER has shallow-cell complexity f if the following holds for every k and m with $1 \le k \le m \le |\mathcal{F}|$, and every sub-family $\mathcal{S} \subseteq \mathcal{F}$ of m sets: All elements that are contained in at most k sets of $\mathcal{S}$ form at most $f(m, k)$ equivalence classes (called *cells*), where two elements are equivalent if they are contained in precisely the same sets of $\mathcal{S}$. A class of instances of weighted SET COVER has shallow-cell complexity f if all its instances have shallow-cell complexity f.

Chan et al. proved that if a set cover problem has low shallow-cell complexity then quasi-uniform sampling yields an LP-relative approximation algorithm with good performance.

Theorem 5.3 (Chan et al. [CGKS12]). *Let $\varphi(m)$ be a non-decreasing function, and let Π be a class of instances of weighted SET COVER. If Π has shallow-cell complexity $m\varphi(m)k^{\mathcal{O}(1)}$, then Π admits an LP-relative approximation algorithm (based on quasi-uniform sampling) with approximation ratio $\mathcal{O}(\max\{1, \log \varphi(m)\})$.*

Unfortunately, there are instances of STABBING (and its constrained variants) that have high shallow-cell complexity, so we cannot directly obtain a sub-logarithmic performance via Theorem 5.3. These instances can be constructed as follows; see Fig. 5.4a. Let m be an even positive integer. For $i = 1, \ldots, m$, define the point $p_i = (i, i)$. For each pair i, j with $1 \le i \le m/2 < j \le m$, let r_{ij} be the rectangle with corners p_i and p_j. Now, consider the following set $\mathcal{S}$ of m line segments. For $i = 1, \ldots, m/2$, the set $\mathcal{S}$ contains the segment s_i with endpoints p_i and (m, i). For $i = m/2 + 1, \ldots, m$, the set $\mathcal{S}$ contains the segment s_i with endpoints $(1, i)$ and p_i. We want to count the number of rectangles that are stabbed by at most two segments in $\mathcal{S}$. Consider any i and j satisfying $1 \le i \le m/2 < j \le m$. Observe that the rectangle r_{ij} is stabbed precisely by the segments s_i and s_j in $\mathcal{S}$. Hence, according to Definition 5.1, our instance consists of at least $m^2/4$ equivalence classes for $k = 2$. Thus, if our instance has shallow cell-complexity f for some suitable function f, we have $f(m, 2) = \Omega(m^2)$. Since f is non-decreasing, we also have $f(m, k) = \Omega(m^2)$ for $k \ge 2$. Hence, Theorem 5.3 implies only an $\mathcal{O}(\log n)$-approximation algorithm for STABBING (and its constrained variants) where we use the above-mentioned fact (see Section 5.3.1) that we can restrict ourselves to $m = \mathcal{O}(n^3)$ many candidate segments.

5.3.3 Decomposition Lemma for Set Cover

Our trick is to decompose general instances of STABBING (which may have high shallow-cell complexity) into partial instances of low complexity with a special, laminar structure. We use the following simple decomposition lemma, which holds for arbitrary set cover instances.

Lemma 5.3. *Let Π, Π_1, Π_2 be classes of SET COVER where Π_1 and Π_2 admit LP-relative α_1- and α_2-approximation algorithms, respectively. The class Π admits an LP-relative $(\alpha_1 + \alpha_2)$-approximation algorithm if, for every instance $(U, \mathcal{F}, c) \in \Pi$, the family $\mathcal{F}$ can be partitioned into $\mathcal{F}_1, \mathcal{F}_2$ such that, for any partition of U into U_1, U_2 where U_1 is covered by $\mathcal{F}_1$ and U_2 by $\mathcal{F}_2$, the instances $(U_1, \mathcal{F}_1, c)$ and $(U_2, \mathcal{F}_2, c)$ are instances of Π_1 and Π_2, respectively.*

Proof. Let $\mathbf{z} = (z_S)_{S \in \mathcal{F}}$ be a feasible solution to $\mathrm{LP}(U, \mathcal{F}, c)$. Let $U_1, U_2 = \varnothing$ initially. Consider an element $e \in U$. Because of the constraint $\sum_{S \in \mathcal{F}, S \ni e} z_S \ge 1$ in the LP relaxation and because of $\mathcal{F} = \mathcal{F}_1 \cup \mathcal{F}_2$, at least one of the two cases

$$\sum_{S \in \mathcal{F}_1, S \ni e} z_S \ge \alpha_1/(\alpha_1 + \alpha_2) \quad \text{and} \quad \sum_{S \in \mathcal{F}_2, S \ni e} z_S \ge \alpha_2/(\alpha_1 + \alpha_2)$$

occurs. If the first case holds, then we add e to U_1. Otherwise, the second case holds and we add e to U_2. We execute this step for each element $e \in U$.

Now, consider the instance $(U_1, \mathcal{F}_1, c)$. For each $S \in \mathcal{F}_1$, set $z_S^1 := \min\{z_S(\alpha_1 + \alpha_2)/\alpha_1, 1\}$. Since $\sum_{S \in \mathcal{F}_1, S \ni e} z_S \ge \alpha_1/(\alpha_1 + \alpha_2)$ for all $e \in U_1$, we have that $\mathbf{z}^1 = (z_S^1)_{S \in \mathcal{F}_1}$ forms a feasible solution to $\mathrm{LP}(U_1, \mathcal{F}_1, c)$. Next, we apply the LP-relative α_1-approximation algorithm to this instance to obtain a solution $\mathcal{S}_1 \subseteq \mathcal{F}_1$ that covers U_1 and whose cost is at most

$$\alpha_1 \sum_{S \in \mathcal{F}_1} c(S) z_S^1 \le (\alpha_1 + \alpha_2) \sum_{S \in \mathcal{F}_1} c(S) z_S .$$

Analogously, we can compute a solution $\mathcal{S}_2 \subseteq \mathcal{F}_2$ to $(U_2, \mathcal{F}_2, c)$ of cost at most

$$(\alpha_1 + \alpha_2) \sum_{S \in \mathcal{F}_2} c(S) z_S .$$

To complete the proof, note that $\mathcal{S}_1 \cup \mathcal{S}_2$ is a feasible solution to $(U, \mathcal{F}, c)$ of cost at most

$$(\alpha_1 + \alpha_2) \sum_{S \in \mathcal{F}_1 \cup \mathcal{F}_2} c(S) z_S .$$

Hence, our algorithm is an LP-relative $(\alpha_1 + \alpha_2)$-approximation algorithm. □

5.3.4 x-Laminar Instances

Definition 5.2. An instance of CONSTRAINED STABBING is called x-*laminar* if the projection of the segments in this instance onto the x-axis forms a laminar family of intervals. That is, any two of these intervals are either interior-disjoint or one is contained in the other.

We remark that for an x-laminar instance of CONSTRAINED STABBING the corresponding instance $(U, \mathcal{F}, c)$ of SET COVER does not necessarily have a laminar set family $\mathcal{F}$.

Lemma 5.4. *The shallow-cell complexity of an x-laminar instance of CONSTRAINED STABBING can be upper bounded by $f(m, k) = mk^2$. Hence, such instances admit a constant-factor LP-relative approximation algorithm.*

Proof. To prove the bound on the shallow-cell complexity, consider a set S of m segments. Let $1 \le k \le m$ be an integer. Consider an arbitrary rectangle r that is stabbed by at most k segments in S. Let S_r be the set of these segments. Consider a shortest segment $s \in S_r$. By laminarity, the projection of any segment in S_r onto the x-axis contains the projection of s onto the x-axis. Let $C_s = (s_1, \ldots, s_\ell)$ be the sequence of *all* segments in S whose projection contains the projection of s, ordered from top to bottom. The crucial point is that the set S_r forms a contiguous sub-sequence $s_i, \ldots, s_{i+|S_r|-1}$ of C_s that contains $s = s_j$ for some $i \le j \le i + |S_r| - 1$. Hence, S_r is uniquely determined by the choice of $s \in S$ (for which there are m possibilities), the choice of s_i with $i \in \{j - k, \ldots, j\}$ within the sequence C_s (for which there are at most k possibilities), and the cardinality of S_r (for which there are at most k possibilities). This fact implies that S_r is one of mk^2 many sets that define a cell. This observation completes our proof since r was picked arbitrarily. $\square$

5.3.5   Decomposing General Instances into Laminar Instances

Lemma 5.5. *Given an instance I of (unconstrained) STABBING with rectangle set R, we can compute an instance $I' = (R, F)$ of CONSTRAINED STABBING with the following properties. The set F of segments in I' has cardinality $\mathcal{O}(n^3)$, it can be decomposed into two disjoint x-laminar sets F_1 and F_2, and $\mathrm{OPT}_{I'} \le 6 \cdot \mathrm{OPT}_I$.*

Proof. Let F' be the set of $\mathcal{O}(n^3)$ candidate segments as defined in Sec. 5.3.1: For every segment s of F', the left endpoint of s lies on the left boundary of some rectangle, the right endpoint of s lies on the right boundary of some rectangle, and s contains the top boundary of some rectangle. Recall that F' contains the optimum solution.

Below, we stretch each of the segments in F' by a factor of at most 6 to arrive at a set F of segments having the claimed properties. By scaling the instance we may assume that the longest segment in F' has length $1/3$.

For any $i, j \in \mathbb{Z}$ with $i \ge 0$, let I_{ij} be the interval $[j/2^i, (j+1)/2^i]$. Let $\mathcal{I}_1$ be the family of all such intervals I_{ij}. We say that I_{ij} has level i. Note that $\mathcal{I}_1$ is an x-laminar family of intervals (segments). Let $\mathcal{I}_2$ be the family of intervals that arises if each interval in $\mathcal{I}_1$ is shifted to the right by the amount of $1/3$. That is, $\mathcal{I}_2$ is the family of all intervals of the form $I_{ij} + 1/3 := [j/2^i + 1/3, (j+1)/2^i + 1/3]$ (for any $i, j \in \mathbb{Z}$ with $i \ge 0$). Clearly, $\mathcal{I}_2$ is x-laminar, too.

We claim that any arbitrary interval $J = [a, b]$ of length at most $1/3$ is contained in an interval I that is at most 6 times longer than J and that is contained in $\mathcal{I}_1$ or in $\mathcal{I}_2$. The claim completes the proof of the lemma since then any segment in F' can be stretched by a factor of at most 6 so that its projection on the x-axis lies in $\mathcal{I}_1$ (giving rise to the segment set F_1) or in $\mathcal{I}_2$ (giving rise to the segment set F_2). Setting $F = F_1 \cup F_2$ completes the construction of the instance $I' = (R, F)$.

To show the claim above, let s be the largest non-negative integer with $b - a \leq 1/(3 \cdot 2^s)$. If J is contained in the interval I_{sj} for some integer j, then we are done because of $b - a > 1/(6 \cdot 2^s)$ by the choice of s. If J is not contained in any interval I_{sj}, then there exists some integer j such that $j/2^s \in J = [a, b]$ and thus $a \in I_{s,j-1}$. Since $b - a \leq 1/(3 \cdot 2^s)$, we have that J is completely contained in the interval $I' := I_{s,j-1} + 1/(3 \cdot 2^s)$ and in the interval $I'' := I_{s,j} - 1/(3 \cdot 2^s)$.

We complete the proof by showing that one of the intervals I', I'' is actually contained in $\mathcal{I}_2$. To this end, note that $1/3 = \sum_{\ell=1}^{\infty}(-1)^{\ell-1}/2^\ell$. Hence, if s is even, the interval $I' - 1/3$ lies in $\mathcal{I}_1$, and if s is odd, the interval $I'' - 1/3$ lies in $\mathcal{I}_1$. $\qquad\square$

Applying the decomposition lemma to Lemmas 5.4 and 5.5 yields our main result. We do not give an explicit approximation factor due to our reliance on the result by Chan et al. [CGKS12]. We also cannot apply a decomposition technique similar to CONSTRAINED STABBING since Lemma 5.5 requires a free choice of the set F of stabbing line segments.

Theorem 5.4. STABBING *admits a constant-factor LP-relative approximation algorithm.*

Complementing Lemmas 5.4 and 5.5, Fig. 5.4a shows that the union of two x-laminar families of segments may have shallow-cell complexity with quadratic dependence on m. Hence, the property of having low shallow-cell complexity is not closed under taking unions.

5.4   Further Applications of the Decomposition Lemma

Here we show that our decomposition technique can be applied in other settings, too.

Horizontal–Vertical Stabbing.   In this new variant of STABBING, a rectangle may be stabbed by a horizontal or by a vertical line segment (or by both). Using the results of Section 5.3.5 and the decomposition lemma where we decompose into horizontal and vertical segments, we immediately obtain the following result.

Corollary 5.2. HORIZONTAL–VERTICAL STABBING *admits an LP-relative constant-factor approximation algorithm.*

Figure 5.4b shows that a laminar family of horizontal segments and vertical segments may have a shallow-cell complexity with quadratic dependence on m. Thus, Corollary 5.2 is another natural example where low shallow-cell complexity is not closed under union and where the decomposition lemma gives a constant-factor approximation although the shallow-cell complexity is high.

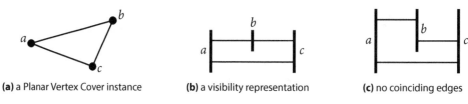

(a) a Planar Vertex Cover instance   **(b)** a visibility representation   **(c)** no coinciding edges

Figure 5.5: Obtaining a visibility representation from a Planar Vertex Cover instance.

Stabbing 3D-Boxes by Squares.   In the 3D-variant of STABBING, we want to stab 3D-boxes with axis-aligned squares, minimizing the sum of the areas or the sum of the perimeters of the squares. Here, "stabbing" means "completely cutting across". By combining the same idea with shifted quadtrees—the 2D-equivalent of laminar families of intervals—we obtain a constant-factor approximation for this problem. It is an interesting question if our approach can be extended to handle also arbitrary rectangles but this seems to require further ideas.

Covering Points by Anchored Squares.   Given a set P of points that need to be covered and a set A of anchor points, we want to find a set of axis-aligned squares such that each square contains at least one anchor point, the union of the squares covers P, and the total area or the total perimeter of the squares is minimized. Again, with the help of shifted quadtrees, we can apply the decomposition lemma. In this case, we do not even need to apply the machinery of quasi-uniform sampling; instead, we can use dynamic programming on the decomposed instances. This approach yields a deterministic algorithm with a concrete constant approximation ratio ($4 \cdot 6^2$, without polishing).

5.5   NP-Hardness of Stabbing

To show that STABBING is NP-hard, we reduce from PLANAR VERTEX COVER: Given a planar graph G and an integer k, decide whether G has a vertex cover of size at most k. This problem is NP-hard [GJS74].

Theorem 5.5. *STABBING is* NP-*hard, even for interior-disjoint rectangles.*

Let $G = (V, E)$ be a planar graph with n vertices, and let k be a positive integer. Our reduction will map G to a set R of rectangles and k to another integer $k^\star$ such that (G, k) is a yes-instance of PLANAR VERTEX COVER if and only if $(R, k^\star)$ is a yes-instance of STABBING. Consider a *visibility representation* of G, which represents the vertices of G by non-overlapping vertical line segments (called *vertex segments*), and each edge of G by a horizontal line segment (called *edge segment*) that touches the vertex segments of its endpoints; see Figs. 5.5a and 5.5b. Any planar graph admits a visibility representation on a grid of size $\mathcal{O}(n) \times \mathcal{O}(n)$, which can be found in polynomial time [LLS04]. We compute such a visibility representation for G. Then we stretch the vertex segments and vertically shift the edge segments so that no two edge segments coincide (on a vertex segment); see Fig. 5.5c. The height of the visibility representation remains linear in n.

In the next step, we create a STABBING instance based on this visibility representation, using the edge segments and vertex segments as indication for where to put our rectangles.

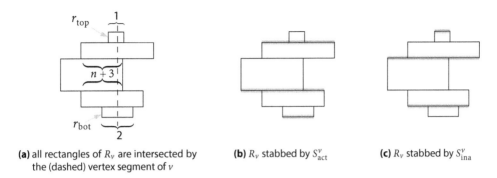

(a) all rectangles of R_v are intersected by the (dashed) vertex segment of v

(b) R_v stabbed by S^v_{act}

(c) R_v stabbed by S^v_{ina}

Figure 5.6: The vertex gadget R_v of vertex v.

All rectangles will be interior-disjoint, have positive area and lie on an integer grid that we obtain by scaling the visibility representation by a sufficiently large factor (linear in n). A vertex segment will intersect $\mathcal{O}(n)$ rectangles (lying above each other since they are disjoint), and each rectangle will have width $\mathcal{O}(n)$. The precise number of rectangles and their sizes will depend on the constraints formulated below. Our construction will be polynomial in n.

For each edge e in G, we introduce an *edge gadget* r_e, which is a rectangle that we place such that it is stabbed by the edge segment of e in the visibility representation.

For each vertex v in G, we introduce a *vertex gadget* R_v as shown in Fig. 5.6a. It consists of an odd number of rectangles that are (vertically) stabbed by the vertex segment of v in the visibility representation. Any two neighboring rectangles share a horizontal line segment. Its length is exactly $n + 3$ if neither of the rectangles is the top-most rectangle r_{top} or the bottom-most rectangle r_{bot}. Otherwise, the intersection length equals the width of the respective rectangle r_{top} or r_{bot}. We set the widths of r_{top} and r_{bot} to 1 and 2, respectively. A vertex gadget R_v is called *incident* to an edge gadget r_e if v is incident to e.

Before we describe the gadgets and their relation to each other in more detail, we construct, in two steps, a set S^v of line segments for each vertex gadget R_v. First, let S^v be the set of line segments that correspond to the top and bottom edges of the rectangles in R_v. Second, replace each pair of overlapping line segments in S^v by its union. Then number the line segments in S^v from top to bottom starting with 1. Let S^v_{ina} be the set of the odd-numbered line segments, and let S^v_{act} be the set of the even-numbered ones; see Figs. 5.6b and 5.6c. By construction, S^v_{act} and S^v_{ina} are feasible stabbings for R_v. Furthermore, $|S^v_{ina}| = |S^v_{act}|$ as $|R_v|$ is odd and, hence, $|S^v|$ is even. Given the difference in the widths of r_{top} and r_{bot}, we have that $\|S^v_{act}\| = \|S^v_{ina}\| + 1$. Note that this equation holds regardless of the widths of the rectangles in $R_v \setminus \{r_{top}, r_{bot}\}$.

The rectangles of all gadgets together form a STABBING instance R. They meet two further constraints: First, no two rectangles of different vertex gadgets intersect. We can achieve this by scaling the visibility representation by an appropriate factor linear in n. Second, each edge gadget r_e intersects exactly two rectangles, one of its incident left vertex gadgets, R_v, and one of its incident right vertex gadgets, R_u. The top edge of r_e touches a segment of S^v_{act} and the bottom edge of r_e touches a segment of S^u_{act}. The length of each of the two intersections is exactly $n + 3$; see Fig. 5.7. Thus, we have $|R_v| = \mathcal{O}(\deg(v)) = \mathcal{O}(n)$.

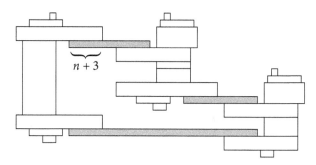

Figure 5.7: The Stabbing instance that encodes the Planar Vertex Cover instance of Fig. 5.5; edge gadgets are shaded gray.

Let S be a feasible solution to the instance R. We call a vertex gadget R_v *active* in S if $\{s \cap \bigcup R_v \mid s \in S\} = S^v_{\text{act}}$, and *inactive* in S if $\{s \cap \bigcup R_v \mid s \in S\} = S^v_{\text{ina}}$. We will see that in any optimum solution each vertex gadget is either active or inactive. Furthermore, we will establish a direct correspondence between the PLANAR VERTEX COVER instance G and the STABBING instance R: Every optimum solution to R *covers* each edge gadget by an active vertex gadget while minimizing the number of active vertex gadgets.

Let OPT_G denote the size of a minimum vertex cover for G, let OPT_R denote the length of an optimum solution to R, let $\text{width}(r)$ denote the width of a rectangle r, and finally let $c = \sum_{e \in E} (\text{width}(r_e) - n - 3) + \sum_{v \in V} \|S^v_{\text{ina}}\|$. To show NP-hardness of STABBING, we prove that $\text{OPT}_G \le k$ if and only if $\text{OPT}_R \le c + k$. We show the two directions separately.

Lemma 5.6. $\text{OPT}_G \le k$ *implies* $\text{OPT}_R \le c + k$.

Proof. Given a vertex cover of size $k' \le k$, we set all vertex gadgets that correspond to vertices in the vertex cover to active and all the other ones to inactive. Then for each edge gadget r_e, at least one incident vertex gadget is active, say R_v. By our construction of R, there is a line segment s in S^v_{act} with $\|s \cap r_e\| = n + 3$. We increase the length of s by $\text{width}(r_e) - n - 3$ so that r_e is stabbed. Hence, we obtained a feasible solution to R. Recall that there are k' active vertex gadgets and that, for each vertex v, we have $\|S^v_{\text{act}}\| = \|S^v_{\text{ina}}\| + 1$. Thus, the total length of our solution is

$$\sum_{v \in V} \|S^v_{\text{ina}}\| + k' + \sum_{e \in E} (\text{width}(r_e) - n - 3) \le c + k' \le c + k$$

and the lemma follows. $\square$

Next we show the other, more challenging direction. Consider an optimum solution S_{OPT} to R and choose $k \le n$ such that $\text{OPT}_R \le c + k$ is satisfied. Let R_v be any vertex gadget, let r_{top} and r_{bot} be its top- and bottom-most rectangles, respectively, and let

$$S^v_{\text{OPT}} = \{s \cap \bigcup R_v \mid s \in S_{\text{OPT}}\}.$$

We transform S_{OPT} as follows without increasing its total length. Let $s \in S_{\text{OPT}}$ be a line segment stabbing r_{top}. If s stabs only r_{top}, then we move s to the top edge of r_{top}. If s also stabs other rectangles, then one of these rectangles must touch r_{top} (otherwise we could split s and shrink its subsegments, contradicting optimality). Note that the only rectangle touching r_{top} lies below it and belongs to R_v. A similar argument holds for r_{bot}.

Observation 5.1. *Without loss of generality, it holds that:*

(i) *Any segment in S_{OPT} stabbing r_{top} either stabs r_{top} through its top edge, or also stabs another rectangle in R_v.*

(ii) *The same holds for the rectangle r_{bot} and its bottom edge.*

Observation 5.2. *Every line segment in S_{OPT}^v that does not stab a rectangle in $\{r_{\text{top}}, r_{\text{bot}}\}$ has length at least $n + 3$.*

Note that Observation 5.2 also holds for line segments that stab only rectangles belonging to edge gadgets as those rectangles have length at least $n + 3$. In the following, we prove that S_{OPT}^v equals either S_{ina}^v or S_{act}^v.

Lemma 5.7. *If $S_{\text{ina}}^v \not\subseteq S_{\text{OPT}}^v$ and $S_{\text{act}}^v \not\subseteq S_{\text{OPT}}^v$, then $\|S_{\text{OPT}}^v\| > \|S_{\text{act}}^v\| + n$.*

Proof. We say that a pair of rectangles is *stabbed* by a line segment if the line segment stabs both rectangles. Let P be a maximum-cardinality set of rectangle pairs of R_v where each pair is stabbed by a line segment in S_{OPT}^v and each rectangle appears in at most one pair. For S_{ina}^v and S_{act}^v, such a maximum-cardinality set of pairs is unique and excludes exactly one rectangle, namely r_{top} or r_{bot}, respectively.

Now, as R_v contains an odd number of rectangles, the number of rectangles not in P is odd and at least one. If there is exactly one rectangle not in P, this rectangle is different from r_{top} and r_{bot}, as otherwise Observation 5.1 would yield $S_{\text{ina}}^v \subseteq S_{\text{OPT}}^v$ or $S_{\text{act}}^v \subseteq S_{\text{OPT}}^v$; a contradiction since $S_{\text{ina}}^v \not\subseteq S_{\text{OPT}}^v$ and $S_{\text{act}}^v \not\subseteq S_{\text{OPT}}^v$. If there are at least three rectangles not in P, then one among them is different from r_{top} and r_{bot}. Hence, in both cases, there is at least one rectangle r' not in P that is different from r_{top} and r_{bot}.

Thus, S_{OPT}^v contains a line segment that stabs r' and that does not stab any other rectangle pair in P. The line segment is not shorter than $\text{width}(r')$. Furthermore, for each pair $(r_1, r_2) \in P$, S_{OPT}^v contains a line segment of length

$$\text{width}(r_1) + \text{width}(r_2) - \text{width}(r_1 \cap r_2)$$

that stabs r_1 and r_2. Putting things together, we bound $\|S_{\text{OPT}}^v\|$ from below by

$$\sum_{r \in R_v} \text{width}(r) - \sum_{(r_1, r_2) \in P} \text{width}(r_1 \cap r_2). \tag{5.2}$$

The first sum is independent of S_{OPT}^v. Thus, bound (5.2) is minimized by maximizing the second sum. Let's examine the value of $\text{width}(r_1 \cap r_2)$ for various pairs (r_1, r_2). For the unique pair containing r_{top}, the value is 1, for the unique pair containing r_{bot}, it is 2. For all the other pairs, by construction it is $n + 3$. Thus, the second sum is maximized when r_{top} is the only rectangle not in P. This is exactly the case for S_{ina}^v. As S_{ina}^v contains one line segment for each pair and one line segment for r_{top}, and each line segment is only as long as necessary, $\|S_{\text{ina}}^v\|$ reaches bound (5.2) and is consequently optimal.

Due to the assumption of the lemma, there is a rectangle r' that is not in P. Note that the second sum is maximized if r' is the *only* rectangle not in P. Compared to the optimal situation when $S_{\mathrm{OPT}}^v = S_{\mathrm{ina}}^v$, the value of the sum changes by $1 - (n + 3)$: replace the pair with r' in S_{ina}^v by the pair with r_{top}. Consequently, under the assumption of the lemma, bound (5.2) for S_{OPT}^v is at least $\|S_{\mathrm{ina}}^v\| + n + 2 = \|S_{\mathrm{act}}^v\| + n + 1$, and the claim follows. $\qquad\square$

Lemma 5.8. *Exactly one of the following three statements holds:*

    (i) $S_{\mathrm{OPT}}^v = S_{\mathrm{ina}}^v$, *or*

    (ii) $S_{\mathrm{OPT}}^v = S_{\mathrm{act}}^v$, *or*

    (iii) $\|S_{\mathrm{OPT}}^v\| > \|S_{\mathrm{ina}}^v\| + n$.

Proof. Suppose that S_{ina}^v is a proper subset of S_{OPT}^v for some vertex v, and let $s \in S_{\mathrm{OPT}}^v \setminus S_{\mathrm{ina}}^v$. Consider the segment $s' \in S_{\mathrm{OPT}}$ that "induces" s, that is, $s = s' \cap \bigcup R_v$. If s stabs only a rectangle in $\{r_{\mathrm{top}}, r_{\mathrm{bot}}\}$, then, by Observation 5.1, s' stabs no other rectangle in R. Hence, we can safely remove s' from S_{OPT}, as r_{top} and r_{bot} are already stabbed in S_{ina}^v; a contradiction to the optimality of S_{OPT}. Consequently, s must stab a rectangle in $R_v \setminus \{r_{\mathrm{top}}, r_{\mathrm{bot}}\}$. By Observation 5.2, we get

$$\|S_{\mathrm{OPT}}^v\| \geq \|S_{\mathrm{ina}}^v\| + n + 3 > \|S_{\mathrm{ina}}^v\| + n \, .$$

The same holds for $S_{\mathrm{act}}^v \not\subseteq S_{\mathrm{OPT}}^v$. Together with Lemma 5.7, these observations yield the claim. $\qquad\square$

Now, we show that S_{OPT} forces each vertex gadget to be either active or inactive.

Lemma 5.9. *In S_{OPT}, each vertex gadget is either active or inactive.*

Proof. Suppose that there is a vertex gadget R_u that is neither active nor inactive in S_{OPT}. This implies $\mathrm{OPT}_R > c + n$ and contradicts our previous assumption $\mathrm{OPT}_R \leq c + k \leq c + n$.

To this end, we give a lower bound on OPT_R. Since R_u is neither active nor inactive, we have $S_{\mathrm{OPT}}^u > \|S_{\mathrm{ina}}^u\| + n$ by Lemma 5.8. Thus, $\sum_{v \in V} \|S_{\mathrm{OPT}}^v\| > \sum_{v \in V} \|S_{\mathrm{ina}}^v\| + n$. Let $S_{\mathrm{OPT}}^{\mathrm{out}}$ be the set of all segment fragments of S_{OPT} lying outside of $\bigcup_{v \in V} S_{\mathrm{OPT}}^v$. Each edge gadget r_v contains a segment fragment from $S_{\mathrm{OPT}}^{\mathrm{out}}$ of length at least $\mathrm{width}(r_v) - n - 3$ since, by construction, it can share a line segment with only one of its incident vertex gadgets. Since all edge gadgets are interior-disjoint, we have $\|S_{\mathrm{OPT}}^{\mathrm{out}}\| \geq \sum_{e \in E} \mathrm{width}(r_v) - n - 3$. Hence,

$$\mathrm{OPT}_R \geq \|S_{\mathrm{OPT}}^{\mathrm{out}}\| + \sum_{v \in V} \|S_{\mathrm{OPT}}^v\| > \sum_{e \in E}(\mathrm{width}(r_e) - n - 3) + \sum_{v \in V} \|S_{\mathrm{ina}}^v\| + n \; = \; c + n. \; \square$$

Lemma 5.10. *For each edge gadget, one of its incident vertex gadgets is active in S_{OPT}.*

Proof. Suppose that for an edge gadget r_e both vertex gadgets are not active in S_{OPT}. By Lemma 5.9, they are inactive. Without loss of generality, the line segment s stabbing r_e lies on the top or bottom edge of r_e. Then s intersects a vertex gadget to the left or right, say R_v, and hence $S_{\mathrm{OPT}}^v \neq S_{\mathrm{ina}}^v$ and $S_{\mathrm{OPT}}^v \neq S_{\mathrm{act}}^v$. A contradiction to Lemma 5.9. $\qquad\square$

Lemma 5.11. $OPT_R = c + k'$, where k' is the number of active vertex gadgets in S_{OPT}.

Proof. Consider any edge gadget r_e. It is stabbed by only one line segment s, and, without loss of generality, the line segment s lies on the top or bottom edge of r_e. Thus, it intersects a vertex gadget R_v on a rectangle r. Then $R_v \neq S^v_{ina}$ and R_v is active according to Lemma 5.9. By our construction of R, there is exactly one segment in S^v_{act} intersecting r_e, which also stabs r. Hence, this segment is a subsegment of s and we have

$$\|s\| = \text{width}(r) + \text{width}(r_e) - \text{width}(r \cap r_e) = \text{width}(r) + \text{width}(r_e) - n - 3.$$

Thus, by Lemma 5.9 and $\|S^v_{act}\| = \|S^v_{ina}\| + 1$,

$$OPT_R = \sum_{e \in E} (\text{width}(r_e) - n - 3) + \sum_{v \in V} \|S^v_{ina}\| + k' = c + k'$$

where k' is the number of active vertex gadgets in S_{OPT}. $\qquad\square$

Given S_{OPT}, we put exactly those vertices in the vertex cover whose vertex gadgets are active. By Lemma 5.10, this yields a vertex cover of G. By Lemma 5.11, the size of the vertex cover is exactly $OPT_R - c$, which is bounded from above by k given that $OPT_R \leq c + k$.

Lemma 5.12. $OPT_R \leq c + k$ implies that $OPT_G \leq k$.

By our construction, we represent R on a grid of size polynomial in n, hence, all numerical values are upperbounded by a polynomial in n. Our construction is polynomial. With Lemmas 5.6 and 5.12, we conclude that STABBING is NP-hard.

5.6 APX-Hardness of Cardinality and Constrained Stabbing

In this section, we consider CARDINALITY STABBING and CONSTRAINED STABBING. The latter is the variant of STABBING, where the solution is constrained to be some subset of a given set of line segments. By reducing a restricted APX-hard variant of SET COVER to these problems, we show that neither CARDINALITY STABBING nor CONSTRAINED STABBING admits a PTAS unless P = NP. The following lemma follows directly from Definition 1.2 and Lemma 1.3 by Grant and Chan [CG14].

Lemma 5.13 (Grant and Chan [CG14]). *SPECIAL-3SC is APX-hard, where SPECIAL-3SC is defined as unweighted SET COVER with the following properties: The input is a family S of subsets of a universe $U = A \cup W \cup X \cup Y \cup Z$ that comprises the disjoint sets (which are part of the input)*

$$A = \{a_1, \ldots, a_n\}, W = \{w_1, \ldots, w_m\}, X = \{x_1, \ldots, x_m\}, Y = \{y_1, \ldots, y_m\}, Z = \{z_1, \ldots, z_m\}$$

where $2n = 3m$. The family S consists of $5m$ sets and satisfies the following two conditions:

- *For every t with $1 \leq t \leq m$, there are integers i and j with $1 \leq i < j < k \leq n$ such that S contains the sets $\{a_i, w_t\}, \{w_t, x_t\}, \{a_j, x_t, y_t\}, \{y_t, z_t\}$, and $\{a_k, z_t\}$. (See Fig. 5.8a.)*

- *For every i with $1 \leq i \leq n$, the element a_i is in exactly two sets in S.*

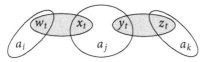

(a) For $1 \leq t \leq m$, there are five sets. Each element appears in exactly two sets.

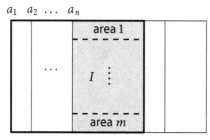

(b) Distinct rectangles $a_1, \ldots, a_n$ (a_1 is bold) have intersection I (shaded) which is subdivided into areas $1, \ldots, m$.

(c) For $1 \leq t \leq m$, there are five line segments (thick gray horizontal line segments). Every line segment stabs exactly one of $\{a_i, w_t\}$, $\{w_t, x_t\}$, $\{a_j, x_t, y_t\}$, $\{y_t, z_t\}$, and $\{a_k, z_t\}$.

Figure 5.8: Encoding of Special-3sc via Stabbing.

We begin with CARDINALITY STABBING.

Theorem 5.6. *CARDINALITY STABBING is* APX-*hard.*

Proof. Given a SPECIAL-3SC instance $(\mathcal{U}, \mathcal{S})$ with $\mathcal{U} = A \cup W \cup X \cup Y \cup Z$, we efficiently encode it as a STABBING instance by creating a rectangle for each element of the universe $\mathcal{U}$ and adding a line segment for each set of $\mathcal{S}$. We will achieve the property that a line segment corresponding to a set s stabs exactly those rectangles that correspond to the elements of s.

Let $n = |A|$ and $m = |W|$ (recall $2n = 3m$). To encode $(\mathcal{U}, \mathcal{S})$, we place n rectangles of equal size on one spot and then shift them one by one to the right such that all rectangles are distinct and their total intersection $\mathcal{I}$ is not empty. For $1 \leq i \leq n$, the i-th rectangle from the left corresponds to element a_i; see Fig. 5.8b.

Next, we horizontally subdivide the intersection $\mathcal{I}$ into m areas. For $1 \leq t \leq m$, we place four thin rectangles inside the t-th area from the top such that the vertical projections of the rectangles intersect sequentially and only pairwise as in Fig. 5.8c. From top to bottom they correspond to w_t, x_t, y_t, and z_t.

Now, we show that our rectangle configuration allows a feasible set of line segments that corresponds to $\mathcal{S}$. Recall the definition of SPECIAL-3SC. For $1 \leq t \leq m$, the input contains the sets $\{a_i, w_t\}$, $\{w_t, x_t\}$, $\{a_j, x_t, y_t\}$, $\{y_t, z_t\}$ and $\{a_k, z_t\}$. Consider the first set. As the rectangle w_t is inside the rectangle a_i, we can stab both with one line segment. We can even stab them exclusively if we place the line segment above the rectangle x_t and do not leave the rectangle a_i (note that no rectangle of A is contained in another one). Hence, the line segment corresponds to the set $\{a_i, w_t\}$. With a similar discussion, we can find line segments that correspond to the sets $\{w_t, x_t\}$, $\{a_j, x_t, y_t\}$, $\{y_t, z_t\}$ and $\{a_k, z_t\}$, respectively; see Fig. 5.8c.

Since the objective is to minimize the cardinality of line segments, there is a cost-preserving correspondence between solutions to the SPECIAL-3SC instance and the generated STABBING instance. Hence, CARDINALITY STABBING is APX-hard. □

Next, we show that there is an *L-reduction* [PY91] from SPECIAL-3SC onto CONSTRAINED STABBING (where we minimize the total segment length). This reduction implies APX-hardness [PY91].

Theorem 5.7. CONSTRAINED STABBING *is* APX-*hard*.

Proof. For an *L*-reduction, it suffices to find two constants α and β such that for every SPECIAL-3SC instance I_{3SC} it holds:

(1) We can efficiently construct a CONSTRAINED STABBING instance I_{stab} with

$$\mathrm{OPT}(I_{stab}) \leq \alpha \cdot \mathrm{OPT}(I_{3SC})$$

where $\mathrm{OPT}(I_{stab})$ is the total length of an optimum solution to I_{stab} and $\mathrm{OPT}(I_{3SC})$ is the cardinality of a minimum set cover to I_{3SC}.

(2) For every feasible solution S_{stab} to I_{stab}, we can efficiently construct a feasible solution S_{3SC} to I_{3SC} with

$$\mathrm{cost}(S_{3SC}) - \mathrm{OPT}(I_{3SC}) \leq \beta \cdot (\mathrm{cost}(S_{stab}) - \mathrm{OPT}(I_{stab})) \,,$$

where $\mathrm{cost}(S_{3SC})$ denotes the cardinality of S_{3SC}, and $\mathrm{cost}(S_{stab})$ denotes the total length of S_{stab}.

Given a SPECIAL-3SC instance I_{3SC} with $5m$ subsets we construct a STABBING instance I_{stab} as in the proof of Theorem 5.6 with the following specifications: Every rectangle corresponding to elements in A has width equal to $1 + \delta$ for $\delta = 1/10m$ and the intersection $\mathcal{I}$ of all these rectangles has width equal to 1. For $1 \leq t \leq m$, we choose the lengths of the line segments corresponding to $\{w_t, x_t\}$ and $\{y_t, z_t\}$ to be equal 1. Thus, every line segment has length either 1 or $1 + \delta$.

Consequently, any optimum solution to I_{3SC} implies a feasible solution to I_{stab} with cost at most $(1 + \delta) \cdot \mathrm{OPT}(I_{3SC})$. Hence, we can bound $\mathrm{OPT}(I_{stab})$ from above by

$$(1 + \delta) \cdot \mathrm{OPT}(I_{3SC}) < 2 \cdot \mathrm{OPT}(I_{3SC}) \,.$$

This bound shows Property (1) of *L*-reduction with $\alpha = 2$.

Now, given a feasible solution S_{stab}, we will first observe that it cannot consist of less line segments than an optimum solution. Let x be the cardinality of any optimum solution to I_{stab}. Recall that every line segment has length 1 or $1 + \delta$ and that any feasible solution has at most $5m$ line segments. Thus, $x \leq \text{OPT}(I_{\text{stab}})$ and, consequently,

$$
\begin{aligned}
x &\leq \text{cost}(S_{\text{stab}}) \\
&\leq |S_{\text{stab}}|(1 + \delta) \\
&\leq |S_{\text{stab}}| + 5m\delta \\
&= |S_{\text{stab}}| + \frac{1}{2} \, .
\end{aligned}
$$

Hence, the inequality holds only if S_{stab} contains at least x lines segments.

Next, let S_{3SC} consist of all sets corresponding to the line segments in S_{stab}. Observe that S_{3SC} is feasible. To show Property (2), we consider two cases. In the first case, S_{stab} has the same number of line segments as the optimum solution. We immediately get

$$
\text{cost}(S_{\text{3SC}}) - \text{OPT}(I_{\text{3SC}}) \ = \ 0
$$

and the inequality of Property (2) holds. In the second case, S_{stab} has more line segments than the optimum solution. Thus, $x < |S_{\text{stab}}| \leq 5m$. With the definition of δ we, obtain

$$
\begin{aligned}
\text{cost}(S_{\text{stab}}) - \text{OPT}(I_{\text{stab}}) &> |S_{\text{stab}}| - x(1 + \delta) \\
&\geq 1 - x\delta \\
&\geq 1 - 5m\delta \\
&= \frac{1}{2} \, .
\end{aligned}
$$

Furthermore, we have

$$
\begin{aligned}
\text{OPT}(I_{\text{stab}}) &\leq (1 + \delta) \cdot \text{OPT}(I_{\text{3SC}}) \\
&\leq \text{OPT}(I_{\text{3SC}}) + \delta 5m \\
&\leq \text{OPT}(I_{\text{3SC}}) + \frac{1}{2} \, .
\end{aligned}
$$

On the other hand, $\text{cost}(S_{\text{3SC}}) \leq \text{cost}(S_{\text{stab}})$. Putting things together, we get

$$
\begin{aligned}
\text{cost}(S_{\text{3SC}}) - \text{OPT}(I_{\text{3SC}}) &\leq \text{cost}(S_{\text{stab}}) - \text{OPT}(I_{\text{stab}}) + \frac{1}{2} \\
&\leq 2 \cdot (\text{cost}(S_{\text{stab}}) - \text{OPT}(I_{\text{stab}}))
\end{aligned}
$$

and Property (2) holds for $\beta = 2$. $\qquad\square$

5.7   Conclusion

We have seen that STABBING is NP-hard and that it admits an $\mathcal{O}(1)$-approximation algorithm. Since our positive results relies on a general result regarding the shallow-cell complexity of the problem, it would be interesting to design a direct, combinatorial c-approximation algorithm with a concrete constant c that makes use of the geometry underlying the problem.

On the negative side, it remains open whether STABBING is APX-hard, which is the case for CONSTRAINED STABBING and CARDINALITY STABBING (see Theorems 5.6 and 5.7 in Section 5.6). Do the latter two problems admit constant-factor approximation algorithms? So far, we have only an $\mathcal{O}(\log\log \text{OPT})$-approximation algorithm for CARDINALITY STABBING via an existing approximation algorithm for piercing 3D-boxes [AES10], see Corollary 5.1 in Section 5.2.2. (Here, OPT denotes the size of an optimum solution.)

Finally, it would be interesting to examine natural problems of high shallow-cell complexity of unsettled approximability and try to partition them (possibly by our decomposition technique) into instances of low-shallow cell complexity, as in Section 5.4.

Colored Non-Crossing Euclidean Steiner Forest

Given a set of k-colored points in the plane, we consider the problem of finding k trees such that each tree connects all points of one color class, no two trees cross, and the total edge length of the trees is minimized. For $k = 1$, this task is the well-known EUCLIDEAN STEINER TREE problem. For general k, only a $(1.21k)$-approximation algorithm is known [EHKP15].

We present a PTAS for $k = 2$, a $(5/3 + \varepsilon)$-approximation algorithm for $k = 3$, and two approximation algorithms for general k, with ratios $\mathcal{O}(\sqrt{n}\log k)$ and $k + \varepsilon$. The first two algorithms are substantial modifications of Arora's [Aro98] PTAS for EUCLIDEAN STEINER TREE. For the third algorithm, the underlying idea is to compute a path connecting all terminals such that terminals of the same color have small distance along the path. In the forth algorithm, we successively compute a tree for each color, thereby creating "shells" around present trees in order to bypass them without crossings.

6.1 Introduction

STEINER TREE IN GRAPHS is a fundamental problem in combinatorial optimization. Given an edge-weighted graph and a set of vertices called *terminals*, the task is to find a minimum-weight subgraph that connects the terminals. In its generalization STEINER FOREST IN GRAPHS, the terminals are colored, and the desired subgraph must connect, for each color, the terminals of that color.

The most famous problem variant is the EUCLIDEAN STEINER TREE (EST) problem. In its generalization EUCLIDEAN STEINER FOREST, the input consists of n colored points in the plane, which we also call *terminals*, and the output is a drawing of minimum length connecting all terminals of the same color. Throughout this chapter, we call a cycle-free drawing connecting a set of terminals an *(Euclidean Steiner) tree*. If a tree is of minimum length, then we also call it a *minimum* Euclidean Steiner tree. Hence, a solution to EUCLIDEAN STEINER FOREST either consists of one minimum Euclidean Steiner tree or of two or more Euclidean Steiner trees.

In this chapter, we consider a new and natural variant of EUCLIDEAN STEINER FOREST where we add the constraint of planarity and require that terminals with distinct colors lie in distinct (connected) components. More precisely, we consider the problem of computing, for a k-colored set of terminals in the plane, k pairwise non-crossing planar Euclidean Steiner trees, one for each color. Such trees exist for every given set of points. We call the problem of minimizing the total length of these trees k-COLORED NON-CROSSING EUCLIDEAN STEINER FOREST (k-CESF). Figure 6.1 shows some interesting instances. Note that for $k = 1$, our problem is the same as EST.

The problem is motivated by a method that Efrat et al. [EHKP15] suggested recently for visualizing embedded and clustered graphs. They visualize clusters by regions in the plane that enclose related graph vertices. Their method attempts to reduce visual clutter and optimize "convexity" of the resulting regions by reducing the amount of "ink" necessary to connect

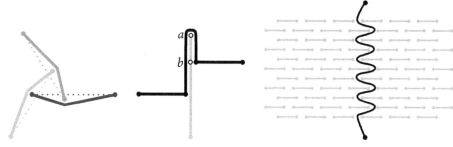

(a) The optimum contains no straight-line edge.

(b) Segment ab is used twice by the black curve.

(c) In the optimum, the black curve can be made arbitrarily longer than the corresponding straight-line segment (if every gray segment represents a different color).

Figure 6.1: Difficult examples for k-CESF.

all elements of a cluster. Efrat et al. [EHKP15] proposed the problem k-CESF and provided a simple $k\rho$-approximation algorithm, where ρ is the *Steiner ratio*. The Steiner ratio is the supremum, over all finite point sets in the plane, of the ratio of the total edge length of a minimum spanning tree to the total edge length of a Euclidean Steiner tree. Chung and Graham [CG85] showed $\rho \leq 1.21$.

Our contribution. The middle column of Table 6.1 shows our results. For k-CESF, we present a deterministic $(k+\varepsilon)$- and a randomized $\mathcal{O}(\sqrt{n}\log k)$-approximation algorithm; see Section 6.2. Our main result states that 2-CESF admits a PTAS; see Section 6.3. By a non-trivial modification of the PTAS, we prove that 3-CESF admits a $(5/3+\varepsilon)$-approximation algorithm; see Section 6.4.

Our PTAS for 2-CESF uses some ideas of Arora's algorithm [Aro98] for EST, which is equivalent to 1-CESF. Since, in a solution to 2-CESF, the two trees are not allowed to cross, our approach differs from Arora's algorithm in several respects. Informally speaking, Arora's algorithm lays a quadtree grid over the instance, snaps the instance to the grid, and searches, by dynamic programming, for a solution that crosses the quatree edges only in a specific way. At the end, the solution is snapped to the origin vertices. For our case, we have to modify the first and the last step carefully to avoid crossings of trees. We also use different constraints on how a solution may cross a quadtree edge. This difference forces us to change the dynamic programming and to prove the existence of a near-optimum solution that satisfies these new constraints. In the beginning of Section 6.3, we explain the differences between our and Arora's algorithm in more detail.

Related Work. Apart from the result of Efrat et al. [EHKP15], so far the only two variants of k-CESF that have been studied are those with extreme values of k. As mentioned above, 1-CESF is the same as EST, which is NP-hard [GJ79]. Arora [Aro98] and Mitchell [Mit99] showed independently that EST admits a PTAS. The other extreme value of k, for which k-CESF has been considered, is $k = n/2$. This case is the problem of joining specified pairs of points via non-crossing curves of minimum total length. Liebling et al. [LMM$^+$95] gave some heuristics for this problem. Bastert and Fekete [BF98] claimed that $(n/2)$-CESF is NP-hard, but their proof has not been formally published. Recently, Chan et al. [CHKL13] considered $(n/2)$-CESF in the context of drawing planar graphs at fixed vertex locations. They gave an $\mathcal{O}(\sqrt{n}\log n)$-approximation algorithm based on an idea of Liebling et al. [LMM+95] for computing a short non-crossing tour of all given points.

Several set visualization techniques assume also the setting where the input is a multi-colored point set [ARRC11, HKvK+18, CPC09, RBvK+08]. These techniques allow regions to cross, while the regions that correspond to (the geodesic hulls of) the trees in our approach are non-crossing. Reinbacher et al. [RBvK+08] consider the problem of computing a minimum-perimeter polygon that connects a specific set of uncolored points while separating all red from all blue points.

There is substantial work on the case where there are obstacles in the plane. Note that, in contrast to k-CESF, a valid solution may not exist in that setting. For a single color (that is, 1-CESF with obstacles), Müller-Hannemann and Tazari [MHT10] give a PTAS. The same variant is considered by Razaghpour [Raz08]. Papadopoulou [Pap99] gave an algorithm for finding minimum-length non-crossing paths joining pairs of points (that is, $n/2$-CESF) on the boundary of a single polygon. Erickson and Nayyeri [EN11] generalize the problem to the case of points on the boundaries of h polygonal obstacles; their algorithm is exponential in h. A practical aspect of the problem—computing non-crossing paths of specified thickness—was studied by Polishchuk and Mitchell [PM07]. Their algorithm computes a representation of the thick paths inside a simple polygon; they also show how to find shortest thick disjoint paths joining endpoints on the boundaries of polygonal obstacles (with exponential dependence on the number of obstacles). They also prove that the problem is hard to approximate. The main difficulty with multiple obstacles is deciding which homotopy class of the paths gives the minimum length. If the homotopy class of the paths is specified, then the problem is significantly easier [Bes03, EKL06, Ver13].

The graph version of k-CESF has been studied in the context of VLSI design. Given an edge-weighted plane graph G and a family of k vertex sets (called nets), the goal is to find a set of k non-crossing subgraphs interconnecting the nets such that the total weight is minimized. The problem is clearly NP-hard, as the special case $k = 1$ is STEINER TREE IN PLANAR GRAPHS (STP), a problem known to be NP-hard [GJ79]. STP admits a PTAS [BKM09]. For k terminal pairs (that is, size-2 nets) where all terminals lie on h faces of the given n-vertex plane graph, k-CESF can be solved in $\mathcal{O}(2^{\mathcal{O}(h^2)} n \log k)$ time [EN11]. If we allow k constant-size nets and restrict h to 2, then the problem is solvable even in $\mathcal{O}(n \log n)$ time [KMN01]. We list these results in Table 6.1; many entries are still open.

In the GROUP STEINER TREE problem, one is given a k-colored point set and the task is to find a minimum-length tree that connects at least one point of each color. The problem is discussed in a survey by Mitchell [Mit00]. Recently, Bateni et al. [BDHM16] gave a PTAS for the planar case. They also show APX-hardness of the planar GROUP STEINER FOREST problem, where only specified pairs of colors need to fulfill the connectivity requirement. Another related problem is that of constructing a minimum-length non-crossing path through a given sequence of points in the plane. Its complexity status remains open [PM05, Löfl1].

Table 6.1: Known and new results for k-CESF (hardness and approximation ratios).

k	k-CESF in Euclidean space	k-CESF in planar graphs
1	EST: NP-hard [GJ79], $1 + \varepsilon$ [Aro98, Mit99]	STP: NP-hard [GJ79], $1 + \varepsilon$ [BKM09]
2	$1 + \varepsilon$ (Theorem 6.4)	
3	$5/3 + \varepsilon$ (Theorem 6.5)	
general k	$k + \varepsilon$ (Theorem 6.1), $\mathcal{O}(\sqrt{n} \log k)$ (Theorem 6.3)	k const.-size nets on 2 faces, exact [KMN01]
$n/2$	NP-hard [BF98], $\mathcal{O}(\sqrt{n} \log n)$ [CHKL13]	k size-2 nets on const. many faces, exact [EN11]

6.2 Algorithms for k-CESF

Despite its simple formulation, the k-CESF problem seems to be rather difficult. There are instances where the optimum contains no straight-line edges or contains paths with repeated line segments; see Fig. 6.1a and 6.1b. This fact shows that obvious greedy algorithms fail to find an optimal solution, as Liebling et al. [LMM+95] observed. They also provided an instance of the problem in a unit square for $k = n/2$ in which the length of an optimal solution is in $\Omega(n\sqrt{n})$, whereas the trivial lower bound (the sum of lengths of straight-line segments connecting the pairs of terminals) is only $\mathcal{O}(n)$. The example is based on the existence of expander graphs with a quadratic number of edge crossings. In Fig. 6.1c, we provide an example in which the length of one of the curves in the optimal solution can be arbitrarily bigger than the trivial lower bound for the corresponding color.

In some cases, cycles will arise in our drawings. We will *cut* them by removing a longest segment from each cycle such that all terminals that were on a cycle remain connected. For any geometric graph G, we let $\|G\|$ denote its total edge length.

Efrat et al. [EHKP15] suggested an approximation algorithm for k-CESF. The key ingredient of their algorithm is the following observation, which shows how to make a pair of given trees non-crossing: reroute one of the trees using a "shell" around the other tree.

Lemma 6.1 (Efrat et al. [EHKP15]). *Let R and B be two trees in the plane spanning red and blue terminals, respectively. There exists a tree R' spanning the red terminals such that*

(i) *R' and B are non-crossing and*

(ii) *$\|R'\| \le \|R\| + 2\|B\|$.*

Efrat et al. [EHKP15] start with k (possibly intersecting) minimum spanning trees, one for each color. Then, they iteratively go through these trees in order of non-decreasing length. In every step, they reroute the next tree by laying a shell around the current solution as in Lemma 6.1. Their algorithm has approximation factor $k\rho$. We now show that the algorithm even yields approximation factor $k + \varepsilon$ if we use a PTAS for EST for the initial solution to each color.

Theorem 6.1. *For every positive ε, there is a $(k+\varepsilon)$-approximation algorithm for k-CESF.*

Proof. Fix an optimal solution $\mathcal{T}$. For $i = 1, \ldots, k$, let T_i be the length of the Steiner tree spanning color i in $\mathcal{T}$. Hence, OPT $= \sum_{i=1}^{k} T_i$. For each color $i = 1, \ldots, k$, use a PTAS to compute a Steiner tree of length $P_i \le (1+\varepsilon)T_i$. Now, consider the trees one by one in non-decreasing order of their lengths. Without loss of generality, we have $P_1 \le \ldots \le P_k$.

Let S_i denote the length of the Steiner tree spanning color $i \in \{1, \ldots, k\}$ in our solution $\mathcal{S}$. Lemma 6.1 yields $S_1 = P_1$ and $S_2 \le P_2 + 2P_1$. For the i-th tree with $2 \le i \le k$, we add a shell around every tree j with $j < i$. Observe that the tree and the shell give us a Steiner tree (after cutting any cycles) for i that does not intersect any tree built in a step j with $j < i$. Thus, we get $S_i \le P_i + \sum_{j=1}^{i-1} 2P_j$ and $\|\mathcal{S}\| = \sum_{i=1}^{k}(P_i + \sum_{j=1}^{i-1} 2P_j)$. Let $\overline{P} = (\sum_{i=1}^{k} P_i)/k$ be the average length of the Steiner trees. Since the Steiner trees P_i are ordered by non-decreasing lengths, we have $\sum_{j=1}^{i} P_j \le i \cdot \overline{P}$ for every $i \in \{1, \ldots, k\}$. This inequality yields

$$S_i = P_i + \sum_{j=1}^{i-1} 2P_j = \sum_{j=1}^{i-1} P_j + \sum_{j=1}^{i} P_j \le (2i-1)\overline{P},$$

which sums up to

$$\|\mathcal{S}\| \le \sum_{i=1}^{k}(2i-1)\overline{P} = k^2 \cdot \overline{P}.$$

Since $k \cdot \overline{P} = \sum_i P_i \le (1+\varepsilon)$ OPT, we have $\overline{P} \le (1+\varepsilon)$ OPT $/k$. Hence, the total length of our solution is

$$\|\mathcal{S}\| \le k^2 \cdot \overline{P} \le (1+\varepsilon)k \text{ OPT}. \qquad \square$$

For even k, we can slightly improve on this by using our PTAS for 2-CESF (Theorem 6.4).

Theorem 6.2. *For every positive ε, there is a $(k-1+\varepsilon)$-approximation algorithm for k-CESF if k is even.*

Proof. Fix an optimal solution $\mathcal{T}$. For $1 \le i \le k$, let P_i be the set of terminals of color i. Let $Q_1 = \bigcup_{i=1}^{k/2} P_i$ and $Q_2 = \bigcup_{j=1+k/2}^{k} P_j$. Call the terminals in Q_1 red and those in Q_2 blue. Further, let $\mathcal{T}^*$ be an optimal solution to the resulting 2-CESF instance I^*. Obviously, we have $\|\mathcal{T}^*\| \le \|\mathcal{T}\|$.

Let $\varepsilon' = \varepsilon/(k-1)$. We use the PTAS for 2-CESF of Theorem 6.4 to compute a solution $\mathcal{S}^*$ to I^* with $\|\mathcal{S}^*\| \le (1+\varepsilon')\|\mathcal{T}^*\|$. In general, $\mathcal{S}^*$ is not a valid solution to I. Let S_1 and S_2 be the Steiner trees connecting Q_1 and Q_2 in $\mathcal{S}^*$, respectively. We now create, for $1 \le i \le k/2$, a Steiner tree R_i connecting the terminals in P_i, as follows. Let R_1 be the smallest subtree of S_1 spanning the terminals in P_1. Thus, $\|R_1\| \le \|S_1\|$. We create R_2 by laying a shell around R_1 that goes through all terminals in P_2. Note that, at this point, R_2 still contains a cycle that has R_1 in its interior. For $3 \le i \le k/2$, we iteratively create R_i by laying a shell around the outer boundary of R_{i-1} that goes through all terminals in P_i. Finally, we cut the cycles of $R_2, \ldots, R_{k/2}$ at some point to create trees. Since each of these Steiner trees consists of a shell around S_1, the inequality $\|R_i\| \le 2\|S_1\|$ holds for $2 \le i \le k/2$. Analogously, we compute $R_{1+k/2}, \ldots, R_k$ with $\|R_{1+k/2}\| \le \|S_2\|$ and $\|R_j\| \le 2\|S_2\|$ for $2+k/2 \le j \le k$.

Our solution $\mathcal{R}$ to I consists of $R_1, \ldots, R_k$; its total length is

$$\|\mathcal{R}\| = \|R_1\| + \sum_{i=2}^{k/2} \|R_i\| + \|R_{1+k/2}\| + \sum_{j=2+k/2}^{k} \|R_j\|$$

$$\leq \|S_1\| + (\frac{k}{2} - 1) \cdot 2 \|S_1\| + \|S_2\| + (\frac{k}{2} - 1) \cdot 2 \|S_2\|$$

$$= (k-1) \|S_1\| + (k-1) \|S_2\|$$

$$= (k-1) \|S^*\|$$

$$\leq (k-1)(1+\varepsilon') \|\mathcal{T}^*\|$$

$$\leq (k-1 + (k-1)\varepsilon') \|\mathcal{T}\|$$

$$= (k-1+\varepsilon) \|\mathcal{T}\| \ . \qquad \square$$

Next, we present an approximation algorithm for k-CESF whose ratio depends only logarithmically on k but also depends on $\sqrt{n}$. The algorithm employs a space-filling curve through a set of given points. The curve was utilized in a heuristic for $(n/2)$-CESF by Liebling et al. [LMM+95]. Recently, Chan et al. [CHKL13] showed that the approach yields an $\mathcal{O}(\sqrt{n} \log n)$-approximation for $(n/2)$-CESF. We show that similar arguments yield an approximation ratio $\mathcal{O}(\sqrt{n} \log k)$ for general k.

Theorem 6.3. *k-CESF admits a (randomized) $\mathcal{O}(\sqrt{n} \log k)$-approximation algorithm.*

Proof. Chan et al. [CHKL13] gave a randomized algorithm to construct a curve C through the given set P of n points. Their curve has small *stretch*, that is, the ratio between the Euclidean distance $d(p, q)$ of two points $p, q \in P$ and their distance $d_C(p, q)$ along the curve is small. Assuming that the points are scaled to lie in a unit square, Chan et al. showed, for a fixed pair of points $p, q \in P$,

$$\mathbb{E}[d_C(p, q)] = \mathcal{O}\left(\sqrt{n} \log(\frac{1}{d(p, q)})\right) \cdot d(p, q) \ .$$

Using C, we construct a solution to k-CESF so that, for every color, the terminals are visited in the order given by the curve; and thus, the solution to every color is a path. All paths can be wrapped around the curve without intersecting each other; see Fig. 6.2.

If the order of the points along the curve for a specific color i is $p_1^i, \ldots, p_{n_i}^i$, then the length of the corresponding path is

$$\sum_{j=1}^{n_i-1} d_C(p_j^i, p_{j+1}^i) = d_C(p_1^i, p_{n_i}^i) \ .$$

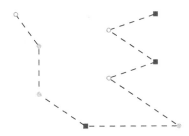
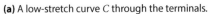
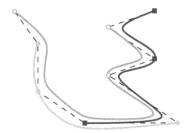

(a) A low-stretch curve C through the terminals.

(b) A 3-CESF solution to the instance created by wrapping paths around C.

Figure 6.2: Obtaining a solution to k-CESF by using a low-stretch curve. Depicted is the case $k = 3$.

Let $\overline{d} = \sum_{i=1}^{k} d(p_1^i, p_{n_i}^i)/k$. The total (expected) length of the solution is

$$\text{ALG} = \sum_{i=1}^{k} \mathbb{E}\left[d_C(p_1^i, p_{n_i}^i)\right] = \sum_{i=1}^{k} \mathcal{O}\left(\sqrt{n}\log(1/d(p_1^i, p_{n_i}^i))\right) \cdot d(p_1^i, p_{n_i}^i)$$

$$= \sum_{i=1}^{k} \mathcal{O}\left(\sqrt{n}\log(1/\overline{d})\right) \cdot \overline{d} .$$

Since the optimal solution to P connects all pairs of terminals of the same color (possibly using non-straight-line curves),

$$\text{OPT} \geq \sum_{i=1}^{k} d(p_1^i, p_{n_i}^i) = k\overline{d} .$$

Hence,

$$\text{ALG} = \sum_{i=1}^{k} \mathcal{O}\left(\sqrt{n}\log\left(\frac{k}{\text{OPT}}\right)\right) \cdot \frac{\text{OPT}}{k} = \mathcal{O}(\sqrt{n}\log k)\,\text{OPT} . \qquad \square$$

6.3 PTAS for 2-CESF

In this section, we show that 2-CESF admits a PTAS. We follow Arora's approach for computing EST [Aro98], which consists of the following steps. First, Arora performs a recursive geometric partitioning of the plane using a quadtree and snaps the input points to the corners of the tree. Next, he defines an *r-light* solution, which is allowed to cross an edge of a square in the quadtree at most r times and only at so-called *portals*. Then he builds an optimal *portal-respecting* solution using dynamic programming, and finally trims the edges of the solution to get the result. To get an algorithm for 2-CESF, we modify these steps as follows:

(i) The perturbation step, which snaps the terminal to a grid, is modified to avoid crossings between trees. Similarly, the reverse step transforming a perturbed instance solution into one to the original instance is different; see Lemmas 6.2 and 6.3.

(ii) We use a different notion of an r-light solution in which every *portal* is crossed at most r times. We devise a *portal-crossing reduction* that reduces the number of crossings to $r = 3$; see Lemma 6.5.

(iii) The base case of dynamic programming needs a special modification; it computes a set of crossing-free Steiner trees of minimum total length (see Lemma 6.6).

We assume that the bounding rectangles of the two sets of input terminals overlap; otherwise, we can use a PTAS to obtain a Steiner tree for each input set individually. We first snap the instance to an $(L \times L)$-grid with $L = \mathcal{O}(n)$. We proceed as follows. Let L_0 be the diameter of the smallest bounding box of the given 2-CESF instance. We place an $(L \times L)$-grid of granularity (grid cell size) $g = L_0/L$ inside the bounding box. By scaling the instance appropriately, we can assume that the granularity $g = 1$. We move each terminal of one color to the closest grid point in an even row and column (without loss of generality, we assume there is only one such closest grid point), and each terminal of the other color to the closest grid point in an odd row and column. Thus, the grid point for each terminal is uniquely defined, and no terminals of different color end up at the same location. If there are more terminals of the same color on a grid point, we remove all but one of them. We call the resulting instance a *perturbed* instance.

In what follows, let ε denote an arbitrarily small positive constant. We will fix its value at the end.

Lemma 6.2. *Let* OPT_I *be the length of an optimal solution to a 2-CESF instance I of n terminals. There is an* $(L \times L)$-*grid with* $L = \mathcal{O}(n/\varepsilon)$ *such that* $\mathrm{OPT}_{I^*} \leq (1 + \varepsilon)\,\mathrm{OPT}_I$ *holds, where* OPT_{I^*} *is the length of an optimal solution to the perturbed instance* I^*.

Proof. Choose L to be a power of 2 within the interval $[3\sqrt{2}n/\varepsilon, 6\sqrt{2}n/\varepsilon]$ and perturb the instance as described above. Consider an optimal solution to I. Iteratively, we connect every terminal in I^* to the optimum solution as follows: Connect the terminal to the closest point of the tree in the optimum solution that has the same color. If this line segment crosses the tree of the other color, then reroute this tree around the line segment by using two copies of the line segment. Two copies suffice even if the other tree is crossed more than once since all crossing edges can be connected to the two new line segments. The distance between the terminal and the tree is at most the distance between the terminal and the corresponding terminal in I, which is bounded by $\sqrt{2}$ as we are assuming the unit grid. Hence, we pay at most $3\sqrt{2}$ for connecting the terminal. Since the bounding rectangles of the input terminals overlap, $\mathrm{OPT}_I \geq L$. Thus, the additional length of an optimal solution to I^* is

$$\mathrm{OPT}_{I^*} - \mathrm{OPT}_I \leq 3\sqrt{2}n \leq \varepsilon\,\mathrm{OPT}_I \,. \qquad \square$$

The next lemma, proven analogously to Lemma 6.2, shows that a solution to the perturbed instance can be transformed into one to the original instance.

Lemma 6.3. *Given a solution* $\mathcal{T}$ *to the perturbed instance as defined in Lemma 6.2, we can transform* $\mathcal{T}$ *into a solution to the original instance, increasing its length by at most* $\varepsilon\,\mathrm{OPT}_I$.

In the following, we assume that the instance is perturbed. We place a quadtree in dependence of two integers $a, b \in [0, \dots, L-1]$ that we choose independently uniformly at random.

We place the origin of the coordinate system on the bottom left corner of the bounding box of our instance. Then we take a box B whose width and height is twice the width and height of the bounding box. We place it such that its bottom left corner has coordinates $(-a, -b)$. Note that the bounding box is inside B. We extend the $(L \times L)$-grid to cover B. Thus, we have an $(L' \times L')$-grid with $L' = 2L$.

Next, we partition B with a quadtree along the $(L' \times L')$-grid. The partition is stopped when the current quadtree box coincides with a grid cell. We define the *level of a quadtree square* to be its depth in the quadtree. Thus, B has level 0, whereas the level of a leaf is bounded by $\log L' = \log(2L) = \mathcal{O}(\log n)$. Then, for each grid line ℓ, we define its *level* as the highest (that is, of minimum value) level of all the quadtree squares that touch ℓ (but which are not crossed by it).

Let $m = \lceil 4 \log L'/\varepsilon \rceil$. On each grid line ℓ of level i, we place $2^i m$ equally spaced points. We call these points *portals*. Thus, each square contains at most m portals on each of its edges. A solution that crosses the grid lines only at portals is called *portal-respecting*. We show that there is a close-to-optimal portal-respecting solution. Note that, in contrast to Arora, we first make the solution portal-respecting before reducing the number of crossings on each grid line. The proof of the following lemma is similar to the Arora's prove.

Lemma 6.4. *Let* OPT_I *be the length of an optimal solution to a 2-CESF instance I. There exists a position of the quadtree and a portal-respecting solution to I of length at most* $(1 + \varepsilon)\,\mathrm{OPT}_I$.

Proof. Fix an optimal solution $\mathcal{T}$. Move all crossings on the grid lines to the closest portals by adding a line segment on each side of the grid. Note that the modified solution remains crossing-free.

Consider a grid line ℓ that has a non-empty intersection with the bounding box B. Let $t(\ell)$ be the number of crossing points between ℓ and $\mathcal{T}$. If i is the level of ℓ, then the inter-portal distance on ℓ is $L'/(2^i m)$. Since the position of the quadtree has been chosen uniformly at random, the probability that the level of ℓ is i is at most $2^i/L'$. Thus, the expected length increase of $\mathcal{T}$ due to moving the crossings to the portals of ℓ is at most

$$\sum_{i=1}^{\log L'} \frac{2^i}{L'} \cdot t(\ell) \cdot \frac{L'}{2^i m} \leq \frac{t(\ell) \log L'}{m} \leq \frac{\varepsilon}{4} \cdot t(\ell),$$

where the last inequality follows from $m \geq 4 \log L'/\varepsilon$. Thus, the expected total increase in length is at most $\varepsilon/4 \sum_{\text{gridline } \ell} t(\ell)$.
Next, we show

$$\sum_{\text{gridline } \ell} t(\ell) \leq 4\,\mathrm{OPT}.$$

Consider any line segment of the solution. Let l be the length of the line segment. Given the granularity $g = 1$ of the grid, the line segment crosses at most $l + 1$ horizontal grid lines and at most $l + 1$ vertical grid lines; hence, its contribution to the left-hand side of the equation is at most $4l$.

Thus, we have shown that the expected length increase is at most $\varepsilon\,\mathrm{OPT}$. But then, there exists a position of the quadtree for which the total length increase is bounded by $\varepsilon\,\mathrm{OPT}$. We can try out all positions of the quadtree which increases the total run time by a factor of $\mathcal{O}(n^2)$. $\qquad\square$

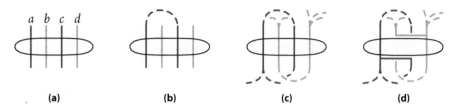

Figure 6.3: A portal modification for four passes.

The last ingredient for our dynamic programming is to reduce the number of crossings in every portal. We call a solution *r-light* if each portal is crossed at most *r* times. (Note that we use a different definition than Arora. He defined a solution to be *r*-light if a grid line is crossed at most *r* times.)

In the following, we explain an operation which we call a *portal-crossing reduction*. We are given a portal-respecting solution consisting of two Steiner trees R and B (red and blue) and we want to reduce (that is, modify without increasing its length) it such that R and B pass through each portal at most three times in total.

Lemma 6.5. *Every portal-respecting solution of 2-CESF can be transformed into a 3-light portal-respecting solution without increasing its length.*

Proof. Consider a sequence of passes through a portal. We assume that there are no terminals in the portals. If two adjacent passes belong to the same tree, then we can eliminate one of them by snapping it to the other one. If this operation creates cycles, we cut them. Therefore, we can assume that the passes form an alternating sequence. It suffices to show that any alternating sequence of four passes can be reduced to two passes by shortening the trees. Let a, b, c, and d be such a sequence as shown in Fig. 6.3a, where the passes a and c belong to B and b and d to R. We cut the passes b and c. This cut results in two components in each tree. Without loss of generality, the pass a and the upper part of c belong to the same component; see Fig. 6.3b. Otherwise, we can change the colors because (i) a and the lower part of c are connected, and (ii) the upper part of b and d are connected.

Since R and B are disjoint, d and the lower part of b are in the same component; see Fig. 6.3c. We connect the component as shown in Fig. 6.3d and shorten the trees (for instance, the lower part of b can be reduced to a terminal of R). Note that the passes a and d remain in the solution, while the passes b and c are eliminated. We repeat the procedure for the remaining passes, until there are at most three passes left. The length of the solution does not increase because the portal has width 0.   □

With the next Lemma 6.6, we show how to find a close-to-optimal 3-light portal-respecting solution to the perturbed instance. We assume that an appropriate quadtree (as defined in Lemma 6.4) is given.

Lemma 6.6. *Given a perturbed instance I^* of an n-terminal 2-CESF instance, we can compute, in $\mathcal{O}(n^{\mathcal{O}(1/\varepsilon)})$ time and $\mathcal{O}(n^{\mathcal{O}(1/\varepsilon)})$ space, a solution of length at most $(1 + \varepsilon)\,\mathrm{OPT}_{I^*}$, where OPT_{I^*} is the length of an optimal 3-light portal-respecting solution to I^*.*

Proof. We use dynamic programming where a subproblem consists of

(a) a square A of the quadtree,

(b) a set B of point sequences, one on each portal on the border of the square, where each sequence consists of up to three red and blue points, and

(c) a *non-crossing* partition C of these points into sets of the same color.

A partition of the points yielded by B is non-crossing if for no four points a, b, c, d, occurring in that order on the boundary of the square, it holds that a and c belong to one set of the partition, and b and d to another one. The goal is to find an optimal collection of crossing-free red and blue Steiner trees, such that each set of the partition and each terminal inside the square is contained in a tree of the same color.

The base case of dynamic programming is a unit square, which is either empty or contains terminals only at corners of the square. If the square is empty, we consider each set of the partition as an instance of 1-CESF and solve it by the PTAS for EST [Aro98]. For each point set, we force its Steiner tree to lie inside its convex hull by projecting any part of the solution outside the convex hull to its border. Since the partition is non-crossing, the convex hulls of its point sets are pairwise disjoint. Therefore, the Steiner trees and their union is also a close-to-optimal solution to the base case. If the square contains (up to four) terminals at the corners, these terminals are treated in a similar way as portals.

For composite squares in the quadtree, we proceed as follows. For the four squares that subdivide the composite square, we consider all combinations of all possible sequences for B and partitions for C that match together and match the subproblem. In the dynamic programming, we have already computed a close-to-optimal solution to every choice of the sequences for B and partition for C of each of the four squares; taking the best combination gives a close-to-optimal solution.

The size of the dynamic programming table is proportional to the number "(a)×(b)×(c)" of subproblems. There are $\mathcal{O}(n^2)$ possibilities for A as there are $\mathcal{O}(n^2)$ squares in the quadtree in total. Each square contains $\mathcal{O}(\log n/\varepsilon)$ portals. For each portal, there is a constant number of possible sequences of up to three colored points. Thus, there are $2^{\mathcal{O}(\log n/\varepsilon)} = n^{\mathcal{O}(1/\varepsilon)}$ possibilities for the set B of sequences. Since the number of non-crossing partitions of a set of k elements is the k-th Catalan number $\mathbf{C}_k$, we have

$$\mathbf{C}_{\mathcal{O}(\log n/\varepsilon)} = 2^{\mathcal{O}(\log n/\varepsilon)} = n^{\mathcal{O}(1/\varepsilon)}$$

possibilities for the partition C. In total, we consider $n^{\mathcal{O}(1/\varepsilon)}$ subproblems in the dynamic programming.

The run time to solve an instance of the base case is polynomial in $\mathcal{O}(\log n/\varepsilon)$. The run time to handle a composite square is polynomial in $(n^{\mathcal{O}(1/\varepsilon)})^4$, which is $n^{\mathcal{O}(1/\varepsilon)}$. Thus, the total run time is bounded by $n^{\mathcal{O}(1/\varepsilon)}$. $\qquad\square$

Now, we prove the main result of this section.

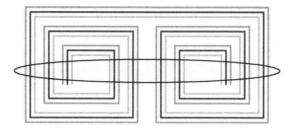

Figure 6.4: A difficult portal crossing of a 3-CESF instance.

Theorem 6.4. *2-CESF admits a PTAS.*

Proof. Consider a 2-CESF instance I. Let OPT be the length of an optimum solution. For any positive ε, by Lemmas 6.2, 6.4 and 6.5, the length OPT' of an optimal 3-light portal-respecting solution to the perturbed version of I is a most $(1+\varepsilon)$ OPT. Using Lemma 6.6, we find a 3-light portal-respecting solution to the perturbed instance of length at most

$$(1+\varepsilon)\,\mathrm{OPT}' \;\leq\; (1+\varepsilon)(1+\varepsilon)\,\mathrm{OPT}\,.$$

By Lemma 6.3, we transform the solution into a solution to I by increasing its length by at most ε OPT. Therefore, for every positive ε', we can construct a solution to I of length

$$(1+\varepsilon)(1+\varepsilon)\,\mathrm{OPT} + \varepsilon\,\mathrm{OPT} \;\leq\; (1+\varepsilon')\,\mathrm{OPT}$$

by choosing an appropriate value for ε. □

6.4 Algorithm for 3-CESF

The approach for 2-CESF described in Section 6.3 cannot be directly applied to 3-CESF since optimal trees may need to pass portals many times. For example, the three paths crossing the portal in Fig. 6.4 are difficult because we cannot locally reroute them to make them $\mathcal{O}(1)$-light as in Lemma 6.5.

Instead, we now improve the approximation ratio of $3+\varepsilon$ (from Theorem 6.1) to $5/3+\varepsilon$. We re-use some ideas of the approach for 2-CESF.

To this end, take an optimal solution T for 3-CESF. The terminals are red, green, and blue; we call the corresponding trees R, G, and B. We assume that B is the cheapest among the three trees. In the beginning, we construct a quadtree partitioning the plane and choose the portals, for a given ε, as described in Section 6.3. We then make the solution portal-respecting, which results in a solution T^* consisting of trees R^*, G^*, and B^*. In expectation, this operation increases the length of each of the trees (and hence, of T) by a factor at most $1+\varepsilon$.

First, we show that we have few portal passes if the blue and the green tree do not *meet* at any portal, that is, no blue and green passes are adjacent.

Lemma 6.7. *Consider a portal-respecting solution T^* to 3-CESF consisting of trees R^*, G^*, B^*. If B^* and G^* do not meet at any portal, then T^* can be transformed into a 7-light portal-respecting solution.*

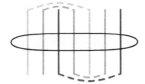 

Figure 6.5: Constructing a 7-light solution to an instance without adjacent blue-green passes (one of several possible cases).

Proof. Apply the portal-crossing reduction from Lemma 6.5 and consider a portal. Recall that, after this operation, there are no *rbrb* and *rgrg* subsequences in the passes of the portal. Here, r, b, and g correspond to the passes of the trees R^*, B^*, and G^*, respectively. If the portal has only one blue or one green pass, then the solution is already 7-light at the portal (with the longest possible sequences *rgrbrgr* and *rbrgrbr*, respectively). Otherwise, it contains at least two blue and at least two green passes. Notice that the sequence of passes must be *r-alternate*, that is, of the form $\ldots r \vartriangle r \vartriangle r \ldots$, where $\vartriangle \in \{g, b\}$, since blue and green do not meet. Thus, a sequence of more than seven passes must contain a subsequence *grbrgrb* (or a symmetric one, *brgrbrg*). These subsequences are reducible. See Fig. 6.5 for one of the possible cases, the other cases are analogous. □

Now, we show that T^* can be transformed into a 10-light portal-respecting solution T' of length at most $\|R^*\| + \|G^*\| + 3\|B^*\|$.

Lemma 6.8. *A portal-respecting solution T^* to 3-CESF, consisting of trees B^*, R^*, and G^*, can be transformed into a portal-respecting solution T' such that*

(i) T' passes at most ten times through each portal, and

(ii) $\|T'\| \le \|R^*\| + \|G^*\| + 3\|B^*\|$.

Proof. We define a BG-*solution*; informally, this is a solution in which we are allowed to connect green branches to the blue tree (if they never meet, we can apply Lemma 6.7). Formally, a BG-solution is a set of crossing-free trees consisting of a blue tree, a red tree and a forest of green trees. Every terminal is contained in a tree of its color and every green tree is attached to the blue tree. Note that, in general, a BG-solution is not a valid 3-CESF solution. We prove the lemma in two steps. First, we show that T can be transformed to a portal-respecting BG-solution T^{BG} with at most six passes per portal having the same (or smaller) length. Then, we show how T^{BG} can be further modified to get a portal-respecting solution T^* with at most 10 passes per portal and the desired length.

In order to construct T^{BG} from T^*, we first replace, as in Lemma 6.5, all uni-colored sequences of passes (that is, consisting of passes of the same color) in a portal by a single pass, and all bi-colored sequences of passes by at most three passes. We call this procedure the *initial reduction*. Consequently, uni-colored and bi-colored portals have at most three passes; hence, we focus on the portals containing passes of all three colors.

We can assume that there is a portal in which a blue and a green pass are adjacent (otherwise, we already have a 7-light instance by Lemma 6.7.). We eliminate the green pass by connecting it to its neighboring blue pass; see Fig. 6.6b. We thus may consider the blue and the green tree

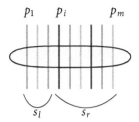
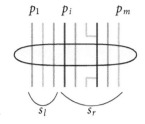
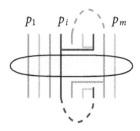

(a) A tri-colored portal after the initial reduction.

(b) Eliminating the green passes that meet a blue pass.

(c) Applying the portal reduction to s_l and s_r.

Figure 6.6: Construction of a BG-solution to a portal.

to be connected and together to form a blue-green tree. Its length is $\|B^*\| + \|G^*\|$. After this step, the sequence of passes is r-alternate.

Consider now a tri-colored portal in T after the initial reduction. Let $(p_1, \ldots, p_m)$ be a sequence of passes through the portal and suppose that pass p_i (for $1 \le i \le m$) is the leftmost blue pass; see Fig. 6.6a. Split the sequence into two subsequences $s_l = (p_1, \ldots, p_{i-1})$ and $s_r = (p_i, \ldots, p_m)$. Since p_i is the leftmost blue pass, it holds that s_l is bi-colored and, by the initial reduction, satisfies $\|s_l\| \le 3$. Regarding s_r, we apply the portal-crossing reduction according to Lemma 6.5 by viewing the blue and the green passes as passes of a single blue-green tree; see Fig. 6.6c. As a result, we get a new instance s_r' with $\|s_r'\| \le 3$. Recall that, before this step, the blue and the green tree are connected; thus, every blue and green pass is connected to the leftmost pass p_i. Furthermore, after disconnecting a blue pass in the proof of Lemma 6.5, one part remains connected to p_i by a blue path, and the other part gets connected to p_i by a blue segment. For the green passes, one part remains connected to p_i, while the other part gets connected to p_i by a green segment. Since the blue segments where connected before this step, the blue tree remains connected after the portal-crossing reduction. The green tree is split into subtrees that are connected to the blue tree. Therefore, the new instance is a BG-solution. The sequence of passes in the portal for T^{BG} is a concatenation of s_l and s_r' and, hence, has at most six passes per portal.

Note that the constructed solution T^{BG} has at most two blue passes per portal. We add a green shell to B to connect green branches. This operation increases the number of passes per portal by at most 4. The resulting solution T^* has length bounded by $\|R^*\| + \|G^*\| + 3\|B^*\|$ and at most ten passes per portal. □

Before we describe our approximation algorithm, we first need to discuss the perturbation step. The perturbation itself is the same as in Section 6.3: We move each terminal to a uniquely defined grid point (we assign the grid points of even row and odd column to the third color) and merge terminals of the same color to one terminal. However, we need a different technique to transform a solution to the original instance into a solution to the perturbed instance and vice versa.

Lemma 6.9. *Let I be a 3-CESF instance with n terminals, let OPT_I be the length of an optimal solution to I. For every positive ε, we can place an $(L \times L)$-grid with $L = \mathcal{O}(n/\varepsilon)$ such that, for the perturbed instance I^* of I, $\mathrm{OPT}_{I^*} \le (1 + \varepsilon)\,\mathrm{OPT}_I$.*

Proof. We proceed similar as in the proof of Lemma 6.2 by connecting each terminal of I^* to the closest point of its corresponding tree. Since this connection can cross segments of two colors, we have to be more careful with the rerouting. We choose L as a power of 2 within the interval $[7\sqrt{2}n/\varepsilon, 14\sqrt{2}n/\varepsilon]$.

Fix an optimal solution to I. Consider a terminal v of I^* of, say, green color. Connect it to the closest point of the green tree by a straight-line segment s. Note that the length $\|s\|$ of this segment is bounded from above by the distance of v to its corresponding terminal in I, which is at most $\sqrt{2}$ as we have a unit grid.

Assume that s intersects red or blue segments. Their intersection points with s impose a unique ordering of the segments where the segment with the intersection point closest to v is defined as the last segment; see Fig. 6.7 for an example. We reroute the first three segments along s going around v. This operation yields a 3-layer shell around v. Consider the next segment according to the ordering and reroute it along s and around v. We can view the crossing point of this segment with the shell as a portal on one side of s. This portal contains four bi-colored passes. Using Lemma 6.5, we reduce the number of passes to at most three. Now, we stretch this portal around v along s until it reaches the crossing point on the other side of s. Since the portal has at most three passes, the shell around v still consists of three layers. We repeat this procedure until all segments are rerouted around v.

By using this rerouting for every terminal in I^*, the total length of the solution increases by at most $(\sqrt{2} + 6 \cdot \sqrt{2})n = 7\sqrt{2}n$. Since $\mathrm{OPT}_I \geq L$, the length of an optimal solution to I^* is at most

$$\mathrm{OPT}_I + 7\sqrt{2}n \leq (1+\varepsilon)\,\mathrm{OPT}_I . \qquad \square$$

Analogously to the proof of Lemma 6.9, we transform a solution to a perturbed instance back into one to the original instance by not increasing the length too much. Then, we combine the lemmas to prove the main result of this section.

Lemma 6.10. *We can transform a solution $\mathcal{T}$ to the perturbed instance I^* into a solution to the original instance I, increasing the length by at most $\varepsilon\,\mathrm{OPT}_I$.*

Proof. Iteratively connect each terminal of the original instance to the solution $\mathcal{T}$ analogously to the proof of Lemma 6.9. Again, we pay at most 14 units per terminal, which yields the claim. $\qquad \square$

Using Lemmas 6.8, 6.9 and 6.10, we are ready to prove the main result of this section.

Theorem 6.5. *For every positive ε, 3-CESF admits a $(5/3 + \varepsilon)$-approximation algorithm.*

Proof. Let $\varepsilon' = \sqrt[3]{1 + 3\varepsilon/5} - 1$. Let T be an optimal solution to a 3-CESF instance I with trees R, G and B. Without loss of generality, assume $\|B\| \leq \|R\|$ and $\|B\| \leq \|G\|$. Let OPT_I denote the length $\|R\| + \|G\| + \|B\|$ of T. We first construct a portal-respecting solution T^* of length

$$\|T^*\| = \|R^*\| + \|G^*\| + \|B^*\| \leq (1+\varepsilon')(\|R\| + \|G\| + \|B\|) .$$

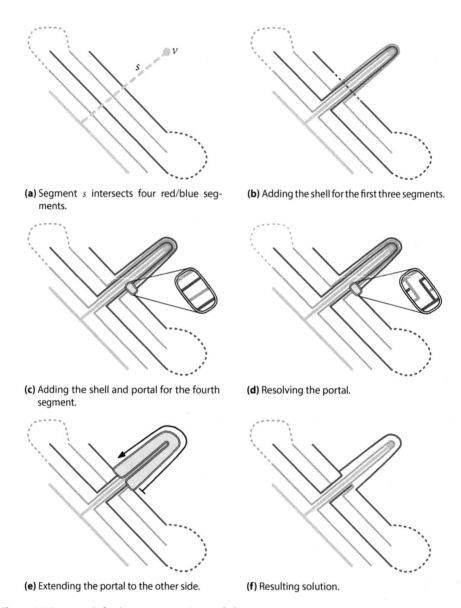

(a) Segment s intersects four red/blue segments.

(b) Adding the shell for the first three segments.

(c) Adding the shell and portal for the fourth segment.

(d) Resolving the portal.

(e) Extending the portal to the other side.

(f) Resulting solution.

Figure 6.7: An example for the rerouting in the proof of Lemma 6.9.

Then we obtain by Lemma 6.8 an optimal 10-light portal-respecting solution T' of length

$$\|T'\| \leq \|R^*\| + \|G^*\| + 3\|B^*\|$$
$$\leq \frac{5}{3}\|T^*\|$$
$$\leq \frac{5}{3}(1 + \varepsilon') \cdot (\|R\| + \|G\| + \|B\|)$$
$$= \frac{5}{3}(1 + \varepsilon') \cdot \mathrm{OPT}_I .$$

Using a dynamic program similar to the one described in Section 6.3 and Lemma 6.9, we find a 10-light portal-respecting solution of length $(1 + \varepsilon')\|T'\|$ to the perturbed instance I^* of I. By Lemma 6.10, we can transform our solution to I^* into a solution to I whose total length is bounded by

$$(1 + \varepsilon')^2 \|T'\| \leq \frac{5}{3}(1 + \varepsilon')^3 \, \mathrm{OPT}_I < \left(\frac{5}{3} + \varepsilon\right) \mathrm{OPT}_I . \qquad \square$$

6.5 Conclusion

We have presented approximation algorithms for k-CESF. For $k = 2$, we achieved a PTAS, for $k = 3$, a ratio of $5/3 + \varepsilon$, and for general k, ratios $k + \varepsilon$ and $\mathcal{O}(\sqrt{n}\log k)$.

We leave a number of interesting questions open. Is k-CESF APX-hard for some $k \geq 3$? Can we improve the run time of the PTAS for 2-CESF from $\mathcal{O}(n^{\mathcal{O}(1/\varepsilon)})$ to $\mathcal{O}(n(\log n)^{\mathcal{O}(1/\varepsilon)})$ as Arora [Aro98] did for EST? Can we obtain better approximation ratios for k-CESF when k greater than 2?

Another inviting direction is to study an "anchored" version of k-CESF where we are only allowed to draw straight line segments between input points of any colors. Any α-approximation algorithm for k-CESF yields an $\alpha(1 + \sqrt{3})/2$- approximation algorithm for the anchored version.

7 Minimum Rectilinear Polygons for Given Angle Sequences

A rectilinear polygon is a polygon whose edges are axis-aligned. Walking counterclockwise on the boundary of such a polygon yields a sequence of left turns and right turns, The number of left turns always equals the number of right turns plus 4. It is known that every sequence of $r + 4$ left and r right turns can be realized by a rectilinear polygon. In this chapter, we consider the problem of finding realizations that minimize the perimeter, or the area of the polygon, or the area of the bounding box of the polygon. We show that all three problems are NP-hard in general and we consider the special cases of x-monotone and xy-monotone rectilinear polygons. For these, we can optimize the three objectives efficiently.

7.1 Introduction

In this chapter, we consider the problem of computing, for a given *rectilinear angle sequence*, a "small" rectilinear polygon that realizes the sequence. A rectilinear angle sequence S is a sequence of left ($+90°$) turns, denoted by L, and right ($-90°$) turns, denoted by R. We write $S = (s_1, \ldots, s_n) \in \{L, R\}^n$, where n is the *length* of S. As we consider only rectilinear angle sequences, we usually drop the term "rectilinear." A polygon P *realizes* an angle sequence S if there is a counterclockwise (*ccw*) walk along the boundary of P such that the turns at the vertices of P, encountered during the walk, form the sequence S. The turn at a vertex v of P is a left or right turn if the interior angle at v is $90°$ (v is convex) or, respectively, $270°$ (v is reflex). We call the problem MINIMUM RECTILINEAR POLYGON FOR GIVEN ANGLE SEQUENCE.

In order to measure the size of a polygon, we only consider polygons that lie on the integer grid. In this context, the *area* of a polygon P corresponds to the number of grid cells that lie in the interior of P. The *bounding box* of P is the smallest axis-parallel enclosing rectangle of P. The *perimeter* of P is the sum of the lengths of the edges of P. The task is, for a given angle sequence S, to find a simple[1] polygon that realizes S and minimizes

(a) its bounding box,

(b) its area, or

(c) its perimeter.

Thereby, *minimizing the bounding box* is short for *minimizing the area of the bounding box*. Figure 7.1 shows that, in general, the three criteria cannot be minimized simultaneously.

Obviously, the angle sequence of a polygon is unique (up to rotation), but the number of polygons that realize a given angle sequence is unbounded. The formula for the angle sum of a

---

[1] We use the following strong notion of simplicity: A polyline is *simple* if it visits every grid point at most once. Thus, neither crossings nor revisits of a same point are allowed. Similarly, a polygon is simple if the (closed) polyline realizing its boundary is simple.

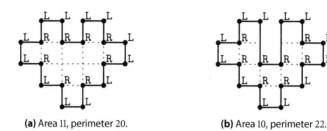

(a) Area 11, perimeter 20.   **(b)** Area 10, perimeter 22.

Figure 7.1: Two polygons realizing the same angle sequence. The bounding box of both polygons has area 20, but (a) shows a polygon of minimum perimeter and (b) one of minimum area.

polygon implies that, in any angle sequence, $n = 2r + 4$, where n is the length of the sequence and r is the number of right turns. In other words, the number of right turns is exactly four less than the number of left turns.

Related Work.   Bae et al. [BOS12] considered, for a given angle sequence S, the polygon $P(S)$ that realizes S and minimizes its area. They studied the following question: Given a number n, find an angle sequence S of length n such that the area of $P(S)$ is minimized, or maximized. Let $\delta(n)$ denote the minimum area and let $\Delta(n)$ denote the maximum area for n. They showed

(i) $\delta(n) = n/2 - 1$ if $n \equiv 4 \bmod 8$, $\delta(n) = n/2$ otherwise, and

(ii) $\Delta(n) = (n - 2)(n + 4)/8$ for any n with $n \geq 4$.

The result for $\Delta(n)$ tells us that any angle sequence S of length n can be realized by a polygon with area at most $(n - 2)(n + 4)/8$.

Several authors have explored the problem of realizing a turn sequence. Culberson and Rawlins [CR85] and Hartley [Har89] described algorithms that, given a sequence of exterior angles summing up to 2π, construct a simple polygon realizing that angle sequence. Culberson and Rawlins' algorithm, when constrained to $\pm 90°$ angles, produces polygons with no colinear edges, implying that any n-vertex polygon can be drawn with area approximately $(n/2 - 1)^2$. However, as Bae et al. [BOS12] showed, the bound is not tight.

In his PhD thesis, Sack [Sac84] introduced label sequences (which are equivalent to turn sequences) and, among others, developed a grammar for label sequences that can be realized as simple rectilinear polygons.

Vijayan and Wigderson [VW85] considered the problem of efficiently drawing *rectilinear graphs*, of which rectilinear polygons are a special case, using an edge labeling that is equivalent to a turn sequence in the case of paths and cycles.

In graph drawing, the standard approach to drawing a graph of maximum degree 4 orthogonally (that is, with rectilinear edges) is the topology–shape–metrics approach of Tamassia [Tam87]:

(1) Compute a planar(ized) embedding, that is, a circular order of edges around each vertex that admits a crossing-free drawing;

Table 7.1: Summary of our results.

Type of sequences	Minimum area	Min. bounding box	Minimum perimeter
general	NP-hard	NP-hard	NP-hard
x-monotone	$\mathcal{O}(n^4)$	$\mathcal{O}(n^3)$	$\mathcal{O}(n^2)$
xy-monotone	$\mathcal{O}(n)$	$\mathcal{O}(n)$	$\mathcal{O}(n)$

(2) compute an *orthogonal representation*, that is, an angle sequence for each edge and an angle for each vertex;

(3) *compact* the graph, that is, draw it inside a bounding box of minimum area.

Unless P = NP, Step (3) does not admit a PTAS for planar graphs, as shown by Patrignani [Pat01], and it is inapproximable within a polynomial factor for non-planar graphs, as shown by Bannister et al. [BES12]. Note that an orthogonal representation computed in step (2) is essentially an angle sequence for each face of the planarized embedding, so our problem corresponds to step (3) in the special case that the input graph is a simple cycle.

Another related work contains the reconstruction of a simple (non-rectilinear) polygon from partial geometric information. Disser et al. [DMW11] constructed a simple polygon in $\mathcal{O}(n^3 \log n)$ time from an ordered sequence of angles measured at the vertices visible from each vertex. The run time was improved to $\mathcal{O}(n^2)$, which is optimal in the worst-case [CW12]. Biedl et al. [BDS11] considered polygon reconstruction from points (instead of angles) captured by laser scanning devices. Very recently, Asaeedi et al. [ADA18] encloses a given set of points by a simple polygon whose vertices are a subset of the points and that optimizes some criteria (minimum area, maximum perimeter or maximum number of vertices). The vertex angles are constrained to lie below a threshold.

Our Contribution.   First, we show that finding a minimum polygon that realizes a given angle sequence is NP-hard for any of the three measures: bounding box area, polygon area, and polygon perimeter; see Section 7.2. This hardness result extends the one of Patrignani [Pat01] and settles an open question that he posed. We note that in a previous abstract [EFK+16], on which this chapter is based, there were some inaccuracies in our proof that now have been addressed.

In this chapter, we also give efficient algorithms for special types of angle sequences, namely xy- and *x-monotone sequences*, which are realized by xy-monotone and x-monotone polygons, respectively. For example, Figure 7.1 depicts an x-monotone polygon realizing the x-monotone sequence LLRRLLRLLRLRLRLLRLRLLR. Our algorithms for these angle sequences minimize the bounding box and the area (Section 7.3) and the perimeter (Section 7.4). For an overview of our results, see Table 7.1. Throughout this chapter, a *segment* is always an axis-aligned line segment.

7.2 NP-Hardness of the General Case

In contrast to the special cases that we efficiently solve in later sections, the general case of our problem turns out to be NP-hard. In two steps, we show NP-hardness for all three objectives: minimizing the perimeter of the polygon, the area occupied by the polygon, and the area of the bounding box. First, in Section 7.2.1, we consider the base problem defined below (Definition 7.1) from whose NP-hardness we then derive the three desired results in Section 7.2.1.

The setting of the base problem is a little different from the general case. Given an angle sequence S, we do not look for a polygon that realizes it while minimizing one of the three objectives, but for a polyline that lies within some given rectangle. We say that a (simple rectilinear) polyline P *realizes* S if we can walk along P from one of its endpoints to the other one and observe exactly the same angle sequence as S. Note that the endpoints of P do not have angles, hence, a polyline that realizes S has $|S| + 2$ vertices (including its endpoints) and $|S| + 1$ edges. Furthermore, if all edges of P have unit length, then $\mathrm{peri}(P) = |S| + 1$. For polylines in this section, we define $|P|$ as the number of inner vertices of P, that is, $|P| = |S|$. Throughout the section, we will interchangeably use the names of angle sequences to refer to fixed polylines realizing them. For example, $\mathrm{peri}(S)$ would denote the perimeter of a polyline realizing S that we fixed before.

Definition 7.1 (FITBOUNDINGBOX). An instance $\langle S, W, H \rangle$ of FITBOUNDINGBOX consists of an angle sequence S and positive even integers W and H. A *feasible drawing* of S (with respect to W and H) is a simple rectilinear polyline P realizing S within an axis-parallel rectangle of width $W + 10$ and height $H + 10$ such that the first and last edge of P are horizontal and such that P can be extended to a simple polygon (not necessarily within the rectangle) by connecting its endpoints with a simple rectilinear polyline. An instance is called a *no-instance* if there is no feasible drawing of S. An instance is called a *yes-instance* if there is a feasible drawing of S within an (even smaller) axis-parallel rectangle R of width W and height H such that the first vertex of P lies in the upper-left corner of R and the last vertex of P lies in the lower-right corner of R. An instance is *valid* if it is a yes- or a no-instance (note that not every instance is valid). The problem is to decide whether a given valid instance of FITBOUNDINGBOX is a yes- or a no-instance.

The "gap" between yes- and no-instances will help us to differentiate among them in our hardness proof: To classify a valid instance as a yes-instance, it suffices to show that it admits a feasible drawing and, similarly, to classify it as a no-instance, it suffices to show that it does not admit a feasible drawing in the smaller $(W \times H)$-rectangle.

7.2.1 NP-Hardness of FitBoundingBox

To show the NP-hardness of FITBOUNDINGBOX, we reduce from 3-PARTITION: Given a multiset A of $3m$ integers $a_1, \ldots, a_{3m}$ with $\sum_{i=1}^{3m} a_i = Bm$, is there a partition of A into m subsets such that, for each subset A', $\sum_{a \in A'} a = B$? It is known that 3-PARTITION is NP-hard even if B is polynomially bounded in m and, for every $a \in A$, we have $B/4 < a < B/2$, which implies that every subset must contain exactly three numbers [GJ79].

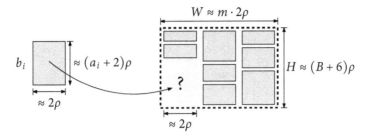

Figure 7.2: Overview of our reduction for $m = 3$. The boxes are shaded.

Equivalently, we can ask the question whether we can pack $3m$ boxes, where the i-th box has width 1 and height a_i, into a rectangle of width m and height B. The problem remains the same if, for some ρ, we scale the boxes and the rectangle horizontally by 2ρ and vertically by ρ. Assuming $B/4 < a_i$, the vertical space allows at most three boxes above each other. Hence, the problem remains equivalent even if we further add 2ρ to the height of each box and $3 \cdot 2\rho$ to the height of the rectangle. Thus, the question is, can we pack $3m$ boxes $b_1, \ldots, b_{3m}$, where b_i has width 2ρ and height $a_i\rho + 2\rho$, into a rectangle of width $W \approx m \cdot 2\rho$ and height $H \approx (B+6)\rho$? See Fig. 7.2 for an overview of our reduction. We create an angle sequence S that contains, for each b_i, a subsequence called a *snail* whose minimum bounding box is b_i. By ensuring that the snails are "more or less" disjoint, 3-PARTITION reduces to FITBOUNDINGBOX via the following question: Can we draw S inside a $(W \times H)$-rectangle?

Theorem 7.1. *FITBOUNDINGBOX is NP-hard.*

We now prove Theorem 7.1. Let c_W and c_H be sufficiently big even constants that we discuss at the end of the proof. Given an instance for 3-PARTITION as defined above, we set $\rho = 4B^3 m^7$ and assume that m is larger than a sufficiently big constant depending on c_W and c_H. We set

$$W' = 2m\rho + c_W m^2$$

and

$$H' = (B+6)\rho + c_H m$$

and choose $W = W' - 10$ and $H = H' - 10$ for our $(W \times H)$-rectangle R (note that W and H are even as desired). In the following, we create step by step an angle sequence S for FIT-BOUNDINGBOX consisting of $3m$ subsequences, called *snails*, each corresponding to an (integer) number a_i in A. We will show that $\langle S, W, H \rangle$ is a valid instance with the property that it is a yes-instance of FITBOUNDINGBOX if and only if the 3-PARTITION instance is a yes-instance. The number of angles in S (as well as the time to construct S) will be polynomially bounded in m.

Before we define S, let us consider the snails. For $a_i \in A$, a snail has the property that if we draw it with minimum perimeter, then its bounding box has roughly width 2ρ and height $(a_i + 2)\rho$. Observe that W provides enough width to draw m snails next to each other along a horizontal line, but not more than that (for sufficiently big values of m). Furthermore, H provides enough height to draw three snails above each other (along a vertical line) if and only if the corresponding numbers in A add up to at most B, provided m is sufficiently

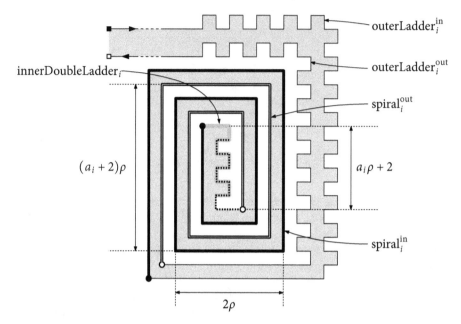

Figure 7.3: A compact drawing of snail$_i$, $i \in \{1, \ldots, 3m\}$. Here, $\rho = 4$. The shaded area depicts the exterior of the polygon that one obtains by interconnecting the endpoints of S. Note that innerDoubleLadder$_i$ consists of two overlapping inner ladders (bold gray and bold dashed) that we define later.

big; see Fig. 7.2. By forcing that, in any feasible drawing of S, each snail is drawn with roughly minimum perimeter, we will get the property that all the bounding boxes of the snails are basically disjoint and drawn in one of m "columns" with three boxes per column. Hence, given the heights of the boxes, this will allow us to directly "read" a solution to the underlying 3-PARTITION-instance.

We now describe a snail in more detail. Let a_i be the corresponding number in A. The "heart" of a snail is its *inner double ladder*. This is a y-monotone sequence built by alternating two left and two right turns, and it has minimum width 1 and minimum height $a_i\rho + 2$. It consists of two overlapping *inner ladders* that we define later. The inner double ladder is placed in the center of two *spirals* that wind around it approximately ρ times (later we'll give a precise definition of winding that depends on the number of horizontal spiral edges); see Fig. 7.3. The bounding box of the spirals will have width at least 2ρ and height at least $(a_i + 2)\rho$. In order to ensure that a spiral is winding around the inner double ladder, each spiral will end with a so called *outer ladder*, a combination of a y- and an x-monotone sequence of some large minimum length. A spiral winding around its outer ladder is thus much longer than when winding around its inner ladder. Hence, it consumes many more grid points than in the other case. By ensuring that the number of grid points in a $(W \times H)$-rectangle (and even in a $(W' \times H')$-rectangle) is just big enough for every spiral being drawn with its minimum perimeter (that is, winding around its inner double ladder), there won't be enough free grid points for any spiral to be drawn in a "bad way" (several times around the outer ladder). We will use the following upper bound on the number of grid points in a $(W' \times H')$-rectangle (that also bounds its area $W' \cdot H'$):

$$(W'+1) \cdot (H'+1) = (2m\rho + c_W m^2) \cdot ((B+6)\rho + c_H m) + W' + H'$$
$$\leq 2(B+6)m\rho^2 + c_{WH}Bm^2\rho \qquad (7.1)$$

where c_{WH} is some sufficiently large constant.

Formally, we define the angle sequence snail_i. The superscript "in" denotes that the respective angle sequence comes in S before the inner double ladder, whereas the superscript "out" denotes that the sequence comes after the ladder. (Recall that the first and last vertex of a polyline have no angles and are omitted in the angle sequence.) Note that snail_i has exactly two more right turns than left ones.

$$\text{snail}_i \; = \; (\text{outerLadder}_i^{\text{in}}) \, R \, (\text{spiral}_i^{\text{in}})$$
$$R \, (\text{innerDoubleLadder}_i) \, L$$
$$(\text{spiral}_i^{\text{out}}) \, L \, (\text{outerLadder}_i^{\text{out}}),$$

where

$$\text{outerLadder}_i^{\text{in}} \; = \; LR(RLLR)^\rho R(LRRL)^{(a_i+2)\rho/2+3}R,$$
$$\text{spiral}_i^{\text{in}} \; = \; R^{2\rho},$$
$$\text{innerDoubleLadder}_i \; = \; (RRLL)^{a_i\rho/2+1},$$
$$\text{spiral}_i^{\text{out}} \; = \; L^{2\rho-2},$$
$$\text{outerLadder}_i^{\text{out}} \; = \; L(LRRL)^{(a_i+2)\rho/2+1}L(RLLR)^\rho.$$

Independently of how we complete our definition of the whole angle sequence S, as long as all spiral drawings are rotated such that the inner double ladders start (and end) with horizontal edges oriented to the right (as in Fig. 7.3), we can prove the following, using a number of intermediate lemmas.

Proposition 7.1. *Given a feasible drawing of S, we can efficiently decode a solution to the underlying 3-PARTITION instance. In other words, if $\langle S, W, H \rangle$ is a yes-instance, then the underlying 3-PARTITION instance is a yes-instance.*

Fix some feasible drawing of S inside an axis-aligned $(W' \times H')$-rectangle R'. (Recall that we have $W' = W + 10$ and $H' = H + 10$.) Let $\kappa = 1/(Bm^2)$, and let $\iota = (1-3\kappa)$. Note that for increasing m, κ gets arbitrarily close to 0 and ι arbitrarily close to 1. Let the *center* of an inner double ladder denote the center point of its bounding box. For $1 \leq i \leq 3m$, let R_i be the box of width $2\iota\rho$ and height $2\iota\rho + a_i\rho$ centered at the center of innerDoubleLadder$_i$. Let $\mathcal{R}$ denote the set of all these boxes.

Observe that, by definition of ι, a box R_i has width slightly smaller than 2ρ and height slightly smaller than $(a_i+2)\rho$. Later we use this fact to prove that these boxes are pairwise disjoint if the drawing is feasible. If the boxes were slightly bigger, they possibly might overlap.

We now show a special case of Proposition 7.1. Later we will see that we can always assume this "special case", which will prove Proposition 7.1.

Lemma 7.1. *If all boxes in $\mathcal{R}$ are pairwise disjoint and lie completely inside R', then we can efficiently decode a solution to the underlying 3-PARTITION instance.*

Proof. We place the origin in the upper-left corner of R' and, for $1 \leq j \leq m$, we place a vertical line at x-coordinate $(2j-1)\rho$.

First, suppose that there is a box $R_i \in \mathcal{R}$ not intersected by any of these vertical lines. Then R_i lies between two vertical lines as it is too wide ($2\iota\rho$) to fit before the leftmost or after the rightmost vertical line (which offer only ρ and $\rho + c_W m^2$ horizontal space, respectively). Recall that the distance between two vertical lines is 2ρ. Let j be the number of vertical lines to the left of R_i. Observe that the distance between the left edge of R_i and the j-th vertical line from the left is at most $2\rho - 2\iota\rho = 2(1 - \iota)\rho = 6\kappa\rho$. Hence, the distance between the left edge of R_i and the left edge of R' is at most $(2j - 1 + 6\kappa)\rho$. Consider any horizontal line that intersects R_i. The number of boxes to the left of R_i intersected by this line is at most $j - 1$ since j boxes have total width

$$j \cdot 2\iota\rho = 2j(1 - 3\kappa)\rho = (2j - 6j\kappa)\rho > (2j - 1 + 6\kappa)\rho.$$

By repeating the same argument for the right side of R_i, we observe that any horizontal line intersecting R_i intersects at most $m - 1$ boxes including R_i. Consider the parts of such a line not covered by the boxes. Their total length inside R' is at least $W' - (m - 1)2\iota\rho \geq 2\rho$. Given that R_i has height $2\iota\rho + a_i\rho \geq 2\rho$, taking the integral over the uncovered parts of all horizontal lines intersecting R_i gives us $2\rho \cdot 2\rho = 4\rho^2$ as a lower bound on the total area to the left and to the right of R_i (inside R') that is not covered by the boxes. However, this is a contradiction as the total area of R' is

$$2(B + 6)m\rho^2 + c_{WH}Bm^2\rho$$

by Inequality 7.1, and the total area occupied by all the boxes is at least

$$\sum_{i=1}^{3m} 2\iota\rho \cdot (2\iota\rho + a_i\rho)$$

$$= \sum_{i=1}^{3m} 4\iota^2\rho^2 + 2\iota\rho^2 \sum_{i=1}^{3m} a_i$$

$$= 12m(1 - 6\kappa + 9\kappa^2)\rho^2 + 2Bm(1 - 3\kappa)\rho^2$$

$$\geq 2(B + 6)m\rho^2 - 72m\kappa\rho^2 - 6Bm\kappa\rho^2$$

$$\geq 2(B + 6)m\rho^2 - 78\rho^2/m$$

implying an upper bound of $c_{WH}Bm^2\rho + 78\rho^2/m \leq 79\rho^2/m$ (if ρ is sufficiently large) on the total area not covered by the boxes. This, however, is less than the area of $4\rho^2$ that we lose to the left and to the right of R_i if R_i is not intersected by a vertical line. Consequently, each box in $\mathcal{R}$ is intersected by one of the m vertical lines.

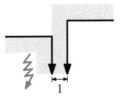

Figure 7.4: Two parallel edges with the same orientation must have distance at least 2. The interior of the polygon is shaded.

Next, assume that each vertical line intersects exactly three boxes of $\mathcal{R}$. These three boxes correspond to three numbers in A, so each vertical line corresponds to a subset of A of cardinality 3. Since there are $3m$ boxes and m vertical lines, and since each box is intersected by at least one vertical line, these subsets form a partition of the numbers in A. We claim that in each such subset A', the numbers sum up to at most B. This holds as otherwise $\sum_{a \in A'} a \geq B + 1$ and, thus, the total height of the three corresponding boxes would be at least

$$\sum_{a \in A'} (2\iota\rho + a\rho) \geq 6\iota\rho + (B+1)\rho > (B+6)\rho + c_H m = H' \qquad (7.2)$$

(by using $\iota > 5/6 + 1/7$ and $6/7\rho > c_H m$), which would be strictly greater than the height of R'; a contradiction. Hence, given the total sum Bm of all numbers in A, the numbers of each subset sum up to exactly B. Our partition is therefore a feasible solution to the underlying 3-PARTITION instance.

Finally, suppose that a vertical line intersects four boxes. Recall that for any a_i in A we have $B/4 < a_i < B/2$. Hence, the numbers corresponding to these four boxes sum up to a value strictly larger than B. By a similar calculation as in Inequality (7.2), we can show that the total height of the four boxes is strictly greater than the height of R'; a contradiction. $\square$

We will now show that the boxes in $\mathcal{R}$ are indeed pairwise disjoint and lie inside R'. We begin with a simple observation about feasible drawings of S.

Observation 7.1. *In a feasible drawing of S, if two edges are oriented in the same way and their projections on a line parallel to both edges overlap, then their distance is at least 2.*

Proof. By assumption, the endpoints of S can be appropriately connected to obtain a drawing of a simple polygon. The orientation of an edge determines on which side the interior of the polygon lies. Now consider two edges that are oriented in the same way and whose projections on a line parallel to both edges overlap; see Fig. 7.4. If the distance of the two edges was 1 then, for one of the two edges, the interior of the polygon would lie on both of its sides; a contradiction. $\square$

To facilitate the arguments in the following proofs, we introduce several notions. An inner double ladder consists of two overlapping *inner ladders* that we obtain by either removing the first two or last two vertices from it; see Fig. 7.3. Thus, each inner ladder is incident to one spiral and its minimum height is $a_i\rho + 1$ where a_i is the corresponding number in A. In the context of a fixed spiral, the inner ladder refers always to the inner ladder incident to the

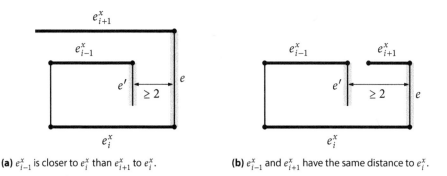

(a) e_{i-1}^x is closer to e_i^x than e_{i+1}^x to e_i^x.

(b) e_{i-1}^x and e_{i+1}^x have the same distance to e_i^x.

Figure 7.5: At least one of both, e_{i-1}^x and e_{i+1}^x, is shorter than e_i^x. The edges e and e' (highlighted) are parallel and have the same orientation. Therefore, their distance is at least 2.

spiral. Furthermore, we use the following notation concerning the edges of the (fixed) spiral. Let ρ'_x and ρ'_y denote the number of its horizontal and vertical edges, respectively ($\rho'_x = \rho'_y - 1$ and $\rho'_y \in \{\rho, \rho + 1\}$). Let $z \in \{x, y\}$ and consider all edges of the spiral parallel to the z-axis. We define two orders on the edges along the spiral. In the *inner order*, the first edge is incident to the inner ladder, in the *outer order*, the first edge is incident to the outer ladder. For a given order, let $e_1^z, \dots, e_{\rho_z}^z$ denote the z-axis-parallel spiral edges in this order and let defLadder denote the ladder defining the order. For an edge e_i^z, we call i its *level* with respect to the order, and denote its length by $\|e_i^z\|$.

Throughout the proof, we fix a spiral and a $z \in \{x, y\}$. Note that all claims shown hold for any spiral and coordinate axis.

Lemma 7.2. *Let* $1 < i < \rho'_z$. *We have* $\|e_i^z\| \geq \|e_{i-1}^z\| + 2$ *or* $\|e_i^z\| \geq \|e_{i+1}^z\| + 2$.

Proof. Assume that e_{i-1}^z has the smallest distance to e_i^z among $\{e_{i-1}^z, e_{i+1}^z\}$; see Fig. 7.5. We have $\|e_{i-1}^z\| < \|e_i^z\|$, as otherwise e_{i-1}^z would intersect the edge e connecting e_i^z with e_{i+1}^z; a contradiction to the drawing being simple. Furthermore, consider the edge e' that is incident to e_{i-1}^z and not incident to e_i^z. The edges e and e' are parallel and oriented in the same way. Since e_{i-1}^z has the smallest distance to e_i^z among $\{e_{i-1}^z, e_{i+1}^z\}$, the projection of e' on the line through e is contained in e. Thus, by Observation 7.1, the distance between e and e' is at least 2; hence, $\|e_i^z\| \geq \|e_{i-1}^z\| + 2$. By repeating the same argument for the case that e_{i+1}^z is closer to e_i^z than e_{i-1}^z, the claim follows. □

Note that both inequalities of Lemma 7.2 can be fulfilled for at most one edge since, in a cascading manner, it forces all other edges to satisfy exactly one of the two inequalities. Consequently, one of the following three cases holds (see Fig. 7.6).

Corollary 7.1. *One of the following three cases holds:*

1. $\|e_1^z\| < \dots < \|e_{\rho'_z - 1}^z\|$, *or*

2. $\|e_2^z\| > \dots > \|e_{\rho'_z}^z\|$, *or*

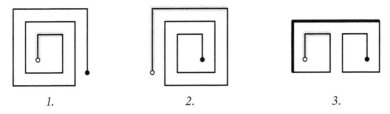

Figure 7.6: The three cases of Corollary 7.1 (gray: e_1^x, e_1^y; bold: e_i^x, e_i^y of case (3)).

3. *there is an i with $1 < i < \rho_z' - 1$ such that*

$$\|e_1^z\| < \cdots < \|e_i^z\| \qquad and \qquad \|e_{i+1}^z\| > \cdots > \left\|e_{\rho_z'}^z\right\| \qquad holds.$$

If $\|e_i^x\| > \|e_{i-1}^x\|$, then we say that the spiral *winds i times* around defLadder. Although we use this definition only for horizontal edges, note that $\|e_i^x\| > \|e_{i-1}^x\|$ implies $\|e_i^y\| > \|e_{i-1}^y\|$.

Observation 7.2. *Let b_x and b_y denote the width and height of the bounding box of defLadder, respectively. Let $1 < i \le \rho_z'$. If $\|e_i^z\| \ge \|e_{i-1}^z\| + 2$, then $\|e_i^z\| \ge 2i + b_z$.*

Proof. By Corollary 7.1 and Lemma 7.2, we have $\left\|e_j^z\right\| \ge \left\|e_{j-1}^z\right\| + 2$ for $1 < j \le i$. Hence, we have $\|e_i^z\| \ge \|e_1^z\| + 2(i-1)$. We now show $\|e_1^z\| \ge b_z + 2$ and the claim will follow.

Let e_1, e_2, e_3, e_4 denote the first four edges of the spiral in the order defined by defLadder; see Fig. 7.7a. Note that e_1 is vertical, so $e_1^y = e_1$ and $e_1^x = e_2$. Recall $\|e_3\| = \|e_2^y\| > \|e_1^y\| = \|e_1\|$. Thus, by monotonicity, defLadder lies completely inside the bounding box of e_1 and e_2. Consider any horizontal edge of defLadder with smallest distance to e_2. Observe that in the case of the outer ladder as well as in the case of the inner ladder, this edge lies on the border of the bounding box of defLadder and has the same orientation as e_2. Furthermore, observe that the same holds for e_3: Any vertical edge of defLadder with smallest distance to e_3 lies on the border of the bounding box of defLadder and has the same orientation as e_3. Hence, by Observation 7.1, the bounding box of defLadder has distance at least 2 to e_2 and to e_3. Now, observe that the height b_y of this bounding box and its distance to e_2 sum up to exactly $\|e_1\|$. Thus, $\|e_1\| \ge b_y + 2$ and, similarly, $\|e_2\| \ge b_x + 2$. $\qquad\square$

Definition 7.2. For $1 \le i \le 3m$, we define for every spiral edge e belonging to snail$_i$ its *lower value* as

- $\text{low}(e) = 2j$ if e is horizontal and

- $\text{low}(e) = 2j + a_i\rho$ otherwise

where j is the level of e with respect to the inner order. We denote by lowSpirals the sum of the lower values over all edges of all spirals.

Now we show that the lower values of the edges are proper lower bounds on their lengths.

Lemma 7.3. *In any feasible drawing, every spiral edge e has length at least* $\text{low}(e)$ *and the total perimeter of all spirals is at least* $\text{lowSpirals} \geq 2(B+6)mp^2$.

Proof. Consider any spiral edge e and its spiral belonging to snail$_i$. For a moment, consider any order of the spiral edges and let b_x and b_y denote the width and height, respectively, of the bounding box of the ladder defining the order. In case of the inner order, we have

$$b_x \geq 1 \quad \text{and} \quad b_y \geq a_i\rho,$$

and in case of the outer order, we have

$$b_x \geq 2\rho'_x \quad \text{and} \quad b_y \geq 2\rho'_y + a_i\rho.$$

To see the latter case, observe that the x-monotone parts of outerLadder$_i^{\text{in}}$ and outerLadder$_i^{\text{out}}$ consist of at least 2ρ horizontal edges, and the y-monotone parts consist of at least

$$(a_i + 2)\rho + 2 = 2(\rho + 1) + a_i\rho$$

vertical edges.

Thus, in any case, we have

$$b_z \geq \text{low}(e) - 2j$$

where j is the level of e in the respective order and z is the axis to which e is parallel. If, for one of the two orders, we have $\left\|e_j^z\right\| \geq \left\|e_{j-1}^z\right\| + 2$ where $e_j^z = e$, then Observation 7.2 implies $\left\|e_j^z\right\| \geq 2j + b_z \geq \text{low}(e)$. Otherwise, Lemma 7.2 implies that e is the first edge in one of the two orders and we have $\left\|e_1^z\right\| < \left\|e_2^z\right\| + 2$ in that order (where $e_1^z = e$). Fix this order and let $e_1, \ldots, e_4$ denote the first four edges of the spiral in the order when starting at e ($e_1 = e = e_1^z$, $e_3 = e_2^z$, and, by assumption, $\|e_1\| < \|e_3\| + 2$); see Fig. 7.7b. Let e_0 be the edge before e_1 (either belonging to defLadder or being adjacent to defLadder). Observe that e_0 has to stop before e_3 as otherwise it would either intersect e_3 (if $\|e_3\| \geq \|e_1\|$) or lie opposite to e_4 with distance 1 (if $\|e_3\| = \|e_1\| - 1$) and thus contradict Observation 7.1. Therefore, by monotonicity, defLadder lies completely in the bounding box of e_1 and e_2. As in the proof of Observation 7.2, this containment implies $\|e_1\| \geq b_z + 2 \geq \text{low}(e)$.

We are ready to show the second claim. The perimeter of the spiral is at least

$$\sum_{j=1}^{\rho'_x} \text{low}(e_j^x) + \sum_{j=1}^{\rho'_y} \text{low}(e_j^y) \geq \sum_{j=1}^{\rho-1} 2j + \sum_{j=1}^{\rho} (2j + a_i\rho)$$

$$= 2\sum_{j=1}^{\rho-1} 2j + 2\rho + a_i\rho^2 = (2 + a_i)\rho^2.$$

Recall that $\sum_{i=1}^{3m} a_i = Bm$ holds and that, for each $a_i \in A$, there are two spirals (namely spiral$_i^{\text{in}}$ and spiral$_i^{\text{out}}$). Thus, summing up over all spirals, we obtain

$$\text{lowSpirals} \geq \sum_{i=1}^{3m} 2 \cdot (2 + a_i)\rho^2 = 2(B+6)mp^2. \qquad \square$$

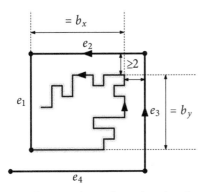

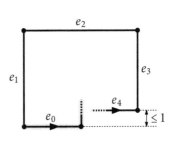

(a) The spiral edges e_2 and e_3 are longer by 2 than the respective bounding box edges of the ladder (lengths b_x and b_y).

(b) The edge e_0 has to make a turn before reaching e_4.

Figure 7.7: The spiral winds around the ladder (highlighted). By monotonicity, the ladder cannot leave the bounding box of e_1 and e_2.

Definition 7.3. For $1 \leq i \leq \rho_x'$ and the inner order, we define the *spiral box* BB_i as the bounding box of e_i^x and e_{i+1}^y. For $i \geq 3$, the *entrance* of BB_i is defined as the area between e_{i-1}^x and e_{i+1}^x (that is, as the bounding box of e_{i-1}^x and its vertical projection onto e_{i+1}^x); see Fig. 7.8a. The *height* of the entrance is the distance between e_{i-1}^x and e_{i+1}^x. We call BB_i closed if and only if its entrance has height 2. If BB_i is closed, we say that the spiral is *closed at level i*.

By Observation 7.1, the height of an entrance cannot be smaller than 2. Also observe that a spiral entering a spiral box of another spiral has to do so through the entrance. We formulate this observation as follows.

Observation 7.3. *Consider a spiral box BB_i of a spiral. If there is a polyline distinct to the spiral containing a point inside and outside BB_i, then it contains a horizontal line segment intersecting the entrance of BB_i; see Fig. 7.8a.*

Recall that we set $\kappa = 1/(Bm^2)$; $\iota = 1 - 3\kappa$; and $\rho = 4B^3 m^7$.

Lemma 7.4. *For every spiral, there is a j with $\iota\rho + 2 \leq j \leq \iota\rho + \kappa\rho$ such that the spiral is closed at level j and winds at least $j + \kappa\rho$ times around the inner ladder.*

Proof. Consider any spiral. We first show the second claim: If the spiral winds fewer than

$$\iota\rho + 2\kappa\rho = \rho - \kappa\rho$$

times around the inner ladder, then it winds at least $\kappa\rho$ times around the outer ladder. Recall that the width of the bounding box of the outer ladder is at least $2\rho_x'$. Thus, by Lemma 7.2 and Observation 7.2, for any spiral edge e_i^x with $1 < i < \kappa\rho$ in the outer order, we have

$$\|e_i^x\| \geq 2\rho_x' + 2i \geq 2(\rho_x' - i + 1) + i = \mathrm{low}(e_i^x) + i .$$

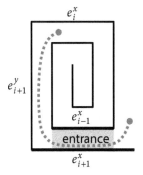
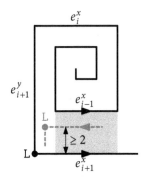

(a) The dashed polyline contains a point outside and inside BB_i, therefore it has to go through the entrance.

(b) The vertical dashed segment forces the entrance to have height at least 3.

Figure 7.8: The shaded area depicts the entrance of the spiral box BB_i.

Hence, the perimeter of the drawing is at least

$$\text{lowSpirals} + \sum_{i=2}^{\kappa\rho-1} i \geq 2(B+6)m\rho^2 + (\kappa\rho-2)^2/2$$

$$= 2(B+6)m\rho^2 + (\kappa^2\rho^2 - 4\kappa\rho + 4)/2$$

$$= 2(B+6)m\rho^2 + \kappa^2\rho^2/4 + (\kappa^2\rho^2/2 - 4\kappa\rho + 4)/2$$

$$\geq 2(B+6)m\rho^2 + (\kappa^2\rho)\rho/4$$

$$= 2(B+6)m\rho^2 + Bm^3\rho .$$

However, this is strictly greater than $2(B+6)m\rho^2 + c_{WH}Bm^2\rho$ (recall that c_{WH} is a constant), which again, for a sufficiently big constant value of c_{WH}, is greater than the total number $(W'+1) \cdot (H'+1)$ of grid points offered by R' (see Inequality 7.1); a contradiction.

Next, we show the first claim. Consider the inner order. If the spiral were not closed at any level between $\iota\rho+2$ and $\iota\rho+\kappa\rho$, then, for $1 \leq i \leq \kappa\rho - 2$, we have

$$\left\|e^y_{\iota\rho+i+2}\right\| \geq \left\|e^y_{\iota\rho+i+1}\right\| + 3$$

$$\geq \left\|e^y_{\iota\rho+2}\right\| + 3i$$

$$\geq \text{low}(e^y_{\iota\rho+2}) + 3i$$

$$= \text{low}(e^y_{\iota\rho+i+2}) + i .$$

Again, the perimeter of the drawing is larger than $(W'+1) \cdot (H'+1)$; a contradiction. $\square$

Let j be as in Lemma 7.4. We call BB_j the *closing box* of the respective spiral.

Corollary 7.2. *For $1 \leq i \leq 3m$, the box R_i is contained in each of the closing boxes of* spiral^{in}_i *and* spiral^{out}_i.

Proof. Recall that the closing box of any of the two spirals is closed at some level $j \geq \iota\rho + 2$. Thus, it contains at least $\iota\rho + 2$ vertical and $\iota\rho + 2$ horizontal edges of the spiral in its interior, where at least $\iota\rho/2 + 1$ many of them are lying on each side (left and right, above and below) of the inner double ladder. Recall that, at each of the four sides, the distance between any two neighboring parallel edges is at least 2 as they have the same orientation (Observation 7.1). Hence, the center of the inner double ladder lies at a distance of at least $\iota\rho$ to the left and to the right edge of the closing box, and at a distance of at least $\iota\rho + a_i\rho/2$ to the top and to the bottom edge of the closing box. Recall that R_i has width $2\iota\rho$ and height $2\iota\rho + a_i\rho$. Thus, R_i fits into the closing box when centered at the center of the inner double ladder. $\square$

Lemma 7.5. *The boxes in $\mathcal{R}$ are pairwise disjoint and lie inside R'.*

Proof. The second statement follows from the fact that, by Corollary 7.2, all boxes lie inside spirals and that all spirals lie inside R'. To show the first statement, suppose for a contradiction that two boxes R_i and R_j intersect. Thus, by Corollary 7.2, the closing boxes b_i and b_j of $\text{spiral}_i^{\text{out}}$ and $\text{spiral}_j^{\text{out}}$, respectively, intersect each other. This intersection implies that one of the closing boxes, say b_i, contains a point of the spiral corresponding to the other closing box, here b_j, in its interior. Consider the entrance of b_j. Suppose that a horizontal line segment s of $\text{spiral}_j^{\text{out}}$ intersects the entrance. By Observation 7.1, s can be oriented only towards the entrance. But then s ends with a left turn inside b_i, forcing the entrance to be higher than 2 (see Fig. 7.8b). This contradicts that the entrance is closed.

By Observation 7.3, $\text{spiral}_j^{\text{out}}$ cannot contain any point outside b_i. Consequently, $\text{spiral}_j^{\text{out}}$ lies completely inside b_i. Hence, the horizontal edge e of $\text{spiral}_i^{\text{out}}$ spanning b_i is longer than the longest horizontal edge of $\text{spiral}_j^{\text{out}}$ whose length is at least $2\rho'_x$ by Lemma 7.3. Since, by Lemma 7.4, the level of e is at most $\iota\rho + \kappa\rho \leq \rho'_x - \kappa\rho$, e is longer by at least $2\kappa\rho$ than its lower value. Also by Lemma 7.4, $\text{spiral}_i^{\text{out}}$ winds at least $\kappa\rho$ times around b_i. Thus, for at least $\kappa\rho$ edges, it holds that their length is larger by at least $2\kappa\rho$ than their lower values. Thus, the perimeter of the drawing is at least

$$\text{lowSpirals} + 2(\kappa\rho)^2 \geq 2(B+6)m\rho^2 + 8Bm^3\rho .$$

However, this is strictly greater than the total number of grid points in R' (see Inequality 7.1); a contradiction. $\square$

Proposition 7.1 follows immediately from Lemmas 7.1 and 7.5. We will now show the other direction of our reduction.

Proposition 7.2. *If the 3-PARTITION instance is a yes-instance, then there is a feasible drawing of S within an axis-parallel rectangle R of width W and height H such that, for the polyline P realizing S, the first vertex of P lies on the upper-left corner of R and the last vertex of P lies in the lower-right corner of R, that is, $\langle S, W, H \rangle$ is a yes-instance.*

Proof. Before we complete our definition of S, let us take another look at the snails. As long as we neglect on how the snails are embedded in S, we can observe that every snail$_i$ can be drawn inside a bounding box of width $2\rho + \mathcal{O}(1)$ and height $(a_i + 2)\rho + \mathcal{O}(1)$ such that the first segment of the inner double ladder is horizontal and oriented to the right; see Figs. 7.3 and 7.9. The idea is now as follows. We subdivide R into m columns of width $2\rho + \Theta(m)$ each.

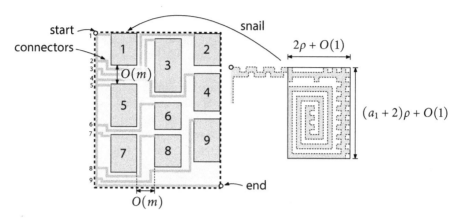

Figure 7.9: The polyline realizing S connects the upper-left corner (start) of the ($W \times H$)-rectangle R with the lower-right one (end). It consists of nine snails enumerated from 1 to 9. For readability, we shaded one part of the rectangle separated by the polyline in light gray, the other part in dark gray. The widths of all spirals, when tightly wound around their inner ladders, are the same. Their heights depend on the corresponding numbers in the 3-Partition instance. Here, $m = 3$. All snails are packed into three columns, each one accommodates three snails.

In each column, we will draw three snails as described above, one above another. The way we choose which snail to draw in which column depends on our solution to the 3-PARTITION instance. Let $(A_j)_{j=1}^m$ be our partition of A where $\sum_{a \in A_j} a = B$ for every A_j. In the j-th column from the left, we draw the three snails corresponding to the three numbers in A_j. We draw them such that their right border is aligned to the right border of the column. Hence, the left part of the column of width $\Theta(m)$ is unused. As the vertical order of the three snails, we choose the order of the corresponding numbers in the input. That is, for two snails snail_i and snail_k belonging to the same column, snail_i is drawn above snail_k if and only if $i < k$. Note that such a drawing fits into R: The total height of the three spirals in each column is only $(B + 6)\rho + \Theta(1)$. Hence, the total height of the unused space in the columns is $\Theta(m)$.

We will use the unused space to the left and between the snails to interconnect them. This will give us the complete angle sequence S. We will do it by modifying our drawings of the snails by redrawing their outer ladders to connect the snails to the left edge of R; see the snail in Fig. 7.9. More precisely, only the x-monotone part of the outer ladders leaves the current bounding box of the snails. We call this part *connector*. At the left edge of R, these connector pairs will be ordered from top to bottom relative to the order of the corresponding numbers in A. For any connector pair, the connector oriented towards the snail will be drawn above the other one. Consecutive pairs will be connected by a vertical edge. The bottommost connector is connected to a vertical and then a horizontal line segment allowing us to reach the lower-right corner of R. Observe that a connector consists of at least ρ up-and-down curves, hence, of enough curves to bypass all the snails encountered in the at most $m - 1$ columns between the left edge of R and the spiral it is connected to. We are ready to complete the definition of S.

$$S \;=\; \text{RL} \left(\text{snail}_1 \text{LL}\right) \ldots \left(\text{snail}_{3m} \text{LL}\right).$$

Finally, observe that we can draw the connectors such that the total height of all connectors going through a column below or above the snails is $\mathcal{O}(m)$. Since a connector does not need to change its y-position more than once in each column (in order to bypass or to connect to a snail), a total extra width of $\mathcal{O}(m)$ per column is sufficient to allow the connectors to change their y-positions (which happens in each column to the left of the snails). Hence, we choose the constants c_W and c_H in $W = 2m\rho + c_W m^2 - 10$ and $H = (B+6)\rho + c_H m - 10$ big enough such that R gives enough space to draw S in the way described above. Also note that our drawing is feasible as it can be easily extended to a simple polygon by appropriately connecting its endpoints around R. We conclude that $\langle S, W, H \rangle$ is a yes-instance.   □

7.2.2   Extension to the Optimization Versions

In this section, we show for each of the three objectives (minimum perimeter, area, and bounding box) that it is NP-hard to draw a rectilinear polygon of minimum cost that real-izes a given angle sequence. Our proof is a reduction from FitBoundingBox. Given an instance $\langle S, W, H \rangle$ of FitBoundingBox, we define an angle sequence T (with $|T|$ polynomial in $|S|$) and, for each objective, a threshold value Y such that T can be drawn with cost at most Y (with respect to the objective) if and only if S is a yes-instance. We consider only drawings that are *feasible* in the general case (without the restrictions of Section 7.2.1), that is, a simple rectilinear polygon or polyline on the grid realizing a given angle sequence.

At first glance, one might think that FitBoundingBox directly implies NP-hardness for the objective of minimizing the area of the bounding box. However, the question of whether an angle sequence S can be drawn within a rectangle of width W and height H does not directly translate to the question of whether S can be drawn in a rectangle of area $W \cdot H$. For instance, suppose that S is a no-instance that we obtained by our reduction from 3-Partition. Draw the snails of S as tight as possible below each other in the order of their indices and connect them on the left side. Observe that such a drawing fits into a rectangle of width $2\rho + \mathcal{O}(1)$ and height $\left(\sum_{i=1}^{3m}(a_i + 2)\rho + \mathcal{O}(1)\right) = (B+6)m\rho + \mathcal{O}(m)$ (the variables are defined as in Section 7.2.1). Hence, S fits into a rectangle of area even smaller than $W \cdot H$.

Outline of the proof.   We define T by simultaneously constructing a "reference drawing" for the case that S is a yes-instance. It, roughly speaking, consists of two snail subsequences with S in between, where each snail is formed by ladder and spiral subsequences similar to Section 7.2.1. The notions *spirals*, *snails* and *ladders* throughout this section refer only to the subsequences of T excluding S, unless otherwise mentioned. After defining the thresholds, we use the reference drawing as a certificate in the first direction of the proof that a cheap drawing exists if S is a yes-instance. In the second direction of the proof, we show, for each objective, that if a drawing does not surpass the respective threshold Y, then S is a yes-instance. For this, we first observe that, in any drawing of T, certain subsequences (for instance, spirals) have certain lower bounds on the cost of drawing them. We use these lower bounds to show that a drawing respecting the threshold Y has some special structure: If it doesn't, then some part of it is very expensive and, *together* with the lower bounds on the other parts, the total cost is above the threshold; a contradiction. Generally speaking, T consists of two long spirals. Step by step, we show that spiral edges are not much longer than certain lower bounds and that spirals wind sufficiently enough in the "right" direction. This again will help us to observe

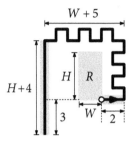

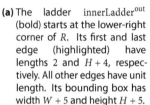

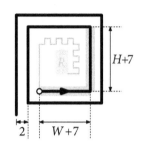

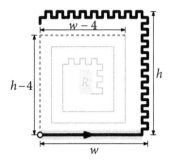

(a) The ladder innerLadder^{out} (bold) starts at the lower-right corner of R. Its first and last edge (highlighted) have lengths 2 and $H + 4$, respectively. All other edges have unit length. Its bounding box has width $W + 5$ and height $H + 5$.

(b) The spiral spiral^{out} (bold) starts at the endpoint of innerLadder^{out} and winds around it with edge lengths increasing in steps of 2. The first two edges (highlighted) have lengths $W + 7$ and $H + 7$, respectively.

(c) The last two spiral edges (dashed) have lengths $w - 4$ and $h - 4$, respectively. outerLadder^{out} (bold) starts at the endpoint of the spiral, and its bounding box has width w and height h. All but its first edge (highlighted) have unit length.

Figure 7.10: The construction of snail^{out}.

that the spirals interleave until the inner-most level. Together with the upper bounds on the spiral edges, we will see that S cannot leave the center of the spirals and is closed in a box of relatively small size, which implies that S is a yes-instance.

Definition of the instance T. Recall that W and H are even. Without loss of generality, we assume $\min\{W, H\} > 5$. Let

$$\text{maxCenterCost} = 2(W + 7)(H + 7)$$

and let

$$\rho = (\text{maxCenterCost} + 12)^2 .$$

Finally, set

$$w = W + 2\rho + 11 \qquad \text{and} \qquad h = H + 2\rho + 11 .$$

We define T constructively by giving a drawing of two polylines, called *snails*, whose angle sequences together with S form T.

We begin with the first snail that we call snail^{out}. Place an axis-aligned rectangle R of width W and height H in the grid. Starting at its lower-right corner, draw a ladder around it, as in Fig. 7.10a, such that the first edge (horizontal) has length 2, the last edge (vertical) has length $H + 4$, and all the other edges have unit length, and the bounding box of the ladder has width $W + 5$ and height $H + 5$. We call the ladder innerLadder^{out}. Formally,

$$\text{innerLadder}^{\text{out}} = L(\text{LRRL})^{\frac{H}{2}} L(\text{RLLR})^{\frac{W+4}{2}} L .$$

We continue the sequence by a left turn followed by a spiral, called spiral^{out}, of $2\rho + 1$ left turns winding around the rectangle (and innerLadder^{out}) in such a way that the first edge has length $W + 7$, the second edge has length $H + 7$, and the $(i + 2)$-th edge is longer by exactly 2 than the i-th edge; see Fig. 7.10b. Note that the spiral consists of $\rho + 1$ horizontal and $\rho + 1$ vertical edges. Thus, in our drawing, the last horizontal and vertical edges of spiral^{out} have the lengths $W + 7 + 2\rho = w - 4$ and $H + 7 + 2\rho = h - 4$, respectively. Formally,

$$\text{spiral}^{out} \quad = \quad L^{2\rho+1}.$$

We finish the snail by a left turn and a following ladder, called outerLadder^{out}. We draw the ladder around the spiral such that all edges but the first one have unit length and the bounding box of the ladder has width w and height h. The length of the first edge is $w - 1$; see Fig. 7.10c. Formally,

$$\text{outerLadder}^{out} \quad = \quad L(\text{RLLR})^{\frac{h-1}{2}} L(\text{LRRL})^{\frac{w-3}{2}} \text{LRL}.$$

Summarized,

$$\text{snail}^{out} \quad = \quad \text{innerLadder}^{out} \text{ L spiral}^{out} \text{ L outerLadder}^{out}.$$

In a similar way, we define the second snail snail^{in}; see Fig. 7.11. The biggest difference is that snail^{in} winds in the other direction and ends at the upper-left corner of the rectangle R. In detail, the polyline of innerLadder^{in} is a copy of innerLadder^{out} turned by $180°$ with reversed orientation. Another difference is that the spiral spiral^{in} contains only $2\rho - 1$ right turns (instead of $2\rho + 1$ turns). Thus, it consists of ρ horizontal and ρ vertical edges which also increase in lengths by steps of 2. Therefore, in our drawing, the last horizontal and vertical edges of spiral^{in} have lengths $W + 7 + 2(\rho - 1) = w - 6$ and $H + 7 + 2(\rho - 1) = h - 6$, respectively. Regarding outerLadder^{in}, it has width $w - 2$, height $h - 3$, and it starts and ends with a horizontal edge. Formally,

$$\text{snail}^{in} \quad = \quad \text{outerLadder}^{in} \text{ R spiral}^{in} \text{ R innerLadder}^{in},$$
$$\text{outerLadder}^{in} \quad = \quad (\text{LRRL})^{\frac{w-3}{2}} R(\text{RLLR})^{\frac{h-5}{2}} R,$$
$$\text{spiral}^{in} \quad = \quad R^{2\rho-1},$$
$$\text{innerLadder}^{in} \quad = \quad R(\text{LRRL})^{\frac{W+4}{2}} R(\text{RLLR})^{\frac{H}{2}} R.$$

Finally, we complete our definition of T as follows:

$$T \quad = \quad \text{snail}^{in} \text{ S snail}^{out} \text{ L}.$$

Note that, if S is a yes-instance, then there exists the following drawing of T: We draw snail^{in} and snail^{out} as above and place S inside R such that the first vertex of S touches the last vertex of snail^{in} and the last vertex of S touches the first vertex of snail^{out} (in other words, the first and last edge of S—which are horizontal—extend the first and last edge of snail^{in} and snail^{out}, respectively). Finally, we connect both snails on the outside by prolonging the last (vertical) edge of snail^{out} one unit to the bottom such that it touches the first vertex of snail^{in}; see Fig. 7.11. We call this drawing the *reference drawing*.

Throughout this section, we say *inner ladder* to refer to innerLadder^{in} or innerLadder^{out} (the ladders incident to S) and *outer ladder* to refer to outerLadder^{in} or outerLadder^{out}.

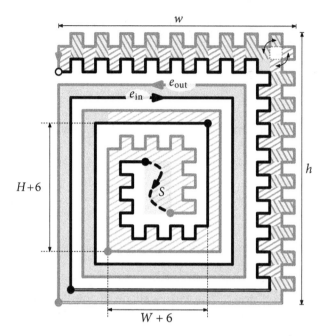

Figure 7.11: The reference drawing of T (when S is a yes-instance). The snails $\text{snail}^{\text{out}}$ (gray) and snail^{in} (black) wind around R (shaded rectangle in the center). The endpoints of the ladders and spirals are depicted as nodes; the common endpoint of the snails is white. The other two endpoints are connected via S (dashed curve) within R. The bounding box containing both inner ladders has size $(W + 6) \times (H + 6)$. The edges of the outer ladders that are incident to the spirals (edges with white filling) are longer by 3 than e_{in} and e_{out}, respectively. To ease the estimation of the area, the grid cells of the polygon are highlighted as follows: (i) All grid cells within the bounding box of the first vertical edge of $\text{spiral}^{\text{out}}$ and both inner ladders (size $(W + 7) \times (H + 7)$) are hatched. (ii) Almost all remaining grid cells surrounded by exactly two edges of the drawing are shaded in gray. (iii) with the exception of one grid cell (dashed white box), all other remaining grid cells are grouped into pairs that are hatched in one of two patterns (the pairs around the white box are indicated with arrows).

Lower Bounds and Thresholds.   Next, we provide lower bounds and thresholds on the cost of any feasible drawing of T that depend only on W and H. The thresholds will be defined on each of the three objectives. They will be essential for our reduction: There exists a drawing of T (in particular our reference drawing) that does not surpass the threshold of the respective objective if and only if S is a yes-instance. In the reduction, we prove by contradiction that any drawing having the threshold as an upper bound has some specific properties. Our proof will use that any drawing of T has a lower bound on the perimeter (that influences also the other objectives) that is very close to the threshold. We will see that if a drawing lacks a desired property, then it has to be much more expensive than its lower bound, and thus above the respective threshold.

We begin by providing lower bounds on the perimeter of any drawing of T. We will first consider spiral edges, then whole spirals, and finally the ladders. We will see that, in the reference drawing, the respective parts meet the lower bound or are very close to them. (Generously, we will use the lower bound of 0 for the remaining part of T, which is S.) We will also give a lower bound on the area of the bounding box.

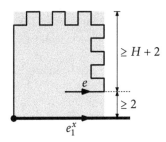

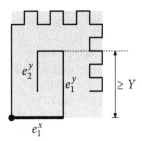

(a) e_1^x (bold) leaves the bounding box

(b) e_1^x (bold) stays completely inside

Figure 7.12: In each of the two cases, the bounding box b (shaded) of innerLadder^{out} has height at least $Y = H + 4$.

In the following, we use the same notation as in Section 7.2.1 for the spirals and ladders of snail^{in} and snail^{out}. Consider a spiral. Note that, in contrast to Section 7.2.1, $\|e_i^y\| > \|e_{i-1}^y\|$ implies $\|e_i^x\| > \|e_{i-1}^x\|$ in the inner order. Therefore, in this section, we redefine winding and say that a spiral winds i times around the ladder defining the order if $\|e_i^y\| > \|e_{i-1}^y\|$. Note that Observation 7.1, Lemma 7.2, Observation 7.2, and Corollary 7.1 hold also for the spirals of snail^{in} and snail^{out}.

We begin with a definition similar to Definition 7.2.

Definition 7.4. We define for every spiral edge e its *lower value* as

- $\text{low}(e) = 2j + X$ if e is horizontal and

- $\text{low}(e) = 2j + Y$ otherwise

where j is the level of e with respect to the inner order, $X = W + 5$, and $Y = H + 4$.

- Let lowSpirals denote the sum of the lower values over all edges of both spirals.

- Let lowLadders = $|\text{outerLadder}^{\text{out}}| + |\text{outerLadder}^{\text{in}}| + \text{low}(e_{\text{in}}) + \text{low}(e_{\text{out}})$, where e_{in} and e_{out} denote the first horizontal edge of spiral^{in} and spiral^{out}, respectively, in the outer order.

- Let lowBBArea = $w \cdot h$.

In the following, we observe that the lower values defined in Definition 7.4 are proper lower bounds for any feasible drawing. First, we observe that X and Y correspond to the minimum width and height of the bounding box of the inner ladders, respectively. We also examine the width and height of the outer ladders.

Lemma 7.6. *In any feasible drawing, outerLadder^{out} has width at least w and height at least h, outerLadder^{in} has width at least $w - 2$ and height at least $h - 3$, and the bounding box of an inner ladder has minimum width X and minimum height Y.*

Proof. A ladder consists of an x-monotone and a y-monotone part (that overlap). The width of an x-monotone polyline is at least the number of its horizontal edges, the height of a y-monotone polyline is at least the number of its vertical edges. Hence, by the definition of the ladders, the first claim follows.

The second claim follows only partially by this observation: The bounding box of an inner ladder has minimum width $W + 5 = X$ and minimum height $H + 2 = Y - 2$. We now show that the height is at least Y. Without loss of generality, consider innerLadder^{out}, its bounding box b, and its incident spiral in the inner order. The ladder starts with a right-oriented edge e and ends with a vertical edge that is incident to the right-oriented spiral edge e_1^x; see Fig. 7.12a. We have two cases: In the first case, e_1^x leaves b. Since the left endpoint of e_1^x lies on the left edge of b, its right endpoint has to be to the right of b. Furthermore, the bottom edge of b is contained in e_1^x since e_1^x lies below the vertical ladder edge it is incident to. Thus, e_1^x goes below e. By Observation 7.1, the vertical distance between e and e_1^x is at least 2. Note that the y-monotone part of innerLadder^{out} starts at e and goes upward for at least $H + 2$ units. Hence, the height of the bounding box of innerLadder^{out} is at least $H + 4 = Y$.

In the second case, $e_1^x \in b$; see Fig. 7.12b. Then, also $e_1^y \in b$ and, by monotonicity of the ladder, $\|e_1^y\| > \|e_2^y\|$. Recall that the level of e_1^y is at least ρ in the outer order and that the outer ladder has height at least $h - 3$. Thus, Lemma 7.2 and Observation 7.2 imply

$$\|e_1^y\| \geq 2\rho + (h - 3) \geq Y .$$

Hence, the height of b is at least Y.   □

The following lemma is a consequence of the lemma above.

Lemma 7.7. *For any feasible drawing, the area of its bounding box is at least* lowBBArea.

Proof. By Lemma 7.6, the bounding box b of outerLadder^{out} has width and height at least w and h, respectively. Thus, b has area at least $w \cdot h = $ lowBBArea. Since b is contained in the bounding box of the whole drawing, the claim follows.   □

By using the same arguments as in the proof of Lemma 7.3, we obtain the following lemma.

Lemma 7.8. *In any feasible drawing, every spiral edge e has length at least* low(e) *and the total perimeter of the spirals is at least* lowSpirals.

Lemma 7.9. *In any feasible drawing, the total perimeter of the two outer ladders is at least* lowLadders.

Proof. Given a feasible drawing, consider a spiral and its incident outer ladder L. A natural lower bound on peri(L) is $|L| + 1$ (as L consists of $|L| + 1$ edges). However, this is not enough. Therefore we show that some of the edges are longer than 1. We define the *remainder* of an edge e to be $\|e\| - 1$ and we let r denote the total remainder of the edges of L, that is, $r = $ peri(L) $- |L| - 1$. In the following, we bound r from below.

Let v_1 and v_2 denote the first two vertices (including the endpoint) of the spiral in the outer order, and let e denote the first horizontal spiral edge. Furthermore, let w denote a right-most vertex of L and let d denote the horizontal distance between w and v_1 (and v_2); see Fig. 7.13.

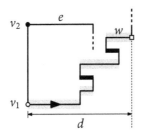

Figure 7.13: The distance d between the spiral endpoint v_1 (white node) and the right-most vertex w (white square) of the incident outer ladder (here $\text{outerLadder}^{\text{out}}$) is $d \geq \text{low}(e)$. The polyline $v_1 - w$ has at most two more right-oriented edges (highlighted) than left-oriented ones (bold).

Suppose $d \leq \|e\|$. Then, by monotonicity of L, L lies completely inside the bounding box of v_1, v_2, and w. However, the width of this bounding box is $d \leq \text{low}(e) \leq 2(\rho + 1) + X = w - 4$ and the minimum width of L is at least $w - 2$; a contradiction. Hence, we have $d \geq \text{low}(e) + 1$.

Consider the part of L between v_1 and w, and orient the edges of this polyline such that it is directed from v_1 to w. Observe that the polyline is y-monotone and that it has at most two right-oriented edges more than left-oriented edges. Since its width is d, the total length of its right-oriented edges is bigger by d than the total length of its left-oriented edges. Hence, the total remainder of the right-oriented edges is at least $d - 2$. Thus, $r \geq d - 2 \geq \text{low}(e) - 1$, and $\text{peri}(L) = r + |L| + 1 \geq |L| + \text{low}(e)$. We repeat the proof above for the other spiral and its outer ladder and the claim follows. □

Definition 7.5. We define the following *thresholds* for each objective:

- $Y_p = \text{lowLadders} + \text{lowSpirals} + \text{maxCenterCost} + 2\rho + 12$ for minimizing the perimeter of the drawing,

- $Y_a = Y_p/2 - 1$ for minimizing the area of the drawing, and

- $Y_b = \text{lowBBArea}$ for minimizing the area of the bounding box of the drawing.

We use the thresholds for our reduction.

Theorem 7.2. *For each of the three objectives it holds: There is a drawing of T that does not surpass the threshold (as defined in Definition 7.5) of the given objective if and only if S is a yes-instance.*

We first show that if S is a yes-instance, then there is a drawing of T that does not surpass the threshold of the respective objective. Consider the reference drawing and recall that we drew S inside the empty $(W \times H)$-rectangle R and connected it to the two snails accordingly. We now show that the reference drawing respects all three thresholds.

Perimeter. First, consider S and the inner ladders. Given that S and the inner ladders lie in a $((W + 6) \times (H + 6))$-rectangle (see Fig. 7.11), the total perimeter of S and the inner ladders is bounded from above by

$$2(W + 7)(H + 7) = \text{maxCenterCost} .$$

Next, consider the spirals. Observe that in the reference drawing, each horizontal spiral edge e has length $\mathrm{low}(e)$, and each vertical spiral edge e has length $\mathrm{low}(e) + 1$. Recall that spiral^{in} has ρ vertical edges and spiral^{out} has $\rho + 1$ vertical edges. Thus, the total perimeter of the spirals is $\mathrm{lowSpirals} + 2\rho + 1$. Finally, consider the outer ladders. with the exception of the edges incident to the spirals and the last edge of outerLadder^{out} (which has length 2), all edges of the outer ladders have unit length. The two edges incident to the spirals are exactly 3 units longer than the first horizontal edge of the respective incident spiral in the outer order. Hence, using the notation of Definition 7.4, the two edges have total length $\mathrm{low}(e_{\mathrm{in}}) + \mathrm{low}(e_{\mathrm{out}}) + 6$. Thus, the total perimeter of the outer ladders is

$$|\text{outerLadder}^{\mathrm{in}}| + |\text{outerLadder}^{\mathrm{out}}| + \mathrm{low}(e_{\mathrm{in}}) + \mathrm{low}(e_{\mathrm{out}}) + 6 + 1 \;\leq\; \mathrm{lowLadders} + 7 .$$

Summing up, the total perimeter of the reference drawing is at most

$$\mathrm{lowLadders} + \mathrm{lowSpirals} + \mathrm{maxCenterCost} + 2\rho + 8 \;<\; Y_p .$$

Area.   Regarding the area, we subdivide the grid cells of the reference drawing into three parts: The first part is the intersection of our polygon with the $((W + 7) \times (H + 7))$-rectangle containing S, the inner ladders, and the first vertical edge of spiral^{out} in the inner order. Hence, the intersection contains at most

$$(W + 7) \cdot (H + 7) \;=\; \mathrm{maxCenterCost}/2$$

grid cells. The second part consists of almost all grid cells outside this rectangle touching exactly two edges of the polyline P that realizes the spirals and the outer ladders. The third part consists of all the remaining grid cells. with the exception of one grid cell, we can group the grid cells of the third part into pairs that touch four or five edges of P; see Fig. 7.11. Hence, with the exception of one grid cell, each grid cell of the second and third part touches at least two edges of P on average. Since each unit-line segment of P is touched by exactly one grid cell, the number of grid cells belonging to the second and third part is at most $1 + \mathrm{peri}(P)/2 \leq (\mathrm{lowLadders} + \mathrm{lowSpirals} + 2\rho + 10)/2$. Hence, the total area of the reference drawing is at most

$$\frac{\mathrm{lowLadders} + \mathrm{lowSpirals} + \mathrm{maxCenterCost} + 2\rho + 10}{2} \;\leq\; \frac{Y_p - 2}{2} \;=\; Y_a .$$

Bounding Box.   Regarding the bounding box of the reference drawing, note that it is identical to the bounding box of outerLadder^{out}. Following the proof of Lemma 7.7, the area of the bounding box of the drawing is $\mathrm{lowBBArea} = Y_b$.

Now, to prove the other direction of Theorem 7.2, assume that T can be drawn such that (at least) one of the three thresholds of Definition 7.5 is not surpassed. We show that this fact implies that T is a yes-instance. Until the remainder of this section, we fix such a drawing that respects a threshold and refer to it as *our drawing*. We begin by making a helpful observation that will allow us to focus only on the perimeter and the bounding box of our drawing:

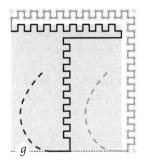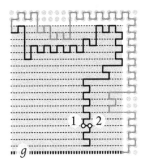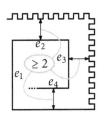

(a) If outerLadder^{in} visits the grid line g (dashed), then Γ consists of two disconnected polylines; a contradiction as the whole drawing is a polygon.

(b) Within BB(Γ), the outer ladders occupy at least two grid points from every horizontal (dashed) and vertical (not depicted) grid line with the exception of g (bold dashed).

(c) Given the orientation of the edges, the spiral edges e_2, e_3, and e_4 have distance at least 2 to the outer ladder.

Figure 7.14: If the bounding box of the drawing has height h and width w, then every grid point (gray nodes) at distance at most 1 to the top or right border of the bounding box is visited only by outerLadder^{out} (gray). This forces the remaining part Γ of the drawing to lie in the box (shaded) of width $w - 2$ and height $h - 2$, which has several implications on outerLadder^{in} (black) and the spirals, for instance, forcing outerLadder^{in} to have its minimum height $h - 3$.

Lemma 7.10. *If the area of our drawing is at most Y_a, then the perimeter is at most Y_p.*

Proof. The claim follows from $Y_a = Y_p/2 - 1$ and the following observation that we prove below: For any simple rectilinear polygon P on the grid,

$$\mathrm{area}(P) \geq \mathrm{peri}(P)/2 - 1.$$

We scale P by a factor of 2 and obtain a new polygon P'. In P', there are #L grid cells touching exactly two edge segments (which happens only at L vertices), peri(P') − 2#L grid cells touching exactly one edge segment, and at least #R grid cells touching no edges (every R vertex is exclusively incident to one such grid cell due to the simplicity and upscaling of P). Thus, area(P') $\geq$ #L + peri(P') − 2#L + #R = peri(P') − 4 using #L = #R + 4. The claim follows by substituting area(P') = 4 · area(P) and peri(P') = 2 · peri(P). $\square$

Our assumption that at least one of the three thresholds of Definition 7.5 is not surpassed has a number of implications that we consider one by one.

Lemma 7.11. *If the bounding box of the drawing has area at most Y_b, then the spirals wind at least ρ times around their inner ladders and for every spiral edge e, $\|e\| \leq \mathrm{low}(e) + 1$.*

Proof. Consider outerLadder^{out}. By Lemma 7.6, the area of its bounding box is at least

$$w \cdot h = \mathrm{lowBBArea} = Y_b .$$

Thus, the bounding box of outerLadder^{out} is exactly the bounding box of the whole drawing (see Lemma 7.7). Let Γ denote the part of the drawing that excludes the edges of outerLadder^{out}. Recall that outerLadder^{out} consists of an x-monotone and a y-monotone part of minimum width w and height h, respectively. Given the orientation of the first and the last edge of outerLadder^{out}, Γ has to lie entirely to the bottom of the x-monotone part and to the left of the y-monotone part. Observe that all horizontal edges of the x-monotone part as well as the vertical edges of the y-monotone part have unit length. Thus, every grid point with distance at most 1 to the top or right border of the bounding box of the drawing either belongs to outerLadder^{out}, or is not visited by the drawing; see Fig. 7.14b. Consequently, the bounding box of Γ, which includes spiral^{out} as well as spiral^{in} and outerLadder^{in}, has width and height at most $w - 2$ and $h - 2$.

Consider outerLadder^{in}. It cannot visit any grid point on the bottom-most grid line g, as otherwise it would separate spiral^{in} from spiral^{out} (see Fig. 7.14a); a contradiction as Γ is a (connected) polyline. Thus, outerLadder^{in} lies in a bounding box of width $w - 2$ and height $h - 3$. Given that its x-monotone part has width at least $w - 2$ and its y-monotone part has height at least $h - 3$, all horizontal line segments of the x-monotone part and all vertical line segments of the y-monotone part are of unit length. Therefore, every (vertical and horizontal) grid line that goes through $BB(\Gamma)$—with the exception of g—contains at least two grid points within $BB(\Gamma)$ that are covered by the outer ladders[2]. Consequently, every vertical and horizontal grid line —with the exception of g—contains within $BB(\Gamma)$ at most $h - 4$ and $w - 4$ free grid points, respectively; see Fig. 7.14b.

For the remainder of the proof, consider any of the two spirals. Let $e_1, \ldots, e_4$ denote the first four spiral edges in the outer order. Recall that the spiral is contained in $BB(\Gamma)$ and observe that e_2 lies above g. Consequently, given the number of free grid points, $\|e_1\| \leq h - 4$ and $\|e_2\| \leq w - 4$. For spiral^{in}, we even have sharper upper bounds. Observe that e_1 starts on a grid point above g. Given the orientation of e_2 and Observation 7.1, e_1 ends two units below the x-monotone part of outerLadder^{in}; see Fig. 7.14c. Thus, $\|e_1\| \leq h - 6$. By a similar argument, $\|e_2\| \leq w - 5$.

Now, we show that $\|e_i\| \geq \|e_{i+2}\| + 2$ holds for $i \in \{1, 2\}$. By our previous observations and by the winding direction of the spiral, the spiral is contained in the bounding box of its outer ladder. Since the outer ladder is connected to e_1, its y-monotone part contains a left-oriented line segment below e_4. Thus, by monotonicity and by Observation 7.1, e_4 has to lie at least two units above the bottom endpoint of e_1; see Fig. 7.14c. Given that the top endpoints of e_1 and e_3 have the same y-coordinate, the claim holds for $i = 1$, and, by a similar argument, for $i = 2$. Given Corollary 7.1, the first claim of the lemma follows.

Regarding the second claim, suppose that, for a spiral edge e, $\|e\| \geq low(e) + 2$. Then, by Corollary 7.1, Lemma 7.2 and Definition 7.4, we have in a cascading manner $\|e_1\| \geq low(e_1) + 2$ if e_1 is parallel to e, and $\|e_2\| \geq low(e_2) + 2$ otherwise. Thus, if our spiral is spiral^{out}, then we have $\|e_1\| \geq h - 3$ or $\|e_2\| \geq w - 2$. If our spiral is spiral^{in}, then $\|e_1\| \geq h - 5$ or $\|e_2\| \geq w - 4$. In either case, we have a contradiction to our upper bounds on the spiral edges. $\qquad\square$

Lemma 7.12. *The spirals wind at least $\rho - \sqrt{\rho}$ times around their inner ladders.*

Proof. By Lemma 7.10 and Lemma 7.11, we have to consider only the case that the total perimeter is at most Y_ρ. Consider any of the two spirals. If the spiral winds only around the inner ladder, then we are done. Otherwise, the spiral winds $\alpha \geq 1$ times around its outer ladder (see

---

[2] We consider both outer ladders as outerLadder^{in} possibly visits only one grid point of the left-most vertical line; see Fig. 7.14b.

Corollary 7.1). Consider any vertical spiral edge e of a level i with $1 \le i \le \alpha$ in the outer order. Note that its level is at most $\rho - i + 2$ in the inner order, hence, $\mathrm{low}(e) \le 2(\rho - i + 2) + Y$ by Definition 7.4. Recall that the bounding box of the outer ladder has height at least

$$h - 3 = 2\rho + Y + 4$$

(see Lemma 7.6). Thus, by Observation 7.2, we have

$$\|e\| \ge 2i + (2\rho + Y + 4) \ge 2(\rho - i + 2) + Y + 4i \ge \mathrm{low}(e) + 4i .$$

Consequently, the perimeter of the drawing is at least

$$\mathrm{lowLadders} + \mathrm{lowSpirals} + \sum_{i=1}^{\alpha} 4i$$

$$\ge \mathrm{lowLadders} + \mathrm{lowSpirals} + 2\alpha(\alpha + 1) .$$

Thus, $\alpha \le \sqrt{\rho}$, as otherwise $2\alpha(\alpha + 1) > \mathrm{maxCenterCost} + 2\rho + 12$ (here, recall that we have set $\rho = (\mathrm{maxCenterCost} + 12)^2$) and the perimeter is greater than Y_ρ; a contradiction. We conclude by Corollary 7.1 that the spiral winds at least

$$\rho - \alpha \ge \rho - \sqrt{\rho}$$

times around the inner ladder. □

Lemma 7.13. *For every spiral edge e of level at most $\sqrt{\rho}$ with respect to the inner order, we have $\|e\| \le \mathrm{low}(e) + 2$.*

Proof. By Lemma 7.10 and Lemma 7.11, we have to consider only the case that the total perimeter is at most Y_ρ. Suppose that there is a horizontal edge e of a level $j \le \sqrt{\rho}$ for which $\|e\| \ge \mathrm{low}(e) + 3$ holds. Then, by Lemma 7.12, Definition 7.4, and Lemma 7.2, we also have $\|g\| \ge \mathrm{low}(g) + 3$ for every horizontal edge g of the same spiral of a level between j and $\rho - \sqrt{\rho}$. Hence, the total perimeter of the drawing is at least

$$\mathrm{lowLadders} + \mathrm{lowSpirals} + 3(\rho - 2\sqrt{\rho})$$
$$> \mathrm{lowLadders} + \mathrm{lowSpirals} + \mathrm{maxCenterCost} + 2\rho + 12$$
$$= Y_\rho ;$$

a contradiction to the upper bound Y_ρ. In a similar way, we get a contradiction if e is vertical. □

Now we will see that the spirals interleave until the first level (with respect to the inner ladders). Let $v_1, \ldots, v_{2\rho+1}$ be the vertices (including the endpoints) and let $e_1, \ldots, e_{2\rho}$ be the edges of spiral^{in} in the inner order. Similarly, let $w_1, \ldots, w_{2\rho+3}$ be the vertices (including the endpoints) and let $f_1, \ldots, f_{2\rho+2}$ be the edges of spiral^{out} in the inner order. For $1 \le i < 2\sqrt{\rho}$, we define $\mathrm{BB}_i^{\mathrm{in}}$ as the bounding box of e_i and e_{i+1}, and $\mathrm{BB}_i^{\mathrm{out}}$ as the bounding box of f_i and f_{i+1}.

Lemma 7.14. *For $1 \leq i < 2\sqrt{\rho}$, v_i lies in the interior of BB_i^{out} and w_i lies in the interior of BB_i^{in}.*

Proof. We show the lemma by induction in two steps. First, we prove the claim for $i = 2\sqrt{\rho} - 1$, and then, by induction, for $1 \leq i < 2\sqrt{\rho} - 1$.

Let $i = 2\sqrt{\rho} - 1$. We begin by proving the following observation that will lead us to the first claim: The *interiors* of BB_i^{in} and BB_i^{out} intersect. Recall that both spirals are connected to each other by the polyline realizing S and the inner ladders. If BB_i^{in} and BB_i^{out} were interior-disjoint, then the polyline, starting inside BB_1^{in}, had to leave BB_i^{in} before entering BB_i^{out}. However, such a polyline requires[3] i vertices just for leaving BB_i^{in}, which is more than the number of vertices provided by S and the two inner ladders[4]; a contradiction.

Now, suppose that the claim is violated by v_i not being in the interior of BB_i^{out}. To ease the description, we temporarily rotate the drawing (if needed) such that e_i is a right oriented edge. Since the interiors of the two bounding boxes intersect and given our assumption, v_i lies above w_{i+3} and to the right of w_i and, consequently, also to the right of w_{i+3} (note that we have $\|f_{i+2}\| > \|f_i\|$ by Lemma 7.12); see Fig. 7.15a. In particular, w_{i+3} lies in BB_i^{in}. Observe that the edge f_{i+3} starting at w_{i+3} cannot leave BB_i^{in} and has distance at least 1 to the border of BB_i^{in}. Also note that the levels of e_{i+3} and e_{i+1} differ by one. Thus, the border edge e_{i+1} of BB_i^{in} has length

$$
\begin{aligned}
\|e_{i+1}\| &\geq \|f_{i+3}\| + 2 \\
&\geq \text{low}(f_{i+3}) + 2 \\
&= \text{low}(e_{i+3}) + 2 \\
&= \text{low}(e_{i+1}) + 4 .
\end{aligned}
$$

Since the level of e_{i+1} is $\lceil (i+1)/2 \rceil = \sqrt{\rho}$, the inequality contradicts Lemma 7.13. In a similar way, we show the case for v_i not being in the interior of BB_i^{in}. Thus, our claim holds for $i = 2\sqrt{\rho} - 1$; see Fig. 7.15b.

Now, assume that our claim holds for an i with $2 \leq i \leq 2\sqrt{\rho} - 1$. Temporarily rotate the drawing (if needed) such that e_{i-1} and f_{i-1} are vertical edges facing downwards; see Fig. 7.15b. Consider the bounding boxes BB_{i-1}^{out} and BB_{i-1}^{in}. The vertex w_{i-1} lies in the interior of BB_{i-1}^{in} if and only if v_{i-1} lies below the horizontal line through w_{i-1}. Hence, if the induction hypothesis does not hold for $i - 1$, then v_{i-1} does not lie below w_{i-1} and, thus, the heights of both BB_i^{in} and BB_i^{out} are at least $\|e_{i-1}\| + \|f_{i-1}\|$. Hence, $\|e_{i+1}\| \geq \|e_{i-1}\| + \|f_{i-1}\|$. Therefore, using $\text{low}(f_{i+1}) \geq 5$ (which holds as every spiral edge is longer than $\min\{W, H\} \geq 5$), we have

$$
\begin{aligned}
\|e_{i+1}\| &\geq \|e_{i-1}\| + \|f_{i-1}\| \\
&\geq \text{low}(e_{i-1}) + 5 \\
&= \text{low}(e_{i+1}) + 3 .
\end{aligned}
$$

But this inequality contradicts Lemma 7.13. □

---

[3] Proof sketch: The polyline goes through interior-disjoint regions of type $BB_i^{in} \setminus BB_{i-1}^{in}$ and in order to visit three consecutive such regions, it needs a separate vertex inside the interior of each of the three regions.

[4] Without loss of generality, S has at most $(W+1)(H+1)$ vertices and the inner ladders have at most $4X + 4Y$ vertices in total. Since $i \geq \sqrt{\rho} > \text{maxCenterCost} > (W+1)(H+1) + 4X + 4Y$, i is greater than the number of vertices.

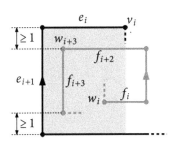

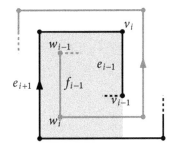

(a) If $v_i \notin \mathrm{BB}_i^{\mathrm{out}}$, then $w_{i+3} \in \mathrm{BB}_i^{\mathrm{in}}$.

(b) The claim: $v_i \in \mathrm{BB}_i^{\mathrm{out}}$ and $w_i \in \mathrm{BB}_i^{\mathrm{in}}$.

Figure 7.15: The bounding boxes $\mathrm{BB}_i^{\mathrm{in}}$ (shaded) and $\mathrm{BB}_i^{\mathrm{out}}$ intersect (for $i = 2\sqrt{\rho} - 1$).

Corollary 7.3. *For every spiral edge e of level at most $\sqrt{\rho}$ with respect to the inner order, we have $\|e\| \leq \mathrm{low}(e) + 1$.*

Proof. By Lemmas 7.10 and 7.11, we have to consider only the case that the total perimeter is at most Υ_p. Suppose that the claim is violated by an edge e_j of $\mathrm{spiral}^{\mathrm{in}}$ (the argument is similar for $\mathrm{spiral}^{\mathrm{out}}$). Thus, $\|e_j\| \geq \mathrm{low}(e_j) + 2$. Recall that $e_j = (v_j, v_{j+1})$. By Lemma 7.14, v_j lies in the interior of $\mathrm{BB}_j^{\mathrm{out}}$ and v_{j+1} lies in the interior of $\mathrm{BB}_{j+1}^{\mathrm{out}}$. Since $\mathrm{BB}_j^{\mathrm{out}} \subset \mathrm{BB}_{j+1}^{\mathrm{out}}$ (as, by Lemma 7.12, we have $\|f_{j+2}\| > \|f_j\|$), e_j lies in the interior of $\mathrm{BB}_{j+1}^{\mathrm{out}}$ and both its endpoints have distance at least 1 to the border of $\mathrm{BB}_{j+1}^{\mathrm{out}}$. Note that the border edge f_{j+2} of $\mathrm{BB}_{j+1}^{\mathrm{out}}$ and e_j are parallel and the level of f_{j+2} is one more than that of e_j. Consequently,

$$\|f_{j+2}\| \geq \|e_j\| + 2 \geq \mathrm{low}(e_j) + 4 = \mathrm{low}(f_{j+2}) + 2 .$$

Recall that the level of e_j is at most $\sqrt{\rho}$. Hence, as in the proof of Lemma 7.13, consider any edge g (of any of the two spirals) that is parallel to e_j and of a level between $\sqrt{\rho} + 1$ and $\rho - \sqrt{\rho}$. For such an edge g, we have $\|g\| \geq \mathrm{low}(g) + 2$. Then, however, the total perimeter of the drawing is at least

$$\mathrm{lowLadders} + \mathrm{lowSpirals} + 2 \cdot 2(\rho - 2\sqrt{\rho})$$
$$> \mathrm{lowLadders} + \mathrm{lowSpirals} + \mathrm{maxCenterCost} + 2\rho + 13$$
$$= \Upsilon_p ;$$

a contradiction to the upper bound Υ_p. $\qquad\square$

Lemma 7.15. *The polyline realizing S lies completely inside a rectangle of width $W + 10$ and height $H + 7$.*

Proof. Let e_0 and f_0 be the vertical edges incident to v_1 and w_1, respectively. We claim that the polyline P connecting v_1 to w_1 (it realizes the inner ladders and S) lies completely in the bounding box of v_2 and w_2; see Fig. 7.16. Note that as a consequence of Lemma 7.14, e_1 lies in the bounding box of f_2 and f_3, and f_1 lies in the bounding box of e_2 and e_3. Hence, the

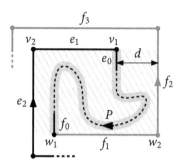

Figure 7.16: The inner-most levels of the spirals. Their endpoints v_1 and w_1 are connected by a highlighted polyline P realizing S and the inner ladders. The polyline has to lie in the bounding box of v_2 and w_2 (hashed area).

relative positions of the elements are as depicted in Fig. 7.16: v_2 lies to the top-left of w_2, f_2 lies to the right of e_0, and e_2 lies to the left of f_0.

First, observe that P can leave the box only between e_0 and f_2 and between e_2 and f_0. Suppose that it leaves the box between e_0 and f_2; the other case is similar. Thus, P contains a vertical line segment between e_0 and f_2 oriented in the same direction as f_2 (to the top). Hence, by Observation 7.1, the distance between the vertical line segment and f_2 is at least 2. Consequently, the distance d between e_0 and f_2 is at least 3. However, given that v_2 is contained in the interior of the bounding box of f_2 and f_3 (Lemma 7.14), we have

$$\|f_3\| \geq \|e_1\| + d + 1 \geq \mathrm{low}(e_1) + 4 = \mathrm{low}(f_1) + 4 = \mathrm{low}(f_3) + 2 .$$

This contradicts Corollary 7.3.

Thus, S lies completely in the bounding box of v_2 and w_2, which itself is contained in the bounding box of f_2 and f_3. By Corollary 7.3, the width of the box is at most

$$\mathrm{low}(f_3) + 1 = X + 5 = W + 10$$

and the height is at most

$$\mathrm{low}(f_2) + 1 = Y + 3 = H + 7 . \qquad \square$$

Hence, S can be drawn within a $((W + 10) \times (H + 10))$-rectangle such that the first and last edge of S are horizontal and such that S can be extended to a simple polygon (given its embedding in T). Hence, $\langle S, W, H \rangle$ is a yes-instance. This conclusion finishes the second direction of our proof of Theorem 7.2.

7.3   The Monotone Case: Minimum Area

In this section, we show how to compute, for a monotone angle sequence, a polygon of minimum bounding box and of minimum area. We start with the simple xy-monotone case and then consider the more general x-monotone case.

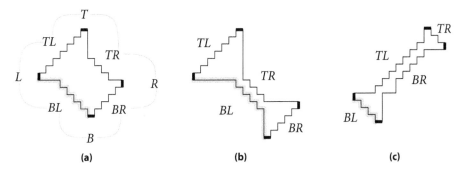

Figure 7.17: Extreme edges are bold. Stair *BL* is highlighted. (a) The four stairs *TL*, *TR*, *BR*, and *BL* of an xy-monotone polygon. The sequences *T*, *R*, *B*, and *L* are unions of neighboring stairs. (b) & (c) Two possibly optimum configurations of the polygon.

7.3.1   The xy-Monotone Case

An xy-monotone polygon has four *extreme edges*; its leftmost and rightmost vertical edge, and its topmost and bottommost horizontal edge. Two consecutive extreme edges are connected by a (possible empty) xy-monotone chain that we will call a *stair*. Starting at the top extreme edge, we let *TL*, *BL*, *BR*, and *TR* denote the four stairs in ccw order; see Fig. 7.17a. We say that an angle sequence consists of k nonempty *stair sequences* if any xy-monotone polygon that realizes it consists of k nonempty stairs; we also call it a *k-stair sequence*. The extreme edges correspond to the exactly four LL-sequences in an xy-monotone angle sequence and are unique up to rotation. Any xy-monotone angle sequence is of the form $[L(LR)^*]^4$, where the single L describes the turn before an extreme edge and $(LR)^*$ describes a stair sequence. Without loss of generality, we assume that an xy-monotone sequence always begins with LL and that we always draw the first LL as the topmost edge (the top extreme edge). Therefore, we can also use *TL*, *BL*, *BR*, and *TR* to denote the corresponding stair sequences, namely the first, second, third and fourth $(LR)^*$ subsequence after the first LL in cyclic order. Let T be the concatenation of *TL*, the top extreme edge, and *TR*; let L, B, and R be defined analogously following Fig. 7.17a. For a chain C, let the *R-length* $r(C)$ be the number of reflex vertices on C. If $C \in \{TR, TL, BL, BR\}$, then $r(C)$ corresponds to the number of horizontal line segments and the number of vertical line segments in C. When we say that a line segment lies above or below another one, we also require implicitly that both line segments share a grid column.

In this section, we obtain the following two results.

Theorem 7.3. *Given an xy-monotone angle sequence S of length n, we can find a polygon P that realizes S and minimizes its (i) bounding box or (ii) area in $\mathcal{O}(n)$ time, and in constant time we can find the optimum objective value if the R-lengths of the stair sequences are given.*

Part (i) of Theorem 7.3 follows from the following observation: The bounding box of every polygon that realizes S has width at least

$$\max\{r(T), r(B)\} + 1$$

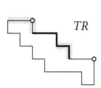
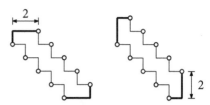

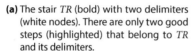

(a) The stair TR (bold) with two delimiters (white nodes). There are only two good steps (highlighted) that belong to TR and its delimiters.

(b) The (only) two optimum polygons realizing the 2-stair instance with $r(BL) = r(TR) = 4$. The nodes depict skew convex vertices. The extreme edges are bold.

Figure 7.18: A stair with good and bad steps (a), and two optimum polygons realizing a 2-stair instance (b).

and height at least

$$\max\{r(L), r(R)\} + 1 .$$

Since we can always draw three stairs with edges of unit length, we can meet these lower bounds.

For part (ii), we first consider angle sequences with at most two nonempty stairs. Here, the only non-trivial case is when the angle sequence consists of two opposite stair sequences, that is, TL and BR, or BL and TR. Without loss of generality, consider the second case.

A stair has two *delimiters* which are the two vertices outside the stair that are adjacent to the endpoints of the stair; see Figure 7.18a. Note that a delimiter is a convex vertex (L vertex). For each convex vertex of a stair and its delimiters, a *step* is the polyline consisting of its two adjacent edges. For a convex vertex of a stair, its step is *good* if both edges have the same length. For a delimiter, its step is *good* if the edge adjacent to the stair is shorter by 1 than the other edge. A step that is not good is *bad*. The *size* of a step is the minimum of the lengths of its two edges.

Lemma 7.16. *Let S be an xy-monotone angle sequence of length n consisting of exactly two nonempty opposite stair sequences BL and TR. If $r(BL) = r(TR)$, then we can choose any extreme edge and, in $\mathcal{O}(n)$ time, we can compute a minimum-area polygon realizing S such that the chosen extreme edge has length 1.*

Proof. Fix a minimum-area polygon P^* that realizes S. Let $a = r(TR)$ and $b = r(BL)$. If $a = b$, then any two parallel extreme edges have length 2 and all other edges have length 1; see Fig. 7.18b. To see this, we use a charging argument. Call a convex vertex *skew* if it is the top right corner or the bottom left corner of the bounding box of its two adjacent edges. Observe that a grid cell lying in the interior of a polygon can touch at most one skew convex vertex of the polygon, assuming that the polygon has more than four vertices. As each convex vertex is touched by exactly one grid cell from the interior, the number of skew convex vertices is a lower bound on the area. Thus, the two polygons of our construction are optimum as every grid cell is touching a skew convex vertex. Hence, if $a = b$, the minimum area is

$$\operatorname{area}(P^*) = 2(b + 1) .$$

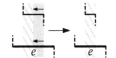

(a) If two segments share two grid columns (hatched and shaded), contract both by one unit.

(b) If a segments shares two grid columns (hatched and shaded) adjacent to a reflex vertex of a long segment, contract both segments by one unit.

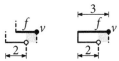

(c) If there is a vertex (white node) one unit left and to the bottom of v, then its incident horizontal segment has length at least 2.

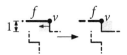

(d) If the vertical segment adjacent to v has length only 1, then decrease the area.

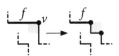

(e) If the vertical segment adjacent to v has length at least 2, then decrease the area by introducing a new reflex vertex (black node).

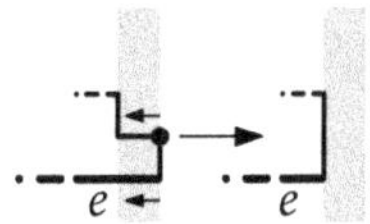

(f) Then remove one reflex vertex (black node) by removing one unit of the right end of the polygon.

Figure 7.19: Forbidden configurations for P^* as they allow to decrease the area. In (c)–(f), we assume that the only segment in $\widehat{BL}$ of length greater than 1 is the bottom extreme edge.

Also note that these two polygons are the only optimum ones as any other polygon contains at least one grid cell not adjacent to any skew convex vertex.   □

Lemma 7.17. *Let S be an xy-monotone angle sequence of length n consisting of exactly two nonempty opposite stair sequences BL and TR. If $r(BL) \neq r(TR)$, let $X \in \{BL, TR\}$ be the stair with the smaller number of reflex vertices. Given any priorities on the steps belonging to X and its delimiters, in $\mathcal{O}(n)$ time, we can compute a minimum-area polygon realizing S that minimizes the sizes of the steps according to the priorities.*

Proof. Fix a minimum-area polygon P^* that realizes S. Let $a = r(TR)$ and $b = r(BL)$. Assume $a < b$ (by rotation if necessary). Let $\widehat{BL}$ denote the polyline consisting of BL and the bottom and left extreme edge, and let $\widehat{TR}$ denote the polyline consisting of TR and the top and right extreme edge.

First, we show that all segments of $\widehat{BL}$ are of unit length. Suppose that the claim were false and that there is, without loss of generality, a horizontal line segment in $\widehat{BL}$ longer than 1. Consider the leftmost such segment e and let $l(e)$ and $r(e)$ denote its left and right endpoint, respectively. If there were a horizontal segment in $\widehat{TR}$ sharing at least two grid columns with e, we could contract both segments by one unit and decrease the area of P^* without causing $\widehat{BL}$ and $\widehat{TR}$ to intersect; a contradiction to the optimality of P^*; see Fig. 7.19a. There is also no horizontal segment in $\widehat{TR}$ passing through the two grid columns left and right of $r(e)$, as, again, we could contract and obtain a contradiction; see Fig. 7.19b.

We will now show that e is not the bottom extreme edge. If it were, we could modify P^* as follows to decrease its area. First, we will observe that there is a convex vertex v of $\widehat{TR}$ whose both incident edges have length at least 2 and that there is no vertex of $\widehat{BL}$ one unit to the left and to the bottom of it. Given $a < b$, there is a horizontal line segment in $\widehat{TR}$ of length at

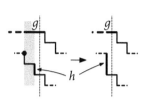

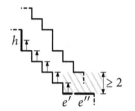

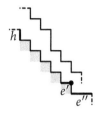

(a) The sweepline (dotted) stabbed a long segment g of $\widehat{TR}$. Contract g and the horizontal segment of $\widehat{BL}$ left to the sweepline by one unit. The vertical segment h gets longer and we loose one reflex vertex (black node).

(b) Move all segments that were stabbed by the sweepline up by one unit, including e'. There are not intersections as they have vertical distance at least 2 to $\widehat{TR}$.

(c) The resulting polygon is simple, has less area and contains one new reflex vertex (black node).

Figure 7.20: If there is a line segment in $\widehat{BL}$ of length greater than 1, then we can decrease the area of P^* in several steps.

least 2. Consider the rightmost such segment f and let v denote the right endpoint of f. If f is the top extreme edge, then all horizontal edges, with the exception of e and f, have length 1. Given $a < b$, that fact implies $\|f\| > \|e\|$. Hence, $\|f\| \geq 3$. In both cases of whether f is the top extreme edge or not, if there were a vertex of $\widehat{BL}$ lying one unit to the left and to the bottom of v, then there is an incident horizontal edge of length at least 2; see Fig. 7.19c. This, however is a contradiction as the only edge in $\widehat{BL}$ of length bigger than 1 is e and its right endpoint is the rightmost vertex in $\widehat{BL}$. Suppose that the vertical edge incident to v had length only 1. Then we could move the vertical edge by one unit to the left without causing any intersections; see Fig. 7.19d. This, however, is a contradiction to the optimality of P^*. Consider the grid cell inside P^* that has v as an endpoint. As argued above, it intersects no vertices of $\widehat{BL}$ and, consequently, no line segments of $\widehat{BL}$. Rotate the grid cell, together with the line drawings on its boundary, by 180°; see Fig. 7.19e. The resulting polygon $P^{*'}$ has less area than P^*, but one reflex vertex more. To remove one reflex vertex from $P^{*'}$, we contract one unit of e and we contract the rightmost edge of $\widehat{TR}$, which has length 1; see Fig. 7.19f. Hence, the area decreases again, and we obtain a contradiction to the optimality of P^*, as our resulting polygon realizes the same angle sequence. We conclude that e is not the bottom extreme edge.

Next, using the fact that e is not the bottom extreme edge, we will decrease the area of the polygon by removing a carefully chosen reflex vertex from $\widehat{BL}$. Later, we will restore the angle sequence of $\widehat{BL}$ without increasing the area and thus obtain a contradiction. We cut e one unit right to $l(e)$ into two segments, e' and e'', where e' denotes the left part. All the facts above imply that the vertical distance between e' and $\widehat{TR}$ is at least $\|e\|$, hence, at least 2. Place a vertical line through e', that we call a *sweepline*, and move the line to the left until, for the first time, one of the two events occurs: (a) The horizontal line segment of $\widehat{TR}$ stabbed by the line has length greater than 1, or (b) the horizontal line segment of $\widehat{BL}$ stabbed by the line has an (left) incident vertical segment of length greater than 1. Note that one of the two events will occur since, in our case, the left and top extreme edge cannot simultaneously attend length 1. Let h denote the left vertical line segment incident to the last horizontal line segment of $\widehat{BL}$ stabbed by the sweepline; see Fig. 7.20a. If the sweep process terminates with event (a), take the horizontal line segment g in $\widehat{TR}$ of length at least 2 that has been stabbed by the sweep line.

Contract one unit of this segment and contract the rightmost horizontal line segment of $\widehat{BL}$ left to e' that has not been stabbed. The latter segment has to be a unit-length segment. By this operation, we decrease the area of P^*, we increase the length of h, and we loose one reflex vertex in BL. We proceed similarly if the sweep process does not terminate with event (a). We take any horizontal line segment g in $\widehat{TR}$ of length at least 2, which exists given $a < b$, and which lies left to the sweep line or right to e. Then we contract one unit of g and we contract the leftmost horizontal line segment lying below g. As a result, we decrease the area and loose one reflex vertex.

In both cases, the vertical edge h has length at least 2. Now, in order to reintroduce the missing reflex vertex, we take the subsequence of all segments of $\widehat{BL}$ that where stabbed by the line at some moment, and shift all these segments up by one unit. In the same time, we shrink h by one unit and connect the right endpoint of e' via a vertical segment to e''; see Fig. 7.20b and 7.20c. To see that we do not cause any intersections, recall that the distance between e' and $\widehat{TR}$ is at least 2. Also, recall that all line segments of our subsequence have unit length, the horizontal ones as well as the vertical ones. Together with the fact that all horizontal line segments of $\widehat{TR}$ lying above the subsequence, with possible exception of the last segment, also have unit length, we conclude that every line segment of our subsequence had distance at least 2 to $\widehat{TR}$ before the up-shifting. Hence, we have obtained a feasible polygon for the same angle sequence as P^* but with smaller area; a contradiction.

Next, we express the area of P^* as a function of the edge lengths of $\widehat{TR}$. We will use the function to find out which values for the edge lengths minimize the area. For $1 \le i \le a + 1$, let τ_i denote the i-th horizontal segment in $\widehat{TR}$ from the left. Given our assumption that all horizontal segments of $\widehat{BL}$ are of unit-length, we can express the length $\|\tau_i\|$ of τ_i as the number of horizontal segments of $\widehat{BL}$ lying below τ_i. Thus, we have $\sum_{i=1}^{a+1} \|\tau_i\| = b + 1$. Let area($i$) denote the area below τ_i in P^*, that is, the number of grid cells in P^* sharing a grid column with τ_i. Since the left extreme edge in P^* has length 1, the area in P^* under τ_1 is

$$\text{area}(1) \;=\; \sum_{j=1}^{\|\tau_1\|} j \;=\; \frac{\|\tau_1\|\,(\|\tau_1\| + 1)}{2} \,.$$

For $2 \le i \le a + 1$, the distance between τ_i and any horizontal segment below it is 2; it cannot be less, and if it were more, we could feasibly shift τ_i to the bottom by at least one unit, contradicting the optimality of P^*. Thus, we have

$$\text{area}(i) \;=\; \sum_{j=1}^{\|\tau_i\|} (j + 1) \;=\; \frac{(\|\tau_i\| + 1)(\|\tau_i\| + 2)}{2} - 1 \,.$$

We can overcome the difference between $i = 1$ and $i \ge 2$ by splitting τ_1 into τ_0' and τ_1', such that $\|\tau_0'\| = 1$ and $\|\tau_1'\| = \|\tau_1\| - 1$ holds. Note that $\|\tau_1'\|$ can be 0. For $2 \le i \le a + 1$, let $\tau_i' = \tau_i$. Observe that now we have

$$\sum_{i=1}^{a+1} \|\tau_i'\| = b \,.$$

Thus,

$$\text{area}(P^*) = 1 + \sum_{i=1}^{a+1} \left(\frac{(\|\tau_i'\| + 1)(\|\tau_i'\| + 2)}{2} - 1 \right)$$

$$= 1 + \sum_{i=1}^{a+1} \left(\frac{1}{2} \|\tau_i'\|^2 + \frac{3}{2} \|\tau_i'\| \right)$$

$$= 1 + \frac{3}{2} b + \frac{1}{2} \sum_{i=1}^{a+1} \|\tau_i'\|^2 \, ,$$

which is minimized if $\sum_{i=1}^{a+1} \|\tau_i'\|^2$ is minimal. By Cauchy-Schwarz, we know that this is the case if, for every $i \in \{1, \dots, a+1\}$, the length $\|\tau_i'\|$ is equal to the arithmetic mean; since we have to use integers, the convexity of the function tells us that, for every $i \in \{1, \dots, a+1\}$, the length $\|\tau_i'\|$ has to be as close to the arithmetic mean as possible, that is,

$$\|\tau_i'\| \in \{\lfloor b/(a+1) \rfloor, \lceil b/(a+1) \rceil \} \, .$$

Let q bet the quotient and r the remainder when b is divided by $a + 1$. Hence,

$$\text{area}(P^*) = \frac{(a+1)(q+1)(q+2)}{2} - a + r(q+2) \, .$$

Repeating the same discussion for the vertical segment, we obtain the fact that every line segments of TR is of length $\lfloor b/(a+1) \rfloor$ or $\lceil b/(a+1) \rceil$, and the top and right extreme edge is of length $\lfloor b/(a+1) \rfloor + 1$ or $\lceil b/(a+1) \rceil + 1$ (the latter fact follows from $\|\tau_1\| = \|\tau_1'\| + 1$). Observe that, in P^*, all steps belonging to TL and its delimiters are good steps. Otherwise, we could take one of the two edges belonging to a bad step and move it towards the interior of the polygon and thus contradict the optimality of P^*. Further, observe that, for $1 \le i \le a + 1$, the size of the i-th step from the left corresponds to $\|\tau_i'\|$. Hence, all steps are of size $\lfloor b/(a+1) \rfloor$ or $\lceil b/(a+1) \rceil$. We conclude that we can arbitrarily assign the values $\lfloor b/(a+1) \rfloor$ or $\lceil b/(a+1) \rceil$ to the steps sizes as long as they sum up to b and in this way obtain a feasible, and, hence, minimum polygon realizing S. Thereby, we can take into account any priority on the steps given by the input. Thus, we can construct a minimum-area polygon realizing S in $\mathcal{O}(n)$ time. □

Note that the proofs of Lemma 7.16 and 7.17 also allow us to obtain, in $\mathcal{O}(1)$ time, the exact area of a minimum polygon without having to construct it. We summarize our results in the following corollary.

Corollary 7.4. *Let S be an xy-monotone angle sequence of length n consisting of exactly two nonempty opposite stair sequences BL and TR. We can find a minimum-area polygon that realizes S in $\mathcal{O}(n)$ time. If $\mathrm{r}(BL)$ and $\mathrm{r}(TR)$ are given, we can compute the area of such a polygon in $\mathcal{O}(1)$ time.*

The proofs of Lemmas 7.16 and 7.17 also lead to the following observation.

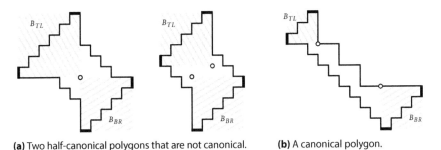

(a) Two half-canonical polygons that are not canonical.   (b) A canonical polygon.

Figure 7.21: Examples of half-canonical and canonical polygons. The nodes depict the interior corners of the bounding boxes (hatched).

Observation 7.4. *Let P be any polygon realizing an angle sequence S consisting of exactly two nonempty opposite stairs TR and BL with $a = r(TR)$ and $b = r(BL)$. The polygon P is a polygon of minimum area realizing S if and only if the following holds: If $a < b$, then*

  (i) *the steps of TR and its delimiters are good and have size $\lfloor b/(a+1) \rfloor$ or $\lceil b/(a+1) \rceil$.*

  (ii) *the bottom and right extreme edge and all edges of BL have length 1.*

If $a = b$, then

  (iii) *two parallel extreme edges have length 2, and*

  (iv) *all other edges have length 1.*

We now consider the case of four nonempty stairs. (The case of three nonempty stairs can be solved analogously.) We begin by defining a special class of four-stairs polygons that fulfil certain properties.

Definition 7.6. Let P be any xy-monotone polygon P with four nonempty stairs TL, TR, BL, and BR. For $X \in \{TL, TR, BL, BR\}$, let B_X denote the bounding box of X and its adjacent extreme edges. An *interior corner* of B_X is the corner of B_X that lies inside P and not on the extension of any extreme edge adjacent to X. We call P *half-canonical* if P has two non-adjacent nonempty stairs $(X, Y) \in \{(TL, BR), (TR, BL)\}$ such that

  (C1) B_X and B_Y do not intersect in more than one point,

and we call it *canonical* if even

  (C2) each of the two interior corners of B_X and B_Y lies on a line segment of P that also contains an endpoint of one the two stairs in $\{TL, BR, TR, BL\} \setminus X \cup Y$.

Figure 7.21 depicts some examples for the case that $X = B_{TL}$ and $Y = B_{BR}$ holds. In Property (C2), the interior corner of the bounding box may coincide with the endpoint of the respective stair; see B_{TL} in Fig. 7.21b. Also note that Property (C1) is a necessary condition for Property (C2).

Now we show that an optimum polygon realizing S can be assumed to be canonical. This fact will help us to argue that an optimum polygon can be partitioned into simpler subinstances.

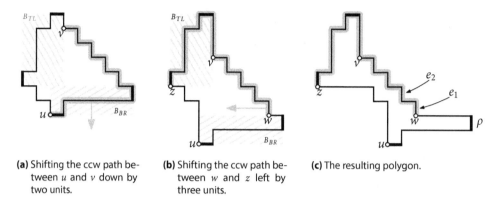

(a) Shifting the ccw path between u and v down by two units.

(b) Shifting the ccw path between w and z left by three units.

(c) The resulting polygon.

Figure 7.22: Transforming an xy-monotone polygon to a polygon that satisfies (C1) and has less area.

Hence, it will suffice to enumerate all compatible subinstances, to solve them and to put them together in order to obtain an optimum polygon.

Lemma 7.18. *For every four-stair sequence S with $|S| > 36$, there exists a polygon of minimum area realizing S that is canonical.*

Proof. Consider an optimum polygon P^* realizing the angle sequence S. Suppose it is not canonical. Observe that all four extreme edges are of length 1, otherwise the polygon is not optimum.

First, suppose that Property (C1) does not hold. Then, for any pair of two opposite stairs, the bounding boxes of their adjacent extreme edges intersect in more than one point. Hence, the (closed) x-ranges of the horizontal extreme edges intersect and the (closed) y-ranges of the vertical extreme edges intersect. Since the extreme edges have length 1, and the bounding boxes intersect in more than one point, we even have that the (closed) x-ranges of the top and bottom extreme edges are the same, or the (closed) y-ranges of the left and right extreme edges are the same. Suppose (by rotation if necessary) it is the latter and also suppose (by temporary vertical or horizontal reflection and, afterwards, backward reflection) that the stair TR has R-length greater than 4 (since $|S| > 36$, this is possible). Let u be the left endpoint of the bottom extreme edge and let v be the reflex vertex that precedes, in ccw order, the top extreme edge; see Fig. 7.22a.

We shift the boundary of P^* that lies on the ccw walk from u to v down by two units, stretching the vertical edges adjacent to u and v. The new polygon P' still realizes the angle sequence and its area is larger by two units than the area of P. However, now B_{TL} and B_{BR} are intersection-free. Let w be the reflex vertex that follows, in ccw order, the right extreme edge and let z be the bottom endpoint of the left extreme edge; see Fig. 7.22b. We shift the boundary of P' that lies on the ccw walk from w to z to the left by three units, stretching the horizontal edges adjacent to w and z. The new polygon still realizes the angle sequence and is still simple: The only crossings that can occur by this operation are between TR and BL. The left extreme edge lies at most three rows above the right extreme edge ρ; hence, any crossing must involve the vertical edge e_1 of TR in the row above ρ or the vertical edge e_2 of TR two rows above ρ;

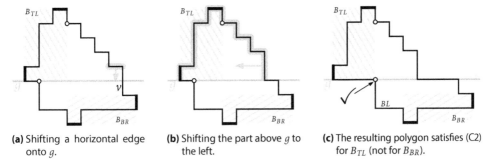

(a) Shifting a horizontal edge onto g.

(b) Shifting the part above g to the left.

(c) The resulting polygon satisfies (C2) for B_{TL} (not for B_{BR}).

Figure 7.23: Transforming an xy-monotone polygon to a polygon that satisfies (C2) and has the same area.

see Fig. 7.22. Let the x-axis go from left to right and let $x(v)$ denote the x-coordinate of v where v is a vertex or a vertical segment. Since $r(TR) > 4$, we have after the shift

$$x(e_1) \geq x(e_2) \geq x(v) + r(TR) - 2 \geq x(v) + 3 = x(u) + 1.$$

Since each vertical edge of BL has x-coordinate at most $x(u)$, there can be no crossing. However, now the area of the polygon decreased by three units; a contradiction to the fact that P^* is optimum. Hence, Property (C1) has to hold for P^*.

Now, assume that there is a bounding box pair having at most one point in common, without loss of generality, B_{TL} and B_{BR}. Since the optimum polygon P^* is not canonical, Property (C2) has to be violated by at least one of the two bounding boxes, say B_{TL}. Then the interior corner (bottom right corner) of B_{TL} does not lie on a line segment that also contains an endpoint of TR or BL. Hence, the endpoints of TR or BL have to lie on the boundary of B_{TL} "behind" the interior corner, that is, they lie on two different edges of B_{TL} and, for each one of them, its distance to the closest corner of B_{TL} is at least 1. Then, for at least one of the two edges, it holds that the line going through the edge does not cross the interior of B_{BR} (it can happen that only one such line exists as Fig. 7.21a indicates). Without loss of generality, this holds for the line g that goes through the horizontal edge of B_{TL}.

Next, we observe that g does not cross any vertical line segment of TR; instead, there is a horizontal line segment of TR lying on g. To see this, suppose the contrary. Thus, there exists a vertical line segment v of TR that is cut by g; see Fig. 7.23a. Thus, the two endpoints of v lie at least one unit above and below g, respectively. Consider the horizontal line segment of TR starting at the top endpoint of v. We can move the horizontal segment downwards and place it on g. By this operation, the angle sequence does not change and the polygon remains simple as all line segments of BL, the only segments that might cross TR after his operation, lie below g by at least one unit. Hence, by moving the horizontal edge downwards, we in fact shrink the area of the polygon; a contradiction to its optimality. Thus, g contains a horizontal line segment of TR.

Now, we cut the polygon through g into two parts; see Fig. 7.23b. Then, we shift the upper part to the left until the endpoint of BL coincides with the bottom right corner of B_{TL}; see Fig. 7.23c. Hence, Property (C2) is satisfied for B_{TL}. Moreover, the resulting polygon realizes the same angle sequence as before and has the same area as before. Note that if B_{BR} satisfied

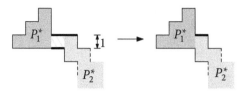

Figure 7.24: If P_2^* connects to P_1^* via two horizontal segments (bold) of distance 1, then the top one of them has length at least 2. Thus, we can contract both by one unit and reduce the area by one grid cell (hatched).

Property (C2) before the shift operation, then it also satisfies the property afterwards: If its interior corner (top left corner) lies below g, then any edge containing the corner will remain unchanged as we do not change anything below g. If its interior corner lies on g, then B_{BR} can only satisfy Property (C2) by an endpoint of TR which has also to lie on g. During the shift operation, we move this endpoint only to the left, thus the property remains fulfilled for B_{BR}.

If the polygon is not yet canonical, then we repeat the procedure with B_{BR} (without losing Property (C2) for B_{TL}) and obtain a canonical optimum polygon. Hence, Property (C2) holds. □

Let P^* be a canonical optimum polygon. Without loss of generality, Property (C2) is satisfied for B_{TL} and B_{BR}. Consider the line segment of TR and the line segment of BL that connect to B_{TL} in a canonical polygon. The two line segments are connected to a same edge of B_{TL} and are

(i) both horizontal,

(ii) both vertical, or

(iii) perpendicular to each other.

The same holds for B_{BR}. Consequently, there is only a constant number of ways in which the stairs outside the two bounding boxes are connected to them. Even more, the three cases cannot appear arbitrarily in an optimum polygon as we will see below.

We cut the optimum polygon P^* along the edge of B_{TL} to which BL and TR are connected. We also cut along the respective edge of B_{BR}. We get three polygons P_1^*, P_2^* and P_3^*. The polygons P_1^* and P_3^*, which lie on the outside, realize the 1-stair sequence defined by TL and BR (including adjacent extreme edges), respectively, whereas the middle polygon P_2^* realizes the 2-stair sequence defined by the concatenation of BL, TR, and the edge segments of B_{TL} and B_{BR} that connect them.

Let $a = r(TR)$ and $b = r(BL)$. If $a = b$, then, for at least one of the two bounding boxes B_{TL} and B_{BR}, Case (iii) holds. To see this, suppose the contrary. Then, for P_1^* and P_3^*, the two parallel segments of TR an BL attached to it have distance at least 2, as otherwise we could shrink the area; see Fig. 7.24. This fact implies that the extreme edges of B_{TL} and B_{BR} to which we attached P_2^* have length at least 3. Let e and f denote the extreme edges in the angle sequence of P_2^* to which we attached P_1^* and P_3^*, respectively. By Observation 7.4, we compute a minimum-area polygon P_2 for the angle sequence of P_2^* such that e has length 1 and f has length at most 2. Then, we can feasibly attach P_1^* and P_3^* to P_2 yielding a polygon for S of area at most area(P^*). However, now the two parallel segments of TR an BL touching P_1^* have only distance 1. As discussed above, we can shrink the area; a contradiction to the optimality of P^*.

This observation leads to the following algorithm: For $|S| \leq 36$, we find a solution in constant time by exhaustive search. For larger $|S|$, we guess which pair of opposite bounding boxes in $\{(TL, BR), (TR, BL)\}$ is intersection-free in the canonical optimum polygon P^* that we want to compute. Without loss of generality, we guessed B_{TL} and B_{BR} (the other case is symmetric). Then, we guess how TR and BL, the two stairs outside B_{TL} and B_{BR}, are connected to each of the two bounding boxes (see Cases (i)–(iii)). The guessed information gives us two 1-stair instances and a 2-stair instance. We solve the instances independently and then put the solutions together to form a solution to the whole instance.

Whereas the 1-stair instances are trivial to solve, we apply Lemmas 7.16 and 7.17 to obtain a solution to the middle instance. For this purpose, we will also fix some edge lengths and assign priorities to steps as follows. Let $a = r(TR)$ and $b = r(BL)$. Without loss of generality, $a \leq b$ and $r(TL) \leq r(BR)$ (the other cases are symmetric). Assume $a = b$. If we guessed Case (iii) for both B_{TL} and B_{BR}, then we choose an arbitrary extreme edge to have length 1. Otherwise, exactly one of the two bounding boxes is in Case (i) or (ii). When its corresponding instance has been solved, we have to attach the solution to a particular extreme edge of the solution of the middle instance. We choose this extreme edge to have length 1 in the solution (see Lemma 7.16). Next, assume $a < b$. Recall that for this case, the algorithm of Lemma 7.17 takes any priorities into account that we have assigned to the steps. The algorithm guarantees that steps of higher priority are not smaller than steps of lower priority. We will assign the priorities in the following way. If we guessed Case (ii) for B_{TL}, then we assign the highest priority to the step of the left delimiter of TR, and the second-highest priority to the step of the right delimiter of TR. In all other cases, we give the highest priority to the step of the right delimiter of TR.

In detail, we put our three solutions together as follows. Let P_1 denote our solution to the instance corresponding to B_{TL}, let P_2 denote our solution to the middle instance, and let P_3 denote our solution to the instance corresponding to B_{BR}; see Fig. 7.25a. If we guessed Case (ii) for B_{TL}, then we put P_1 and P_2 together along their corresponding horizontal extreme edges. If the bottom extreme edge of P_1 is too short, we make it sufficiently longer by shifting the left extreme edge of P_1 to the left; see Fig.. 7.25b. Case (i) works symmetrically. If we guessed Case (iii) for B_{TL}, then note that the left or top extreme edge of P_2 has length at least 2 (independently of that we are in Case (iii)). We glue P_1 and P_2 together along this extreme edge and the corresponding extreme edge of P_1; see Fig. 7.25a. We repeat the same process with P_2 and P_3.

All in all, we obtain a canonical polygon P which realizes the given angle sequence. To show that it has minimum area, we cut it into three smaller parts and show that the area of each part is upper bounded by the corresponding part of P^*. Our choice of the parts will depend on the following cases.

(1) First, assume that we did not prolong any extreme edges. Consider the optimum polygon P^* realizing S and our guesses and cut it accordingly to obtain three polygons P_1^*, P_2^*, and P_3^*, corresponding to the three instances of P_1, P_2 and P_3, respectively. Note that, by construction, P_2 is a minimum-area polygon. Since we did not prolong

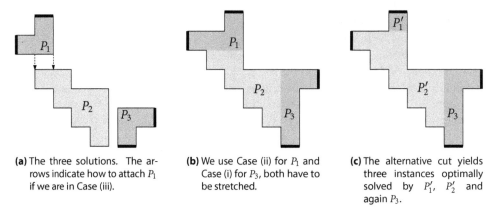

(a) The three solutions. The arrows indicate how to attach P_1 if we are in Case (iii).

(b) We use Case (ii) for P_1 and Case (i) for P_3, both have to be stretched.

(c) The alternative cut yields three instances optimally solved by P_1', P_2' and again P_3.

Figure 7.25: Putting the three solutions P_1, P_2 and P_3 together.

the edges of P_1 and P_2, these polygons are also of minimum area. Hence, for $1 \le i \le 3$, we obtain $\text{area}(P_i) \le \text{area}(P_i^*)$, implying

$$\text{area}(P) \le \text{area}(P^*).$$

(2) Secondly, assume that we did prolong only an extreme edge of P_1. Then we guessed Cases (i) or (ii) for B_{TL}. Note that we did not prolong any edge of P_2 if $a = b$ as otherwise we would have solved P_2 such that the extreme edge on P_2 to which we attached P_1 would have unit length; contradicting the necessity to prolong the corresponding extreme edge of P_1. Thus, we have $a < b$. Further, observe that we did not guess Case (i) for P_1, as otherwise we would attach P_1 to the left extreme edge of P_2. This would, however, contradict the necessity to prolong as the left extreme edge has unit length by Observation 7.4 and the fact $a < b$. We conclude that we prolonged the bottom extreme edge e of P_1 in Case (ii); see Fig. 7.25b. We now cut P^* in a slightly different way. Our first cut goes horizontally through the top endpoint of the left extreme edge (before, we cut through the bottom endpoint), and our second cut is the same as before. Hence, by the second cut, we again obtain P_3^*. The two other polygons that we get, $P_1^{*\prime}$ and $P_2^{*\prime}$, realize a 1- and a 2-stair instance, respectively. We cut P in the same way and obtain three polygons P_1', P_2', and P_3, where P_2' is the polygon realizing the 2 star instance; see Fig. 7.25c. Whereas P_1 is not a minimum-area polygon due to the prolongation of its extreme edge, we have that P_1' as well as P_3 is a minimum-area polygon. Hence, $\text{area}(P_1') \le \text{area}(P_1^*)$ and $\text{area}(P_3) \le \text{area}(P_3^*)$. We now show that $\text{area}(P_2') \le \text{area}(P_2^{*\prime})$ holds by proving that P_2' is a minimum-area polygon. The three inequalities will imply $\text{area}(P) \le \text{area}(P^*)$.

Let BL' be the stair sequence that we obtain by adding one reflex and one convex vertex to BL. Thus, we have $r(BL') = b + 1$. Observe that the 2-stair instance realized by P_2' and $P_2^{*\prime}$ consists of the two stairs TR and BL'. Given that all line segments belonging to BL in P_2 had unit length, so do all the line segments in P_2' belonging to BL'. The same holds for the left and bottom extreme edge of P_2'. Then, note that the step s' of the left delimiter of TR in P_2' is good. Also note that it is bigger by 1 when compared to the step s of the left delimiter of TR in P_2. Given our priorities on the steps when we computed P_2, the size of s is $\lfloor b/(a+1) \rfloor$. Consequently, the size of s' is $\lfloor b/(a+1) \rfloor + 1$. Let S and S' denote all the steps belonging to TR with its delimiters in P_2 and P_2', respectively. As the sizes of the steps in $S \smallsetminus \{s\}$ did not change, all steps in S' have sizes in $\{\lfloor b/(a+1) \rfloor, \lceil b/(a+1) \rceil, \lfloor b/(a+1) \rfloor + 1\}$. If s was the only stair of size $\lfloor b/(a+1) \rfloor$, then, given the total size b of all steps in S, all steps in S' must have the same size $(b+1)/(a+1)$. Otherwise, if s was not the only stair in S of size $\lfloor b/(a+1) \rfloor$, then only two different step sizes occur for S' and, in particular, we have $\lfloor b/(a+1) \rfloor = \lfloor (b+1)/(a+1) \rfloor$. Hence, in every case, all steps in S' have size in $\{\lfloor (b+1)/(a+1) \rfloor, \lceil (b+1)/(a+1) \rceil\}$. Given all these facts, Observation 7.4 implies that P_2' is a minimum-area polygon.

(3) Thirdly, assume that we also prolonged an extreme edge of P_3. By a similar argument that we used for P_1, one can show that this may happen only if we guessed Case (i) for B_{BR} and $a < b$ holds. In what follows, let r be the step of the delimiter of TR in P_2. If we did not prolong any extreme edge of P_1 and if r has size $\lfloor b/(a+1) \rfloor$, then we can conduct a similar discussion as in Case (2) and obtain $\mathrm{area}(P) \leq \mathrm{area}(P^*)$.

To this end, we therefore assume that (a) we did prolong an extreme edge of P_1 (it has to be the bottom one), or that (b) the step r has size $\lfloor b/(a+1) \rfloor + 1$. We cut P^* and P in the same way as in Case (2) and we define, for $1 \leq i \leq 3$, the variables P_i' and $P_i^{*'}$, as well as BL', S, S', s and s' in the same way as in Case (2). Note that r is in S and in S'. Also note that r has the smallest size among all steps in $S \smallsetminus \{s\}$ as it received at least the second-highest priority when computing P_2. We claim that P_2' is a minimum-area polygon and that r is a smallest step in S'. Given this claim, we can conduct a similar discussion as in Case (2) and obtain $\mathrm{area}(P) \leq \mathrm{area}(P^*)$.

If we did prolong the bottom extreme edge e of P_1 (which can happen only in Case (ii) for B_{TL}), then the polygon P_2' is of minimum area by our discussion of Case (2). Given that r has the smallest size among all steps in $S \smallsetminus \{s\}$ and given that s' is greater than s, we conclude that r is a smallest step in S'.

Otherwise, assume that we did not prolong e. There are two immediate consequences. First, e is at least one unit longer than the top extreme edge of P_2. Thus, Observation 7.4 implies $\|e\| \geq \lfloor b/(a+1) \rfloor + 1$. Secondly, $\lfloor b/(a+1) \rfloor + 1$ is the size of the step r as one of the two assumptions (a) or (b) must hold. Hence, given the size of r, the left extreme edge g of P_3 has length $\lfloor b/(a+1) \rfloor + 2$ after its prolongation. Recall our assumption $\mathrm{r}(TL) \leq \mathrm{r}(BR)$ and observe $\|e\| = \mathrm{r}(TL) + 1$ and (after prolongation) $\|g\| > \mathrm{r}(BL) + 1$. Thus,

$$\lfloor b/(a+1) \rfloor + 1 \leq \|e\| < \|g\| = \lfloor b/(a+1) \rfloor + 2 ,$$

and so we have $\|e\| = \lfloor b/(a+1) \rfloor + 1$. Further, observe that all line segments belonging to BL' as well as the left and bottom extreme edge are of unit length in P_2'. Since the top extreme edge of P_2' coincides with e, we conclude that s' is a good step that is bigger than s by exactly one unit. Given that r has the smallest size among all steps in $S \smallsetminus \{s\}$ and size greater than s, all steps in $S \smallsetminus \{s\}$ are of size $\lfloor b/(a+1) \rfloor + 1$. Thus,

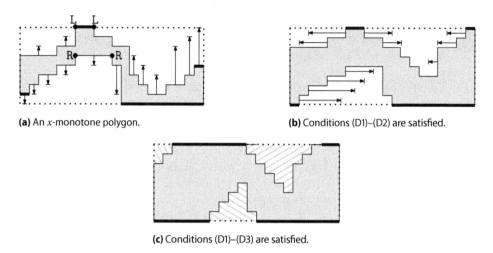

(a) An x-monotone polygon.

(b) Conditions (D1)–(D2) are satisfied.

(c) Conditions (D1)–(D3) are satisfied.

Figure 7.26: Illustration of how to make a polygon canonical. The bold horizontal edges are outer extreme edges, the hashed area marks double stairs (see definition in proof of Theorem 7.4). Note that the illustrating drawing is not optimal.

all steps in S' are good and of the same size, hence, of size $(b+1)/(a+1)$. Therefore, by Observation 7.4, P_2' is a minimum-area polygon and r a smallest step in S'.

We conclude that we computed a polygon of minimum area. The run time is linear in n since our algorithm computes only constantly many 1-stair and 2-stair instances which are each solvable in linear time. Given the number of reflex vertices for the four stairs, we can even compute the minimum area in constant time since this is true for instances with two or less stairs. This observation completes our proof of Theorem 7.3.

7.3.2   The x-Monotone Case

For the x-monotone case, we first give an algorithm that minimizes the bounding box of the polygon, and then an algorithm that minimizes the area.

An x-monotone polygon consists of two *vertical extreme* edges, that is, the leftmost and the rightmost vertical edge, and at least two *horizontal extreme* edges, which are defined to be the horizontal edges of locally maximum or minimum height. The vertical extreme edges divide the polygon into an upper and a lower hull, each of which consists of xy-monotone chains that are connected by the horizontal extreme edges. We call a horizontal extreme edge of type RR an *inner extreme edge*, and a horizontal extreme edge of type LL an *outer extreme edge*; see Fig. 7.26a. Similar to the xy-monotone case, we consider a *stair* to be an xy-monotone chain between any two consecutive extreme edges (outer and inner extreme edges as well as vertical extreme edges) and we let *stair sequence* denote the corresponding angle subsequence $(LR)^*$. Without loss of generality, at least one inner extreme edge exists, otherwise the polygon is xy-monotone and we refer to Section 7.3.1. Given an x-monotone sequence, we always draw the first RR-subsequence as the leftmost inner extreme edge of the lower hull. By this, the correspondence between the angle subsequences and the stairs and extreme edges is unique.

Definition 7.7. An x-monotone polygon is *canonical* if

(D1) all outer extreme edges are lying on the border of the bounding box,

(D2) each vertical non-extreme edge that is not incident to an inner extreme edge has length 1, and

(D3) each horizontal edge that is not an outer extreme edge has length 1.

The following lemma states that it suffices to find a canonical x-monotone polygon of minimum bounding box; see Fig. 7.26 for an illustration.

Lemma 7.19. *Any x-monotone polygon can be transformed into a canonical x-monotone polygon without changing its bounding box.*

Proof. Let P be an x-monotone polygon. We transform it into a canonical polygon in two steps without changing its bounding box.

First, we move all horizontal edges on the upper hull as far up as possible and all horizontal edges on the lower hull as far down as possible; see Fig. 7.26a and 7.26b. This establishes Condition (D1). Furthermore, assume that there is a vertical edge (u, v) on the upper hull with $y(u) > y(v) + 1$. If the (unique) horizontal edge (v, w) is not an inner extreme edge, then it can be moved upwards until $y(u) = y(v) + 1$, which contradicts the assumption that all horizontal edges on the upper hull are moved as far up as possible. This argument applies symmetrically to the edges on the lower hull. Hence, Condition (D2) is established.

Second, we move all vertical edges on a stair as far as possible in the direction of the inner extreme edge bounding the stair, for instance, if the stair lies on the upper hull and is directed downwards, then all vertical edges are moved as far right as possible; see Fig. 7.26b and 7.26c. This movement stretches the outer extreme edges while simultaneously contracting all other horizontal edges to length 1, which satisfies Condition (D3).

Note that in neither step the bounding box changed. Since all conditions are satisfied, the resulting polygon is canonical. □

We observe that the length of the vertical extreme edges depends on the height of the bounding box, while the length of all other vertical edges is fixed by the angle sequence. Thus, a canonical x-monotone polygon is fully described by the height of its bounding box and the length of its outer extreme edges. Furthermore, the y-coordinate of each vertex depends solely on the height of the bounding box.

We use a dynamic program that constructs a canonical polygon of minimum bounding box in time $\mathcal{O}(n^3)$. For each possible height h of the bounding box, the dynamic program populates a table that contains an entry for any pair of an extreme vertex p (that is, an endpoint of an outer extreme edge) and a horizontal edge e of the opposite hull. The value of the entry $T[p, e]$ is the minimum width w such that the part of the polygon left of p can be drawn in a bounding box of height h and width w in such a way that the edge e is intersecting the interior of the grid column left of p.

Theorem 7.4. *Given an x-monotone angle sequence S of length n, we can find a polygon P that realizes S and minimizes its bounding box in $\mathcal{O}(n^3)$ time.*

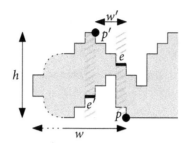

Figure 7.27: Two extreme column pairs (p, e) and (p', e') with $T[p, e] = T[p', e'] + w' = w$. The part of the polygon left of p can be drawn in the bounding box of size $h \times w$.

Proof. To prove the theorem, we present an algorithm that constructs a canonical polygon of minimum bounding box in time $\mathcal{O}(n^3)$. The height of any minimum bounding box is at most n; otherwise, as there are only n vertices, there is a y-coordinate on the grid that contains no vertex and can be "removed". For any height h of the n possible heights of an optimum polygon, we run the following dynamic program in $\mathcal{O}(n^2)$ time.

We call the left and right endpoint of an outer extreme edge the *left extreme vertex* and the *right extreme vertex*, respectively. The dynamic program contains an entry for any pair of an extreme vertex p and a horizontal edge e of the opposite hull. Consider the part of the polygon between p and e that includes the left vertical extreme edge, that is, the chain that goes from p to e over the left vertical extreme edge. The value of the entry $T[p, e]$ is the minimum width w of a bounding box of height h in which this part of the polygon can be drawn in such a way that edge e is intersecting the interior of the grid column left of p and such that e has the same y-coordinate as it has in a canonical drawing of the whole polygon in a bounding box of height h; see Fig. 7.27. We call (p, e) an *extreme column pair*.

We compute $T[p, e]$ as follows. Consider a drawing of the part of the polygon between p and e that includes the left vertical extreme edge in a bounding box of height h and minimum width. Let p' be the rightmost extreme vertex in this drawing to the left of p, let (p', e') be the corresponding extreme column pair, and let w' be the horizontal distance between p and p'; see Fig. 7.27.

We can find (p', e') and w' from the angle sequence as follows. If p is a left extreme vertex, then, by Condition (D3), the pair (p', e') and the distance w' is fully determined. Otherwise, if p is a right extreme vertex, then p' is either the left extreme vertex incident to p, or p' is the horizontally closest extreme vertex on the opposite hull; we test both cases. Again, by Condition (D3), edge e' and distance w' is fully determined.

When determining (p', e') and w', we also test, as we will describe in the next paragraph, whether we can canonically draw the part of the polygon between (p', e') and (p, e) in the given space constraints. If we can, then we call (p', e') a feasible pair for (p, e). We find a feasible pair (p', e') for (p, e) with the smallest value of $T[p', e'] + w'$ and set

$$T[p, e] = T[p', e'] + w'.$$

If all pairs for (p, e) are infeasible, we set $T[p, e] = \infty$.

First, we will argue that if there is such a canonical drawing, then it is unique. We assume $T[p', e'] < \infty$. We group each pair of stairs that share an inner extreme edge as a *double stair*; see Fig. 7.26c. Each remaining stair forms a double stair by itself. Let $P_\top$ denote the part of the upper hull between (p', e') and (p, e). Given the choice of p', it does not contain any endpoint of an outer extreme edge in its interior. Hence, there are only two cases. Either $P_\top$ consists of a single horizontal line segment belonging to an outer extreme edge, or it is a subchain belonging to a double stair. In the first case, by Condition (D1), we have to draw $P_\top$ on the top boundary of the bounding box. Further, its left endpoint has x-coordinate equal to $T[p', e']$ and the length of the segment is w'. Hence, the drawing is unique. In the second case, note that conditions (D1)–(D3) determine the lengths and y-positions of all edges with the exception of the lengths of the outer extreme edges. Thus, given the x-position of any vertex of a double stair, there is only one canonical way to draw the double stair. In our case, the value of $T[p', e']$ is equal to the x-position of the leftmost vertex of $P_\top$. Hence, the drawing of $P_\top$ is unique. By the same arguments, we have to draw the part $P_\perp$ of the lower hull between (p', e') and (p, e) in a unique way.

Now, given the unique drawings of $P_\top$ and $P_\perp$, we check for every x-coordinate whether $P_\top$ is lying above $P_\perp$. If and only if this is the case, then the two drawings together form a feasible canonical drawing and (p', e') is a feasible pair for (p, e).

In the last step, we compute the minimum width w of the bounding box assuming height h. Consider an optimum canonical drawing of the whole polygon in a bounding box of height h. Let p^* be a rightmost (right) extreme vertex. Note that for p^* there are only two candidates, one from the upper hull and one from the lower hull. Since p^* is a rightmost extreme vertex, all horizontal edges to the right of p^* (on the upper and on the lower hull) are segments of length 1. Thus, given p^*, we can compute the distance r^* between p^* and the right vertical extreme edge. Let e^* be the r^*-th horizontal edge from the right on the hull opposite to p^*. Observe that edge e^* is the edge that forms an extreme column pair with p^*. Hence, the width of the polygon is $w = T[p^*, e^*] + r^*$.

We compute width w as follows. For each one of the two candidates for p^*, we determine r^* and e^*. Then we check whether the candidate is feasible. For this, recall that Conditions (D1)–(D3) determine the y-positions of all edges. Also recall that all horizontal edges to the right of (p^*, e^*) are of length 1. Hence, there is only one way to canonically draw the edges right to (p^*, e^*). If the upper hull always stays above the lower hull, candidate p^* is feasible. Thus, we get the width by

$$w = \min_{\text{feasible candidate } p^*} \{T[p^*, e^*] + r^*\} \cup \{\infty\}.$$

For every height h, we compute the minimum width w and find the bounding box of minimum area $w \cdot h$.

It remains to show the run time of the algorithm. The table T consists of $\mathcal{O}(n^2)$ entries. To find the value of an entry $T[p, e]$, we have to find the closest column pair (p', e') to the left, the distance w', and we have to test whether we can canonically draw the polygon between (p', e') and (p, e). We now show that each of these steps is possible in $\mathcal{O}(1)$ time by precomputing some values for each point.

(i) For each point, we store its y-coordinate. As observed above, the y-coordinate is fixed, and it can be computed in $\mathcal{O}(n)$ time in total by traversing the stairs.

(ii) For each point p, we store the next extreme point $\lambda(p)$ to the left on the same hull, as well as the distance $\delta(p)$ to it. These values can be computed in $\mathcal{O}(n)$ time in total by traversing the upper and the lower hull from left to right.

(iii) For each left extreme vertex q, we store an array that contains all horizontal edges between q and $\lambda(q)$ ordered by their appearance on a walk from q to $\lambda(q)$ on the same hull. We also store the index of the inner extreme edge in this array. These arrays can be computed altogether in $\mathcal{O}(n)$ time by traversing the upper and the lower hull from right to left.

The precomputation takes $\mathcal{O}(n)$ time in total. Given an extreme column pair (p, e), let l_e be the left endpoint of e. We can use the precomputation of Step (ii) to find in $\mathcal{O}(1)$ time the closest extreme vertex p' to the left of p, since it is either $\lambda(p)$ or $\lambda(l_e)$, as well as the distance w', which is either $\delta(p)$ or $\delta(l_e)$. To test whether we can canonically draw the polygon between (p', e') and (p, e), we make use of the fact that there is no outer extreme edge between them. Hence, we only have to test whether a pair of opposite double stairs intersects. To this end, we observe that a pair of double stairs can only intersect if the inner extreme edge of the lower hull lies (partially) above the upper hull or the inner extreme edge of the upper hull lies (partially) below the lower hull. With the array precomputed in Step (iii), we can find the edge opposite of the inner extreme edges, and by Step (i), each point (and thus each edge) knows its y-coordinate, which we only have to compare to find out whether an intersection exists. Hence, we can compute each table entry in $\mathcal{O}(1)$ time after a precomputation step that takes $\mathcal{O}(n)$ time.

Since we call the dynamic program $\mathcal{O}(n)$ times—once for each candidate for the height of the bounding box—the algorithm takes $\mathcal{O}(n^3)$ time in total. Following Lemma 7.19, this proves the theorem. $\qquad\square$

For the area minimization, we make two key observations. First, since the polygon is x-monotone, each grid column (properly) intersects either no or exactly two horizontal edges: one edge from the upper hull and one edge from the lower hull. Secondly, a pair of horizontal edges share at most one column; otherwise, the polygon could be drawn with less area by shortening both edges. With the same argument as for the bounding box, the height of any minimum-area polygon is at most n.

We use a dynamic program to solve the problem. To this end, we fill a three-dimensional table T as follows. Let e be a horizontal edge on the upper hull, let f be a horizontal edge of the lower hull, and let h be an integer satisfying $1 \le h \le n$. The entry $T[e, f, h]$ specifies the minimum area required to draw the part of the polygon to the left of (and including) the unique common column of e and f under the condition that e and f share a column and have vertical distance h.

Let $e_1, \ldots, e_k$ be the horizontal edges on the upper hull from left to right and let $f_1, \ldots, f_m$ be the horizontal edges on the lower hull from left to right. For each h with $1 \le h \le n$, we initialize the table with $T[e_1, f_1, h] = h$. To compute any other entry $T[e_i, f_j, h']$, we need to find the correct entry from the column left of the column shared by e_i and f_j. There are

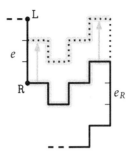

Figure 7.28: First step of transforming P into a canonical form. We decrease $\|e\|$ by increasing $\|e_R\|$.

three possibilities: this column either intersects e_{i-1} and f_{j-1}, it intersects e_i and f_{j-1}, or it intersects e_{i-1} and f_j. For each of these possibilities, we check which height can be realized if e_i and f_j have vertical distance h' and search for the entry of minimum value. We set

$$T[e_i, f_j, h'] = \min_{h'' \text{ valid}} \{T[e_{i-1}, f_{j-1}, h''], T[e_i, f_{j-1}, h''], T[e_{i-1}, f_j, h'']\} + h' .$$

Finally, we can find the optimum solution by finding $\min_{1 \le h \le n}\{T[e_k, f_m, h]\}$. Since the table has $\mathcal{O}(n^3)$ entries each of which we can compute in $\mathcal{O}(n)$ time, the algorithm runs in $\mathcal{O}(n^4)$ time. This proves the following theorem.

Theorem 7.5. *Given an x-monotone angle sequence S of length n, we can find a minimum-area polygon that realizes S in $\mathcal{O}(n^4)$ time.*

7.4 The Monotone Case: Minimum Perimeter

In this section, we show how to compute a polygon of minimum perimeter for any xy-monotone or x-monotone angle sequence S of length n.

Let P be an x-monotone polygon realizing S. Let e_L be the leftmost vertical edge and let e_R be the rightmost vertical edge of P. Recall that P consists of two x-monotone chains; an upper chain T and a lower chain B connected by e_L and e_R. For every $e \in T$, let $T(e_R, e)$ denote the subchain of T consisting of all segments between e_R and e (without e_R and e). Similarly, for every $e' \in B$, let $B(e', e_R)$ denote the subchain of B consisting of all segments between e' and e_R (without e' and e_R). Without loss of generality, we assume that the number of reflex vertices of T and B satisfies $r(T) \ge r(B)$.

Definition 7.8. An x-monotone polygon is *perimeter-canonical* if

(1) every vertical edge except e_R and e_L has unit length, and

(2) every horizontal edge of T has unit length.

We show that it suffices to find a perimeter-canonical polygon of minimum perimeter.

Lemma 7.20. *Any x-monotone polygon can be transformed into a perimeter-canonical x-monotone polygon without increasing its perimeter.*

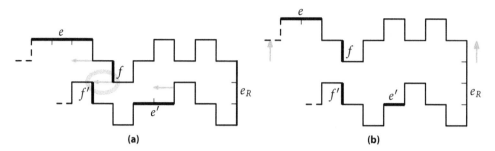

(a)   (b)

Figure 7.29: Steps two and three of transforming P into a canonical form. We decrease the length of e and e' (bold) by increasing $\|e_L\|$ and $\|e_R\|$. Stretching e_l and e_R prevents the crossing of f and f' (bold).

Proof. We transform any minimum-perimeter polygon into a perimeter-canonical form without sacrificing its perimeter in two steps as follows. First, we shorten every *long* vertical edge $e \in T \cup B$ with $\|e\| > 1$ so that $\|e\| = 1$ holds. This shortening is always possible: For any long vertical edge $e \in T \cup B$, say $e \in T$, if its end vertices have turns RL in ccw order, then we proceed as follows; see Fig. 7.28. We move the subchain $T(e_R, e)$ upward by $\|e\| - 1$ units by shortening e and by simultaneously stretching e_R. This movement guarantees that $\|e\|$ decreases and $\|e_R\|$ increases by the same amount of $\|e\| - 1$, so the perimeter remains the same. We can also shorten any long vertical edge whose end vertices have turns LR in a symmetric way.

Secondly, we shorten every long horizontal edge $e \in T$ with $\|e\| > 1$ so that its length becomes 1. Suppose that e is the rightmost long horizontal edge e in T. Since $r(T) \geq r(B)$, there must be a long horizontal edge e' in B. We shorten both e and e' by one unit, and move the two subchains $T(e_R, e)$ and $B(e', e_R)$ together with e_R one unit left. This move may cause two vertical edges, $f \in T$ and $f' \in B$, to intersect; see Fig. 7.29a. Note that exactly one of both vertical edges did not move, say f', as otherwise there would be no intersection between them. This means f' is to the left of e', that is, $f' \in B \setminus B(e', e_R)$. We also know that the x-distance between f and f' prior to the move was one, otherwise they would not intersect. Since f and f' are of unit length, the lower end vertex of f has the same y-coordinate as the upper end vertex of f'. To avoid the intersection, we first move the whole upper chain T one unit upward by stretching e_R and e_L each by one unit, as in Fig. 7.29b. Then we can move $T(e_R, e)$, $B(e', e_R)$, and e_R one unit to the left without causing any intersection. We get rid of two units by shortening e and e', and receive two units by stretching e_R and e_L, so the total perimeter remains unchanged. We repeat this second step until $\|e\| = 1$.   □

Assume that P is a minimum-perimeter canonical polygon that realizes S. Assume further that $r(T) \geq r(B)$ holds. Let peri(P) denote the perimeter of P. By Conditions (1)–(2), every edge in T is of unit length, so the length of T is $2\,r(T) + 1$. This property implies that the width of B should be $r(T) + 1$. By Condition (1), the length of the vertical edges in B is $r(B)$, so the total length of B is $r(T) + r(B) + 1$. Thus, we can observe the following property.

Lemma 7.21. *Given an x-monotone angle sequence S, there is a canonical minimum-perimeter polygon P realizing S with $r(T) \geq r(B)$ such that peri(P) = $3\,r(T) + r(B) + 2 + \|e_L\| + \|e_R\|$ holds.*

The first three terms of peri(P) in Lemma 7.21 are constant, so we need to minimize the sum of the last two terms, $\|e_L\|$ and $\|e_R\|$, to get a minimum perimeter. However, once one of them is fixed, the other is automatically determined by the fact that all vertical edges in T and B are unit-length segments. Even more, minimizing one of them is equivalent to minimizing their sum, consequently minimizing the perimeter. We call the length of the left vertical extreme edge of a polygon the *height* of the polygon.

7.4.1 The xy-Monotone Case

Let P be a minimum-perimeter canonical xy-monotone polygon that realizes an xy-monotone angle sequence S of length n. As before, we assume that $r(T) \geq r(B)$ holds. When $n = 4$, that is, the number r of reflex vertices is 0, then a unit square P achieves the minimum perimeter. Therefore, we assume in the following that we have $r > 0$. Recall that the boundary of P consists of four stairs, TR, TL, BL, and BR. Let (r_1, r_2, r_3, r_4) be a quadruple of the numbers of reflex vertices of TR, TL, BL, and BR, respectively. Then $r = r_1 + r_2 + r_3 + r_4$, where $r_i \geq 0$ for each i with $1 \leq i \leq 4$. Again, we define L as the chain consisting of TL, e_L and BL and R as the chain consisting of BR, e_R and TR. In P, let $w(T)$ and $w(B)$ denote the widths of T and B, respectively, and $h(L)$ and $h(R)$ the heights of L and R, respectively. Hence, the perimeter of P is

$$\text{peri}(P) = w(T) + w(B) + h(L) + h(R).$$

Note that $w(T) = w(B)$ holds and, by Condition (2),

$$w(T) = r_1 + 1 + r_2.$$

Thus, $w(T) + w(B) = 2(r_1 + r_2) + 2$. Similarly, $h(L) = h(R)$, and, by Condition (1),

$$h(L) = r_2 + \|e_L\| + r_3 \quad \text{and} \quad h(R) = r_4 + \|e_R\| + r_1.$$

Thus, if $\|e_L\| = 1$, then

$$h(L) + h(R) = 2(r_2 + r_3) + 2,$$

and, if $\|e_R\| = 1$, then

$$h(L) + h(R) = 2(r_1 + r_4) + 2.$$

Furthermore observe that $\|e_L\| = 1$ implies

$$r_2 + r_3 \geq r_1 + r_4,$$

and that $\|e_R\| = 1$ implies

$$r_2 + r_3 \leq r_1 + r_4.$$

Hence, if $\|e_L\| = 1$ or $\|e_R\| = 1$, then

$$h(L) + h(R) = r + |r_2 + r_3 - r_1 - r_4|$$

and eventually

$$\mathrm{peri}(P) = 3(r_1 + r_2) + (r_3 + r_4) + |r_2 + r_3 - r_1 - r_4| + 4 . \qquad (7.3)$$

Now, consider the remaining case when $\|e_L\| \geq 2$ and $\|e_R\| \geq 2$. We will observe that this case can occur only if (r_1, r_2, r_3, r_4) is $(r_1, 0, r_1, 0)$ or $(0, r_2, 0, r_2)$. We will also observe that then $\|e_L\| = \|e_R\| = 2$. Hence, we obtain that $\mathrm{peri}(P) = 2r_1 + 6$ for case $(r_1, 0, r_1, 0)$, and $\mathrm{peri}(P) = 2r_2 + 6$ for case $(0, r_2, 0, r_2)$. For all other cases, Equation 7.3 holds.

To make these observations, we first apply the same contraction step as depicted in Fig. 7.26b of Lemma 7.19. That is, we contract all horizontal segments of BL to length 1 by moving all their right endpoints as far as possible to the left, and we contract all horizontal segments of BR to length 1 by moving all their left endpoints as far as possible to the right. By this, all edges of B except the bottom extreme edge have length 1, and the perimeter does not change. Next, note that T and B have vertical distance 1 to each other. Otherwise, we could move B at least one unit to the top by simultaneously shrinking e_L and e_B, and thus shrinking the perimeter of P, a contradiction to the minimality of $\mathrm{peri}(P)$. As T consists only of unit-length segments (Conditions (1)–(2)), there is a vertex p in T having distance 1 to B.

First assume that p belongs to TR. We choose the rightmost such p. If p were a convex vertex, then it would be the top endpoint of e_R, and, hence, we would have $\|e_R\| = 1$; a contradiction to $\|e_R\| \geq 2$. Thus, p is a reflex vertex and therefore a left endpoint of a horizontal edge pp'. Hence, the right endpoint p' of pp' is convex. Let e be the edge in B below pp', that is, the edge that crosses the same grid column as pp'. Observe that the distance between pp' and e is at least 2. If it were 1, then the vertical edge $p'p''$ incident to p' would connect to e (recall that p' is convex). Hence, pp' and e would be incident to $e_R = p'p''$, and again we would have $\|e_R\| = 1$; a contradiction. Thus, the distance between p and e is at least 2. Let q be the point of B directly one unit below p. Then e lies at least one unit below q. Hence, q has to connect to e via a vertical edge, and, consequently, q has to be a reflex vertex and belong to BL. By Condition (1), the vertical edge connecting q and e has length 1, hence, the distance between pp' and e is exactly 2. But now, either the bottom endpoint p'' of $p'p''$ has distance 1 to B, or p'' lies on B, that is, $p'p'' = e_R$. The former case contradicts our assumption that p is the rightmost vertex of T having distance 1 to B. Thus, the latter case holds and pp' and e are incident to e_R. Hence, $\|e_R\| = 2$, e is the bottom extreme edge and has length $\|e\| = 1$, and BR is empty, that is, $r_4 = 0$. Thus, all horizontal edges in B have unit length. This property allows us to use the same argument as above to show $r_2 = 0$ and $\|e_L\| = 2$. Given $r_1 + 1 = w(T) = w(B) = r_3 + 1$, we get $r_1 = r_3$.

Finally, assume that p belongs to TL. Then we can show in a similar way as above that we are in case $(0, r_2, 0, r_2)$, and, again, $\|e_L\| = \|e_R\| = 2$. Thus, our observation follows.

Theorem 7.6. *Given an xy-monotone angle sequence S of length n, we can find a polygon P that realizes S and minimizes its perimeter in $\mathcal{O}(n)$ time. Furthermore, if the lengths of the stair sequences are given as above as a tuple ℓ where $\ell = (r_1, r_2, r_3, r_4)$, then $\mathrm{peri}(P)$ can be expressed as:*

$$\mathrm{peri}(P) = \begin{cases} 4r_1 + 6 & \text{if } \ell = (r_1, 0, r_1, 0), \\ 4r_2 + 6 & \text{if } \ell = (0, r_2, 0, r_2), \\ 3(r_1 + r_2) + (r_3 + r_4) + |r_3 - (r_1 - r_2 + r_4)| + 4 & \text{otherwise.} \end{cases}$$

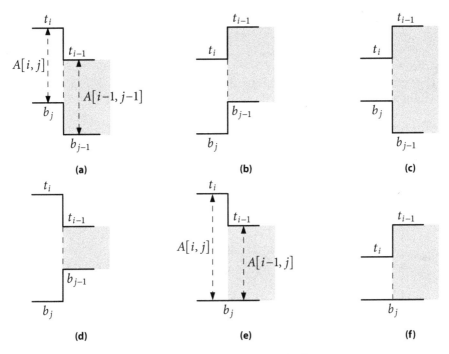

Figure 7.30: Six situations when t_i and b_j are considered to fill $A[i, j]$.

7.4.2 The x-Monotone Case

A minimum height polygon P that realizes S can be computed in $\mathcal{O}(n^2)$ time using dynamic programming. Recall that a perimeter-canonical polygon of minimum height is a polygon of minimum perimeter.

From right to left, let $t_1, \ldots, t_{r(T)}$ be the horizontal edges in T and $b_1, b_2, \ldots, b_{r(B)}$ be the horizontal edges in B. Recall our assumption $r(T) \geq r(B)$. For $i \geq j \geq 1$, let $A[i, j]$ be the minimum height of the subpolygon formed with the first i horizontal edges from T and the first j horizontal edges from B. Note that the leftmost vertical edge of the subpolygon whose minimum height is stored in $A[i, j]$ joins the left endpoints of t_i and b_j. To compute $A[i, j]$, we attach edges t_i and b_j to the upper and lower chains of the subpolygon constructed so far. Since t_i has unit length, either t_i and b_j are attached to the subpolygon with height of $A[i-1, j-1]$ or just t_i is attached to the subpolygon with height of $A[i-1, j]$. Figure 7.30 shows that there are four cases, Cases (a)–(d), for the first attachment and two cases, Cases (e)–(f), for the second attachment, according to the turns formed at the attachments.

Let u and v be the left end vertex of t_{i-1} and the right end vertex of t_i, respectively. Let u' and v' be the right end vertex of b_j and the left end vertex of b_{j-1}, respectively. Notice that both vertical edges (u, v) and (u', v') have unit length. As an example, let us explain how to calculate $A[i, j]$ when $uv = \mathrm{LR}$ and $u'v' = \mathrm{LR}$, which corresponds to Fig. 7.30b and Fig. 7.30f. We set $A[i, j]$ to the minimum height of the two possible attachments of Cases (b) and (f). For now, consider the height for Case (b). If $A[i-1, j-1] > 1$, then t_i and b_j are attached to the subpolygon as illustrated in Fig. 7.30b. Since edges (u, v) and (u', v') have unit length, $A[i, j] = A[i - 1, j - 1]$. In the other case, if $A[i - 1, j - 1] = 1$, then we can move the upper chain of the subpolygon one unit upward without intersection so that t_i and b_j are safely attached to the subpolygon with $A[i, j] = 2$. Note that this is the smallest possible value for $A[i, j]$ given $uv = $ LR and $u'v' = $ LR. Thus, $A[i, j] = \max\{A[i - 1, j - 1], 2\}$. The height for Case (f) should be at least 1, so it is expressed as $\max\{A[i - 1, j] - 1, 1\}$. Therefore,

$$A[i, j] = \min\{\max\{A[i - 1, j - 1], 2\}, \max\{A[i - 1, j] - 1, 1\}\}\ .$$

For the other turns at uv and $u'v'$, we can similarly define the equations as follows:

$$A[i, j] = \begin{cases} \text{undefined} & \text{if } i = 0,\ j = 0 \text{ or } i < j, \\ 1 & \text{if } i = 1,\ j = 1, \\ A[i - 1, j] + 1 & \text{if } uv = \text{RL},\ j = 1, \\ \max\{A[i - 1, j] - 1, 1\} & \text{if } uv = \text{LR},\ j = 1, \\ \min\{\max\{A[i - 1, j - 1], 2\}, A[i - 1, j] + 1\} & \text{if } uv = \text{RL},\ u'v' = \text{RL}, \\ \min\{A[i - 1, j - 1] + 2, A[i - 1, j] + 1\} & \text{if } uv = \text{RL},\ u'v' = \text{LR}, \\ \min\{\max\{A[i - 1, j - 1], 2\}, \\ \qquad \max\{A[i - 1, j] - 1, 1\}\} & \text{if } uv = \text{LR},\ u'v' = \text{LR}, \\ \min\{\max\{A[i - 1, j - 1] - 2, 1\}, \\ \qquad \max\{A[i - 1, j] - 1, 1\}\} & \text{if } uv = \text{LR},\ u'v' = \text{RL}\ . \end{cases}$$

Evaluating each entry takes constant time, so the total time to fill A is $\mathcal{O}(n^2)$. Using A, a minimum-perimeter polygon can be reconstructed within the same time bound.

Theorem 7.7. *Given an x-monotone angle sequence S of length n, we can find a polygon P that realizes S and minimizes its perimeter in $\mathcal{O}(n^2)$ time.*

7.5   Conclusion

In this chapter, we considered the problem of drawing a polygon satisfying a given angle sequence on a rectilinear grid such that its area, its bounding box, or its perimeter is minimized. We have seen several efficient algorithms for x-monotone and xy-monotone variants of the problem and have shown that the general variant is NP-hard for all three objectives. Hence, these results raise the question about the approximability of the general problem. As a next step, one could consider stepwise more complicated objects than polygons. Eventually, one would arrive at the following general question: Given an orthogonal representation of a graph that specifies an angle sequence for each edge and an angle for each vertex, draw the graph without crossings on an integer grid realizing the orthogonal representation while minimizing the bounding box or the perimeter. Patrigani [Pat01] showed that this problem does not admit a PTAS unless P = NP, and Bannister et al. [BES12] even rule out any subpolynomial factors for the non-planar case. It would be interesting to give a non-trivial upper bound on the approximation ratio or to increase the lower bound.

Open Problems

In the preceding chapters, we examined five network design problems related to graphs and the Euclidean plane. In the process, a number of questions were left open. Now, we briefly recall the results that we obtained and summarize the most interesting open problems.

Disjoint Connecting Paths. In Chapter 3, we examined the problems of routing terminal pairs by edge- and node-disjoint paths in graphs of bounded feedback vertex set number r. Our main observation is that r is a parameter that describes the "difficulty" of the problems quite well. We base this observation on lower and upper bounds related to r that are implied by our algorithms as well as our hardness results. On the positive side, we have obtained, among others, the following result for MAXEDP. Let k be the number of terminal pairs, n the number of nodes and OPT* the optimum objective value of the underlying multi-commodity flow relaxation. Up to the logarithmic factor of $\log kr$, our $\Omega(\text{OPT}^* /(\sqrt{r} \log kr))$-approximation algorithm for MAXEDP is improving the best-known approximation ratio of $\Omega(\text{OPT}^* /\sqrt{n})$ [CKS06], since $r \leq n$. Hence, this result leads to our first open problem.

Open Problem 1. Can we get rid of the $\log kr$-factor? That is, can we obtain an approximation algorithm with ratio $\Omega(\text{OPT}^* /\sqrt{r})$ for MAXIMUM EDGE DISJOINT PATHS problem with feedback vertex set number r?

On the negative side, we have shown that the decision variant of MAXEDP is NP-hard already for $r = 2$. In our extended abstract [FMS18], we conjectured that for $r = 1$ the problem is decidable in polynomial time. Recently, Ganian et al. [GOS17] settled this open problem by giving a positive answer.

Capacitated Facility Location. In Chapter 4, we presented constant-factor approximation algorithms for hard-capacitated k-FACILITY LOCATION problems, where we considered either non-uniform capacities or non-uniform opening costs. Hence, it would be interesting to consider the generalization of both.

Open Problem 2. For hard-capacitated k-FACILITY LOCATION where both the capacities and openings are non-uniform, give a constant-factor approximation algorithm with capacity violation bounded by a constant.

Both our algorithms, which are based on the standard LP relaxation, violate the capacities only by small constants. It is known that any standard integer program permitting capacity violation at most $2 - \varepsilon$ has unbounded integrality gap for any sufficiently small positive ε. Our results imply that this lower bound is practically tight for the uniform capacitated case. For the non-uniform capacitated case, we know that the barrier on capacity violation lies in the interval $[2 - \varepsilon, 3 + \varepsilon]$. Hence, the precise location of the barrier is still open.

Open Problem 3. What is the smallest capacity violation that a standard integer program for non-uniform hard-capacitated k-FACILITY LOCATION can permit such that the integrality gap is bounded?

Unsolved remains the important question on the approximability of capacitated k-MEDIAN when no constraints are relaxed.

Open Problem 4. Does capacitated k-MEDIAN admit a constant-factor approximation algorithm?

Stabbing Rectangles with Line Segments. In Chapter 5, we first showed that STABBING is an NP-hard problem and two variants of it are even APX-hard. Next, we tried various approaches to obtain good approximation algorithms. However, the combinatorial algorithm that we obtained, a greedy one, yields only a logarithmic approximation ratio. Thus, there is a significant gap to the approximation ratio of $\mathcal{O}(1)$ that we obtained by an applications of Varadarajan's [Var10] quasi-uniform sampling method. Thus, we ask for the following.

Open Problem 5. Give a combinatorial $\mathcal{O}(1)$-approximation algorithm for STABBING and determine its precise approximation ratio.

Colored Steiner Problem. In Chapter 6, we studied the k-COLORED NON-CROSSING EU-CLIDEAN STEINER FOREST problem. Thereby, we obtained several approximation algorithms for different values of k. For $k = 2$, we achieved a PTAS modifying Arora's PTAS for EUCLIDEAN STEINER TREE [Aro98]. In this context, we ask:

Open Problem 6. Can we improve the run time of the PTAS for 2-CESF from $\mathcal{O}(n^{\mathcal{O}(1/\varepsilon)})$ to $\mathcal{O}(n(\log n)^{\mathcal{O}(1/\varepsilon)})$ as Arora [Aro98] did for EUCLIDEAN STEINER TREE?

For $k = 3$, we achieved a ratio of $5/3 + \varepsilon$ and were not able to obtain a PTAS. Hence, this fact raises the following question.

Open Problem 7. Is k-CESF APX-hard for some k with $k \geq 3$?

For general k, we achieved ratios $k + \varepsilon$ and $\mathcal{O}(\sqrt{n} \log k)$.

Open Problem 8. Can we obtain better approximation ratios for k-CESF with $k \geq 3$?

Drawing Rectilinear Polygons for Given Angle Sequences. In Chapter 7, we asked for a rectilinear polygon realizing a given angle sequence while minimizing the area of the bounding box, the area of the polygon, or its perimeter. We showed that the problem is NP-hard. In the same chapter, we obtained several exact algorithms for special variants of the problem. Hence, it would be interesting to design algorithms for the general case and study its approximability.

Open Problem 9. Examine the approximability of MINIMUM RECTILINEAR POLYGON FOR GIVEN ANGLE SEQUENCE. Does it admit a constant-factor approximation algorithm? Is it APX-hard?

Another direction worth to be studied is to generalize the problem.

Open Problem 10. Examine the complexity and approximability of the following problem: Given an orthogonal representation of a graph that specifies an angle sequence for each edge and an angle for each vertex, draw the graph without crossings on an integer grid realizing the orthogonal representation while minimizing the bounding box or the perimeter.

It is known that this problem does not admit a PTAS unless $P = NP$ [Pat01].

Bibliography

[AB09]   Sanjeev Arora and Boaz Barak. *Computational Complexity: A Modern Approach*. Cambridge University Press, 1st edition, 2009. [see pages 9 and 15]

[ABC⁺15]   Hyung-Chan An, Aditya Bhaskara, Chandra Chekuri, Shalmoli Gupta, Vivek Madan, and Ola Svensson. Centrality of trees for capacitated k-center. *Math. Program.*, 154(1):29–53, 2015. [see page 48]

[ADA18]   Saeed Asaeedi, Farzad Didehvar, and Mohades Ali. NLP formulation for polygon optimization problems, 2018. Preprint available at https://www.preprints.org/manuscript/201811.0300 . [see page 137]

[AES10]   Boris Aronov, Esther Ezra, and Micha Sharir. Small-size ε-nets for axis-parallel rectangles and boxes. *SIAM J. Comput.*, 39(7):3248–3282, 2010. [see pages 94, 99, and 115]

[AGK⁺01]   Vijay Arya, Naveen Garg, Rohit Khandekar, Adam Meyerson, Kamesh Munagala, and Vinayaka Pandit. Local search heuristic for k-median and facility location problems. In *Proc. 33th ACM Symp. Theory Comput. (STOC'01)*, pages 21–29, 2001. [see page 49]

[AGLR94]   Baruch Awerbuch, Rainer Gawlick, Tom Leighton, and Yuval Rabani. On-line admission control and circuit routing for high performance computing and communication. In *Proc. IEEE 35rd Symp. Found. Comput. Sci. (FOCS'94)*, pages 412–423, 1994. [see page 26]

[AKK⁺11]   Isolde Adler, Stavros G. Kolliopoulos, Philipp Klaus Krause, Daniel Lokshtanov, Saket Saurabh, and Dimitrios Thilikos. Tight bounds for linkages in planar graphs. In *Proc. 38th Int. Colloq. Aut. Lang. Prog. (ICALP'11)*, pages 110–121, 2011. [see page 25]

[ALB⁺13]   Ankit Aggarwal, Anand Louis, Manisha Bansal, Naveen Garg, Neelima Gupta, Shubham Gupta, and Surabhi Jain. A 3-approximation algorithm for the facility location problem with uniform capacities. *Math. Program.*, 141(1):527–547, 2013. [see page 48]

[And10]   Matthew Andrews. Approximation algorithms for the edge-disjoint paths problem via Räcke decompositions. In *Proc. IEEE 51st Symp. Found. Comput. Sci. (FOCS'10)*, pages 277–286, 2010. [see page 22]

[AR95]   Yonatan Aumann and Yuval Rabani. Improved bounds for all optical routing. In *Proc. 6th ACM-SIAM Symp. Discrete Algorithms (SODA'95)*, pages 567–576, 1995. [see page 26]

[AR98]   Yonatan Aumann and Yuval Rabani. An $\mathcal{O}(\log k)$ approximate min-cut max-flow theorem and approximation algorithm. *SIAM J. Comput.*, 27(1):291–301, 1998. [see page 26]

[Aro98]   Sanjeev Arora. Polynomial time approximation schemes for Euclidean traveling salesman and other geometric problems. *J. ACM*, 45(5):753–782, 1998. [see pages 2, 6, 117, 118, 120, 123, 127, 133, and 190]

[ARRC11]   Basak Alper, Nathalie Henry Riche, Gonzalo Ramos, and Mary Czerwinski. Design study of LineSets, a novel set visualization technique. *IEEE Trans. Vis. Comput. Graphics*, 17(12):2259–2267, 2011. [see page 119]

[AS04]   Alexander A. Ageev and Maxim I. Sviridenko. Pipage rounding: A new method of constructing algorithms with proven performance guarantee. *J. Comb. Optim.*, 8(3):307–328, 2004. [see page 62]

[ASS17]   Hyung-Chan An, Mohit Singh, and Ola Svensson. LP-based algorithms for capacitated facility location. *SIAM J. Comput.*, 46(1):272–306, 2017. [see page 48]

[AvdBGL15]   Karen Aardal, Pieter L. van den Berg, Dion Gijswijt, and Shanfei Li. Approximation algorithms for hard capacitated k-facility location problems. *Europ. J. Operational Research*, 242(2):358–368, 2015. [see page 49]

[BBF99]   Vineet Bafna, Piotr Berman, and Toshihiro Fujito. A 2-approximation algorithm for the undirected feedback vertex set problem. *SIAM J. Discrete Math.*, 12(3):289–297, 1999. [see pages 28 and 34]

[BDHM16]   Mohammad Hossein Bateni, Erik D. Demaine, Mohammad Taghi Hajiaghayi, and Dániel Marx. A PTAS for planar group Steiner tree via spanner bootstrapping and prize collecting. In *Proc. 48th ACM Symp. Theory Comput. (STOC'16)*, pages 570–583, 2016. [see page 119]

[BDS11]   Therese C. Biedl, Stephane Durocher, and Jack Snoeyink. Reconstructing polygons from scanner data. *Theor. Comput. Sci.*, 412(32):4161–4172, 2011. [see page 137]

[Bes03]   Sergey Bespamyatnikh. Computing homotopic shortest paths in the plane. *J. Algorithms*, 49(2):284–303, 2003. [see page 119]

[BES12]   Michael J. Bannister, David Eppstein, and Joseph A. Simons. Inapproximability of orthogonal compaction. *J. Graph Algorithms and Applications*, 16(3):651–673, 2012. [see pages 137 and 188]

[BF98]   Oliver Bastert and Sandor P. Fekete. Geometric wire routing. Technical Report 96.247, Universität zu Köln, 1998. Available at http://e-archive. informatik.uni-koeln.de/247 . [see pages 119 and 120]

[BFK+15]   Sergey Bereg, Krzysztof Fleszar, Philipp Kindermann, Sergey Pupyrev, Joachim
           Spoerhase, and Alexander Wolff. Colored non-crossing Euclidean Steiner forest.
           In *Proc. 26th Int. Symp. Algorithms Comput. (ISAAC'15)*, pages 429–441, 2015.
           [see page 6]

[BFRS15]   Jarosław Byrka, Krzysztof Fleszar, Bartosz Rybicki, and Joachim Spoerhase.
           Bi-factor approximation algorithms for hard capacitated k-median problems.
           In *Proc. 26th ACM-SIAM Symp. Discrete Algorithms (SODA'15)*, pages 722–736,
           2015. [see pages 5, 49, and 50]

[BFSU99]   Andrei Z. Broder, Alan M. Frieze, Stephen Suen, and Eli Upfal. Optimal construc-
           tion of edge-disjoint paths in random graphs. *SIAM J. Comput.*, 28(2):541–573,
           1999. [see page 26]

[BFU94]   Andrei Z. Broder, Alan M. Frieze, and Eli Upfal. Existence and construction of
           edge-disjoint paths on expander graphs. *SIAM J. Comput.*, 23(5):976–989, 1994.
           [see page 26]

[BG95]   Hervé Brönnimann and Michael T. Goodrich. Almost optimal set covers in
           finite VC-dimension. *Discrete Comput. Geom.*, 14(4):463–479, 1995.   [see
           page 94]

[BGG12]   Manisha Bansal, Naveen Garg, and Neelima Gupta. A 5-approximation for
           capacitated facility location. In *Proc. 20th Europ. Conf. Algorithms (ESA'12)*,
           pages 133–144, 2012. [see page 48]

[BKM09]   Glencora Borradaile, Philip Klein, and Claire Mathieu. An $\mathcal{O}(n \log n)$ approx-
           imation scheme for Steiner tree in planar graphs. *ACM Trans. Algorithms*,
           5(3):31:1–31:31, 2009. [see pages 119 and 120]

[BOS12]   Sang Won Bae, Yoshio Okamoto, and Chan-Su Shin. Area bounds of rectilinear
           polygons realized by angle sequences. In *Proc. 23rd Int. Symp. Algorithms
           Comput. (ISAAC'12)*, pages 629–638, 2012. [see page 136]

[BP14]   Nikhil Bansal and Kirk Pruhs. The geometry of scheduling. *SIAM J. Comput.*,
           43(5):1684–1698, 2014. [see page 95]

[BPR+17]   Jarosław Byrka, Thomas Pensyl, Bartosz Rybicki, Aravind Srinivasan, and Khoa
           Trinh. An improved approximation for k-median and positive correlation in
           budgeted optimization. *ACM Trans. Algorithms*, 13(2):23:1–23:31, 2017. [see
           page 49]

[BRU16]   Jarosław Byrka, Bartosz Rybicki, and Sumedha Uniyal. An approximation algo-
           rithm for uniform capacitated k-median problem with $1 + \varepsilon$ capacity viola-
           tion. In *Proc. 18th Int. Conf. Integer Prog. Comb. Optim. (IPCO'16)*, pages 262–274,
           2016. [see page 50]

[BTY11]   Hans L. Bodlaender, Stéphan Thomassé, and Anders Yeo. Kernel bounds for
           disjoint cycles and disjoint paths. *Theoret. Comput. Sci.*, 412(35):4570–4578,
           2011. [see pages 25 and 26]

[CE13]   Chandra Chekuri and Alina Ene. Poly-logarithmic approximation for maximum node disjoint paths with constant congestion. In *Proc. 24th ACM-SIAM Symp. Discrete Algorithms (SODA'13)*, pages 326–341, 2013. [see page 22]

[CFK+15]   Marek Cygan, Fedor V. Fomin, Lukasz Kowalik, Daniel Lokshtanov, Daniel Marx, Marcin Pilipczuk, Michal Pilipczuk, and Saket Saurabh. *Parameterized Algorithms*. Springer Publishing Company, Incorporated, 1st edition, 2015. [see pages 2, 9, 12, and 15]

[CG85]   Fan R. K. Chung and Ronald L. Graham. A new bound for Euclidean Steiner minimal trees. *Annals New York Acad. Sci.*, 440(1):328–346, 1985. [see pages 2 and 118]

[CG14]   Timothy M. Chan and Elyot Grant. Exact algorithms and APX-hardness results for geometric packing and covering problems. *Comput. Geom. Theory Appl.*, 47(2):112–124, 2014. [see pages 95 and 111]

[CGKS12]   Timothy M. Chan, Elyot Grant, Jochen Könemann, and Malcolm Sharpe. Weighted capacitated, priority, and geometric set cover via improved quasi-uniform sampling. In *Proc. 23th ACM-SIAM Symp. Discrete Algorithms (SODA'12)*, pages 1576–1585, 2012. [see pages 95, 101, 102, and 105]

[CGTS99]   Moses Charikar, Sudipto Guha, Éva Tardos, and David B. Shmoys. A constant-factor approximation algorithm for the k-median problem (extended abstract). In *Proc. 31st ACM Symp. Theory Comput. (STOC'99)*, pages 1–10, 1999. [see pages 47, 49, 55, 56, and 85]

[CHK12]   Marek Cygan, Mohammad Taghi Hajiaghayi, and Samir Khuller. LP rounding for k-centers with non-uniform hard capacities. In *Proc. IEEE 53rd Symp. Found. Comput. Sci. (FOCS'12)*, pages 273–282, 2012. [see page 48]

[CHKL13]   Timothy M. Chan, Hella-Franziska Hoffmann, Stephen Kiazyk, and Anna Lubiw. Minimum length embedding of planar graphs at fixed vertex locations. In *Graph Drawing (GD'13)*, pages 376–387, 2013. [see pages 119, 120, and 122]

[Chu16]   Julia Chuzhoy. Routing in undirected graphs with constant congestion. *SIAM J. Comput.*, 45(4):1490–1532, 2016. [see page 22]

[CKL16]   Julia Chuzhoy, David H. K. Kim, and Shi Li. Improved approximation for node-disjoint paths in planar graphs. In *Proc. 47th ACM Symp. Theory Comput. (STOC'16)*, pages 556–569, 2016. [see page 26]

[CKN18]   Julia Chuzhoy, David H. K. Kim, and Rachit Nimavat. Almost polynomial hardness of node-disjoint paths in grids. In *Proc. 50th ACM Symp. Theory Comput. (STOC'18)*, pages 1220–1233, 2018. [see page 22]

[CKS06]   Chandra Chekuri, Sanjeev Khanna, and F. Bruce Shepherd. An $\mathcal{O}(\sqrt{n})$ approximation and integrality gap for disjoint paths and unsplittable flow. *Theory Comput.*, 2:137–146, 2006. [see pages 21, 22, 23, 24, 27, 45, and 189]

[CKS09]   Chandra Chekuri, Sanjeev Khanna, and F Bruce Shepherd. A note on multiflows and treewidth. *Algorithmica*, 54(3):400–412, 2009. [see page 22]

[CL12]   Moses Charikar and Shi Li. A dependent LP-rounding approach for the k-median problem. In *Proc. 39th Int. Colloq. Aut. Lang. Prog. (ICALP'12)*, pages 194–205, 2012. [see pages 49 and 50]

[CL16]   Julia Chuzhoy and Shi Li. A polylogarithmic approximation algorithm for edge-disjoint paths with congestion 2. *J. ACM*, 63(5):45:1–45:51, 2016. [see page 22]

[CLRS09]   Thomas H. Cormen, Charles E. Leiserson, Ronald L. Rivest, and Clifford Stein. *Introduction to Algorithms*. The MIT Press, 3rd edition, 2009. [see page 9]

[CMS07]   Chandra Chekuri, Marcelo Mydlarz, and F. Bruce Shepherd. Multicommodity demand flow in a tree and packing integer programs. *ACM Trans. Algorithms*, 3(3):27:1–27:23, 2007. [see page 26]

[CNS13a]   Chandra Chekuri, Guyslain Naves, and F. Bruce Shepherd. Maximum edge-disjoint paths in k-sums of graphs. In *Proc. 40th Int. Colloq. Aut. Lang. Prog. (ICALP'13)*, pages 328–339, 2013. [see page 22]

[CNS13b]   Chandra Chekuri, Guyslain Naves, and F. Bruce Shepherd. Maximum edge-disjoint paths in k-sums of graphs. Arxiv report, 2013. Available at http://arxiv.org/abs/1303.4897 . [see page 27]

[CPC09]   Christopher Collins, Gerald Penn, and Sheelagh Carpendale. Bubble sets: Revealing set relations with isocontours over existing visualizations. *IEEE Trans. Vis. Comput. Graphics*, 15(6):1009–1016, 2009. [see page 119]

[CR85]   Joseph C. Culberson and Gregory J. E. Rawlins. Turtlegons: Generating simple polygons from sequences of angles. In *Proc. 1st ACM Symp. Comp. Geom. (SoCG'85)*, pages 305–310, 1985. [see page 136]

[CR05]   Julia Chuzhoy and Yuval Rabani. Approximating k-median with non-uniform capacities. In *Proc. 16th ACM-SIAM Symp. Discrete Algorithms (SODA'05)*, pages 952–958, 2005. [see page 49]

[Cre97]   P. Crescenzi. A short guide to approximation preserving reductions. In *Proc. 12th IEEE Conf. Comput. Compl. (CCC'97)*, 1997. [see page 15]

[CSW13]   Chandra Chekuri, F. Bruce Shepherd, and Christophe Weibel. Flow-cut gaps for integer and fractional multiflows. *J. Comb. Theory, Ser. B*, 103(2):248–273, 2013. [see page 26]

[CvDF⁺18]   Timothy Chan, Thomas C. van Dijk, Krzysztof Fleszar, Joachim Spoerhase, and Alexander Wolff. Stabbing rectangles by line segments. In *Proc. 29th Int. Symp. Algorithms Comput. (ISAAC'18)*, 2018. To appear. [see page 6]

[CW12]   Danny Z. Chen and Haitao Wang. An improved algorithm for reconstructing a simple polygon from its visibility angles. *Comput. Geom.*, 45(5):254–257, 2012. [see page 137]

[DFK⁺18]   Aparna Das, Krzysztof Fleszar, Stephen G. Kobourov, Joachim Spoerhase, Sankar Veeramoni, and Alexander Wolff. Approximating the generalized minimum Manhattan network problem. *Algorithmica*, 80(4):1170–1190, 2018. [see pages 6, 94, and 96]

[DL16]   Gökalp Demirci and Shi Li. Constant approximation for capacitated k-median with $(1 + \varepsilon)$-capacity violation. In *Proc. 43th Int. Colloq. Aut. Lang. Prog. (ICALP'16)*, pages 73:1–73:14, 2016. [see pages 49 and 50]

[DMW11]   Yann Disser, Matús Mihalák, and Peter Widmayer. A polygon is determined by its angles. *Comput. Geom.*, 44(8):418–426, 2011. [see page 137]

[DS14]   Irit Dinur and David Steurer. Analytical approach to parallel repetition. In *Proc. 46th ACM Symp. Theory Comput. (STOC'14)*, pages 624–633, 2014. [see page 94]

[EFK⁺16]   William S. Evans, Krzysztof Fleszar, Philipp Kindermann, Noushin Saeedi, Chan-Su Shin, and Alexander Wolff. Minimum rectilinear polygons for given angle sequences. In *Proc. 18th Japan Conf. Discrete Comput. Geom. Graphs (JCDCGG'15), Revised Selected Papers*, pages 105–119, 2016. [see pages 7 and 137]

[EHKP15]   Alon Efrat, Yifan Hu, Stephen Kobourov, and Sergey Pupyrev. Mapsets: Visualizing embedded and clustered graphs. *J. Graph Algorithms and Applications*, 19(2):571–593, 2015. [see pages 117, 118, and 120]

[EIS75]   Shimon Even, Alon Itai, and Adi Shamir. On the complexity of time table and multi-commodity flow problems. In *Proc. IEEE 16th Symp. Found. Comput. Sci. (FOCS'75)*, pages 184–193, 1975. [see page 21]

[EKL06]   Alon Efrat, Stephen G. Kobourov, and Anna Lubiw. Computing homotopic shortest paths efficiently. *Comput. Geom. Theory Appl.*, 35(3):162–172, 2006. [see page 119]

[ELR⁺08]   Guy Even, Retsef Levi, Dror Rawitz, Baruch Schieber, Shimon Shahar, and Maxim Sviridenko. Algorithms for capacitated rectangle stabbing and lot sizing with joint set-up costs. *ACM Trans. Algorithms*, 4(3):34:1–34:17, 2008. [see page 95]

[EMPR16]   Alina Ene, Matthias Mnich, Marcin Pilipczuk, and Andrej Risteski. On routing disjoint paths in bounded treewidth graphs. In *Proc. 10th Scand. Workshop Algorithm Theory (SWAT'06)*, pages 15:1–15:15, 2016. [see pages 22, 26, and 41]

[EN11]   Jeff Erickson and Amir Nayyeri. Shortest non-crossing walks in the plane. In *Proc. 22nd ACM-SIAM Symp. Discrete Algorithms (SODA'11)*, pages 297–308, 2011. [see pages 119 and 120]

[Fei98]   Uriel Feige. A threshold of ln n for approximating set cover. *J. ACM*, 45(4):634–652, 1998. [see pages 94 and 96]

[FG06]   J. Flum and M. Grohe. *Parameterized Complexity Theory*. Texts in Theoretical Computer Science. An EATCS Series. Springer-Verlag New York, Inc., 2006. [see pages 9 and 15]

[FHRV09]   Michael R. Fellows, Danny Hermelin, Frances Rosamond, and Stéphane Vialette. On the parameterized complexity of multiple-interval graph problems. *Theoret. Comput. Sci.*, 410(1):53–61, 2009. [see page 41]

[FJQS08]   Gerd Finke, Vincent Jost, Maurice Queyranne, and András Sebö. Batch processing with interval graph compatibilities between tasks. *Discrete Appl. Math.*, 156(5):556–568, 2008. [see pages 6 and 94]

[FMS18]   Krzysztof Fleszar, Matthias Mnich, and Joachim Spoerhase. New algorithms for maximum disjoint paths based on tree-likeness. *Math. Program.*, 171(1):433–461, 2018. [see pages 4, 26, and 189]

[Fri01]   Alan M. Frieze. Edge-disjoint paths in expander graphs. *SIAM J. Comput.*, 30(6):1790–1801, 2001. [see page 26]

[Gas12]   William I. Gasarch. Guest column: The second P =?NP poll. *SIGACT News*, 43(2):53–77, 2012. [see page 13]

[GGP17a]   Sapna Grover, Neelima Gupta, and Aditya Pancholi. Private communication, 2017. [see page 49]

[GGP17b]   Sapna Grover, Neelima Gupta, and Aditya Pancholi. Constant factor approximation algorithms for uniform hard capacitated facility location problems: Natural LP is not too bad. Arxiv report, 2017. Available at http://arxiv.org/abs/1606.08022 . [see page 49]

[GIK02]   Daya Ram Gaur, Toshihide Ibaraki, and Ramesh Krishnamurti. Constant ratio approximation algorithms for the rectangle stabbing problem and the rectilinear partitioning problem. *J. Algorithms*, 43(1):138–152, 2002. [see page 95]

[GJ79]   Michael R. Garey and David S. Johnson. *Computers and Intractability: A Guide to the Theory of NP-Completeness*. W. H. Freeman & Co., 1979. [see pages 118, 119, 120, and 138]

[GJS74]   Michael R. Garey, David S. Johnson, and Larry Stockmeyer. Some simplified NP-complete problems. In *Proc. 6th ACM Symp. Theory Comput. (STOC'74)*, pages 47–63, 1974. [see page 106]

[GK99]   Sudipto Guha and Samir Khuller. Greedy strikes back. *J. Algorithms*, 31(1):228–248, 1999. [see page 48]

[GKPS06]   Rajiv Gandhi, Samir Khuller, Srinivasan Parthasarathy, and Aravind Srinivasan. Dependent rounding and its applications to approximation algorithms. *J. ACM*, 53(3):324–360, 2006. [see page 62]

[GKRW13]   Panos Giannopoulos, Christian Knauer, Günter Rote, and Daniel Werner. Fixed-parameter tractability and lower bounds for stabbing problems. *Comput. Geom. Theory Appl.*, 46(7):839–860, 2013. [see page 95]

[GOS17]   Robert Ganian, Sebastian Ordyniak, and Ramanujan Sridharan. On structural parameterizations of the edge disjoint paths problem. In *Proc. 28th Int. Symp. Algorithms Comput. (ISAAC'17)*, pages 36:1–36:13, 2017.   [see pages 25, 26, and 189]

[Gün07]   Oktay Günlük. A new min-cut max-flow ratio for multicommodity flows. *SIAM J. Discrete Math.*, 21(1):1–15, 2007. [see page 26]

[GVY97]   Naveen Garg, Vijay V. Vazirani, and Mihalis Yannakakis. Primal-dual approximation algorithms for integral flow and multicut in trees. *Algorithmica*, 18(1):3–20, 1997. [see pages 22, 23, 25, 26, and 27]

[Har89]   Richard I. Hartley. Drawing polygons given angle sequences. *Inform. Process. Lett.*, 31(1):31–33, 1989. [see page 136]

[HKvK+18]   Ferran Hurtado, Matias Korman, Marc J. van Kreveld, Maarten Löffler, Vera Sacristán, Akiyoshi Shioura, Rodrigo I. Silveira, Bettina Speckmann, and Takeshi Tokuyama. Colored spanning graphs for set visualization. *Comput. Geom.*, 68:262–276, 2018. Special issue in memory of Ferran Hurtado. [see page 119]

[Hol81]   Ian Holyer. The NP-completeness of edge-coloring. *SIAM J. Comput.*, 10(4):718–720, 1981. [see page 44]

[HS85]   Dorit S. Hochbaum and David B. Shmoys. A best possible heuristic for the k-center problem. *Math. Oper. Res.*, 10(2):180–184, 1985. [see page 48]

[JMM+03]   Kamal Jain, Mohammad Mahdian, Evangelos Markakis, Amin Saberi, and Vijay V. Vazirani. Greedy facility location algorithms analyzed using dual fitting with factor-revealing LP. *J. ACM*, 50(6):795–824, 2003. [see page 48]

[Kar75]   Richard M. Karp. On the computational complexity of combinatorial problems. *Networks*, 5:45–68, 1975. [see page 21]

[KK10]   Ken-ichi Kawarabayashi and Yusuke Kobayashi. An $\mathcal{O}(\log n)$-approximation algorithm for the disjoint paths problem in eulerian planar graphs and 4-edge-connected planar graphs. In *Proc. APPROX-RANDOM'10*, pages 274–286, 2010. [see pages 22 and 26]

[KMN01]   Yoshiyuki Kusakari, Daisuke Masubuchi, and Takao Nishizeki. Finding a non-crossing Steiner forest in plane graphs under a 2-face condition. *J. Comb. Optim.*, 5(2):249–266, 2001. [see pages 119 and 120]

[Knu76]   Donald E. Knuth. Big omicron and big omega and big theta. *SIGACT News*, 8(2):18–24, 1976. [see page 10]

[KR96]   Jon Kleinberg and Ronitt Rubinfeld. Short paths in expander graphs. In *Proc. IEEE 37rd Symp. Found. Comput. Sci. (FOCS'96)*, pages 86–95, 1996. [see page 26]

[Kru56]   Joseph B. Kruskal. On the shortest spanning subtree of a graph and the traveling salesman problem. *Proc. Amer. Math. Soc.*, 7(1):48–50, 1956. [see page 1]

[KS04]   Stavros G. Kolliopoulos and Clifford Stein. Approximating disjoint-path problems using packing integer programs. *Math. Program.*, 99(1):63–87, 2004. [see page 22]

[KS06]   Sofia Kovaleva and Frits C. R. Spieksma. Approximation algorithms for rectangle stabbing and interval stabbing problems. *SIAM J. Discrete Math.*, 20(3):748–768, 2006. [see page 95]

[KT95]   Jon Kleinberg and Éva Tardos. Disjoint paths in densely embedded graphs. In *Proc. IEEE 36th Symp. Found. Comput. Sci. (FOCS'95)*, pages 52–61, 1995. [see page 26]

[KT98]   Jon Kleinberg and Éva Tardos. Approximations for the disjoint paths problem in high-diameter planar networks. *J. Comput. Syst. Sci.*, 57(1):61–73, 1998. [see page 26]

[KW10]   Ken-ichi Kawarabayashi and Paul Wollan. A shorter proof of the graph minor algorithm: the unique linkage theorem. In *Proc. 42nd ACM Symp. Theory Comput. (STOC'10)*, pages 687–694, 2010. [see page 24]

[Li13]   Shi Li. A 1.488 approximation algorithm for the uncapacitated facility location problem. *Inform. Comput.*, 222:45–58, 2013. [see page 48]

[Li14]   Shanfei Li. An improved approximation algorithm for the hard uniform capacitated k-median problem. In *Proc. APPROX-RANDOM'14*, pages 325–338, 2014. [see page 85]

[Li16]   Shi Li. Approximating capacitated k-median with $(1 + \varepsilon)k$ open facilities. In *Proc. 27th ACM-SIAM Symp. Discrete Algorithms (SODA'16)*, pages 786–796, 2016. [see pages 50 and 89]

[Li17]   Shi Li. On uniform capacitated k-median beyond the natural LP relaxation. *ACM Trans. Algorithms*, 13(2):22:1–22:18, 2017. [see pages 48 and 50]

[LLR95]   Nathan Linial, Eran London, and Yuri Rabinovich. The geometry of graphs and some of its algorithmic applications. *Combinatorica*, 15(2):215–245, 1995. [see page 26]

Bibliography

[LLS04]   Ching-Chi Lin, Hsueh-I Lu, and I-Fan Sun. Improved compact visibility representation of planar graph via Schnyder's realizer. *SIAM J. Discrete Math.*, 18(1):19–29, 2004. [see page 106]

[LMM+95] Thomas M. Liebling, François Margot, Didier Müller, Alain Prodon, and Lynn Stauffer. Disjoint paths in the plane. *ORSA J. Comput.*, 7(1):84–88, 1995. [see pages 118, 119, 120, and 122]

[Löf11]   Maarten Löffler. Existence and computation of tours through imprecise points. *Int. J. Comput. Geom. Appl.*, 21(1):1–24, 2011. [see page 119]

[LR99]   Tom Leighton and Satish Rao. Multicommodity max-flow min-cut theorems and their use in designing approximation algorithms. *J. ACM*, 46(6):787–832, 1999. [see page 26]

[LRS18]   Daniel Lokshtanov, M. S. Ramanujan, and Saket Saurabh. Linear time parameterized algorithms for subset feedback vertex set. *ACM Trans. Algorithms*, 14(1):7:1–7:37, 2018. [see page 36]

[LS16]   Shi Li and Ola Svensson. Approximating k-median via pseudo-approximation. *SIAM J. Comput.*, 45(2):530–547, 2016. [see page 49]

[LSS12]   Retsef Levi, David B. Shmoys, and Chaitanya Swamy. LP-based approximation algorithms for capacitated facility location. *Math. Program.*, 131(1):365–379, 2012. [see pages 47, 48, 50, and 57]

[MHT10]   Matthias Müller-Hannemann and Siamak Tazari. A near linear time approximation scheme for Steiner tree among obstacles in the plane. *Comput. Geom. Theory Appl.*, 43(4):395–409, 2010. [see page 119]

[Mit99]   Joseph S.B. Mitchell. Guillotine subdivisions approximate polygonal subdivisions: A simple polynomial-time approximation scheme for geometric TSP, k-MST, and related problems. *SIAM J. Comput.*, 28(4):1298–1309, 1999. [see pages 118 and 120]

[Mit00]   Joseph S.B. Mitchell. Geometric shortest paths and network optimization. In *Handbook of Computational Geometry*, chapter 15. North-Holland, 2000. [see page 119]

[MR10]   Nabil H. Mustafa and Saurabh Ray. Improved results on geometric hitting set problems. *Discrete Comput. Geom.*, 44(4):883–895, 2010. [see page 94]

[MRR15]   Nabil H. Mustafa, Rajiv Raman, and Saurabh Ray. Quasi-polynomial time approximation scheme for weighted geometric set cover on pseudodisks and halfspaces. *SIAM J. Comput.*, 44(6):1650–1669, 2015. [see page 95]

[NVZ01]   Takao Nishizeki, Jens Vygen, and Xiao Zhou. The edge-disjoint paths problem is NP-complete for series-parallel graphs. *Discrete Appl. Math.*, 115(1):177–186, 2001. [see page 22]

[Pap94]   Christos H. Papadimitriou. Computational complexity. In *Encyclopedia of Computer Science*. Addison Wesley Pub Co Inc, 1994. [see pages 9 and 15]

[Pap99]   Evanthia Papadopoulou. k-Pairs non-crossing shortest paths in a simple polygon. *Int. J. Comput. Geom. Appl.*, 9(6):533–552, 1999. [see page 119]

[Pat01]   Maurizio Patrignani. On the complexity of orthogonal compaction. *Comput. Geom. Theory Appl.*, 19(1):47–67, 2001. [see pages 137, 188, and 191]

[PM05]   Valentin Polishchuk and Joseph S. B. Mitchell. Touring convex bodies – A conic programming solution. In *Canadian Conf. Comput. Geom.*, pages 290–293, 2005. [see page 119]

[PM07]   Valentin Polishchuk and Joseph S. B. Mitchell. Thick non-crossing paths and minimum-cost flows in polygonal domains. In *Proc. 23rd ACM Symp. Comput. Geom. (SoCG'07)*, pages 56–65, 2007. [see page 119]

[PY91]   Christos H. Papadimitriou and Mihalis Yannakakis. Optimization, approximation, and complexity classes. *J. Comput. Syst. Sci.*, 43(3):425–440, 1991. [see pages 14 and 113]

[Raz08]   Mina Razaghpour. The Steiner ratio for the obstacle-avoiding Steiner tree problem. Master's thesis, University of Waterloo, 2008. Available at `http://hdl.handle.net/10012/4055` . [see page 119]

[RBvK⁺08] Iris Reinbacher, Marc Benkert, Marc J. van Kreveld, Joseph S. B. Mitchell, Jack Snoeyink, and Alexander Wolff. Delineating boundaries for imprecise regions. *Algorithmica*, 50(3):386–414, 2008. [see page 119]

[RS95]   Neil Robertson and P. D. Seymour. Graph minors. XIII. The disjoint paths problem. *J. Comb. Theory, Ser. B*, 63(1):65–110, 1995. [see pages 22 and 31]

[RS04]   Neil Robertson and P. D. Seymour. Graph minors. XX. Wagner's conjecture. *J. Comb. Theory, Ser. B*, 92(2):325–357, 2004. [see page 16]

[RT87]   Prabhakar Raghavan and Clark D. Tompson. Randomized rounding: A technique for provably good algorithms and algorithmic proofs. *Combinatorica*, 7(4):365–374, 1987. [see pages 22, 23, 24, and 45]

[RZ10]   Satish Rao and Shuheng Zhou. Edge disjoint paths in moderately connected graphs. *SIAM J. Comput.*, 39(5):1856–1887, 2010. [see page 26]

[Sac84]   Jörg-Rüdiger Sack. *Rectilinear Computational Geometry*. PhD thesis, School of Computer Science, McGill University, 1984. Available at `http://digitool.library.mcgill.ca/R/?func=dbin-jump-full&object_id=71872&local_base=GEN01-MCG02` . [see page 136]

[Sch94]   Petra Scheffler. A practical linear time algorithm for disjoint paths in graphs with bounded tree-width. Technical Report TR 396/1994, FU Berlin, Fachbereich 3 Mathematik, 1994. [see pages 21, 25, and 46]

[SCS11]   Loïc Séguin-Charbonneau and F. Bruce Shepherd. Maximum edge-disjoint
            paths in planar graphs with congestion 2. In *Proc. IEEE 52nd Symp. Found.
            Comput. Sci. (FOCS'11)*, pages 200–209, 2011. [see page 26]

[Tam87]   Roberto Tamassia. On embedding a graph in the grid with the minimum
            number of bends. *SIAM J. Comput.*, 16(3):421–444, 1987. [see page 136]

[Tam16]   Roberto Tamassia. *Handbook of Graph Drawing and Visualization*. Chapman &
            Hall/CRC, 2016. [see page 9]

[Tar85]   Éva Tardos. A strongly polynomial minimum cost circulation algorithm. *Com-
            binatorica*, 5(3):247–255, 1985. [see page 51]

[Tru93]   Richard J. Trudeau. *Introduction to Graph Theory*. New York: Dover Pub, 1993.
            [see page 9]

[Var10]   Kasturi Varadarajan. Weighted geometric set cover via quasi-uniform sampling.
            In *Proc. 42nd ACM Symp. Theory Comput. (STOC'10)*, pages 641–648, 2010. [see
            pages 94 and 190]

[Vaz10]   Vijay V. Vazirani. *Approximation Algorithms*. Springer Publishing Company,
            Incorporated, 2010. [see page 9]

[Ver13]   Kevin Verbeek. Homotopic $\mathcal{C}$-oriented routing. In *Graph Drawing (GD'12)*,
            pages 272–278, 2013. [see page 119]

[VW85]   Gopalakrishnan Vijayan and Avi Wigderson. Rectilinear graphs and their
            embeddings. *SIAM J. Comput.*, 14(2):355–372, 1985. [see page 136]

[WS11]   David P. Williamson and David B. Shmoys. *The Design of Approximation Algo-
            rithms*. Cambridge University Press, 1st edition, 2011. [see pages 9 and 48]

www.ingramcontent.com/pod-product-compliance
Lightning Source LLC
LaVergne TN
LVHW080115070326
832902LV00015B/2602

* 9 7 8 3 9 5 8 2 6 0 7 6 4 *